NOT Ten Suggestions

The impossibility of living successfully without assuming the Ten Commandments

Rev. Dr. Curtis I. Crenshaw, Th.M., Th.D.

Footstool Publications
4008 Louetta Rd., Suite 542
Spring, TX 77388

Printed December 2010

ISBN: 978-1-877818-15-8

Righteousness exalts a nation, but sin is a reproach to *any* people (Proverbs 14:34).

To my friend, **David Merriman,** whom I knew from the first grade, until the Lord took him on July 24th, 2008 in a car wreck. He was one of the greatest servants I've ever known. See you around the Throne, my brother in Christ, when the Lord takes me.

Table of Contents:

Endorsements

(See back cover for John Frame.)

The Rt. Rev. Daniel R. Morse, M.Div., D. D.:

"This latest offering by Dr. Curtis Crenshaw — *Not Ten Suggestions* — is certainly not a dry and hard to read treatment of the Ten Commandments. Dr. Crenshaw's usual lively style is full of examples from real life that will make the reader say, 'Oh, is that how the Law of God applies to real life?' In my experience even those who are familiar with the Ten Commandments tend to relegate them to religious ceremony, reciting them in a worship service, instead or bringing them into the middle of the household, school, and work place. Dr. Crenshaw has certainly had enough experience in college, the military, business, and church to know how frequently we would like to cut corners on morality and ethics out of our selfish desire to make things easier or more advantageous for ourselves, and also to know how much such self-interest corrupts life in church and society. Here you will not find an exhaustive list of how the Law of God operates in the practical circumstances of everyday life, but you will read solid exposition of the Bible and enough practical applications to help you understand how to apply it in your own life. Let this book be your guide to understanding how God gives you wise counsel in His Ten Commandments."

The Rt. Rev. Ray R. Sutton, Th.D., Ph.D.:

"One of my professors once told me, 'Certain books on the Christian faith need to be written, or rewritten, for every generation.' He was referring to books on the great creeds of Christendom (Nicene, Apostles' and Athanasian). I believe books on the Ten Commandments also apply to my instructor's comment. The decadent world, indeed the Church, in which we live desperately faces the requirement for an obedient faith. Our Master, Jesus Christ, stated that 'if we love Him we will keep His commandments.' How can we 'keep' them if we do not know them? The Very Rev. Dr. Curtis Crenshaw has provided what has been needed for so long. He has also written his work in a succinct way without neglecting the critical moral issues confronting every Christian in today's world. He offers a particularly refreshing Biblical defense for the historic distinction between worship and reverence of Christian symbols. I highly commend this book to every Christian."

Preface

These were sermons delivered in 2007 to my congregation, and are not meant to be footnoted with scholarly notes, though there are some, especially in Part 1 and Part 3. But I trust the reader will find the material substantial.

There is some redundancy throughout the work that I left both for emphasis and because we'll be printing some parts of the book separately. Hopefully this will give further distribution not only of the parts but also of the whole, for those who read the parts may want the larger work.

I've used the New King James version of the Bible for all quotes, unless stated otherwise. This version uses italics for words that are not in the original Hebrew or Greek but which are needed to make sense. Thus, I have used underlining for emphasis in quoting biblical passages, not italics.

Christian vs. Non-Christian Ethics

If you are not a Christian, try reading this book. Perhaps by the grace of the Triune God you might be challenged and blessed to think a different way, or at least to understand how we think. I pray for your conversion to Christ.

How to Read this Book

It is best if you read it straight through from Chapter 1 to the end, the Conclusion. However, if you choose to jump around, I have designed each chapter to be complete. But you should read the first five chapters to understand the rest of the book, and then Chapters 18-22 are especially necessary. We will print some of the chapters separately to make it easy to give to others. Please see our website for these booklets from this book (www.footstoolpublications.com).

Also, our culture does not mind people speaking of God generically, but it hates definition, especially the Christian definition of God. Therefore, I have often used "Triune God" (Father, Son, and Holy Spirit) for God, not just "God," and also the Name that is above all, Jesus. This is by design.

I have tried to make the book easy to read with humor and illustrations from real life; however, Chapter 1 is somewhat the exception. I deal with some heavier ideas there, especially with point one, "I. Origin of All Things." If you don't understand it, please go to Chapter 2.

Of course, the appendices are optional. But you *must read* the next heading, Why This Book?

Why This Book? Full Disclosure (MUST READ)

I have several assumptions and goals for this book.

First, if you have wondered *what is happening to the USA*, this book offers an explanation. From the tea parties to the town hall meetings to the new laws being enacted against Christianity, we see rapid *change* in the West in general and in the USA in particular. We are in moral free fall. We are being destroyed internally by moral decay; we are rotting like carrion on the roadside. Not one in a thousand even has any clue of the cause. Some will read only this far and put down this book because it is not positive enough, though there is much positive in it, especially in the last chapter. They only want to have their ears tickled, to be told they are wonderful, and that the Triune God is well pleased with us in this country. Yet, we are idolaters, wanting to be our own gods with our own ethics. Man is incurably religious and will worship something, and usually it is the state, self, or some deity.

Second, if you have wondered *what is happening to the Christian Church* with its internal heresies and self-centeredness; TV evangelists who promote health and wealth and personal success, I hope that you'll peruse this volume. The explanation is basically the same: we want our own ethics; we want to be our own gods.

The Church in the USA needs to wake up. Christ is raising up enemies in our culture to make the Church take a stand, for it is a compromised Church. We will never make an impact by saying what people want to hear, for the Gospel, by its very nature, is confrontational. I'm always hearing people say that we need to pray, that if we can get all Christians praying that we'll be restored to some sense of morality. I beg to differ. Prayer without repentance is hypocrisy, and He will not hear such prayers:

> One who turns away his ear from hearing the law, even his prayer is an abomination (Proverbs 28:9).

But one of my *main purposes in writing this book* is this:

> If My people who are called by My name will humble themselves, and pray and seek My face, and turn from their wicked ways, then I will hear from heaven, and will forgive their sin and heal their land (2 Chronicles 7:14).

Notice that we Christians must *both* pray *and* repent, but we are worldly, wanting health, wealth, positive confession to create our own providence, and so forth. Until we are willing to part with our sins, until we are willing to give up all we have and die for Christ, we are salt without savor, good for nothing but judgment, a joke to the world.

Over 35 years ago Francis Schaeffer began to warn us of what is happening in our culture. If you don't know who he was, that is a shame and just part of our problem. We forget so easily. Though I'll never rise to Schaeffer's greatness, I hope that in some small way the Lord will use this work to help awaken His people.

The key to restoration of some semblance of Christian culture to the USA is the Christian Church. *We have two problems*: our immoralities and our formal heresies in denying the faith. We must believe the Gospel of the Triune God, and we must demonstrate that faith by obedience to His law.

The Christian Church is eaten up with moral heresies, *which is one of the main reasons I've written this book*. We Christians are the problem, not liberal politics or Islam. The solution is not conservative politics; rather, it is *our* repentance. The problem is idolatry; the solution is the Triune God. Once we are right with God, the gates of hell will not be able to stand against the Church (Matthew 16:18), and only then our culture will recover. The rest of this book covers God's morality. *The cure for our moral problems is the Ten Commandments.*

The cure for our formal heresies is the Nicene Creed that has been believed by all three branches of Christians for all time: Roman Catholic, Eastern Orthodox, and Protestant. Here it is:

I believe in one God,

the Father Almighty,

> Maker of heaven and earth,
>
> And of all things visible and invisible:

And in one Lord Jesus Christ,

> The only-begotten Son of God;
>
> Begotten of his Father before all worlds,
>
> God of God,
>
> Light of Light,
>
> Very God of very God;
>
> Begotten, not made,
>
> Being of one substance with the Father,
>
> By whom all things were made:
>
> Who for us men and for our salvation came down from heaven,
>
> And was incarnate by the Holy Ghost of the Virgin Mary,
>
> And was made man,
>
> And was crucified also for us under Pontius Pilate.
>
> He suffered and was buried,
>
> And the third day he rose again according to the Scriptures,
>
> And ascended into heaven,
>
> And sitteth on the right hand of the Father.
>
> And he shall come again with glory to judge both the quick and the dead:
>
> Whose kingdom shall have no end.

And I believe in the Holy Ghost,

> The Lord and Giver of life,
>
> Who proceedeth from the Father and the Son, ("and the Son" can be left out),

Who with the Father and the Son together is worshipped and glorified,
Who spake by the prophets.
And I believe one holy Catholic and Apostolic Church.
I acknowledge one baptism for the remission of sins.
And I look for the resurrection of the dead,
And the life of the world to come. *Amen.*

Some people say that doctrine divides people; of course it does, but it also unites. The ancient creeds, like the one just quoted, were designed to eliminate heretics (to divide) and to bring together the truly orthodox (to unite). The nature of truth is the same in any area of life (2 times 2 is 4, not 5). One must not only confess the truth but also deny its opposite; otherwise, there is compromise. But today people want to be tolerant, and that has its place, but we must not be tolerant of heresy, for that is idolatry, the violation of the First Commandment.

Think about what is happening. There is great hope for Christians and for the USA, but we must be willing to count the cost and fight with our spiritual weapons (2 Corinthians 10:3-6). We Christians must repent of our doctrinal, formal heresies and of moral heresies of violating God's Ten Commandments.

In both cases (culture and church), we see that man wants to be his own god. In the Reformation of the 16th century, the main issue was whether man could earn his relationship with God, but now the issue is much deeper—it is whether the Triune God exists or not, or which god is really God, for our culture is inventing new ways to be its own god, which began 150 years ago and is now accelerating. This time, all three branches of Christianity need Reformation, Eastern Orthodoxy, Roman Catholicism, and Protestant.

I've lost much sleep over our culture and over the state of Christianity in America, and there have been days when I could not eat. My soul is exceedingly vexed at times with concern. I love both our country and Christians, and both are going to hell in a hand basket, as we say. I offer an analysis of the problem with the solution.

Therefore, *third*, one of the points in this book is that *mankind cannot be his own god*. The battle lines are drawn; who is god on this planet, the Triune God, or mankind? From politicians in high places to talk show hosts, our culture has a fetish with its own deity. As one friend said in her class, "Those who want to be god, won't need God, and then can be god."[1] The human proclivity to be deity will always sell, for it caters to the wants of sinful humans. This explains why Star Wars with its New Age emphasis on the "force" was so popular because mankind, at least some mankind (the elite), have the ability to rise above others to be gods. It also explains why one female TV talk show host's presentation of the god within us is so popular. This book challenges that, and presents mankind as under the judgment of Almighty God and His law with only one way out: Jesus Christ. To restate, there is a Creator/creature distinction that cannot be bridged. God is God, and we are creatures; nothing will change that. (More on this later.) One may want to get my book against such theology among Christians who think they can create wealth and health for themselves. The title is *Man as God: The Word of Faith Movement*. You may purchase it at this site:

www.footstoolpublications.com.

Wanting to be God is a reflection of what we see in the first temptation in Genesis 3 when the devil told Eve that she could be her own god if she ate the forbidden fruit: "You will be like God, knowing good and evil." The word "knowing" in this context means "determining" good and evil for herself. Though the Hebrew word for "know" does not mean "determine" itself, in this context that seems to be the derived meaning, for Satan challenges Eve to defy God and declare her own ethic, which mankind has been doing ever since.

Therefore, *fourth*, and one of the main theses of this book, is that *only God can give us morality*, that all other morality is rebellion against Him, and that we cannot prosper in this world ethically without assuming His moral law. Just as Satan said to Eve that she could disobey God, eat the fruit, and not die, so a large part of mankind's self-deception is that he thinks he can practice his own ethic in rebellion to the Triune God with no consequences. This book challenges that.

---

[1] Deaconess Teresa Johnson, M.A., M.A.R.

In our culture, we see politicians trying to build the city of man in rebellion to the city of God, man wanting his own kingdom apart from God's kingdom built on the Gospel and the Church. We are at war, spiritually and morally, and everyone is in the battle, whether he knows it or not. One is either a casualty or a warrior. There are no other options. (I highly recommend St. Augustine's (A.D. 354-430) book, *The City of God*, written so many centuries ago, and still as fresh as if written yesterday.)

Fifth, another point of this book is that God's law, the Ten Commandments, is the *only morality that exists*. To restate it, one cannot live life with meaning and with blessing without knowing the Triune God and loving Him through obedience to His law.

Sixth, God's law is equally for the nation as well as for the individual, for Christ is Lord of all. God's character does not change from the single individual in society to many individuals that make up a society. The same principles of righteousness apply equally to individuals and to nations.

Seventh and final, *the only way to know God is through Christ* and in covenant with God through Him. A covenant is an agreement, a relationship established by vows, and lived by faith in the Triune God and in humble submission and love to Him by loving His character as revealed in His Ten Commandments. Though one cannot earn his salvation by trying to keep God's commandments, he demonstrates love for God by keeping them. This life is lived with God's people in His Church, not just as an individual. One cannot cover everything in one book, so this is assumed throughout.

We Win!

I've read the end of the Book, and we Christians win. Earlier in the Bible in Daniel chapter two, we see a rock cut out of a mountain without hands, and the rock hit a statue, which Daniel interpreted as God's kingdom (rock) that would smash the Roman Empire (statue). This kingdom would fill the whole earth. Unlike Islam, Christianity has 100 percent penetration to every country on the globe, which means the leavening of the Gospel is proceeding. Islam increases primarily by birth rate and by forcing others to convert at gun point. Also, they hate one another, as seen in the Iran-Iraq war just a few years ago, and as seen in Osama bin Laden who has his henchmen murder other Moslems.

Western Christianity is passing, but it will be revived by persecution if Christians will respond to God's judgments. "In 1900, more than 80 percent of Christians lived in Europe and America. Today 60 percent live in the developing world. More than two out of three evangelical Christians now live in Asia, Africa, and South America."[2] In Africa 100 years ago, there were ten million Christians, but today there are over 300 million, going from 10 percent of the nation to 50 percent. Uganda, the once pagan culture that offered human sacrifice, now has 20 million Christians, having withstood the Islamic murderer Idi Amin. (Child sacrifice is having a revival among non-Christians there.) While we in America are using all kinds of gimmicks to get people to church — like entertainment, coffee, casual dress and "seeker sensitive" services — African pastors are sometimes asking attendees not to come to church except every third Sunday (or so) to make room for the many converts. Likewise, China can boast of 100 million, mostly underground, even in the midst of the late Mao Zedong. Central and South America are having explosive growth of Pentecostalism. In Brazil a few decades ago there were not enough evangelical Protestants to count, but today there are over 50 million. In 1950 Brazil had 50 million Roman Catholics, but now has 120 million, and let us remember that amid some error, Roman Catholics still formally hold to the Nicene Creed just quoted above. In South Korea not many decades ago Christians were sparse and Buddhists dominated, but today Christians outnumber them with Presbyterians composing a large percentage.

In short, in the days of the Apostles there was one Christian for every 324 people in the world, and today there is one Christian for every 3.5 people. But why is there decline in the West? That is partially what this book is about. An individual, nation, or region of the world cannot prosper by disobedience to God's law; over time, they *necessarily*

---

[2] Dinesh D'Souza, *What's So Great About Christianity?* (Carol Stream, Illinois: Tyndale House Publishers, 2007), p. 10ff.

self-destruct (Proverbs 11:5). The West is turning *from* the Triune God while the rest of the world is turning *to* Him. Yet, that means that the Church in the West will be disciplined severely with persecution, which will, by God's sovereign grace, lead to renewal and revival.

Atheism is on the way out (see the excellent book by Christian scholar and former atheist Alister McGrath, *The Twilight of Atheism*), which is why we have such vehement and anti-intellectual attacks on Christians (such as Sarah Palin) and on Christianity (Richard Dawkins ridiculous name-calling book, *The God Delusion*, which will be discussed more later). Satan is afraid of the truth so he attacks it. (We will consider more of our future in Part 3.) **AMEN**.

Acknowledgements

My special thanks to Deaconess Teresa Johnson (M.A., M.A.R.) for reading this manuscript and making many helpful suggestions. Her expertise as a technical writer has only made this better in grammar and expression.

The Rev. Doug Sangster read some of the beginning chapters to improve the style and clarity. Thank you, Doug.

Thanks also to David Potts, a long time friend who designed the book cover. His skills are greatly appreciated.

Any remaining errors from those who made suggestions are mine, not theirs.

What can one say about one's wife? My beloved Ruth whom I married in 1969 also read this. At times she would say, "That just doesn't make sense," and upon confirmation she would be right. She has been by side these many decades, always encouraging me, believing in me, and is the mother of our two children. We also have four grandchildren. We are truly blessed by the Lord!

This book was the product of a series of sermons I preached at my church, St. Francis Reformed Episcopal Church; the members have been a great encouragement to me. I owe them a debt I can never repay, for they have ministered to me more than I have to them. God bless them, both now and forever. **AMEN**.

Introduction

You are married and have your first child, a son. He is now two years old and beginning to talk. You savor every cute word. You cannot imagine loving anyone so much, and just thinking about losing him makes your heart sink in despair. You want only the best for this little life.

But what makes you love him so much? Is this just an accident, a product of random molecules in motion? Is love real, and if so, where did it come from? Twenty-three of his 46 chromosomes came from you. He even looks like you, and has some of your personality characteristics. Is it any wonder that we love someone made in our image?

You've heard that there are no ethical standards, but you can't imagine allowing this little life to be injured, and you don't want him making "wrong" choices. You plan only the best for your child, which involves choices, morality, which in turn means that you as a person must instruct him as a person. Which morality will you use?

PART 1: THE BEGINNING AND THE LAW

Part 1 is necessary to understand what this book is about. In Chapter 1, we look at the origin of things, meaning to life and the basic Christian morality.

In Chapter 2, we must understand what morality is, the personal aspect to it, and then how morality works with God, man, and His commandments.

Chapter 3 answers the question Who Is God's Law for? Is it for individuals, for nations, for politics, churches, or all those?

In Chapter 4, we explore if morality is relative, just up for grabs, or constant.

Finally in Chapter 5, we summarize the Ten Commandments so the reader can have a basic understanding of them before we look at each commandment separately.

Chapter 1—Creation

Introduction

God is sitting in Heaven when a scientist says to Him, "Lord, we don't need you anymore. Science has finally figured out a way to create life out of nothing. In other words, we can now do what you did in the beginning."

God says: "Oh, is that so? Tell me how you do it."

"Well," says the scientist, "we can take dirt and form it into the likeness of You and breathe life into it, thus creating man."

"Well, that's interesting. Show Me."

So the scientist bends down to the earth and starts to mold the soil.

"Oh no, no, no . . ." interrupts God, "Get your own dirt."[1]

I. Origin of All Things

A. From Nothing or From Something?

Did the universe come from nothing or from something?[2] If it came from nothing, not even from God, how do we explain our existence?

---

[1] I recommend, Alister McGrath, Ph.D (Oxford), *The Twilight of Atheism* (New York: Galilee Book, Doubleday, division of Random House, 2006); and Norman L. Geisler, Ph.D. and Frank Turek, Ph.D., *I Don't Have Enough Faith to be an Atheist* (Wheaton, IL: Crossway Books, 2004).

[2] I had this book completely done and ready to send to my editor when I decided to reread Francis Schaeffer's magisterial work first published in 1972, the year I began seminary. The title is *He Is There and He Is Not Silent*. It is deep reading in places, but I first read it in 1973, several times since then, the latest being 2002 until I read it again early this year (2009) in a reprint. I was surprised how much he had affected me, for much of the argument of my Chapter One is from him. I did not realize that his thought forms, and sometimes even wording, had become a part of me. I cannot footnote every thought, but I give him credit for much of this chapter, though I take credit for all errors

The silence from the scientific, atheistic community regarding why there is something rather than nothing is deafening.[3] That is irrational.

If the universe came from something, was that "something" impersonal or personal? If impersonal, how do we explain the fact that we are personal, rational beings?

Does an impersonal being have concern about morality? How do we explain our concern for morality? How do we explain our need to order the world with moral norms? Even though we may pretend that we don't care about morality, we base our societal structure on it and make laws for all to obey. We can't survive without morality. Hence, it is woven into the warp and woof of society. For example, our civil code *assumes* good and evil, distinctions inherent in a universal code of ethics and morality.

Moreover, an impersonal universe would lead to man as a machine with no will to choose; there would be no morality. Mankind would just be chemistry. If the universe is impersonal with molecules in motion, man is inescapably reduced to a carbon-base machine, forced to eke out an absurd existence in a chaotic world of random events. Moreover, finding meaning in an impersonal, random universe is impossible, and the task of agreeing on a universal standard of morality is hopeless. In this view, might makes right. This is the modern evolutionary perspective, which maintains that everything has come from an impersonal beginning, from random molecules.

If we assume the impersonal, the universe is undeniably silent regarding life, consciousness, rationality, personhood, morals, meaning; in short, we will return to non-personhood at death. But the great irony is that we live as if we are real persons in communion with other persons, with the capacity for meaningful speech and for cooperation. We

---

in thought. Dr. Schaeffer would never have claimed to be a prophet, and he was not in the sense of receiving new revelation from God, but he definitely was a prophet in the sense that he could extrapolate from God's word. Most of what he said would happen in our culture is sadly coming true. Dr. Schaeffer in turn studied under Cornelius Van Til, whom I've also read. For those interested, Schaeffer was not a consistent presuppositionalist.

[3] Ravi Zacharias, *The End of Reason* (Grand Rapids: Zondervan, 2008), p. 32. A very fine work by a Christian scholar, who was reared in India.

assume consciousness, rationality (all those things just given), and we can't do otherwise. It is impossible not to assume these and function, for we are made in God's image. We live in His world. We live with hope for tomorrow. We live with morals and expect others to do the same. We love others. Where did these capacities come from? It should be evident that it is a contradiction to say personal beings came from impersonal matter.

If we say the universe has always existed as matter and with some kind of order, we are making a god of it, which is a faith statement, and still does not answer how logic and persons arose. Moreover, how do we explain that all the galaxies are moving away from one another as from a common point of origin, implying a beginning, if not the "big bang"? (Did God do it that way? I'm not one to speculate.) If the universe has always existed, we have infinite time, which means it would take infinite time to reach any point of time, which in turn means we could not be here. But we are here.

But if the universe came from a personal being, was it one or more personal beings? If more than one, which "god" would have dominion over what area of the universe, and did they coordinate their "creations" to harmonize with one another? We would be back to mythology (Greek, Roman, others) with all their competing gods. We would have the gods relative to one another. No one god would be big enough to give unity to all things. Each god would control his area, and "logic" and "science" would vary over the areas. It is irrational to believe that a *uni*-verse could develop from *multi*-sources.

The god of Islam will not do. How can Allah, who is one "person," love without an object, without another person to love who is equal to Himself? Also, morality exists among persons in relationship, but if Allah is only one person, where is morality? Perhaps this is the reason love is absent from Islam and hate prominent with its adherents carrying hate signs to blow everything up. Before creation, how would there be sympathetic feeling, right action, or mutual trust with only one "person" in god? How could there be a righteous being without fellowship or moral relation? Before creation, there would be only eternal darkness, solitude, communion with oneself, self-love, and after creation only an endless game of solitaire with worlds for cards.

The Islamic apologist might argue that after creation Allah has an object to love, but then Allah needed creation to realize his full potential; therefore, he was incomplete until after creation. God has now created something new, something completely other than himself, further indicating his need of creation to fulfill himself. Mankind would have something Allah does not have: personal relationships. Moreover, one person in God would give us a god completely absorbed in himself, without concern for others, without communion with us, just a far off being who has sovereignty but no personal involvement with his creatures.

In Christianity, however, we have the one true God, one in essence, but three in persons, who have loved one another from all eternity, the Father not existing before the Son, and they not existing before the Holy Spirit, but all eternal in one divine essence. He is capable of interaction with His creatures because of interaction within the divine persons, not only transcendent (not like us, sovereign over us) but also immanent (like us in Christ who was/is human), capable of direct communication with us on our level through the Second Person of the Triune God who added to Himself a perfect human nature, and so is God's peer and our peer in one person. The bridge now is crossed from the infinite God to finite man in the One who is both.

So if the universe came from the *one* God who is also multi-personal, who was He? The Judeo-Christian heritage is the *only* candidate. As Francis Schaeffer would say, it is not that Christianity is the best answer; it is the *only* answer. The Christian God is one God, but He is three persons, the Father and the Son and the Holy Spirit. We know from His revelation to us that He created. Does this comport with what we know in this world? Very much!

For example, how do we account for reason and logic if the universe is just random, physical particles? Everyone has to assume the laws of logic in order to communicate, for communication implies order, distinction, unity, form, consistency, and other things. Thus we have atheists assuming the Triune God, His logic, and His thoughts in order to refute Him, which is contradictory. Because God is infinitely consistent, infinitely rational, and cannot contradict Himself (such as making a square circle), we humans who are made in His image function by *His* laws of logic. Indeed, these laws of logic govern our thoughts and are *immaterial* (like God, not made of matter), *universal* (everyone assumes them in order to communicate and even think), and *invariant* (like God, they do not change). And through logic and even language, our minds mirror the contours of God's mind and so we are confronted with Him every time we think or speak.

Just one example will suffice. When we seek to argue anything, we assume consistency, that one thing cannot be two different things at the same time.[4] If the universe is just molecules in motion, how do we explain the immaterial laws of logic that govern all thought, and immaterial laws of science that govern matter? What makes quantum particles obey these laws? Matter is one thing; immaterial laws that govern matter quite another. Christians have the answer: God, who is spirit, has revealed that He is transcendent (over all), and He is the condition for science to exist.

Moreover, scientific laws did not even exist as a category at the beginning of the universe if it was just "molecules in motion." How do we explain their existence?

B. Evolution?

Antony Flew, who was a scholar in England and for 50 years was the leading atheist against theism, now embraces intelligent design because nothing else explains the design of the universe, the laws of nature, the origin of life itself, our intelligibility,[5] or the balance of nature for us to live on earth. How could something come from nothing, how could life come from lifeless matter, such as stones, how could consciousness come from raw matter (non-consciousness), how could reason come from non-reason, how could self-conscious thought come from physical objects, how could the consistent laws of science come from random particles, how could persons come from non-persons? The atheist tries to argue that random chance begets intelligence, per-

---

[4] We call this the law of non-contradiction, that something cannot be both A and not A at the same time and in the same way.

[5] See the excellent work by Antony Flew, the former atheist, *There Is A God*, published in 2007. Flew announced his change from atheism to theism in 2004, though sadly as far as I know he did not become a Christian before his death on April 8, 2010.

sons, balance of nature, order, and meaning. In short, chance or chaos gave rise to order. At every point, the atheist is irrational, contradictory, and functions by faith that is irrational, and make no mistake that "irrationality is the prelude to destruction."[6] John Dryden, the seventeenth century English poet, said: "For those whom God to ruin has design'd, He fits for fate, and first destroys their mind." Today we might say it this way: "Those whom God would destroy, He first makes mad."

For one to assume that order came from random molecules,[7] that life came from non-life and that happened only once so that all life is related, that persons came from non-persons, that consciousness came from unconsciousness, that the immaterial laws of logic came from matter—all that takes more faith than I can muster. I must have a rational faith, not an irrational faith, or I can't believe. Here are other assumptions that one evolutionist admitted if the theory of evolution is true:

- All life is related: viruses, bacteria, plants, and animals.
- Protozoa (one cell animals) gave rise to Metazoa (many cell animals).
- Invertebrates (no back bone) gave rise to vertebrates (animals with backbones).[8]

There are more assumptions for which evolutionists have no answer: the change from reproducing by cell division to animal copulation, with the incredible coincidence of both males and females coming along at the same time. Another is the spontaneous development of the complexity of the eye with its nerves going from the eye to the brain, without which an organism cannot see and thus cannot live, and so forth. I just don't have that kind of faith to believe something so unsci-

---

[6] Herbert Schlossberg, *Idols for Destruction* (Nashville: Thomas Nelson Publishers, 1983), p. 165.

[7] This is contrary to the Second Law of Thermodynamics to say that chaos becomes order, that disorder becomes order. Just think of our homes and cars that always tend toward disorder and breaking down, not the reverse.

[8] G. A. Kerkut, *Implications of Evolution* (New York: Pergamon Press, 1960), p. 6.

entific.[9] (See my annotated bibliography for books on creation versus evolution at the end of this book.)

The point is that where one begins in his reasoning determines where he ends. If he assumes that man's mind is the measure of all things, he will not begin with God but with himself, which in turn means that he will never find any god bigger than himself. If he begins with himself, naturally he will think good of himself, not believing in sin or in the self-deceiving power of sin, which means his ethics will be skewed. This line of reasoning provides no answer to man's existence, no morality but his own personal code, no love, no meaning, no hope. We are just animals, or worse, just cogs in the machines of the universe.

However, if we begin with the Triune God, we understand our existence; we have life, consciousness, thought, reason, personhood, truth, morality, love, meaning, and hope because God has these. It should be obvious that finite mankind is not big enough to have an integration point in him to make sense of the universe. For man to assume he can figure everything out by unaided reason is to make himself the defining point of reality. It is like trying to pour the ocean into a thimble; too many things are left out and overlooked. To make sense of the universe, we need someone who is greater than creation to tell us what we need to know. The reference point must be outside of creation.

C. Made in the Image of God?

One thing we learn from this "someone" is that *we are made in His image, in the image of the Triune God*, which in turn means that we are like Him at least in these ways:

- We are personal just as the Triune God is *personal*. But personal and otherness must go together or "personal" has no meaning. How can Allah, who is only one "person," be personal since he has no other one to relate to in eternity? To say he is personal in isolation is meaningless. But if he

---

[9] This is not just the "God of the gaps," as some say, meaning that we invoke God when something can't be explained. Rather, the point is that the evidence that exists fits into the Christian model but not the evolutionist model.

is not personal, how did he communicate the Koran to persons?

- Moreover, mankind is *rational*. This means that we have great mental faculty and the ability to use language. Like the Persons of the Holy Trinity, we communicate with one another with abstract ideas, both oral and written form, communicating with ideas that are objective and true. Thus man has rationality that is qualitatively superior to the animal kingdom. (You will never teach monkeys to write books!) Moreover, we use *speech*, which necessarily involves the laws of logic, which are immaterial, universal, and invariant, presupposing a transcendental standard, which presupposes the Triune God. In Genesis chapter one we see God speaking, both to creation and within the Trinity ("Let Us make man in Our image"), so we have the gift of speech, which means that within created limits we as image bearers are self-conscious and self-determining.

- Just as God is three, so we prefer *communities*. From this naturally follows that we humans want to live in community with one another, husbands with wives, children with their natural parents, communities, nations, and so on. We call these relationships *covenants*, holding to ethical standards, bound by oaths (either implicit or explicit), and with a view to the future to assure the continuity of those in covenant. Since God made us personal after Himself, we receive our definition of personhood from Him. The most basic human relationship God created is man and woman, one male and one female in covenant with one another in marriage who are able to reproduce. When people are alienated from God who is love, they become alienated from one another, which is why marriages are breaking down so quickly today.

- The image of God is further seen in that we are *orientated to righteousness, to morality*, for we have moral motions and moral sensibilities, which manifest themselves in our making rules to live by. God is righteous, and before mankind fell into sin, he was righteous. Now we are dominated by sin, but we are still oriented to morality. We are the only creatures on earth who are. We have a sense of what is right and wrong, and we feel moral outrage at acts that defy this moral code. This means we have a conscience and one that can be trained for good or evil.

- We also have *dominion* over the earth, its creatures, and its resources. Speech and dominion go together, for the high intelligence we have is God's gift to us to exercise dominion over the other creatures. God says in Genesis 1:26, 28:

Then God said, "Let Us make man in Our image, according to Our likeness; <u>let them have dominion</u> over the fish of the sea, over the birds of the air, and over the cattle, over all the earth and over every creeping thing that creeps on the earth."

Then God blessed them, and God said to them, "Be fruitful and multiply; fill the earth and subdue it; <u>have dominion</u> over the fish of the sea, over the birds of the air, and over every living thing that moves on the earth."

- Like God who is love (1 John 4:8), we seek to love and to be loved, but we want love without God, which means we distort love. True love is always expressed by some ethical standard, and that standard is God's commandments.

What is interesting is that when someone promotes evolution only (not theistic evolution), and that someone says we are the product of chance and molecules, he does so by using the image of God:

- He does so personally, and uses verbal propositions.

- He does so rationally, assuming the laws of logic that are immaterial, universal, invariant, yet while living in an allegedly material-only universe.

- He does so ethically, assuming that he is not lying.

- He does so with love, assuming that it does matter.

- He does so with speech, assuming the capacity of such from the God who speaks.

In other words, the image of God within mankind, though marred and flawed by sin, still functions. To deny God, we have to assume Him. Fallen image-bearers use the gift of God's intelligence to suppress objective truth. In using his sense of "ought," he tries to deny morality or to remake it. In using the laws of logic, he seeks to deny the transcendent reason of God. By using design and reason, he argues for chaos and non-reason. Thus he creates alternative gods to worship, but all are bound by creation, as St. Paul said (Romans 1:25).

All people naturally hate God, especially His ethical commands, preferring their own morality (Romans 3:9-19). But when the worst sinner looks into the mirror, he is confronted with the Triune God, for he is His image, and he cannot help but function in accordance with that image, even though the image is marred by sin. When we look at the world, its beauty and design, the image of God within us resonates with creation, and we intuitively know God exists. Yet as the Apostle Paul so insightfully stated, we seek to suppress the truth by means of our sin, the very sinful acts themselves being designed unconsciously to keep His truth out of our minds (Romans 1:18-24). The more consistent the non-Christian is with where he begins his thought (with materialism), the more devastating his lifestyle becomes to himself and to others.

My point is to ask what kind of universe we would expect with the infinite personal God. It would be what we have: rational, personal creation governed by immaterial laws of thought (laws of logic) and immaterial laws of creation (laws of science) with us as personal beings who are concerned about morality. Because God loved us, He gave us this world. But modern man has basically given up on finding truth, which is exactly what God said would happen to those who left Him out:

> He has put eternity in their hearts, except that no one can find out the work that God does from beginning to end (Ecclesiastes 3:11).

II. Origin of Morality: God, Man, and the Standard

Our morality is *from God*. Within the Holy Trinity there is one divine essence but three persons, Father, Son, and Holy Spirit, which means there is community. The persons communicate with one another by propositions (and in other ways), and they love one another with infinite capacity, each being the object of the other two persons' love. They do not glorify themselves but one another. The Father honors the Son (John 5:20, 22-23; 1 John 2:23), the Son honors the Father (John 5:19), the Holy Spirit honors the Son (John 16:7-11), and so on. They all have the same attributes, which also means the same holiness. If I may use the word "character" without being misunderstood, this does not change in the Trinity. Yet there is only one divine essence and thus only one God.

Next we have *mankind*. Like God, we also live in community, communicate with abstract propositions, seek love from one another and express it to one another, and live by standards. Before mankind fell into sin, his love and holiness were not soiled. Adam and Eve's relationship with one another was derived from their relationship with God, and it was perfect.

His holiness was their *standard* so Eve told the devil that they were not allowed to eat the fruit from the forbidden tree. She and Adam communicated with God and the devil by verbal propositions based on the truth of God's unchanging, holy character. Thus, the moral standard was God's law-word, His command to Adam and Eve not to eat the forbidden fruit, but given not arbitrarily, being based on the unchangeable holiness of God. God's commands and His holiness are equally important, and one cannot isolate one from the other.

Satan assaulted the character of God to Adam and Eve when he argued that God did not want them to eat from the forbidden tree because He knew they could be like Him, and He did not want the competition. When Eve gave the forbidden fruit to Adam, she violated the vertical standard from God, which affected her relationship with God and with Adam. Adam and Eve were naked and ashamed in one another's presence, and they put on fig leaves to hide from God. Then God came looking for Adam and said, "Where are you?", which meant they were alienated from Him, and were now afraid of God (Genesis 3:10). They hid from God, but were also at odds with one another as we see Adam telling God that he ate because it was "the woman whom You gave to be with me" that was the problem, and the woman in turn blaming Satan. Alienation from God (the vertical relationship) resulted in alienation from one another (the horizontal relationship). It is also resulted in a distortion of the moral standard with man making his own ethic.

In other words, morality involves *persons*, their *character*, some *standard* that is communicated by verbal statements, and *love* (or the lack) for one another. Once mankind through Adam fell into sin, God, of course, did not change, but mankind changed so that now his orientation is to himself, not God, and to his own standard in rebellion to God's commands, and to exploiting one another, not to love. ***One of the worst parts of self-deception is to think that we can violate God's law without consequences.*** We believe the lie of Satan to Eve that we can be our own gods, making up our own ethic.

The only way to heal this breach is to come back to God through the Son of God, to embrace His love for us in Christ, to confess our sins against His holy law, acknowledging His standard to be the only true one. When we come to God through Christ, He restores our capacity to love both Him and one another, and we will be gradually transformed into the moral image of Christ (2 Corinthians 3), who is the perfect image of God (Colossians 1:15). This means that *God's law will be written on his heart* (Jeremiah 31:33; Hebrews 8:10; 10:16). To put this another way, the character of Christ is revealed in the law, and when we are changed, those laws are inscribed in our hearts, making us love Him all the more by observing those laws.

But mankind wants to be his own god, to make up his own morality, and to pretend that he does not have anything wrong with himself. The irony is that man still seeks love, still argues for moral law codes, still communicates by verbal statements, still uses logic, but since he has rejected God's standard, in the process he self-destructs. One cannot live successfully without assuming His moral law. The more consistent the sinner is in rejecting God, His love, and His standard, the quicker he sinks into the quagmire of his own self-destruction. His standard becomes distorted as he seeks to ignore God, to be his own God, and to invent his own standard. [10]

Taken to its logical conclusion, rejecting God means there is no purpose, no tragedy, no pain, no happiness, just nothing. Absolutely nothing matters if God does not exist, so why not pursue hedonism that gives temporary pleasure? No wonder that atheist Sartre announced on his deathbed that atheism is philosophically unlivable.[11]

And if there is no God, who has the authority to say what is "evil"? Hitler? Those who rape? In some cultures, people love their neighbors, and in other cultures they eat them. Which one is moral and why? How can one derive personal, moral principles from impersonal forces and impersonal realities? That famous humanist and agnostic, Aldous Huxley, said this of nothingness:

> . . . the philosophy of meaninglessness was essentially an
> instrument of liberation. The liberation we desired was . . . from
> a certain political and economic system and liberation from a
> certain system or morality. *We objected to [Christian] morality be-*
> *cause it interfered with our sexual freedom. . . .*[12]

Hatred for God's commands regarding sexuality is nearly always on the agenda of those who hate the Triune God and who prefer atheism, agnosticism, or the like. Sexual immorality is an in your face statement to God the Creator that He is not in charge—the sinner is. William Ernest Henley captured the sentiment in his awful poem, "Invictus."

> It matters not how strait the gate,
> How charged with punishments the scroll,
> I am the master of my fate:
> I am the captain of my soul.

More bluntly, if there is no God, no immortality of the soul, no judgment to fear, why should we live righteously, or according to po-

---

[10] How can one derive obligation from reason? Or, how can one derive "ought" from "is"? This is usually referred to as the naturalist fallacy. I would also add that we cannot derive "can" or ability from "ought" or "is."

[11] Zacharias, *The End of Reason*, p. 43.

[12] McGrath, *The Twilight of Atheism*, p. 152, emphasis added.

litical correctness, or why should we not steal or murder or do *anything* that makes us happy? If there is no God, then everything is just my will and your will, and you are in my way.

I heard an interview on Fox news with "Dr. Death," Jack Kevorkian. The interviewer asked how he wanted to be remembered, to which Kevorkian said something like, "It does not matter. When you're dead, you don't exist. Then absolutely nothing matters." He confirmed what the Bible teaches, which is stated crisply by a Christian philosopher: "Without personal immortality there can be no rational justification for morality."[13]

But we all innately believe in justice and goodness. Which one of us does not feel a strong sense of justice and want judgment on the pedophile who rapes a three year old girl? Where does that innate sense of justice come from if we're just "molecules in motion"? Why do we want to reward "good" behavior and punish "evil" behavior? Where do these ideas come from?

They come from our being made in God's image. Though the human race has fallen into sin and the image is marred, it is still there. Therefore, we have a God consciousness, and we function in this world the way God has made it and us, whether we recognize it or not. In fact, *it is impossible not to function in God's world according to His physical and moral laws.* Don't try jumping off a tall building while yelling "I don't believe in gravity." Likewise, we may deny God's morality, but we still suffer the consequences in this life and in the one to come when we disobey His moral laws.

And if we believe there is a God somewhere who is good, we must believe that He disapproves of evil. Some people would approve of His condemnation of evil, but others expect Him to make an exception in their case when He applies the same standard to them. But if He makes an exception, then He must not be so good or consistent to allow for our evil. So we're in a dilemma. We want God and His goodness to give meaning to our lives and to deliver us from evil outside us, but we

---

[13] Surrenda Gangadean, *Philosophical Foundation* (New York: University Press of America, 2008), p. 150.

don't want to be judged. What is the solution? How can God be both just and the justifier of sinners (Romans 3:26)?

There is a great principle in the Bible that the one who forgives is the one who pays. If you steal $100 from me, and I forgive you, I just lost $100. I paid. In a similar way, God forgives sinners, but He does not compromise His goodness or moral character. How can He forgive and not soil His own character? Only Christianity has the answer: the infinite justice required to be poured out on us humans was assumed by God Himself in the person of Christ, who was God incarnate. He would forgive so He would pay. Christ was both God and man in one person. As a human, He could die and represent us. As God, He had infinite merit, and could satisfy God's justice. He was one person so that both God and man cooperated in the one act of salvation. The chasm between us and God is bridged in the One who is both God and man. Thus Christ died for our sins. As God and man He took our penalty of death on the cross and through that event extends mercy to us. Because of the cross, justice has been met, and because of the cross, mercy can now be extended without compromise.

III. Creation Gives Meaning to Life

As your little boy grows up, what will you tell him? Will you teach him about the wonderful beauty and design of creation, the meaning of all this to us, which in turn reveals a God who desires the best for us? Or, will you hand him over to peers at public schools to do drugs, to engage in sex, to do his own thing, to find his own meaning?

The emptiness that results from a denial of God is cavernous, and leaves mankind with nothing to live for but himself as an individual, and even that is empty. A random universe leaves man with randomness and meaninglessness, despair, hopelessness. As atheistic philosopher Friedrich Nietzsche once said, we are straying through infinite nothingness with madness the logical conclusion. Interestingly, Nietzsche spent the last years of his life insane, while his godly mother watched over him at his bedside until she died in 1897. Then his sister took care of him until his death in 1900.[14]

Think about it: if we came from molecules in motion and we're going back to molecules in motion, what difference does the in-between make? And in our pleasure oriented society, meaninglessness does not come from being weary of pain but from being weary of pleasure (G. K. Chesterton). We seek meaning when we have pain, but we give up meaning when we have everything we want. In the West, we have everything we want. Moreover, in contrast to Marx, the true opiate of the people is not belief in the Triune God but belief in nothingness after death. With that belief, one can justify any behavior, and nothing matters. There may be no reward after death, but at least there is no punishment, or so it is thought.

But if there is no meaning to life or to the whole universe, how would we know that?[15] If there was no light in the universe and we had no eyes, how would we know that it is dark? The fact that we assume meaning and search for it or even that we deny meaning implies the Triune God who made us in His image to have purpose.

IV. New Creation Gives Hope Beyond the Grave

One is not prepared to live until he is prepared to die. "New creation" is redemption, God taking us sinners and re-creating us in Christ to be holy like Him, though we never achieve perfection in this life. The atheist Nietzsche understood that there is no hope once the Triune God is removed. As one philosopher stated, "[Nietzsche] has yet to tell us how we can affirm life in the sure knowledge of our own death."[16] But as Christians, we worship One who was dead and is now alive. There is

---

[14] Ravi Zacharias, *The End of Reason*, p. 27; see also Alistar Kee, *Nietzsche Against the Crucified* (London: SCM Press, 1999), pp. 1, 25. The Crucified won, and Nietzsche lost, dying in unbelief. Likewise, Sam Harris's *Letter to a Christian Nation* promotes the same view. He is an atheist who does not understand his own world view or Christianity, and reveals complete incompetence in his use of the Bible. See my comments in the Bibliography at the end of this book.

[15] C. S. Lewis, *Mere Christianity* (New York, NY: The Macmillan Company, 1943), p. 46.

[16] Alister Kee, *Nietzsche Against the Crucified*, p. 103.

as much historical evidence for the bodily resurrection of Christ as for Julius Caesar as a real person.[17] Christians know that this life is very short and that we must enter eternity, and we do so with little fear. We are truly a blessed people!

For a religion to have truth claims, it must validate those claims. One way to validate them would be from historical evidence, revealing that there is objective truth to substantiate their beliefs, and Christianity is the only qualifier. We stake our whole claim on the historical, bodily resurrection of Christ. We may appear to be most unreasonable with our dogmatic claims to truth, morality, and God (though we would deny it). However, try gathering all the world's religions that validate a bodily resurrection from the dead. Christianity is the only religion that can irrefutably validate Christ's bodily resurrection from the dead. Furthermore, at the time of Christ's resurrection there was no discussion regarding *whether* the tomb was empty but only *how* it became empty.

Conclusion

We enjoy a wonderful world that can be understood by logic and science. He has given us balance in nature, and has made us persons who communicate and love. He has given us purpose in life.

Moreover, we Christians have the greatest hope in the world, which is rooted in Christ, who destroyed death. Consequently, we anticipate the future, and live life confidently, to its fullest. When I stood at the casket of one whom I loved, I thanked God that death had not won; through Christ we win, and we are able to see through the grave to the other side, where our Christian relatives are waiting for us, along with Christ, who is our hope. And by hope we do not mean a remote possibility, but a firm assurance that steels and steadies us in this life.

Yes, this is God's world that He has graciously given to us, created it to sustain our lives, created us in His image to think like Him and to have a conscience that should be trained by His Ten Commandments. Life is beautiful! **AMEN.**

---

[17] For evidence for the Lord's resurrection and for all kinds of questions about philosophy, science, evolution, big bang, see Norman Geisler and Frank Turek, *I Don't Have Enough Faith to be an Atheist.*

Chapter 2—God's Law

Introduction

> Moses came down from Mt. Sinai with tablets of stone in
> hand, and announced to the children of Israel: "I've got good
> news and bad news. The good news is that I got God down just
> to ten rules. The bad news is that adultery is still in."

What is morality about? Does it come from some kind of abstract
principles or is it imposed by persons? If imposed by persons, is this
arbitrary, or is it based on character? If from character, what is its
source? We do not naturally think of God's law as His gift to us, but
since His commandments reveal His character, He is giving Himself.
Moreover, He knows us better than we know ourselves and only desires what is best for us; thus, He has given us His commandments so
we can live well.

I. Morality Implies Persons

One of my favorite movies is *Tombstone*, staring Kurt Russell as Wyatt
Earp and Val Kilmer as Doc Holliday. It is the Earps against the cowboys. At the end, Doc Holliday shot Johnny Ringo, who had been the
leader of the cowboy gang. Why? It was over immorality. Why didn't
the moral principles fight? Moral principles do not exist apart from persons. Bad morality confronts us in bad people, and good morality resides in good persons. A good person gives himself to others, thereby
being a blessing to them. Such is the case with God.

Some of the world's major religions, such as Hinduism and Buddhism, do not believe "god" is personal, but that we just reincarnate
forever until we merge back into nothingness. Buddhism basically says
that the life force of the universe resonates in everything, including us.
The only way to know such an impersonal god is to be part of him/it,

to be part of that one impersonal essence, to merge with god, but Christians know the Triune God through His persons who reveal themselves to us.[1] In Buddhist pantheism, "god" animates the universe like our souls animate our bodies so that if the universe did not exist, God would not exist. But one cannot take the distinction between good and evil seriously if "god" is both evil and good. Moreover, in this view, "god" has no existence except in the things continually coming and going, "his" only thought is the sum of the thoughts of all finite beings, "his" only life the sum of the lives of all creatures and only emergences in our consciousness. In short, this "god" is only what we make him/it to be and thus no threat to us.

Here is the point: ***There is no morality without persons***. Moral principles in the abstract do not exist because all morality is the product of persons in *relationship*. It is the *will* of persons that imposes morality. But that does not mean that morality is arbitrarily agreed upon by persons. All morality is the product of the Triune God *personally*, revealing His moral character and imposing that on us *personally*. God says about His commandments and His own holiness:

> [13] Therefore gird up the loins of your mind, be sober, and rest *your* hope fully upon the grace that is to be brought to you at the revelation of Jesus Christ; [14] as obedient children, not conforming yourselves to the former lusts, *as* in your ignorance; [15] but <u>as He who called you is holy, you also be holy in all *your* conduct,</u> [16] because it is written, "<u>Be holy, for I am holy</u>" (1 Peter 1:13-16).

> [2] Speak to all the congregation of the children of Israel, and say to them: "<u>You shall be holy, for I the LORD your God am holy</u>. [3] Every one of you shall revere his mother and his father, and keep My Sabbaths: I am the LORD your God. [4] Do not turn to idols, nor make for yourselves molded gods: I am the LORD your God (Leviticus 19:2-4).

---

[1] We say that the person is distinct from His essence, though inseparable from His essence. In Pantheism, person and essence merge into one.

Notice from Leviticus that God's character is revealed by the Ten Commandments, and other passages could be cited.

When we teach our children morality, we are giving ourselves to them out of love. When we pick up our babies and small children, we are handling them, saying sweet words to them to let them know how much we love them, communicating *ourselves* to them. This is precisely what God does when He gives us His commandments; and when God the Father gave us Himself in the person of His Son, He was demonstrating His incredible love to us. One day, our faith will be sight, and we will be able to touch and feel the incarnate Son of God. God is personal and so are we.

If the personal God created us, *we* would expect to be personal, and so we are, made in His image. God as person has intelligence, compassion, creativity, love, justice, communicates with other persons as in the Father and the Son and the Holy Spirit, and has many other characteristics. God has all these personal characteristics infinitely, and we have them as creatures, finitely. The way we can have a personal relationship with God is through One who was (is) both God's peer and our peer but as one person. That is, of course, the incarnate Son of God.

Remember the garden in Eden. Adam and Eve were created sinless, what we could describe as "normal." There were God, Adam, Eve, and the serpent, who was the devil. Eve told the devil that God had commanded Adam and her not to eat of the tree of the knowledge of good and evil, so obviously she knew what sin was. The devil responded that God was holding out on her, that she could eat of it, thereby being equal with God, making up her own moral rules, and that there would be no consequences if she did. God said that she and Adam would die if they ate from it, but Satan said they would not die.

To put it another way, the devil essentially said that Eve could abstract the moral principle from God, "Don't eat from the tree," and could make it say something like, "Eat from the tree and you will not die." The devil was saying there were neutral, moral principles, common to her and God, and that she could take or leave those principles. But Eve found out when she sinned that she was confronted with *God*, and that very personally. All morality is the product of the Triune God, *personally* revealing His moral character in His commands and imposing that on us *personally*. But Eve, and then her husband Adam also, quickly discovered that when they disobeyed they were confronted with God *personally*, for He came to them to judge them but also to offer mercy with the promise of the coming redeemer (Genesis 3:15). God is not an abstraction. He takes disobedience personally; it can't be otherwise. God's character is tied up in His commands, and a rejection of them is a rejection of Him.

God judged all three (Adam, Eve, Satan), and they were placed under His curse of death. Consequently, Adam and Eve became abnormal, and so mankind continues that way until the Last Day when the curse shall be removed. Those who know Christ have the curse removed from them at death, and even now God is working in their lives to enable them to overcome their sins, to some extent.

It is a given that *we cannot know anyone except by self-revelation*. We can only know God's morality clearly if He tells us. Think of your friends and relatives whom you love. Did you dream up something about them and then declare that is what they were like? No, you spent time with them, and learned their character by their words and actions. Likewise we cannot simply think about God and fashion Him accordingly, which would be creating a god according to our own image. For example, some people think God must approve certain forms of immorality, such as killing babies, but how do they know this? They just invent such ideas, but the only way to know for sure what God approves is for Him to tell us. The Triune God reveals Himself by written self-revelation in Holy Scripture.

In other words, there are only two ways to think about God: according to what one assumes by human reason, or by what God tells us by revelation. Either our reason is the authority of what God is like, or God is His own authority by revelation. If man's finite reason is the final authority for what can exist, we must further assume that his reason is not skewed by sin, and that man is completely neutral about himself, God, and morality. Now God has to be like the human person thinks He is, and if anyone brings up revelation, that must be tested by his reason. That makes him the God-qualifier so that if someone wants to apply for the job of God, He must meet his human standards.

Likewise, Satan tempted Adam and Eve to begin their reasoning with themselves, to reason from their morality to God, saying they could be their own gods. But they learned that God's thoughts were determinative, not their thoughts.

Have you seen the experiment in which four people are put in a room and asked to say which line on a card matches the length of a line on a similar card? Three of the people are told to lie and pick another line. They always go first. Then the fourth person, who always goes last, has to pick which line matches. Will he conform to the others, or will he tell the truth? Seventy percent of the time, he will go against his own eyes to conform to the others. The point is that we can take or leave abstract principles, but we cannot take or leave *someone*— especially if that someone is the Triune God (Father, Son, and Holy Spirit). We have to reckon with Him.

One reason people want to get rid of the infinite personal God is that they don't want to be judged. Abstract moral principles are not threatening. But if there is such a God as we are describing, and He has given us His moral law, which law is a revelation of His own character, and we break His law, that implies judgment. We all know that sinking feeling when we've done something wrong and have to face the boss. If morality were not personal, it would not matter. Some people want objective morality without God because they don't want to be judged.

If morality were just principle and not also personal, there could be no forgiveness. A live wire will shock everyone who touches it without exception. It cannot make a loving decision to give someone immunity from the consequences, but the Triune God can and does.

Some would like to make up their own Ten Commandments, just like our children would like to make up their own rules. But moral law is His commandments to us to obey *Him*. Every law code implies *someone* behind the code to enforce it.

God and His law are inseparable. Thus, for a school teacher to teach students morality apart from relating to God is to teach them how to sin. There is no neutrality in morality. It is a slap in God's face to pretend that we can do what we wish without taking Him into consideration. In this fabrication, there is no one to answer to, only "principles" that we can change to suit ourselves. But with God's Ten Commandments, we will have to answer to *Him*—a person—at the Last Day, and since He does not change, His moral code does not change. That is scary, and we don't like it so we invent ways around this. But God Himself has given us the way out, which is to trust in Christ who took our judgment on the cross.

To conclude this section, if morality is personal so that we make laws regarding one another, where do the moral motions that we have come from? Why do we even think in terms of moral and immoral? The only rational answer is that our moral inclinations come from the personal God who made us like Him, in His image.

II. Morality Implies Principles

God's morality is not just personal; it is also objective and clearly communicated to us. We may call these moral principles or the Ten Commandments. We can observe the Triune God to some extent in His creation (Romans 1:18ff), and we can see that He loves beauty, is infinitely intelligent, and cares for us, but primarily we know God from His revelation to us in Holy Scripture. This revelation is propositional, which means we know Him by words that are rational, historically and objectively true, documented in Holy Scripture.

Someone will object that there are many holy books, but that is not true. There are only two that claim to be a revelation from the infinite personal God; the Old Testament, which we share with the Jews, and the New Testament, which is unique to Christians. Islam is a counterfeit religion with a counterfeit book, the *Koran*, taking ideas from both the Old Testament and the New Testament and adding a lot of imagination, so if we count it, there are three such holy books. Another counterfeit religion is Mormonism with its *Book of Mormon* making claims to be from God. But there are only two original books making such claims, the Old Testament and the New Testament, which are really only one book, since the Old Testament is further explained by the New Testament. (For an astonishing comparison of Mormons and Muslims in free pdf file, please send an email to service@footstool-publications.com.)

One thing that makes the Judeo-Christian heritage unique is that it is rooted in real history, real people who lived in real cities and countries that still exist and are still in the daily news. Moreover, the Bible was written over a period of about 1,500 years by about 40 various human authors, and yet has only one message.

Some will further object that Christians cannot agree on what that message is, but that also is not true. There are three branches of Christianity, Protestant, Roman Catholic, and Eastern Orthodoxy, and all three have always held to God as Trinity (one God in three persons), to Jesus Christ as God in the flesh, that He died in His humanity on the cross for our sins, to His bodily resurrection, and to the Ten Commandments as God's unchangeable morality. Our disagreements are over minor points. In other words, we all hold to the Nicene Creed and its objective, verbal statements about the Christian faith.

III. Morality Implies Personal Responsibility

In our culture, no one wants to assume accountability for his actions. Politicians make a career out of blaming one another. Criminals point to society. The National Organization for Women said it was postpartum depression that caused Andrea Yates in 2001 to drown her five children in the bath tub in Houston. The oldest, a seven year old boy, said "Mommy, have I done something wrong?"[2]

Justifying oneself while blaming others is as old as humanity, but it has become pandemic in the USA. Everyone wants to shift the blame, disavowing any wrong doing, which is what God said people would do:

> If we say that we have no sin, we deceive ourselves, and the truth is not in us.... If we say that we have not sinned, we make Him a liar, and His word is not in us (1 John 1:8, 10).

We are accountable to Him corporately as a nation, and our actions contribute to our national righteousness (or lack thereof). We are ac-

---

[2] Tammy Bruce, *The Death of Right and Wrong* (New York: Three Rivers Press, 2003), p. 62ff. (See my comments on this book in the Bibliography at the end of the book.)

countable to Him as individuals in our private lives; our actions and even our thoughts are subject to His omniscient scrutiny. There is no area of our lives where we have the right of private choice, where we can be autonomous individuals with no accountability to anyone but ourselves. This is God's world, He is the creator, His holy character as revealed in His holy law is the only standard both public and private, and we are accountable to Him for every word (Matthew 12:36). We are all tied together, and whatever what does in public or in private affects our culture.

IV. How Many Moral Systems Are There?

Lewis Carroll the logician (real name: Charles Lutwidge Dodgson) said through the cat and Alice in *Alice in Wonderland*:

> "But I don't want to go among mad people," Alice remarked.
>
> "Oh, you can't help that," said the Cat: "we're all mad here. I'm mad. You're mad."
>
> "How do you know I'm mad?" said Alice.
>
> "You must be," said the Cat, "or you wouldn't have come here."
>
> "And how do you know that you're mad?"
>
> "To begin with," said the Cat, "a dog's not mad. You grant that?"
>
> "I suppose so," said Alice.
>
> "Well, then," the Cat went on, "you see, a dog growls when it's angry, and wags its tail when it's pleased. Now I growl when I'm pleased, and wag my tail when I'm angry. Therefore I'm mad."

Couched in that absurd exchange is an important illustration about relativism. What is the unchanging standard whereby all things are measured and understood? If the dog is the ultimate standard, the cat is mad; but if the cat is the ultimate standard, the dog is mad. Hence, someone is always the standard for someone else, and by some other standard, we're all mad. In other words, if there is no objective, un-changing standard for what is normal, then no one is normal. As I said earlier, if there is no vertical standard, the horizontal cannot be defined.

A. Cannot Create Moral Law

Moreover, *just as we cannot create physical law into existence, so we cannot create moral law into existence*, and to think that we can only re-veals that we believe the lie of the devil to Eve: "You shall be as God, knowing [or determining] good and evil." (Genesis 3:5, for more com-ments on this verse see page 17, and read the paragraph beginning with "Wanting to be God.") Since the fall of man into sin in the garden in Eden, man has deceived himself into thinking that he can make up his own ethics without incurring consequences, but the past few thou-sand years demonstrate otherwise. Nevertheless, he continues his rest-less pursuit of private morality independent from God, so that he does not have to give account. This is why we find people engaging in ra-tionalizing and self-justification when they are caught doing something wrong; they think they are above judgment, living under the system of morality they allegedly created.

It seems that the religion of self is the dominant religion in the USA. In our culture, we are being taught to look for god inside our-selves, and there is nothing more exhilarating in our day than for one to find himself, to find his own true meaning in life, and to find his own ethic, to be true to himself, or to find his own credo. This longing for personal divinity is one reason sexual sins are so eagerly embraced. Once a person "discovers" he is a god, he intuitively understands that he is free to create an ethic of eroticism. Aldous Huxley comes to mind. He was the fierce atheist, who authored *Brave New World* and a number of other popular volumes. In his book *Ends and Means*, Huxley wrote the following, "For myself . . . the philosophy of meaningless was es-sentially an instrument of liberation . . . sexual . . . [and] political."[3] Our culture loves pretended autonomy. For one to challenge such libertine expressions in another's chosen lifestyle is virtually the unpardonable sin, for it attacks his own divinity.

---

[3] Harper & Brothers Publishers; Fifth Edition, (1937), p. 273.

B. Only One Law-Giver

But there is only one God who exists, the Father and the Son and the Holy Spirit. Therefore, there is only one moral law and one law giver, not two or more:

> There is **one** Lawgiver, who is able to save and to destroy (James 4:12).

Thus every "moral law" enacted by mankind (whether Congress or a local church or an individual) is either an *application* of God's law or an *act of rebellion*. Those who pursue their own morality necessarily self-destruct against God's law (Proverbs 11:5), against His morality, under His judgment. Indeed, the battle of the ages is whose moral law rules? All conflicts between Christians and others in society are ultimately rooted in the debate over whose law is supreme. Mankind resents being finite so he pretends his own divinity to invent his own moral law. *This is the main problem in society as a whole.* Our alternatives are God's law or man's law, and man hates God's law because it interferes with his sinful desires, especially sexual desires. Therefore, we have cosmic war over morality. You will notice how our society hates the Bible and prefers its own morality, often making fun of the Bible (which reveals an attitude but is not an argument against it) and those who believe it.

God's Ten Commandments are like electricity: a man can be blessed if he obeys them in the context of believing the Gospel, or the only other option is to be "electrocuted" by them. The "proof" that God's morality is the only one is the impossibility of living life without assuming His morality; otherwise, we are "electrocuted," we self-destruct.

Since all systems of morality imply a person or persons behind that system, multiple and contradicting law systems imply multiple persons in conflict with one another, which is what we have in Western culture. Indeed, multiple law systems imply a god behind each system, which leads to polytheism, many gods, each competing in the market place. Another name for this is pluralism or diversity. Thus, in Western culture, we now have polytheism (many gods), pluralism (many systems of morality), and sweeping moral instability. The only way to have peace in society is for everyone to worship the one true God with His one moral law; otherwise, people have conflicts while trying to impose their morality on others.

To restate this, *a society's god is revealed by the source of its law*, by the highest law of the land. We are at war, spiritually, and each side is exclusive in its claims, Christianity proclaiming the Lordship of Christ, and the secular gods proclaiming "neutrality" with the ACLU and government arbitrating who can say what in the public arena, with hate speech advocates increasingly denying that we can quote the Bible regarding certain sins. Make no mistake, that both sides are exclusive in their claims, "intolerant" for their position of truth. Already one preacher in Canada has been jailed for hate speech when he proclaimed that gay relationships were sinful, even though the Church has been saying that for 2,000 years, and has the mandate to do such under His sovereign Majesty, the King of kings. The issue is which god is God, the secular gods or the Christ, the government or the Son of the living God?

C. No Values

I hate the word "values," for it implies no standard, just arbitrary choices. God does not allow moral neutrality, for *His law is a revelation of His character that cannot change* (1 Peter 1:13-16), and He is not neutral. I'll never forget during the Colonel North hearings on TV back in the late 1980s what one bushy-eyed senator said to Col. North: "God does not take sides in politics." It is difficult to imagine a more ignorant and arrogant statement. If that were true, the Lord God would have to apologize for destroying Sodom and Gomorrah, the Canaanite nations, as well as Rome, and Hitler's Germany. Moreover, neutrality would imply that God's character did not matter; it would imply that it was acceptable for Hitler to murder millions of Jews and many Christians.

But the Scriptures assert that

> Righteousness exalts a nation, but sin is a reproach to *any* people (Proverbs 14:34).

And "sin" is defined by God in His commandments (1 John 3:4). Thus, *Christians do not believe in "values,"* for these are human preferences that can change, created by humans, but the whole world has imposed on it

God's Ten *Commandments*, given by revelation, not His Ten *Suggestions*. Any person or nation that does not live by these will self-destruct, and moreover God's judgment is on him/them to curse them at the Last Day judgment, unless they trust in Christ who took our judgment.

If we are careful in applying the truth that every system of morality originates from a god, it will become clear that believing in "values" is idolatry, for it implies a strange god or gods. "Values" implies that ethics are arbitrary, that there are many legitimate systems and each person or nation may choose his own moral rules. But if any system is legitimate then nothing is absolute, meaning all is arbitrary. If there are many law givers, there are many gods.

According to atheistic philosopher Nietzsche:

> The noble type of man regards HIMSELF as a determiner of values; he does not require to be approved of; he passes the judgment: 'What is injurious to me is injurious in itself'; he knows that it is he himself only who confers honor on things; he is a CREATOR OF VALUES. He honors whatever he recognizes in himself: such morality equals self-glorification.[4]

In other words, Nietzsche gloried in being one who created his own ethics, but then he spent most of his life fighting the Crucified One, hating Christianity with an unholy passion, and died insane.[5]

Nietzsche and others looked at morality as pins in a pin cushion that could be removed or replaced at will. The "pins" were particular moral principles, and the "cushion" would be the moral system. In other words, morality had no unity, but was just more or less arbitrary rules.

D. Only One Moral Law

But *God's law is really not so much the Ten Commandments but one command, for He is one*, the only God, and thus there can only be one moral law. The Ten Commandments are really one law, each com-

---

[4] Frederich Nietzsche, *Beyond Good and Evil*, Planet PDF format, p. 256. Emphasis his.

[5] For an interesting presentation of Nietzsche's life and thought, see Alistair Kee, *Nietzsche Against the Crucified*. I don't recommend this work for the faint of heart, for it glories in Nietzsche's ungodly thought.

mandment containing all the others, each commandment reflecting that one law. His law is like white light: one can put a prism in front of it to break it down into its various hues though it is still just one. Jesus gave two "hues" to the law, to love God and mankind:

> [35] And one of them, a lawyer, asked him a question to test him. [36] "Teacher, which is the great commandment in the Law?" [37] And he said to him, 'You shall **love** the Lord your God with all your heart and with all your soul and with all your mind.' [38] This is the great and first commandment. [39] And a second is like it: 'You shall **love** your neighbor as yourself.' [40] On these two commandments depend all the Law and the Prophets" (Matthew 22:35-40, ESV).

Or we can break this one law into ten "hues," the Ten Commandments. But like white light, the law is really one, each commandment implying the others. It is like a chain; grab any link, and you have the whole chain. The Ten Commandments are not multiple choices.

This means there is a sense in which if we break any of the Ten Commandments we have broken them all:

> For whoever shall keep the whole law, and yet stumble in one *point,* he is guilty of all (James 2:10).

For example, if someone steals, he is an idolater (first command) who has considered creation worth more than God (second command), taken God's name in vain, thinking he can get away with it (third command), made light of sanctifying all his time to God and of the infinite time he'll spend in hell (fourth command), dishonored godly authority (fifth command), not promoted the life and well being of his neighbor (sixth command), dishonored human relationships (seventh command), stolen (eighth command), had to lie to do it (ninth command), and coveted (tenth command). We could do this for each commandment.

The unity of God's law means that if one breaks any command, he comes under the *one* penalty of the one law, physical and spiritual death.

Moreover, there is no sin that is not represented in the Ten Commandments. They are *comprehensive,* for God has not left anything uncovered, at least in principle. To put this another way, in contrast to our laws where the Congress adds thousands of pages to the federal register each year, God has only ten rules, as it were. These are paradigmatic, a model, a pattern. One can extrapolate from them to any situation. God's morality is simple whereas ours is complex. I can just about guarantee that you have broken some federal laws today, and you do even know what they are.

But as one man has succinctly stated:

> "The significance of the Ten Commandments and their influence on American culture can be observed from the White Plains (NY) Reporter, dated September 19, 1929:

> "No man in more than two thousands years has been able to improve upon the Ten Commandments as the rule of life. To no other origin than to Divine Revelation can they be ascribed. Man constantly improves upon his own handiwork. *There never will be a need for an Eleventh Commandment.* The Ten Contain all there is to guide human conduct in the proper channels."

> In more recent American history (January 1983), Federal Judge John C. Knox, whose jurisdiction included New York City, stated in a public address that the laws of this republic were founded on the Ten Commandments.[6]

The Ten Commandments are not only not obsolete, they are absolute.

But non-Christians think of the world as having compartments with various gods over various areas. The Jesus God is over the Church, the anything-goes god over sexuality, the educational god over public schools, and the government god over all as moderator, and each of these gods has its own law code.

Another system of pluralism is that many people seek to have an end-justifies-the-means ethic. (Later, we shall discuss Peter Singer who justifies infanticide and euthanasia with this ethic. See Chapter 12 on the Sixth Commandment.) For now let us just consider how to view

---

[6] Mark F. Rooker, *The Ten Commandments: Ethics for the Twenty-First Century* (Nashville, TN: B&H Academic, 2010), p. 2. Emphasis added.

such an ethic, for it basically says that we should seek the greatest pleasure for the greatest number of people. Here are some objections to this:

- We could justify murdering a sector of the population if
  the majority agreed and it brought them pleasure.
- Should there be an equal distribution of pleasure?
- How can a person determine what brings pleasure to all
  unless he knew what all wanted at any one point in time?
- Would not the definition of pleasure change all the time?
- Moreover, we would have to be able to trace the consequences of an action into the indefinite future to see if it
  continued to bring pleasure.

This type ethic requires the ethicist to be omniscient, to be God, to
be able to know the hearts of all people at any given moment to put the
rule into effect. But unless the rule comes from God, how can we know
that any rule will give more pleasure than pain throughout all history?[7]

Still others have an ethic of self-realization where all reality is one,
as in Hinduism, Buddhism, Taoism where all things merge. In these
religions there is no Creator/creature distinction, just one being, one
reality, which ultimately means no right or wrong, for everything came
from one and will merge back into one regardless what we do.

V. Is There Natural Moral Law?

The Lone Ranger and Tonto went camping in the desert.
After they set up their tent, both men fell sound asleep.

Some hours later, Tonto wakes the Lone Ranger and says.
"Kemo Sabe, look towards sky, what you see?"

The Lone Ranger replies, "I see millions of stars."

"What that tell you?" asked Tonto.

The Lone Ranger ponders for a minute then says, "*Astro-
nomically* speaking, it tells me there are millions of galaxies and

---

[7] John Frame, *The Doctrine of the Christian Life*, p. 99. I discovered this book after I had written mine, and it is amazing how much we think alike. I've used some of
his thoughts in the book in places.

potentially billions of planets. *Astrologically*, it tells me that Saturn is in Leo. *Time wise*, it appears to be approximately a half past three in the morning. *Theologically*, the Lord is all-powerful and we are small and insignificant. *Meteorologically*, it seems we will have a beautiful day tomorrow. What's it tell you Tonto?"

"Kemo Sabe, you dumb as rock. We get in tent earlier, no see stars. Now see stars. It tell me someone stole tent!"

A. What Is Human Natural Law?

But what is natural law? With some, natural law is the right of the individual to decide moral issues without judges or legislation getting in the way. It is just the individual and his conscience. There is no static set of timeless truths, but each individual and each culture morphs into various standards according to the times. Thus for someone to tell a woman that she should not have an abortion is a violation of her right to choose for herself; it is forcing one's morality on another. Of course, they don't want to talk about forcing their morality of choice on a baby who then dies. This choice is especially demanded in the area of sexuality. This is what Judge Bork in his excellent book *Slouching Towards Gomorrah* calls a radical egalitarianism, which means no one can say anyone is wrong about their choices, for all are equal, and there is no God. But if each can choose, what should we do about murder? Government steps in, as it should, but this only reveals that it is impossible to have complete autonomy; there must be limits on what one can choose. How do we define those limits?[8]

With others natural law is the government ruling according to social norms, and the Constitution must be interpreted by those norms. In this view, the Constitution is reinterpreted with each new generation, and this is the way it should be, they think. But this means the Constitution is not really a binding standard, just a wax nose to be manipulated.

---

[8] Another way to say this is to ask if law is normative or descriptive? If it is normative, there is an unchangeable standard; but if it is just descriptive, then it only "describes" what people do.

With still others, natural law can be an unchanging norm that is discovered by some human process that is devoid of divine input. They would say that there are moral absolutes, such as not murdering one another. But there are so many things that people cannot agree to that this seems hopeless.

The problem with natural law in each case is that man *discovers* it based on who he is rather than it being *revealed* based on who God is. Suppose all morality was just natural law, which means we just discover it by ourselves, or make it up as we go along. The first problem is the source for it, for if the world is just molecules in motion, how could immaterial morality arise from matter? If nature is all there is, then the ways things are is the way they should be.[9] Thus if one is born homosexual, that is the way it should be. Of course, we deny that one is born homosexual but that people choose that lifestyle.

A second problem, if morality is just discovered, is that it is just conventions agreed to, for the moment. How do we get others to "discover" it, and who will enforce it? What happens if we can't agree? If no one enforces it, then we have nothing. If we just discover it, how do we explain that all cultures punish people for murder and theft, and look down on adultery? This flux of morality would be like the murderer who thought it was unfair to be prosecuted because he was doing what was "natural," according to what his wisdom had discovered. Some were predators and some prey. He was a predator, so why punish him? We don't punish wolves for being wolves, do we? Moreover, if morality was just a product of people thinking it up, whose thoughts would prevail? It would seem that we would be subject to majority vote so that the next time a Hitler arose, if he had enough votes, murdering Jews and Christians would be acceptable. But we all know that no amount of rational argument can justify murder, or can it? (See Chapter 12 on the Sixth Commandment.)

A third problem is that if moral law is based on human nature, whose human nature? The position usually assumes evolution, which means human nature is constantly changing as it evolves. In fact, some will be more "advanced" than others in their genetic evolution, and all

---

[9] Philosophers say it this way: What is, is the way it ought to be.

will be different a thousand years from now. What will morality be like then? By contrast, we can trace God's absolute moral law back thousands of years from now, and it has not changed because He has not changed.

"Modernist lawmaking is based not on morality but on 'utility' and 'rights.'"[10] In other words, it is very subjective; it is not concerned with righteousness but with what makes people feel good, what people want. When we give up the objective standard of righteousness, society goes to war to fight over whose rights get upheld and whose rights are violated. This view creates moral civil war. People will say dumb things like "people can do what they wish as long as it does not hurt anyone." But that is just the point: All sin hurts those who do it and consequently those around them with whom they have interaction, both public and private.

B. What Is Biblical Natural Law?

But in another sense we can say there is natural moral law if by that we mean that we are made in God's image, consequently we have the "memory" as it were of His morality stamped in us. The Apostle Paul put it this way:

> [14] for when Gentiles, who do not have the law, by nature do the things in the law, these, although not having the law, are a law to themselves, [15] who show the **work** of the law written in their hearts, their conscience also bearing witness, and between themselves *their* thoughts accusing or else excusing *them)* [16] in the day when God will judge the secrets of men by Jesus Christ, according to my gospel (Romans 2:14-16).

The passage teaches us several things. First, the law that Paul says the Gentiles have is nothing other than God's commandments; that is clear from the context. In the verses that follow, Paul mentions stealing, adultery, idolatry, and perhaps other commandments. It is therefore not a different law, a "neutral" moral law that the Gentiles or non-Christians dreamed up or discovered. Second, Paul does not say they

---

[10] Philip E. Johnson, *Reason in the Balance* (Downers Grove, IL: InterVarsity Press, 1995), p. 139.

have the law in their hearts but the *"work* of the law written in their hearts,"* which is its effects. In other words, the very fact that they have a conscience that accuses and excuses indicates that they are made in His image. Animals don't think about and debate morality. Accusations and excuses are activities that evidence moral consciousness, the only rationale of which is the effect of God's law in their hearts.[11] And the fact that their conscience functions with the assumptions of God's Ten Commandments indicates that they really know God, at least in one sense (Romans 1:21). But they don't want to know Him because they love their sin (John 3:19-20) so they suppress the truth about Him and His morality. Here is how Paul put it earlier in Romans:

> [18] For the wrath of God is revealed from heaven against all ungodliness and unrighteousness of men, who <u>suppress the truth</u> in unrighteousness, [19] because what may be known of God is manifest <u>in them,</u> for God has shown *it* to them. [20] For since the creation of the world His invisible *attributes* are <u>clearly seen,</u> <u>being understood by the things that are made,</u> *even* His eternal power and Godhead, so that they are without excuse (Romans 1:18-20).

God's existence and morality are "clearly seen" in creation, but they do not want it so they "suppress" it by means of unrighteous practices, saying that they are "free" to do as they like. Sinning boldly is a challenge to God that He is not in charge; they are. Likewise, the Triune God is "manifest in them," in their conscience as seen in trying to suppress His knowledge as they try to get rid of this constant reminder by giving themselves over to wickedness. Their sinful desires are driving their minds; they are not neutrally investigating morality. Their minds are enslaved to their immorality. What their hearts love, their wills embrace, and their minds justify. They suppress God's existence by devising alternative theories for our existence, such as evolution, which leaves them "free" to devise alternative theories of morality. In the same passage, here is what Paul says they wish to practice:

---

[11] John Murray, *The Epistle to the Romans* (Grand Rapids: Wm. B. Eerdmans Pub. Co., 1959), 1:55-56.

[26] For this reason God gave them up to vile passions. For even their [females] exchanged the natural use for what is against nature. [27] Likewise also the [males], leaving the natural use of the woman, burned in their lust for one another, men with men committing what is shameful, and receiving in themselves the penalty of their error which was due (Romans 1:26-27).

Notice how I translated "women" and "men" above as "females" and "males." There were several choices Paul the Apostle had in words for women and men, but he uses the rare word for "female" and the more certain word for "male" because he is making a deliberate connection to Genesis 1:27 in the Greek translation of the Old Testament where these same Greek words are used:

So God created man in His *own* image; in the image of God He created him; male and female He created them.

The original creation, Paul implies, was one male and one female. That is the standard.

Robert A. J. Gagnon, *The Bible and Homosexual Practice*, demonstrates from dozens of sources from classical Greek (Plato and others), from Jewish sources between the Old and New Testaments, and from those outside the New Testament who nevertheless lived during the time of the Apostles,[12] that "natural use" and "against nature" were set phrases that referred to heterosexual and homosexual behavior respectively with no known exceptions.[13]

But the point is that they cannot live in God's world without assuming His existence and His morality, for they self-destruct ("receiving in themselves the penalty of their error which was due"). This "error" would seem to be apostasy from God, then "burning," which is ever increasing and intense lusts that can never be satisfied, that finally leads to diseases from aberrant sexual practices (Exodus 15:26; Leviticus 26:16) and to final judgment at the Last Day. Moreover, such practices lead them to mental distress, depression, and to suicide, which is very high among homosexuals. Insider Tammy Bruce reports that male

---

[12] Such as Philo and Josephus.

[13] Robert A. J. Gagnon, *The Bible and Homosexual Practice* (Nashville: Abington Press, 2001), 500 plus pages. See especially chapter four.

homosexuals are pursuing unprotected sex even when they know it will lead to disease,[14] which is a death wish. This is a rebellion to God that they can do as they please without consequences. His response is to turn them over to their lusts for destruction and to a warped mind:

> [24] Therefore <u>God also gave them up</u> to uncleanness, in the lusts of their hearts, to dishonor their bodies among themselves . . . [26] For this reason <u>God gave them up</u> to vile passions . . . [28] And even as they did not like to retain God in *their* knowledge, <u>God gave them over</u> to a debased mind, to do those things which are not fitting (Romans 1:24, 26, 28).

This dishonoring of God leads to the dishonoring of self. Though not every idolater gives himself (or herself) to same sex unions, Paul seems to be saying that just as those who reject God suppress the truth about Him (v. 18), so many who reject Him also suppress the truth about same sex unions. Therefore, three times we see that God gave them over to their lusts and to a debased and warped mind. If they reject Him, His creation, and His morality, He will reject them, but if they reach out to Him, He will forgive and heal (1 Corinthians 6:9-11).

Therefore, *in two areas they suppress the truth* so as to distort the natural law of their conscience: (1) they devise alternatives theories of our origin, denying creation and the Creator, (2) which in turn leads them to devise alternative theories of morality, denying their conscience, the image of God within them, and God's morality.

Secularists accuse Christians of trying to impose "religion" on society, for wanting to impose *our* morality. First, as we just saw above, there is only one morality — God's. Second, if God's morality is the only one, He has already imposed it. Third, the secularists are imposing *their* ungodly morality on society, and they are doing so in the name of their god — secularism. It is not a question of imposing; it is only a question of *who* is imposing *what*.

---

[14] Tammy Bruce, *The Death of Right and Wrong* (New York: Three Rivers Press, 2003), p. 96ff. The movement is known as "bareback," risking and even seeking to get some disease as a badge of honor to one's freedom and challenge to God's authority. (See my comments on this book in the Bibliography at the end of the book.)

Of course we can argue for God's morality to our culture without using Scripture, but we cannot argue for it without assuming Scripture.[15] Christians become embarrassed over believing the Bible so they want to distance themselves from it when dealing with non-Christians. It seems better to assume it and then argue one's case, for that is what God Himself does in scripture. Non-Christians don't get to determine the evidence or how we present it to them; God does.

Thus, there is no natural, morally neutral law that is for all faiths. The reason should be obvious: human nature is fallen, which means the hearts of all people are sinful so that there is no neutral moral law code *in* our hearts but rather a law giver *over* our hearts — the Triune God. To assert that there is neutral morality implies a god who is neutral, but we have seen that such thinking is rebellious to the one and only Triune God who is infinitely holy, not neutral. Here is how Jeremiah put it:

> The heart is deceitful above all *things,* and desperately wicked; who can know it? (Jeremiah 17:9).

VI. Law and Love

Most people do not associate God's law with love nor do they think that God's law and freedom go together. But God's law is His gift to show us how to love, what evil is, how to live, and how to have the greatest freedom both personally and in our culture.

First, let us ask what love is. We see an example of true love in the best known verse in the Bible:

> God so **loved** the world that He gave His only begotten Son, that whoever believes in Him should not perish but have everlasting life (John 3:16).

This demonstrates at least one thing that love is: unconditional commitment to another person or persons to do them good, "good" being defined by God. Love is making oneself vulnerable to others for their good. It is willing to be hurt to help those who hurt us, which is

---

[15] John Frame, *The Doctrine of the Christian Life* (Phillipsburg, NJ: P&R Publishing, 2008), p. 242ff.

the ultimate in unselfishness. Christ came to be killed, to give His life for our sins, and then to rise from the dead. At His Second Coming, He will judge others, but for now, He is gracious to us.

But what is love? Where does it come from? What is the standard for love? And why do we consider love so important that we'll even buy pets to love, thus revealing that we want to be loved and have a need to love something else or someone? Now I'll give you ten seconds to answer these questions. Time is up. What is love, and where does it come from? There can be no love without a moral standard. We hear a lot about love, especially towards those who are practicing some sin. A nurse at a doctor's office asked me a pointed question: "Why does your denomination take such a hard nosed stance against gay people?" It was a good question. But I responded that we don't take a mean stance; we take a loving stand.

Since I was in a doctor's office, I used a medical illustration. I said, "Suppose someone comes in here with a disease from which he will die, but there is a cure that works every time. You have to convince the person that he has this disease, which few will admit. But if you don't tell him, is that love?" She got the point. We love the gay community, but God says they must repent of that sin, the same as we must repent of our sins. Love, as defined by God in the Scriptures, and more specifically the Ten Commandments, dictates that we tell them. To do otherwise would be unloving.

Second, how is God's law the standard for love? We might not think that God gave us His law out of love, but He indeed did! This is like you training your two year old son to obey you so he will not be hurt: "Don't touch the hot stove," or "Don't hit your sister," which would be consideration of others and thus love for others. We are loving and protecting our children when we instruct them or spank them. God's moral commandments were given to us because He loves us and wants what is best for us.

To put it another way, *love is obedience to God's law*:

> For the commandments, "You shall not commit adultery,"
> "You shall not murder," "You shall not steal," "You shall not
> bear false witness," "You shall not covet," and if there is any

other commandment, are *all* summed up in this saying, namely, "<u>You shall love your neighbor as yourself.</u>" Love does no harm to a neighbor; therefore <u>love is the fulfillment of the law</u> (Romans 13:9-10).

It is not love to commit adultery. It is not love to murder. It is not love to steal, lie, covet, and so on. Therefore, we see that love is primarily *volition*; that is, it has to do with our will. In obeying God's law. The engine is our determination to obey God, and the caboose is our emotions that are fickle. For example, when two people marry, they make a vow, a commitment, to love one another until death, and since love is volition, they can *choose* to keep their vow. To restate this, *we* control our love; the *object* of our love does not control our love. Indeed, we can even love our enemies since we control our own love (Matthew 5:44-45).

Some would justify anything by love. After 35 years in the ministry, I've heard people justify adultery because they "loved" the new person and fell out of love with the original spouse, but that is love subjectively defined, especially by one's feelings. But if we define love as obedience to God's law, we see that it is objective and volitional. Love *chooses* to keep God's law, and sin *chooses* to break it.

I've watched sitcoms where a son or daughter comes to a parent and asks how one knows if he is in love. There is the usual silence, cough, and then the nonsense: "You *just* know." But we've seen that love is not that way; it is objective, defined by God's law, which also defines evil. We know we're in love when we *choose* to love. We choose to love our parents and siblings without choosing who they would be so we can surely choose to love our spouses.

VII. What Is Sin?

Some think evil is *natural disasters*, such as hurricanes and earthquakes. These surely take their toll, but to define evil in this manner does not address the wrongs we do in our thoughts, words, and actions. We can do little to nothing about preventing natural disasters. We do not think of punishing hurricanes. Natural disasters are the result of evil that has come into the world (Romans 8:20-22), not evil itself. God uses natural disasters to warn us of our immoral behavior, to get us to repent, to call us to Himself (Luke 13:1-5).

Others think it is evil to be *finite*, to be a creature, so they imagine they are god, part of the oneness of all things, as promoted in the New Age movement and in Hinduism. But the Bible presents us as creatures and only the Triune God as sovereign. He is unique; we are not. There is a Creator/creature distinction that cannot be breached. It is not wrong, therefore, to be finite. God made us that way.

Christianity sees evil as *moral*, (not metaphysical), and that being finite is okay. Immorality is defined as rebellion against the Triune God's commandments. Morality is keeping His commands.

Also, since morality is personal, sin is personal, and that means sin is personal *rebellion* against the Triune God. Sin means that we arrange our existence around ourselves, deliberating leaving God out. It is like the teen who comes home from school and tells his mother that he is going out, and when she asks where he is going, he says "None of your business." In other words, he accepts food, clothing, shelter, and even life itself from his mother, but scorns her authority. Is this not what many do today regarding God? They accept His benefits but reject His authority? Evil is rebellion against God's goodness.

VIII. How Universal Is Sin?

How do we explain that everyone has a streak of meanness, selfishness, pride, lust, unjustified anger, lack of love, and just plain bad behavior? No one is exempt, from the baby who is self-centered to the adult who murders or who does so at least in thought, wanting others dead for personal, vindictive reasons. Indeed, we do not love others or the Triune God but love ourselves as the highest good. Like Adam and Eve in their first sin, we all want to be independent of our maker, to be our own god, making up our own rules as we go along.

Some try to explain this away, even saying that babies are born without sin (So why abort them?), but then we must ask why babies die if they are without sin? Christians have the answer: "the wages of sin is death" (Romans 6:23). All people are connected with Adam, the first human; and when he sinned, his disobedience and death were imputed to us. To restate this, we are all connected back to our first parents (Romans 5:12-23).

Some will claim this is not fair, but then think nothing of punishing a whole nation for the sins of its leaders, intuitively knowing there is a connection, a representation of the whole country in its leaders, an implicit approval of the sins of the leaders by the citizens. An Enron goes down, and though the employees are not directly guilty of the sins of the officers of the corporation, they still suffer the penalty of the officers' sins. In a similar way (though not exactly), we are guilty of the first sin of Adam as seen in our embracing other sins as soon as we're born. We identify with his rebellion; we love our sin and hate God's righteousness (John 3:18-21).

People may bellow that such a connection is not fair, but the same is true of our connection with Christ—those who trust in Him have His righteousness imputed to them. They receive the free gift of eternal life by trusting Him as their head. There is only one alternative: make it to heaven on our own, which can't be done (Ephesians 2:8-9), for even one sin disqualifies us, and we come into the world with one sin, Adam's eating of the forbidden fruit.

But we are all born with a sinful character. We may develop that character for better or for worse, but we come into the world already marred. For example, I've never met a parent who said he had to teach his child how to sin; they come into the world as experts!

It seems to me that universal sin is one Christian doctrine that is empirically verifiable, for we no one but Christ had no bad points to his character—not even Mother Teresa. We all find within ourselves a struggle with that which we know to be good, but we don't want to practice it. We are all inconsistent and unrighteous, yelling at others for no good reason or just wanting our way. We all have a streak of meanness in us.[16]

---

[16] A very interesting book on original sin that surveys various persons and cultures is Alan Jacobs, *Original Sin* (New York, NJ: Harper Collins, 2008). This is not just a pragmatic approach, but he delves into various secular and Christian theories, along with great insight into how cultures stand or fall with their view of original sin. Highly recommended; Jacobs is evangelical. A not so good book, written from a secu-

Jean-Jacques Rousseau (1712-1778) popularized John Dryden's (1631-1700) statement of the "noble savage," believing that those who had no contact with the outside world would not learn the sins of the outside world. In other words, sin was not inherent but only leaned by example, which in turn means there is no character, only isolated acts of our wills that do not reveal a sinful bent. If one could control the environment, he could control the isolated acts.

Enter Robert Owen (1771-1858),[17] who in the early 1800s bought property in Indiana and set up a colony (New Harmony) whereby he would create a perfect environment. Owen thought that if he eliminated three evils: traditional religion (attack against the Church), conventional marriage (attack against the family), and private property (attack against free citizenship)—especially private property—that man's so-called sinful problems would disappear. (The Eighth Commandment gives us the right to own private property.) But as soon as the colony was established and a constitution was written, it fell apart. He thought that since man was allegedly born good, controlling the circumstances and educating him would lead to utopia. But he could not get the people to attend his schools without compulsion, which violated his view of the autonomous, good individual. The colony self-destructed in no time, and he returned to his native Britain, having used up his considerable fortune trying to establish other colonies elsewhere with the same results, and died disillusioned and penniless. *He discovered that man cannot be his own savior.*

From the assumption that man is born good, modern day liberals, following Owen, believe that the problem is external, in the environment. Change that and man will be changed, saved from his own problems. Thus, the means to such change is education, for if man is good, he only needs to know what to do, and then he will choose it. Authority is basically not needed in education; each student, being good, is his own authority. The modern educational system, therefore, seeks to save us by getting rid of traditional religion with its authority, redefin-

---

lar view, is Gary A. Anderson, *Sin: A History*. His theory is that almsgiving is how we atone for our sins.

[17] Alan Jacobs, *Original Sin*, pp. 173ff.

ing marriage and sexuality, and promoting the idea that the government owns all things, which means no private property. The government and man is the only savior, with the government claiming to be god. (It is telling that virtually every man-made alternative to God's salvation includes some form of sexual deviance from His norm as given in the Seventh Commandment: one man and one woman in marriage for life.)

Christianity takes the opposite view: man is born sinful; therefore, the problem is internal, we are changed by Christ internally, need godly authority to make us learn godly behavior and to hold us accountable. Christ is the only savior.

These two systems are mutually exclusive and are at war spiritually, and only one can be the final winner. We know that Christ is that winner, for He is Lord of all!

Conclusion

We may not think of God's Ten Commandments as the gift of Himself, but since morality is personal, it is precisely that. The Ten Commandments reveal the loving character of God. Moreover, these laws are principles, by which we mean truth-statements, verbal, objective, clear, unchanging, and revealed by a loving God for our good. Let us love Him by loving His commandments. **AMEN**.

Chapter 3—Who Is God's Law For?

Introduction

Radio announcer states:

> And now, ladies and gentlemen, we have a word from some attorneys, just a little disclaimer. Then we'll go back to the regularly scheduled slamming. Senator Jones' attorneys said that Jones was not really an adulterer, for his wife would have to disapprove of it, but hey, she has her lovers, too. Moreover, his "indiscretions" and cover-ups would not affect his public life, for they are two different spheres. This has been a test of the emergency disclaimer system. Had it not been a test, you would have read about it in the newspaper.

We hear much today about each person having his own morality as if it does not matter what standard we have. Is there a private standard versus a public standard? Does one's private morality affect his public morality? Can we choose our own system? How many moral systems are there? How does secularism contribute to our moral decay? Is there natural moral law apart from any one to enforce it?

People in our culture have a disconnect between private and public morality, based on the assumption that there is no God. Thus, what they do in private is allegedly their own business; they are their own gods there, accountable only to themselves. Public morality, however, is under the scrutiny of others so they must be more careful. If they can get away with something, it is ok; otherwise, they are accountable.

Some Christians call what I'm saying divine command theory,[1] and then proceed to say that we should not "force" our morality on the unbelievers. They proclaim that Christians have God's law, but non-Christians are not under His law. In other words, it is permissible for Christians to use the Bible with other Christians, but we should use some other authority when we approach the non-Christian. (See chapter 2, IV. How Many Moral Systems Are There?)

I. The Ten Commandments Are the Center of Morality

The Ten Commandments run all through the Bible, being the central moral statement in both the Old Testament and the New Testament.[2] For example, if we took time, we could find each of the Ten Commandments in the book of Genesis, but for sure these Ten Commandments are given by God personally, written in the second book of the Bible (Exodus 20), and then repeated in the fifth book for emphasis (Deuteronomy 5). They were personally written by His "finger" (Deuteronomy 9:10). The Lord talked to Israel "face to face," as it were, in giving these commandments which is the only time in the Bible He did such, which means they must be extremely important.

Then the Ten Commandments were placed in the most sacred part of Israel's worship elements, the ark of the covenant (Deuteronomy 10:5), while other legislation was just written on scrolls and placed *beside* the ark, not *in* it (Deuteronomy 31:24-26).

In the New Testament we see the Ten Commandments often invoked, for in the Sermon on the Mount the Lord Jesus taught about them (Matthew 5-7). He told the rich young ruler to keep God's commandments if he wanted to enter life, and then He names several of the

---

[1] Craig A. Boyd, *A Shared Morality: A Narrative Defense of Natural Law Ethics* (Grand Rapids: Brazos Press, 2007). This is a comprehensive survey of natural law ethics from the St. Augustine to today, written for scholars, and not convincing to me. Again, the book you are reading is not designed to go into such matters in detail but is (hopefully) more on the practical side for Christians who are wondering what is happening to the West, especially the USA, to Christianity in our country, and who want to know how to live righteously.

[2] Much of this section came from Patrick D. Miller, *The Ten Commandments* (Louisville: John Knox Press, 2009), p. 3ff.

Ten (Matthew 19:17). (We interpret this to mean covenantal faithfulness, not meriting one's way to heaven.)

Moreover, James states that we will be judged by these commandments:

> 8 If you really fulfill *the* royal law according to the Scripture, "You shall love your neighbor as yourself," you do well; 9 but if you show partiality, you commit sin, and are convicted by the law as transgressors. 10 For whoever shall keep the whole law, and yet stumble in one *point,* he is guilty of all. 11 For He who said, "Do not commit adultery," also said, "Do not murder." Now if you do not commit adultery, but you do murder, you have become a transgressor of the law. 12 So speak and so do as those who will be judged by the law of liberty (James 2:8-12).

Several pages earlier in this book we saw that the Apostle Paul said in Romans 13:9-10 that the Ten Commandments are the summary of the law and that we are bound by them.

Repeatedly throughout Holy Scripture we see the Ten Commandments invoked as God's standard. They are God's enduring standard, a revelation of His own holy character.

II. The Ten Commandments Are for All Nations

Some think that God's commandments are just for God's people and not for those outside His covenant. But if this is so, on what basis will they be judged? Does God have two different standards by which to judge people? If that is true, God's moral law is rather arbitrary, and His moral character inconsistent. But consider these passages about the Gentile nations that Israel was to displace:

> 2 "Speak to the children of Israel, and say to them: 'I am the LORD your God. 3 According to the doings of the land of Egypt, where you dwelt, you shall not do; and according to the doings of the land of Canaan, where I am bringing you, you shall not do; nor shall you walk in their ordinances. 4 You shall observe My judgments and keep My ordinances, to walk in them: I am the LORD your God" (Leviticus 18:2-4).

We can see that God was judging the Gentile nations for disobedience to His moral laws as defined in the Ten Commandments. Just read Leviticus chapters 18-20 to see the contrast from the sins of the Canaanites to God's command to obey His law.

> [24] Do not defile yourselves with any of these things; for by all these the nations are defiled, which I am casting out before you. [25] For the land is defiled; therefore I visit the punishment of its iniquity upon it, and the land vomits out its inhabitants. [26] You shall therefore keep My statutes and My judgments, and shall not commit *any* of these abominations, *either* any of your own nation or any stranger who dwells among you [27] (for all these abominations the men of the land have done, who were before you, and thus the land is defiled), [28] lest the land vomit you out also when you defile it, as it vomited out the nations that were before you. [29] For whoever commits any of these abominations, the persons who commit *them* shall be cut off from among their people. [30] Therefore you shall keep My ordinance, so that *you* do not commit *any* of these abominable customs which were committed before you, and that you do not defile yourselves by them: I am the LORD your God (Leviticus 18:24-30).

Notice from these passages that God judged the Gentile nations that were in the land because they had violated His commandments. Thus, He sent His people to destroy them. Again, we read:

> [22] You shall therefore keep all My statutes and all My judgments, and perform them, that the land where I am bringing you to dwell may not vomit you out. [23] And you shall not walk in the statutes of the nation which I am casting out before you; for they commit all these things, and therefore I abhor them. [24] But I have said to you, "You shall inherit their land, and I will give it to you to possess, a land flowing with milk and honey." I am the LORD your God, who has separated you from the peoples (Leviticus 20:22-24).

In Isaiah chapters 15-30, we see God indicted various Gentile nations because of their disobedience to His moral law. Therefore, God's Ten Commandments are for all nations and all people.

III. The Ten Commandments Are for Ungodly People

Of course, God's moral law is also for all individuals in that it indicts them for their disobedience. Paul says in Romans 3 that both Jews and Gentiles are under His law and thus condemned as under sin because they have broken it (Romans 3:9-19). Indeed, God's high moral standard shows us that we are sinners, which in turn means that we need His mercy in Christ. Again, Paul stated in 1 Timothy 1:9-11:

> 8 But we know that the law is good if one uses it lawfully,
> 9 knowing this: that the <u>law is not made for a righteous person, but for the lawless</u> and insubordinate, for the ungodly and for sinners, for the unholy and profane, for murderers of fathers and murderers of mothers, for manslayers, 10 for fornicators, for sodomites, for kidnappers, for liars, for perjurers, and if there is any other thing that is contrary to sound doctrine, 11 according to the glorious gospel of the blessed God which was committed to my trust (1 Timothy 1:8-11).

This obviously applies to all people, whether Christians or not. Paul's point is not that Christians are not accountable to God's law, but that it is especially for those who are disobedient. For Christians it becomes a blessing as we embrace Christ by embracing His character in His law.

IV. The Ten Commandments Are for Christians

Especially in this day after the cross, Christians have the law of God written in their hearts (Jeremiah 31:33; 2 Corinthians 3:3; Hebrews 8:10; 10:16), which means it becomes a part of us, that we love God by loving His law, that the way in which we are being conformed to Christ is by increasingly loving Him through His law.

The preface to the Ten Commandments begins with this verse in Exodus where they are first given:

> I am the LORD your God, who brought you out of the land of
> Egypt, out of the house of bondage (Exodus 20:2).

First, we have grace, for we see the LORD proclaiming that He is their God and the One who redeemed them by the blood of the lamb from the "house of bondage." Second, it is only *after* the people have been redeemed that God gives them His Ten Commandments. This is like a wedding ceremony where the couple takes vows to be faithful to one another. The commitment comes first and then working out that commitment to one's spouse. God demonstrated His love by having redeemed His people, and the people respond to be obedient to Him, to keep His covenant. In the previous chapter where Moses is said to have given them the commandments, the people promise: "All that the LORD has spoken we will do" (Exodus 19:8).

This is just like Paul in Ephesians when he says that we obey as the proof of grace:

> [8] For by grace you have been saved through faith, and that not of yourselves; *it is* the gift of God, [9] not of works, lest anyone should boast. [10] For we are His workmanship, <u>created in Christ Jesus **for** good works</u>, which God prepared beforehand that we should walk in them. (Ephesians 2:8-10).

We see that good works are the necessary evidence of our faith, not something optional.

Third, Exodus 20:2 occurs immediately *before* the Ten Commandments, and reveals that God had redeemed His people by the blood of the Passover lamb, an animal that pictured the ultimate Lamb to come, the Lord Christ. By "redeemed" we mean that God freed His people from Egypt, which represented bondage to sin, set them free, and made them His people. God established a relationship with His people *first*, and only then gave them His commandments, for it is out of grace that we obey. It is like preparing a room for the new child to be born, and then the child is brought home to live in what has already been prepared. Only then will the child, as he grows up, be expected to do what his parents tell him. The child does not first obey to get the room. Likewise, Christians obey God not to get grace, but because they have it.

Keeping His commands reveals if we know Him or not, but we can never keep His commands so well that we make Him obligated to give us eternal life. That is a free gift, but we reveal whether our faith is genuine or not by what we do, not just in what we say. It is easy to attend church and mechanically say the Nicene Creed, but are we actually keeping God's commands?

Our obedience to God's law demonstrates whether we have faith or not, and 1 John 2:3-4 especially teaches this:

> 3 Now by this we know that we know Him, if we keep His
> commandments. 4 He who says, "I know Him," and does not
> keep His commandments, is a liar, and the truth is not in him.

It is absolutely astonishing to me how often those who claim to be Christians can violate God's commandments with little thought about it. One very common sin, to be discussed more later, is sexual, either committing adultery or living with someone before marriage. I've had an otherwise nice Christian couple tell me that they set the terms for marriage, and that if they said they were married, they were. Thus, they could live together as husband and wife even before marriage. Apparently, God had little to say about the matter. It would seem that they found a loophole in God's Seventh Commandment not to commit sexual sin. They just proclaimed themselves married. We shall discuss this in Chapter 13, but my point is that even those who profess to be Christians are dishonoring God's Ten Commandments.

V. What Are Some Functions of God's Law?

God in His grace states several uses of His law, and all of these are designed by His love to help us.

A. God's Law Restrains from Sin

One purpose of God's commandments is *to restrain evil*. When I was growing up in the 1950s and early 1960s, we had the Ten Commandments on the wall in home room in public school. Each day in high school a student read from the Bible, prayed, and then we all said the Pledge of Allegiance. The constant reminder of God's law molded our consciences as we grew up. Movies were not rated, for there was no need. There was no profanity on TV or radio, no Playboy, and rape was rare. Consider this verse:

> Where there is no revelation, the people cast off restraint; but
> happy is he who keeps the law (Proverbs 29:18).

In other words, when God's commandments (revelation) are kept before the people, it produces moral restraint, protection from one another, Christian cultural conscience; but without it, the people pursue sin with reckless abandonment. As all Christian symbols are being removed from our culture, all restraint to avoid sin is being removed.

B. God's Law Reveals Our Sin and Thus Our Need of Christ

The law is like this Grandma in court:

> Lawyers should never ask a Mississippi grandma a question if they aren't prepared for the answer. In a trial, a Southern small-town prosecuting attorney called his first witness, a grandmotherly woman to the stand. He approached her and asked, "Mrs. Jones, do you know me?" She responded, "Why, yes, I do know you, Mr. Williams. I've known you since you were a young boy, and frankly, you've been a big disappointment to me. You lie, you cheat on your wife, and you manipulate people and talk about them behind their backs. You think you're a big shot when you haven't the brains to realize you never will amount to anything more than a two-bit paper pusher. Yes, I know you."
>
> The lawyer was stunned! Not knowing what else to do, he pointed across the room and asked, "Mrs. Jones, do you know the defense attorney?" She again replied, "Why, yes, I do. I've known Mr. Bradley since he was a youngster, too. He's lazy, bigoted, and he has a drinking problem. He can't build a normal relationship with anyone, not to mention he cheated on his wife with three different women. One of them was your wife. Yes, I know him." The defense attorney almost died.
>
> The judge immediately stopped the proceedings and called for both counselors to approach the bench and, in a very quiet voice, said, "If either of you idiots asks her if she knows me, I'll send you to the electric chair."

The law reveals to us our sinfulness so that we will run to Christ for forgiveness. But we must not play games with God, presuming on His grace, thinking we can violate His law with impunity, mouthing words only to return to our sin with joy. I had a man tell me that he would live it up in sin, and then later in life he would repent. I told him that God was under no obligation to forgive his sins if he had spurned His warnings, His law, and His grace for so many years. He was instantly killed in a car wreck some years later while still living it up.

There are only two possibilities for us to be accepted by God. (1) He could lower His standard of acceptance, adjusting His commandments to our level of morality, but of course that would be an unacceptable compromise to justice. (2) He could offer us justice and mercy at the same time as a free gift, which is what He does in the Lord Jesus Christ. The Lord kept the law for us perfectly and died under the full penalty of God's law (justice), and then He offers us forgiveness of sins based on this, free, just for the asking (mercy).

It is amazing to me how people will bellow against such a free offer. It is like a man in a flood standing on the roof of his car with the waters quickly rising, and a helicopter comes along, lowering the bucket, but the man yells, "I don't like the color of this helicopter, send me another one." It is ridiculous to reject a free gift because of some irrelevant reason. Have you talked to those trained to save people from drowning? You would think the drowning persons would be glad to see the lifeguard. Instead, they fight him, and resist his mercy. Likewise, those drowning in their sins resist the one with the good news. It is irrational.

No one can keep even one of the Ten Commandments perfectly, not even for one hour, *so another purpose of the God's law is to demonstrate our sinfulness* (Romans 3:20) and thus our need of Christ (Romans 3:21-26). "Christ died for our sins" (1 Corinthians 15:3), and "sin is lawlessness" (1 John 3:4). Just as one will not go to a doctor unless he is convinced he is sick, so he will not go to the Great Physician unless he knows he is sinful. We cannot make ourselves acceptable to God by trying to keep His moral law because no one can keep it perfectly, and God will not accept anything but perfection. If He could just compromise sin and overlook it, we did not need the cross. If the cross is unnecessary, God sent His Son for nothing.

Now here is a startling fact: Even though God runs His moral universe by His commandments, we cannot change people by giving them law. In other words, we can command a thief all day long not to steal, but that will not change his heart, the place where decisions are made. Moreover, we can educate a thief in the finest schools, but that will only make him a clever thief. The solution is to have his heart changed by trusting in Christ for forgiveness of sins.

The Church's function is to preach the Gospel of the death and resurrection of Christ, which changes the hearts of people. Commands do not change hearts, but the good news does.

Does keeping the Ten Commandments merit our way to heaven? Can we make God our debtor by worship on Sunday and tithing? Paul answers that clearly: "Knowing that a man is <u>not</u> justified by the works of the law but by faith in Jesus Christ" (Galatians 2:16). In other words, no one can keep God's law perfectly to merit heaven. Then what is one purpose of the Ten Commandments? "For by the law is the knowledge of sin" (Romans 3:20).

C. God's Law Gives Freedom

God's law with the Gospel leads to freedom, or apart from the Gospel it can enslave; it all depends on the context. To restate this, some think that any law is restrictive of freedom. They understand freedom to mean free to do anything we like. We often hear people say, "This is a free country so I can do what I want." But this is a half truth. We are not free to murder, to rape, to bear false witness. No, *freedom has form,* structure. Today we are rearing a whole generation of children to think that freedom means no form, no structure, no boundaries, and that they can practice any morality they choose with no consequences. Suicide and other kinds of death are very high among teens, for lack of structure leads to insecurity and to hopelessness.

In other words, the law has great freedom attached to it if done from the heart, for we humans are the most free when we are doing what we were created to do, love God by keeping His commandments. A duck is most free in the water, a chicken most free on land, and we humans are most free when we are enslaved to righteousness, to God's most holy and wonderful commandments. It is the disobedience to those commands that brings enslavement and self-destruction, like taking illegal drugs enslaves.

Conclusion

Functions of God's law, then, are several. First, His law restrains us from sin if it is constantly held up as the standard for morality, but if it is criticized, denied, and made fun of, people will ignore it.

Second, His law also reveals to us our sin and our need of Christ. One who thinks he is ok the way he is will never go to Christ for forgiveness of sins. We must understand our guilt before we will pursue His forgiveness.

Three, God's law in the right context can be freedom, showing us how to live for Him, how to be morally successful in this life, how to be free and blessed by pleasing Him by faith, a faith that keeps His law (James 2:20). Yet our keeping His law is always imperfect, and we cannot merit our way to heaven. That is a free gift! **AMEN**.

Chapter 4—Is Morality Relative?

Introduction

Groucho Marx once said:

> "These are my principles. If you don't like them, I have others."

The philosopher and logician Lewis Carroll gives us a good view of relativism in *Alice in Wonderland* when Alice meets the Cheshire Cat:

> "Would you tell me, please, which way I ought to go from here?" Alice asked the Cat.
>
> "That depends a good deal on where you want to get to," said the Cat.
>
> "I don't much care where—" said Alice.
>
> "Then it doesn't matter which way you go," said the Cat.
>
> "—so long as I get *somewhere*," Alice added as an explanation.
>
> "Oh, you're sure to do that," said the Cat, "if you only walk long enough."

We could imagine this continued set of dialogues:

> "But I'm somewhere now," Alice objected.
>
> "Yes, and any road will lead you to somewhere *else*."
>
> "Well, then," asked Alice, "which way do I go if I want to get to a *certain* place."
>
> "What place is that?" the Cat responded.
>
> Alice slowly said, "I don't know the name of it."

"In that case, no road will help you get there."

We can see that if a person is searching for nothing, he will continue to find nothing, and if one searches for truth but does not know what it looks like, no path will help him find it.

I. What Morality?

A. Relativism

But let us pose an ethical question to further illustrate the destructive nature of the secular ethic. If someone takes a homeless child and sells him to a corporation that will kill him and harvest his organs, is that wrong, and if so, why? Many secularists reason that the child probably would not live anyway, and if it did, it would not have a reasonable chance for "quality" of life.[1] Is this not the kind of relativism that propels people to sacrifice even younger children? They do it for the greater good of society, or because the child is an inconvenience at this time, or an embarrassment. Now some forms of stem cell research kill millions of babies after conception. Yet latest research indicates that adult stem cells are more useful, but this isn't being funded, even though nobody dies in the process.

To further accentuate the incoherence of moral relativism, consider the fact that most people really don't believe what they claim to believe, for as soon as their car is stolen, or their child is raped, they suddenly believe in objective morality.

Remember the movie *Indecent Proposal*? The situation was that the couple was deeply in debt, and the woman was beautiful. A rich man approached and offers them one million dollars if she'll sleep with him for one night. The movie was designed to challenge our morals, to make us think that it would be permissible for just one night.

God condemns adultery with no exceptions. A covenant has been made between a man and a woman, and the terms of the covenant are His Ten Commandments, and these commandments are the terms for all relationships between God and humans and between humans and

---

[1] In fact, one philosophy book I was reading that presents a relative ethic used this example, saying that it was wrong, but gave no explanation why. Thomas Cathcart and Daniel Klein, *Plato and Platypus*, p. 82.

humans. These Ten Commandments are not optional, not up for debate, *have already been imposed by God,* and we cannot live profitably without assuming them in every moral act, which means every decision.[2]

B. Death and Deciding

When I was majoring in philosophy at a university, the professors loved to present a relative ethic. One example was that a woman during WW2 was commanded to commit adultery with a Nazi officer, or he would kill her children. Allegedly, this meant she should commit adultery. But one assumption to this argument is that death is the worst evil, worse than adultery, in this case. In such a system, survival is the only ethic. Another assumption is that the woman can be made accountable for an act she did not do, such as killing children.

But God takes a different view. Sin is what will cause all of us to die, and it is worse than physical death, for it attaches to us at the Last Day judgment. The book of Daniel provides a great example of men standing for God's truth even in the face of death:

> [15] "Now if you are ready at the time you hear the sound of the horn, flute, harp, lyre, *and* psaltery, in symphony with all kinds of music, and you fall down and worship the image which I have made, *good!* But if you do not worship, you shall be cast immediately into the midst of a burning fiery furnace. And who is the god who will deliver you from my hands?" [16] Shadrach, Meshach, and Abed-nego answered and said to the king, "O Nebuchadnezzar, we have no need to answer you in this matter. [17] If that is the case, our God whom we serve is able to deliver us from the burning fiery furnace, and He will deliver *us* from your hand, O king. [18] But if not, let it be known to you, O king, that we do not serve your gods, nor will we worship the gold image which you have set up" (Daniel 3:15-18).

---

[2] There are legitimately gray areas, and in theology we call these *adiaphora,* things that are indifferent in themselves. One quick example is drinking alcohol, which is not forbidden, unless by it we cause a person with a drinking problem to fall. Drunkenness, though, is forbidden.

Death was not as bad as idolatry for the three Hebrew believers in God, but I understand why non-Christians reason the way they do:

> [14] Inasmuch then as the children have partaken of flesh and blood, He Himself likewise shared in the same, that through death He might destroy him who had the power of death, that is, the devil, [15] and release <u>those who through fear of death were all their lifetime subject to bondage</u> (Hebrews 2:14-15).

Non-Christians are enslaved to death and fear it above all else, but Christians have been delivered from it. Death is not the worst evil; sin is.

C. Deconstructionism

Moreover, in the *deconstructionist* movement postmodernism has been taken to its next logical conclusion, which holds that there is no paradigm[3] by which one can interpret life. A person receives "meaning" from whatever group he associates with, and since there is no paradigm over all the groups to hold them together, there is perpetual cultural war. Each person creates his own reality as he interprets it. It is like the three umpires calling balls and strikes.[4] The first one said, "I call them as they are." The second one boasted, "I call them as I see them." The third one trumped the others: "They are not balls or strikes until I call them." The first one would be a Christian world view; the second one the old liberal view; and the third the modern view of no truth.

Deconstructionism also maintains that language has no meaning, but words are only symbols of the moment that we can interpret any way we choose, especially written language. That means there is no history, for that involves the objective meaning of words to tell a story. Of course, how can its proponents even write against objective meaning without assuming the laws of logic, which are transcendent and have objective meaning? It is like the famous words Lewis Carroll put into the mouth of Humpty Dumpty:

---

[3] The word they use is "metanarrative."

[4] Millard J. Erickson, *The Postmodern World* (Wheaton, IL: Crossway Books, 2002), p. 40.

"When I use a word, it means just what I choose it to mean — neither more nor less."

But if words have no meaning, they cannot write about it. And if they write about it and others understand them, they have defeated their point. Nothing can be done without the laws of logic, and those laws are known, communicated, and articulated by speech. It is absurd to try to communicate by logic that logic does not work. Moreover, deconstructionists who would deny any history defeat themselves. For as soon as they finish writing, their own documents are history, and thus null and void. Once again we see that they cannot avoid functioning in God's world God's way, for they write propositions that are verbal and rational, and if not true, irrelevant, and if true, they destroy themselves.

Language involves the transcendent God, invokes His logic and even the immaterial rules of grammar in our thought processes, which once again testifies to us made in His image.[5] In other words, the rules of language are rational, personal, transcendent, and one cannot function at all without assuming them. Language is personal because "Persons have rational capacities, . . . not rocks, trees. . . ."[6]

If language came from chemicals by evolution, why can't plants talk? But if man is immaterial soul as well as body, the soul having been made in God's image, then language makes sense. Evolution divinizes nature and lowers man to an animal, whereas Scripture divinizes man (in the sense of being in God's image) and puts nature under man.

In fact, man exercises dominion over the earth, over its creatures, in science and other matters, by means of propositions in the use of language. The animals are not capable of doing this. What the unbeliever denies, verbal propositions that reveal the mind of someone, is what they practice, handing down knowledge from one generation to another by written propositions revealing the minds of those who write. In other words, the irony is that non-Christians write books, which are

---

[5] See the excellent work by Vern Poythress, *In the Beginning Was the Word: Language—A God Centered Approach* (Wheaton, IL: Crossway Books, 2009). Not the easiest read.

[6] Poythress, *In the Beginning*, p. 71.

objective, propositional "revelation" from some transcendent standard to readers, from persons to persons. It is impossible to live in God's world, advance in civilization, and not do such. This only reveals, once again, that this is God's world and that no one can live in it without assuming His truth.

II. Secularism

As one Christian scholar has insightfully stated:

> The emergence of the intellectual as a recognized social type is one of the most remarkable developments of recent centuries. Intellectuals became a secular priesthood, unfettered by the dogmas of the religious past. . . . Western society came to believe that it should look elsewhere than to its clergy for guidance.[7]

Secularism is the idea that the elite, especially those in government or the universities, should direct our institutions and practices, and that government should exist separately from religious beliefs. Secularism believes that it should regulate religion, that it is neutral regarding religion, and therefore superior to religious beliefs. Thus we hear even Christian politicians back peddling very strongly when asked how their religious beliefs will affect how they would govern if elected.

The most powerful foe of Christianity today in the USA is secularism composed of elite. These elite deny the existence of God, and do not want any supernaturalism in their world. We can see what they believe with their social engineering. Their agenda is tax, spend with money that is not backed by silver and gold (against the Constitution) thus devaluing the dollar, lie, use their office to gain sexual favors, promote sexual promiscuity among the youth to destroy the family, kill babies and now also the elderly with euthanasia, and make us vulnerable to our military enemies. Regardless of political party, most politicians are just variations of the same theme. (See Part 3.)

Secularism is as much a religion as anything imaginable with its supreme beings to control society, the elite; with its law, humanist anti-

---

[7] Alister McGrath, *The Twilight of Atheism*, p. 49.

commandments, all against God's Ten Commandments. If it is religious to believe in God, it is religious to deny Him. These elite are very intolerant for their religion, and they demand not to be offended by public expressions of views that challenge them.[8]

Everyone, including the secularist, has a religion, which means beliefs about supreme reality, about morality, and about judgment both in this life and in the one to come. It is impossible not to have religious beliefs, and it is time for us Christians to shout: "The emperor has no clothes," to tell others that their religion is not neutral secularism, but anti-Christian to the core. Jesus, the King of kings and Lord of lords, is at the head of every chain of command and system of morality, and He will judge them all. It is in *confrontation* that we will influence our culture for Christ, not in *compromise*.

Secularists do not usually seek to justify the use of reason but consider it as final. We agree that logic is self-validating, but we do not stop there. We use reason to show that God's self-revelation in Scripture cannot be denied without self-destruction. Here is more on secularism:

- Reason is god.
- Evolution is "science" but creation is "faith."
- Evolution is the creator.
- The Book of Nature is inerrant and a revelation of the god of randomness. Infallibility is transferred from the Bible to man and his new "book."
- The public schools are the "churches".
- The teachers are the "priests."
- Ethics are the politically correct beliefs at the moment, only to change later.
- "Salvation" is by knowledge in the classroom, but knowledge without the Triune God.
- Abortion is the holy sacrament, for nothing is more sacred than the right to kill unborn babies.

---

[8] John Frame, *Doctrine of the Christian Life*, p. 437.

- Unlimited sexual promiscuity is the other sacrament.

- Worship is directed toward the politicians who give us new revelation about new morality and new laws.

- Death is what should govern our lives, not life, such as abortion, infanticide, euthanasia, orientation to drugs, and other things that tend toward death.

III. Politicians and Public Education

Politicians want to cure the ills of society, and their cure for evil is education, more education, and more money for education. But anyone with eyes can see that the last 100 years have only produced frightening new levels of wickedness, illiteracy, mental density, functional illiteracy, sexual problems, and delinquency. What has happened?

The government has assumed that people are born good (see Chapter 2, VIII), which means we don't need God who has been dismissed from education. Bureaucrats produce ethics based on personal preference, and create an educated fool. And by "fool," I mean no disrespect, but use God's label for those who say there is no God (Psalm 53:1). As one very wise man of our country said over 100 years ago:

> The Redeemer said, "He that is not with me is against me." There cannot be a moral neutrality. Man is born with an evil and ungodly tendency. Hence a non-religious training must be an anti-religious training. The more of this, the larger the curse.
>
> . . . The result will be, that . . . protests (for free education) will triumph, as they now do, in many States; and *we shall have a generation of practical atheists* reared "on State account."[9]

But our public schools have removed the only cure for sin, the Triune God. Teachers are not even allowed to talk about God or Christ, though they can talk about aberrant sexuality, witchcraft, and other sins. To complicate matters, politicians and secularists not only want to

---

[9] R. L. Dabney, *Discussions* (Harrisonburg, Sprinkle Publications, 1979, originally published 1897), 4:261. Emphasis added.

silence God in the public schools, they also want Him exiled from society.

IV. Character and Choices (Private Morality?)

How often do we hear politicians say that what they do in private is no one's business, and that their private lives do not affect how they function in public? In other words, they have two moralities: one for behind closed doors and one for when the cameras are rolling. Politicians who affirm such things believe that morality can be reduced to making an isolated choice that is not connected with character. Yet our choices reveal who we are, not that we change with each choice into a different human being. Our character determines our choices, and our choices determine our character. One could never know another individual if morality were only isolated choices, for his "character" would be his single choice, only to change with the next choice. But the one who commits adultery in private carries that same deceptive character with him into public life. The one who would abandon a lady in a car to drown in a creek would also promote abortion. The one who is often adulterous and drunk in private life would promote that same lack of self-discipline in legislation for civil unions of gays.

V. Preachers and Morality

> Four preachers got together once to discuss their problems. One said, "You know, people are always coming to us with their guilt and problems, but we have no one to go to." The second preacher confessed, "I find ways to guilt manipulate those who come to see me." The third lamented, "I'm involved in an affair with one of my parishioners." The fourth one stopped the meeting when he admitted, "I can't seem to keep a secret."

Too many preachers are compromising the Gospel and God's commandments. It has become a fad for preachers to give out only positive statements to their people, and one TV preacher of a large church has stated on national TV that he will never mention sin. Other preachers traffic in sexual promiscuity. If there is no sin, there can be no deliverance from it by the Son of God. But the Apostle John stated:

- Whoever commits sin also commits lawlessness, and sin is lawlessness (1 John 3:4).

- If we say that we have no sin, we deceive ourselves, and the truth is not in us (1 John 1:8).

- If we say that we have not sinned, we make Him a liar, and His word is not in us (1 John 1:10).

You know what a flashlight is, but did you ever see a flashdark? Of course not, for nothing emits darkness. When you enter a dark room and turn on the light, the darkness is expelled, for light controls darkness, not darkness light; and if there is a rheostat, then the light can be turned down gradually, which means the darkness grows gradually. This has been happening in the USA over the past 100 years, except that the gospel light is now being turned down in an accelerating manner.

And who is turning it down? Preachers are turning it down, who will not preach the truth without compromise. Christians have the light of the Gospel, so we control the rheostat. But many preachers are more interested in large turnouts and being positive than in proclaiming God's Ten Commandments and the gospel of Christ that will reconcile us to God if we believe in His death and bodily resurrection. Thus, our culture is falling into ever more sinful practices, which are enslaving us. We preachers must rise to the occasion, stop using our positions to gain favors from the government for our ethnic group, and present the Ten Commandments and the gospel.

Conclusion

Thus, we can see that we humans are like the little two year old I mentioned in the Introduction to this book. We cannot find our way. We think that we are masters of our souls and captains of our fate. But all morality, public and private, is subject to the omniscient gaze of Christ. Every individual, every institution, every business, every church or religious organization, and every government is accountable to His sovereign majesty, the King of kings. **AMEN**.

Chapter 5—Summary of God's Law

Introduction

News person Ted Koppel, in a commencement address at Duke University, stated:

> What Moses brought down from Mt. Sinai were not the Ten Suggestions. They are commandments. *Are*, not *were*. The sheer brilliance of the Ten Commandments is that they codify in a handful of words acceptable human behavior, not just for then or now, but for all time. Language evolves. Power shifts from one nation to another. Messages are transmitted with the speed of light. Man erases one frontier after another. And yet we and our behavior and the commandments governing that behavior remain the same. [1]

Indeed, God's Ten Commandments are the greatest summary of moral law in existence, and they are simple, easy to understand, and full of His wisdom.

I. What Is the Summary of the Law?

The Lord gave the summary of the Ten Commandments:

> [36] "Teacher, which is the great commandment in the law?" [37] Jesus said to him, " 'You shall love the LORD your God with all your heart, with all your soul, and with all your mind.' [38] This is the first and great commandment. [39] And the second is like it:

---

[1] Robert H. Bork, *The Tempting of America: The Political Seduction of the Law* (New York: The Free Press, 1990), p. 168. Address given May 10, 1985, emphasis added.

'You shall love your neighbor as yourself.' [40] <u>On these two com-</u>
<u>mandments hang all the Law and the Prophets</u>" (Matthew
22:36-40).

All the Ten Commandments tell us how to love God and mankind,
but the first five especially emphasize love for God and the last five
love for mankind. Indeed, the Ten Commandments define what love is
for God and what justice is toward mankind. Let us look at a summary
of the Ten Commandments.

II. How Are the Ten Commandments Numbered?

This is not a book on technical matters, so we shall only say that there
are basically two ways the Ten Commandments are numbered, but
everyone has the same content. The Roman Catholic Church, following
St. Augustine, makes the first two commandments into one (don't worship other gods and don't worship images) while dividing the last one
into two (don't covet your neighbor's house and don't covet your
neighbor's wife). I follow the early fathers, Eastern Orthodoxy, Philo,
Josephus, and most of the Reformation (excluding the Lutherans who
follow Rome) to number them as given below. (Jewish scholars follow a
different pattern yet.)

Moreover, there is an esoteric issue about how many commands
there are. In one sense, the answer is virtually none, for the verbs in
Hebrew are generally not formally commands, but with a proper understanding of the grammar, we understand that they function as commands. But there are more command verbs than ten in both places
where they are given (Exodus 20:1-21; Deuteronomy 5:1-21). In fact, the
Bible never calls them Ten "Commandments" but literally ten "words,"
even though most translations say "Ten Commandments." (See Exodus
34:28; Deuteronomy 4:13; 10:4). But the Bible does say there are "ten" of
them, and it is not difficult to discover them in their texts in Exodus 20
and Deuteronomy 5. So for thousands of years no one has doubted that
there are indeed Ten Commandments.

III. How Are the Ten Commandments Divided?

A slightly more important issue is how the commandments are grouped, which means do the first four or the first five go together? There is a long tradition in seeing the first four as the First Table of the law, giving us commands about God, and the last six as the Second Table of the law, presenting commands about mankind. Yet some early fathers believed the first five should be together (Philo, Josephus, Irenaeus).[2] In the end, it probably does not matter, especially since God's law is one, being inseparable. But I see them as five and five.

Virtually no one denies that the first four are about God and commands six through ten about man. The only real question is about command five to honor one's parents. Does it go with those commands about God or about mankind? Here are my reasons for grouping the first five together.

(1) I include it with the first four because it is a positive command, like the Fourth Commandment to keep the Sabbath holy is also positive, implying continuity. Commands six through ten are all negative, giving us the impression that they go together.

(2) Both the Fourth (rest) and Fifth Commandments (live long) have motivational clauses that encourage one to keep them, and those clauses occur in the other First Table commands (Second: judgment if one chooses another God and mercy if he does not; Third: not hold the one guiltless who takes His name in vain). Commands six through ten are very short and without motivational clauses.

(3) It is also interesting that in Leviticus 19 God commands Moses to tell the people to be holy for He is holy and also to honor their parents, keep the Sabbath, and not to make idols. This is First Table material, but the Fifth Commandment is included right next to the Fourth Commandment.

> Every one of you shall revere his mother and his father, and
> keep My Sabbaths: I am the LORD your God (v. 3).

---

[2] W. H. Gispen, *Bible Students Commentary* (Grand Rapids: Zondervan, 1982), p. 188.

(4) The first five commandments can be seen in the garden before Adam and Eve led the human race into sin. They were implicitly given the First Commandment to have only one God. Then they were to honor Him and not creation above Him, but they disobeyed when they ate the forbidden fruit. They took God's name in vain when they honored Satan's word above God's word. The example to rest and worship were there in the creation week, for in seven days the Lord God made heaven and earth and then rested. Finally, God told Adam and Eve to multiply and fill the earth, which is the Fifth Command, the blessing of children and their obedience. Commandments six through ten, the negative ones, would never have been needed if our first parents had not sinned. What use would mankind have had of "do not murder," "do not commit adultery," "do not steal," "do not bear false witness," and "do not covet" if there were no sin? But the first five were needful and given before the Fall into sin.

(5) The Fourth and Fifth Commandments also have to do with time, the Fourth is weekly, and the Fifth is generational, thus implying they go together.

(6) Moreover, for reasons to be disclosed when we look at the Fourth Commandment on the Sabbath, I see that one as having to do with mankind's dominion over the enemies of God. The Fifth Commandment on children implies that we are to have His "godly seed" (Malachi 2:5) and a lot of them (Psalm 127:5), which is one very important way to exercise dominion over God's enemies, thus continuing the thought of command four.

(7) Furthermore, obedience to godly authority is very important in exercising dominion and directly relates to God, since all legitimate authority is His. So command five is also very important to present God's authority to us in our parents. If mankind had not fallen into sin, that one would still be needed in the honoring of God. We will have to wait for the Fourth Commandment before we try to prove how it leads naturally into the Fifth Commandment.

(8) There is a grammatical matter in Deuteronomy where the Ten Commandments are repeated (chapter five). Commands six through ten are connected by a particular word not seen in English (*waw*), indicating that they go together. That word is not with commands one

through five. Command six begins the new section so in good Hebrew grammar it does not have the word, then the other sentences continue the thought of command six. Therefore, the Revised Standard Version and the Jewish Publication Society translate after the sixth command "neither" shall your commit adultery, "neither" shall you steal, and so forth to the end of the Ten Commandments.[3]

(9) In other passages of scripture, we see the Fifth Commandment included *after* what is normally called the Second Table of the law (commands 6-10). For example, in Matthew 19:18-19 where the man comes to Jesus to ask what He must do to inherit eternal life, the Lord gives commands six through nine, but then adds "Honor your father and your mother" and "You shall love your neighbor as yourself." In all three Gospel accounts (see also Mark 10:19; Luke 18:20), the command to honor one's parents comes at the end. This leads Old Testament scholar Patrick Miller to conclude that the Fifth Commandment represents the First Table and the command "to love your neighbor as yourself" the Second Table.[4]

(10) Moreover, the name of God as "Lord" is given in the first five commandments but not in the last five. The First Commandment does not have the name Lord, but it is supplied in the previous verse, and continued to the next verse: "I am the *Lord* your God . . . You shall have no other gods before *Me*." But commandments six through ten simply have the second person mentioned ("you"), which ties them together, and commandments one through five have "Lord," tying them together. Indeed, the word "God" occurs seven times from verse one through the Fifth Commandment (verse 12), and the word "Lord" occurs eight times, tying this section off. Commandments six through ten do not have "God" or "Lord."

(11) If we consider the first five together, there is a natural flow to them. The first command means we know the true and living God. The way we know Him is not through any creature (command two) but through His name (command three). As we know Him, we learn to

---

[3] I observed this in the Hebrew text, but also see Patrick D. Miller, *The Ten Commandments* (Louisville, KY: John Knox Press, 2009), p. 129.

[4] Miller, *The Ten Commandments*, p. 169.

rest/worship (command four) and extend His covenant to His seed He gives us, which extends His rule (command five).

To put this yet another way, in Genesis 1-2 we see that there are several creation ordinances that the Lord God gave man *before the fall into sin*. As one made in God's image (command one), mankind was to know this one God only, not to listen to Satan (command one), to have Sabbath rest (command four), have dominion over creation (commands four and five), have a spouse (command five), and the two of them to fill the earth with their seed (command five). They were not to eat the fruit of the forbidden tree, to put creation above God and His name (commands two and three). At that time, commands six through ten were not needed. It was only after the fall into sin that those were needed, especially against covenant breakers who would rebel against God, trying to make their own covenant by disobeying the first five. After the fall into sin, one cannot separate the commands, for they all stand or fall together.

IV. Summary of the Ten Commandments

1A. WORSHIP TOWARD GOD (commands 1-5)

1B. First Commandment (Worship only the True God):
Object of worship is God only

Required:	Worship God only
Forbidden:	Giving glory to the creature
Blessing:	Knowing the Triune God
Penalty:	Eternal separation from God
Verse:	Matthew 22:17

2B. Second Commandment (Do not worship creation):
Manner of worship: worship God, not creation

Required:	Worship as God says
Forbidden:	Worshipping creation
Blessing:	Mercy from God for many generations
Penalty:	Judgment to the 3rd and 4th generations
Verse:	Romans 1:25

3B. Third Commandment (Not take God's Name in vain):

Attitude of worship: reverence and fear

Required:	Using God's name with fear, reverence, awe
Forbidden:	Taking God lightly or for granted, presumption, denying His word in the Bible
Blessing:	Confidence toward God and man
Penalty:	God will judge all evil thoughts (Matthew 12:36-37)
Verse:	Matthew 5:37

4B. Fourth Commandment (Remember Sabbath):

Time of worship: one day in seven/rest/dominion

Required:	Gospel rest on Lord's Day
Forbidden:	Lack of worship, putting other things before Him
Blessing:	Rest for body and soul
Penalty:	Sick in body and soul; God brings unrest
Verse:	Colossians 2:16-17

5B. Fifth Commandment (Honor Parents):

Goal of Worship: godly seed (dominion)

Required:	Obey and respect God given authority
Forbidden:	To disobey or disrespect God's authority
Blessing:	Long life, security
Penalty:	Shortened life
Verse:	Ephesians 6:2-3

2A. DUTY TOWARD MAN (commands 6-10)

6B. Sixth Commandment (Do Not Murder):

Rule of Life: High value of human life

Required:	Honor and preserve human life; justice for all
Forbidden:	Murder or unjust anger at someone
Blessing:	Right to life
Penalty:	Forfeit one's life for actual murder
Verse:	1 John 3:15

7B. Seventh Commandment (Do Not Commit Adultery):
Rule of <u>Chastity</u>: Respect for self and others

Required:	Preserve one's own and others chastity
Forbidden:	Any sexual thought or act contrary to marriage of one man and one woman
Blessing:	Right to marry and have a spouse
Penalty:	Destruction of oneself, others, and one's home
Verse:	1 Peter 2:11

8B. Eighth Commandment (Do Not Steal):
Rule of <u>Property</u>: Right to own property

Required:	Honor our and other's property, protect it
Forbidden:	Theft in any form either by government or individual persons. We are not even to steal time, either God's or our employer's.
Blessing:	Right to own property and enjoy God's daily provision
Penalty:	Restoration is double, two fold; being possessed by things
Verse:	Ephesians 4:28

9B. Ninth Commandment (Do Not Bear False Witness):
Rule of <u>Speech</u>: right to one's reputation

Required:	To promote ours and others' reputation
Forbidden:	To injure one's reputation by lying, half truth, or by withholding some truth
Blessing:	Good name, trustworthiness
Penalty:	Bad name, loss of trust, broken relationships
Verse:	Ephesians 4:29

10. Tenth Commandment (Do Not Covet):
Rule of <u>Desire</u>: Contentment

Required:	Content with our position in life and with our neighbor's place; satisfied with God

Forbidden: All murmuring, complaining, and
              covetousness

Blessing: True riches in heaven

Penalty: Anxiety, God's displeasure, being
              consumed by desire

Verse: 1 Timothy 6:6

There is a hierarchy in God's Ten Commandments. The first five proceed from the worst sin (idolatry) to lesser ones (idols, taking God's name in vain, worship on His day, and obedience to godly authority). The next five also have a hierarchy: significance of human life, significance of the marriage bond, right to private property, reliability of public testimony, and keeping one's mind clear of coveting, which is idolatry, as St. Paul said (Colossians 3:5). Thus we begin and end with idolatry so that commandments one and ten function as book ends.

PART 2: THE TEN COMMANDMENTS

Part 2 covers each of the Ten Commandments separately, seeking to understand their meaning and application. One may skip around in this section, though it is always good to read in chapter order. This covers chapters 6-17.

Chapter 6—First Commandment: "No other gods"

You shall have no other gods before Me (Exodus 20:3).

14 You shall not go after other gods, the gods of the peoples who are all around you 15 (for the LORD your God is a jealous God among you), lest the anger of the LORD your God be aroused against you and destroy you from the face of the earth (Deuteronomy 6:14-15).

18 For the wrath of God is revealed from heaven against all ungodliness and unrighteousness of men, who suppress the truth in unrighteousness, 19 because what may be known of God is manifest in them, for God has shown *it* to them. 20 For since the creation of the world His invisible *attributes* are clearly seen, being understood by the things that are made, *even* His eternal power and Godhead, so that they are without excuse, 21 because, although they knew God, they did not glorify *Him* as God, nor were thankful, but became futile in their thoughts, and their foolish hearts were darkened. 22 Professing to be wise, they became fools, 23 and changed the glory of the incorruptible God into an image made like corruptible man — and birds and four-footed animals and creeping things. 24 Therefore God also gave them up to uncleanness, in the lusts of their hearts, to dishonor their bodies among themselves, 25 who exchanged the truth of God for the lie, and worshiped and served the creature rather than the Creator, who is blessed forever. 26 For this reason God gave them up to vile passions. For even their women exchanged the natural use for what is against nature. 27 Likewise also the

men, leaving the natural use of the woman, burned in their lust for one another, men with men committing what is shameful, and receiving in themselves the penalty of their error which was due (Romans 1:18-27).

[4] Therefore concerning the eating of things offered to idols, we know that an idol is nothing in the world, and that there is no other God but one. [5] For even if there are so-called gods, whether in heaven or on earth (as there are many gods and many lords), [6] yet for us there is one God, the Father, of whom are all things, and we for Him; and one Lord Jesus Christ, through whom are all things, and through whom we *exist* (1 Corinthians 8:4-6).

My duty towards God is to believe in him, to fear him, and to love him with all my heart, with all my soul, with all my mind, and with all my strength: To worship him, to give him thanks: To put my whole trust in him, to call upon him. (Book of Common Prayer)

Introduction

Shortly after noon on Fridays, the Rev. Ann (last name withheld) ties on a black headscarf, preparing to pray with her Muslim group on First Hill.

On Sunday mornings, she puts on the white collar of an Episcopal priest.

She does both, she says, because she's Christian and Muslim.

[Rev Ann], who until recently was director of faith formation at St. Mark's Episcopal Cathedral, has been a priest[ess] for more than 20 years. Now she's ready to tell people that, for the last 15 months, she's also been a Muslim — drawn to the faith after an introduction to Islamic prayers left her profoundly moved.

Her announcement has provoked surprise and bewilderment in many, raising an obvious question: How can someone be both a Christian *and* a Muslim?

But it has drawn other reactions too. Friends generally say they support her, while religious scholars are mixed: Some say that, depending on how one interprets the tenets of the two faiths, it is, indeed, possible to be both. Others consider the two faiths mutually exclusive.

"There are tenets of the faiths that are very, very different," said Kurt Fredrickson, director of the doctor of ministry program at Fuller Theological Seminary in Pasadena, Calif. "The most basic would be: What do you do with Jesus?"

Indeed, sir, that is *the* question, and this priestess is a classic example of idolatry. (To his credit, her bishop told her to choose the Christian God or Allah.) *Idolatry is compromising* the worship of the one and *only* God, the Triune God, who is not Allah. We are to trust in this God *only*, to rely on Him *only*, to pray to Him *only*, and to believe in Him *only*.

So what is idolatry? According to Exodus 20:3 above, it is having some other god than the true and living Triune God. But what does that mean? The wording in the Hebrew commonly meant to take a wife,[1] and was used for the spiritual marriage between God and His people.[2] Thus idolatry is having a third party in one's relationship with the Triune God. The relationship that determines all other relationships reveals one's true God. Spiritual adultery is worshipping something or someone other than the Triune God, taking orders from someone else than Him. As the Lord Jesus Himself said to Satan:

> Then Jesus said to him, "Away with you, Satan! For it is written, 'You shall worship the LORD your God, and Him only you shall serve'" (Matthew 4:10).

---

[1] Leviticus 21:3; Deuteronomy 24:2, 4; Judges 14:20; 15:2; Ruth 1:13; Ezekiel 16:8; Hosea 3:3, from Mark F. Rooker, *The Ten Commandments: Ethics for the Twenty-First Century* (Nashville, TN: B&H Academic, 2010), p. 25.

[2] Genesis 17:7; Exodus 6:7; Leviticus 11:45; 20:26; 22:33; 25:38; 26:12, etc, also from Rooker, *The Ten Commandments*, p. 25.

Moreover, to have "no other gods" is not an admission that other gods actually exist. The Bible is very clear that there is only one God.[3] So why the statement not to pursue "other" gods? Obviously, many think there are other gods so God is warning not to go after *false* gods.

Our culture does not mind us talking about God as long as we do not say He is the only One, and especially they despise us when we say He is the Father and the Son and the Holy Spirit. They want us to speak of a generic God so that everyone can fill in the blank as they wish. A polytheistic culture is tolerant of other gods, such as our culture is tolerant, but a culture is hostile to those who deny many gods and only proclaim one, as we Christians do. In the culture in which this First Commandment was first proclaimed, it was a novel idea, for all cultures held to many gods. Tolerance of all things is the mandate today, but this command requires intolerance, requires the truth of one God only.

According to the Romans one passage, idolatry means to worship and/or serve something that is created rather than God. Today, this often means that we consider ourselves as more important and our ideas more determinative that God and His thoughts. The aggressive atheists of today think that they can determine, by the power of their logic, if there is a god, and if so, what he/it must be like; and if he/it does not conform, he/it does not exists. In other words, man is the god qualifier. Moreover, an idol is whatever we cling to, love, devote ourselves to, the one we depend on for "our daily bread" and for our security in life.

To restate this, idolatry is making a god in our image, one we can control, who will approve our conduct. In the process, we become like that god, for that god was like us from the moment we created it. Furthermore, if idolatry is worshipping something manmade, then we have blurred the distinction between the true God, the creator, and our idol, the creation. True worship means that we always maintain the creator/creature distinction. The Triune God is not part of His creation, and we as His creatures are not divine. We want to invent our own

---

[3] Isaiah 40:12-31; 43:8-13; 45:5-6; 46:5-13; 1 Timothy 2:5, 1 Corinthians 8:6, and a hundred other places.

ethic, which makes as like God, "[determining] good and evil" (Genesis 3:5).

People want to believe that nature gave rise to us by evolution, which means there is no distinction between us and the animals, but just as there is a creator/creature distinction, there is also a human/animal distinction. To make ourselves part of the animal kingdom is to deny any transcendent ethic, to make ethics just arbitrary choices as the products of chemicals. Now mankind is considered the central meaning of the universe, not the Triune God.[4] Anyone who would introduce order into this assumed chaos will be hated as an idolater, a promoter of a strange god that the elite do not want. Our idolatrous society sees man as the one who brings order out of the chaos of the universe, and if an outside God is introduced it would mean man is not only wrong, but accountable. That will never do.

But as soon as man and nature are identified, man having come from nature, we destroy order and ethics. Order is allegedly only what we make it, and ethics means little when it comes from molecules in motion. But at least man is in control, which is what he wants—the worship of self and his intellect. "The individual believes himself to be the measure of both reality and moral principle. Thus, there are no standards, no belief in eternal truth, no objective measure of right and wrong; norms are delusions, and self-discipline serves no purpose."[5]

Since each individual is seen as autonomous, since there is no overriding principle of order or ethics, the only thing that matters is each person's experience. Thus, people—even Christians—are always basing beliefs on their private experience rather than God's revelation. This is nothing short of making experience one's private idol.

Once nature or creation is seen to be all there is, it becomes an idol. It is worshipped through environmentalist extremes. Mankind must control nature to predestine his future, and the global warming movement is just such a plan to create a crisis so that the state can assume more power. Man is blamed for his misuse of the environment, and

---

[4] Herbert Schlossberg, *Idols for Destruction* (Nashville: Thomas Nelson Publishers, 1983), p. 157.
[5] Ibid., p. 167.

man is hated for it, but our less intelligent "relatives," the animals, are loved. Love for animals and hatred for humans is a product of making nature an idol. I recall some years ago seeing a young woman driving in front of me with stickers on her car that said: "Keep your laws off my body." "Eat plants, not animals." The first one meant that she was free to kill her babies by abortion, and the second one meant that we should not hurt animals. When we hate the Triune God, we necessarily hate His image in mankind.

When man is not distinguished from nature, there is little restraint on barbarism and cruelty to one another. The reason should be clear; nature is all there is, and nature has no order, no ethic. Therefore, to make things "better," those who are in control at the top of the food chain will define right and wrong. A system that bases itself on nature can justify any behavior, for nature knows no morality. If nature is all there is, the difference between maggots and men is only one of degree, not kind. In kind, we all came from the same "creator": chaos, chemicals, and natural selection.

If there are no moral rules except what individuals arbitrarily adopt, the only way for many individuals to co-exist is to have the state be the ultimate law-giver. Now the state is divine, an idol, and the poor in our society are being trained to look to it for their "daily bread." If someone goes "bad" in society, it is society's fault, the only god most know, for society did not raise him "right." A society that adopts nature as its god can hardly escape violence, for that is the only way to make things equal, and since man is just another animal, he will act as one.

In most academic circles today, science is the faith and evolution is the creator. This is the faith that must be adhered to at all times under penalty of losing one academic position or not making tenure. But Exodus tells us that we must worship the living God only, and Paul states that we are not to worship anything made, even if God made it. In other words, God is separate from and high above His creation. But what does worship mean?

It means that we are to consider only God to be ultimate being, the determiner of all things, the Creator, the highest good, the only One worthy of our devotion, the supplier of all our needs. His moral standard is the highest standard in our lives so that even death is not as important as He is. We would rather die than offend Him. With idolaters, death is final, not God, so they compromise to avoid it.

We can see how idolatry plays out in the other commands. In the Second Commandment, we are not to approach God through some manmade or created object, but to honor Him directly. In the Third Commandment, we are not to seek power over God through some other name. In the Fourth Commandment, we will regulate our time by His standard, which means we will sanctify our time by giving Him one day in seven. His priorities with time will be our priorities, such as worship on the Lord's Day, spending time with our families, and not being frantic over our jobs. In the Fifth Commandment, we will honor godly authority and not try to rebel against His commandments. In the Sixth Commandment, we must honor the image of God in other humans by not murdering. In the Seventh Commandment, we will honor His definition of marriage and not disobey His sexual laws. In the Eighth Commandment, we will be content with what He gives us by not making money and things our highest priority. In the Ninth Commandment, we will not seek to destroy others with our tongues, for they are made in His image. We will Honor His word about all else. And in the Tenth Commandment, we shall be content with God and with what He gives us on earth to use for Him.

Some common idols today are power, both political and military. Moreover, it is idolatrous to worship the state, such as looking to Washington to "give us this day our daily bread." Citizens look to politicians as the gods who will pass enough laws to feed us, take care of us, but by doing that we become their slaves.

Others are given to explosive anger, and behind such anger is usually an idol that needs protecting. The exposure of one's true self through his idol is often maddening; or perhaps the anger is because the false god is too weak to bring about what is wanted, and the person does not want to admit it.

There are basically only two gods possible: the one true Triune God or self. All the above false gods come down to one thing: self. Narcissism is the god of most people in the USA today, the pleasing of self.

In addition, idolatry is not loving God just for who He is, but for what we can get out of Him, like the modern word-faith movement that says we can get from God what we want if we have enough faith. But we must affirm God for His own sake, not to get something else. Remember that Satan told God that Job would curse Him if he took his possessions and health. God allowed Satan to do that, but Job maintained faith in God. The essence, then, of the First Commandment is that we must honor God and His law above everything else, worshipping Him as the only God, looking to Him as our highest good. Idolatry consists in divinizing some aspect of creation, such as making nature, man's mind, or government to be god.

I. Idolatry Is the Mother of All Sins

God begins His Ten Commandments with the sin of idolatry because it is the mother of all sins. Adam and Eve's sin in the garden in Eden was that they wanted to be their own God, to make up their own ethics. In our culture, spiritual warfare is accelerating, and it revolves around who is God. Presuming ourselves to be god is causing self-destruction.

One thing that makes us different from the animals is that we were made in the image of God, which means we are oriented to worship. Mankind will indeed worship something. It may be the politicians who promise they can save society by their laws; it may be gods of their own making, such as sex, power, drugs, or making money. These are temporal gods that shall not last. But we *will* worship something, for this is a result of God's image in us. Our worship is revealed by the standard that we use to run our lives. The sin of idolatry is really *the sin of self-sufficiency*, living by our own wits and standards. Thanksgiving to the Triune God demonstrates dependency, love for Him who has given us all things, while not being thankful shows that we are "captain of our souls," looking to creation itself as our supplier. Let us revisit what the Apostle Paul said:

> [20] For since the creation of the world His invisible *attributes* are clearly seen, being understood by the things that are made, *even* His eternal power and Godhead, so that they are without excuse,
> [21] because, although they knew God, they did not glorify *Him* as

God, <u>nor were thankful</u>, but became futile in their thoughts, and
their foolish hearts were darkened (Romans 1:20-21).

Idolaters refuse to accept God as creator; consequently, they do not
thank Him, for that is an act of worship. They thank themselves.

Moreover, we are in a conflict of world views, Christianity versus
everything else. The political worldview is at war with the Lord God
Almighty and cannot win, but the devil convinces his subjects that they
will win by the means of their own ethic, which is the opposite of God's
ethic. Every attempt to devise a plan for living that is contrary to God's
revealed will in His Ten Commandments is an attempt at godhood.
God warns against such in this First Commandment. The USA is neo-
pagan, not just atheistic, chasing after other gods and false religions
with every increasing speed, like a train going down hill faster and faster until it jumps the tracks.

Idolatry can take several forms. It can be *polytheistic*, which means
many gods, such as Mormonism, or such as many Christians today in
the USA who consider their own personal interests more important
that God's interests. If one would keep a log for a week to see where his
time goes, especially his time when he is not working at his job, he
would see who his real God is.

Idolatry can be *syncretistic*, which means it pulls together different
beliefs, merging them into one mixture of opposite things. We see this
with Christians merging standards of the world with Christianity, such
as allowing for people to live together before marriage, allowing for
same sex "marriages," and thinking that people who do not believe in
Jesus might make it to heaven in the end. (See the Third Commandment, IV. The Only Name for Salvation.)

Idolatry can be *pantheistic*, which means the whole universe is
"God." Buddhism and Hinduism are examples of this, and if all is one,
then good and evil are one, which means there is no right and wrong.

II. The Attractions of Idolatry[6]

Idolatry is attractive because it tends to be *materialistic,* and we love our toys and physical things. Now creation—physical things—are not evil in themselves, but when we live our lives to gain them, that is sin.

Moreover, idolatry is attractive because it nearly always *minimizes the importance of ethical behavior.* In one Episcopal denomination that has left the faith, ritual is the important thing. With them unity is more important than doctrine.

With the word-faith movement, *speaking positive words* into the air will bring you health and wealth. One gets the idea from these self-proclaimed prophets that faith without cash is dead. What is conspicuous by its absence is God's law, His commandments. Some denominations even ordain same sex partners into the ministry, thus completely dismissing God's law. (Purchase my book on the word-faith movement from the web site in the front of this book. The title is *Man as God: The Word of Faith Movement.*)

Idolatry can be *indulgent to the flesh,* which means that all forms of sex, drunkenness, and other kinds of "pigging out" (obesity) can be justified with the idea that God affirms us as we are. Such people conveniently forget that God is holy and that those who know Him must be holy. God loves us the way we are, but He loves us too much to let us stay that way. We must enter a life of repentance to honor Him. Using God to justify one's disobedience to God's wonderful sexual laws is like the temple prostitution that was pervasive in Old Testament times. The idea was that one was in union with the god represented by a statue if he was in union with the temple prostitute. Like then, now illicit sex is a regular aspect of "worship."

III. The Privilege to Know God

The First Commandment means that we can be in communion with the Triune God, the Father, and the Son, and the Holy Spirit. We can be in covenant with Him through faith in the death and resurrection of the

---

[6] Many of these thoughts came from Douglas K. Stuart, *The New American Commentary: Exodus* (Nashville: Broadmand & Holman Publishers, 2006), p. 450ff.

Son of God, the Second Person of the Holy Trinity. *This is what life is all about, knowing God and enjoying Him!*

If we are not to have any other gods but the true and living one, then we get to have Him if we trust in Him! He is our God by covenant, by trusting in Jesus. A covenant is an agreement between persons, and a commitment to one another made by vows and kept by obedience to the terms of those vows. We were "married" to God by vows when we believed in Jesus and/or when we were baptized into the name of the Triune God, Father, Son, and Holy Spirit. The agreement was that He would be our God and that we would keep His commandments.

How is your retirement program? I mean real long range, like 100 years from now, or 1,000 years from now? Have you planned well by loving God, by living for Him, by rearing your kids so that *He* is their highest priority?

IV. What We Must Do

We are required to be sorrowful when anything offends Him. We must not feel superior to others who engage in idolatry, such as the priestess mentioned earlier, but we must be sorrowful, to love such a one for the glory of God, and hopefully to bring her to repentance.

We are required to live for God on a daily basis. In the morning, our first thought should be for God, and we must teach our children the same. Our last thought at night should be to God. Every priority in our lives should be with Him at the center.

What is required is to honor God's law above all else. Behind every system of law is an implied law-giver. Thus having many systems of laws is polytheism, having many gods. All human law systems should be based on the one God's one law: Love God, which can be broken down into two commands: Love God and love your neighbor as yourself. And in turn that can be broken down into the Ten Commandments, and so on. Our law in this country against murder is righteously based on God's Sixth Commandment: "Thou shalt not murder." But when the Supreme Court ruled that abortion was permissible, that made them lawbreakers, idolaters, worshippers of false gods. There is *no neutrality: every moral law made by mankind is either an application of God's law or an act of rebellion.*

Since there is only one true God, and His revealed law is an expression of who He is, then *to change law systems is to change gods*, which is what has happened in the USA. We are required to recognize His law as the only moral law that exists, for He is the only God who exists.

What is required is to pursue the knowledge of God at every opportunity. I have never understood the mentality to learn as little about God as possible. That is living for this life only, not planning for future retirement. What would we say if someone was going to have to live from age 30 and for the rest of his life in a foreign country, but this person rarely learned about that country? Would not that seem near sighted?

V. What We Should Avoid

(1) We are not allowed to give glory to anything created, whether that is something tangible, such as houses or cars, or something intangible, such as false concepts of God. By giving glory we mean to honor something more with our time, money, and thoughts than we do the Triune God. Someone may *say* he honors God, but let him write down how he spends his time each week to see if it is true or not.

(2) We are forbidden to have subtle, personal idols. Idolatry is the favorite past time in America. Sports, which have become a god for many, are not wrong in themselves. They use their time and energy to follow their favorite team, yet ignore God in their daily lives. Sunday morning is too precious for these people to give to God. They want to sleep in, turn on the TV to "worship" as they enjoy their sports from the couch. They want God to take them to heaven, but they would not like heaven since they don't like it now.

(3) We are forbidden to love ourselves above God. If you haven't noticed, there has been a revival in the USA in the past generation but not a good one. It is the affirmation of self. It is like the lie Satan told Eve in the Garden:

> Then the serpent said to the woman, "You will not surely
> die. For God knows that in the day you eat of it your eyes will be

opened, and you will be like God, knowing good and evil"
(Genesis 3:4-5).

In other words, *affirm yourself.* Believe in yourself, and you can do
anything. Feel good about yourself. Love the lord *thyself* with all your
heart, mind, soul, body, time, and money. The whole face of Christianity has changed, and now people will build mega-churches if you'll affirm them, not talk of sin, but just make them the center of attention.
Christianity has become pop psychology, not the great acts of God in
redemptive history.

Physical happiness and personal fulfillment are the goals of modern religion, not self-denial. Jesus said:

"If anyone desires to come after Me, let him <u>deny himself</u>, and
take up his cross <u>daily</u>, and follow Me" (Luke 9:23).

In 1878 a 26 year old Episcopal priest named Louis heard of the
yellow fever epidemic in Memphis, Tennessee. He asked his bishop if
he could go there to be comfort for the people, and at first his bishop
refused, saying he might die. But then as Louis pushed, stating that in
Christ he had already died, the bishop allowed it. He went to Memphis
and ministered to the dying, then succumbed to yellow fever himself.
Where is this kind of commitment today? We don't want a god who
requires *anything,* but a god who gives us *everything.*

Faith is something optional we think, for we can live just fine without God, and faith is certainly not something to die for. But even the
Muslims will die for their faith, and they don't have the true God.

(4) Then another god is *hedonism,* the worship of the human body,
such as illicit sex, sex before marriage, obesity, and drugs. We have giv-
en our bodies over to enslavement for physical gratification.

God's judgment on America is NOW . . . and increasing daily. For
all these idols in our culture are part of God's judgment. The idols bring
more judgment, of course, but the idols themselves are judgment, for
they enslave us. One cannot continually transgress God's commands
and prosper long term. He will not allow it. (See Part 3.)

These gods obey those who have invented them, and these gods
only declare what their masters say. These gods morph into whatever
their creators want, for these gods are made in their image.

(5) We are forbidden to have cultural gods. As Judge Bork said in his most enlightening book, *Slouching toward Gomorrah*, we now have radical egalitarianism, which means the push to reduce everything to its lowest common denominator, and radical individualism, the push to ever more tolerance. Or, to put this another way, there can be no moral superiority, just competing gods on a level playing field, with the government god being the referee, of course.

Did you see the prayer service in the National Cathedral the day after President Obama was sworn in? If you have not noticed, we have a new god in the USA, and I do not mean our new president. Even though there were some very good hymns sung, including *Amazing Grace* written by John Newton the former slave and slave trader who came to know the Triune God, these were nullified by the content of the prayers and the sermon preached by a woman pastor.

Conspicuous by its absence was the Name that is above every name, the *only* Name in whom there is salvation—Jesus. Prayers were offered to the "Great Creator," not to the Father, for saying "father" is allegedly sexist. Prayers were offered by an Islamic woman with her sari, then a Jewish rabbi, a Hindu woman, several Christian priests, a Roman Catholic bishop, and others. *Not a single prayer addressed the Father through the Son.* Not a single prayer mentioned the Name "Jesus." Do you get it? Who was the god of gods?

Likewise the sermon preached by the woman priest never quoted the Scriptures, never mentioned God the Son or His death and resurrection, never mentioned the Name Jesus. She quoted Ghandi, Martin Luther King, and others, but not the Triune God in His written word.

So which god controlled the day of prayer, the prayers, and the sermon? It was not Allah, for he/it was only one of the gods. It was not the Hindu gods (300 million of them), for they were only some of the gods. It was not the Jewish god, for he was only one of many. It was not the Christian God, for He was only one of many. In the midst of all this polytheism, there was one god very conspicuous over all the others, who controlled what people said and how they worshipped, and that was the ***politically correct god***, the one invented by those who hate the Triune God, who will have nothing to do with Jesus the Christ.

The interesting thing is that by excluding the Triune God, they implied that He is powerful. These other gods can be controlled, but He demands allegiance. As C. S. Lewis stated of the lion Asland in his *Lion, Witch, and Wardrobe*, "He is not a tame lion."

(6) We are forbidden to know the future or to try to control the future, for that is God's domain. Thus we are forbidden to complain against God and His providence, for He is the author of it. Hating Him for His providence is idolatry, setting ourselves up as the one who will manufacture our own providence. And if things don't go our way, we'll hate Him for it, like the children of Israel in the wilderness who complained when they did not get their way.

(7) We are forbidden to withhold from God His tithe, for this is the love of money more than the love of God. Charles Spurgeon, that great Baptist preacher in the late 1800s in London, used to say a man needs two conversions: one for his soul, and one for his pocketbook. That is so true. We tend to give God tips.

> Covetousness is <u>idolatry</u> (Colossians 3:5).
>
> For this you know, that no fornicator, unclean person, nor <u>covetous man</u>, who is an <u>idolater</u>, has any inheritance in the kingdom of Christ and God (Ephesians 5:5).
>
> [8] And having food and clothing, with these <u>we shall be content</u>. [9] But those who <u>desire to be rich</u> fall into temptation and a snare, and *into* many foolish and harmful lusts which drown men in destruction and perdition. [10] For the <u>love of money</u> is a root of all *kinds of* evil, for which some have strayed from the faith in their greediness, and pierced themselves through with many sorrows (1 Timothy 6:8-10).
>
> But seek ye first the kingdom of God, and his righteousness; and all these things shall be added unto you (Matthew 6:33, KJV).

God put Job through terrible suffering when He allowed Satan to take his children, his wealth, and his health, and yet Job refused to worship God as a sugar daddy, but for who He is. We cannot out-give God, but some don't want to take any chances, so they withhold the tithe.

(8) We are forbidden to live by sight, but we are required to live by faith. When we have only the bare word of God, and still believe it, like Abraham, we are worshipping God properly in our lives. In the USA we are so used to being self-sufficient, living by our wits, living by sight, that we have a difficult time believing that God can supply our needs.

(9) We are forbidden to seek the knowledge of God from any source but His infallible written word:

> [19] And when they say to you, "Seek those who are mediums and wizards, who whisper and mutter," should not a people seek their God? *Should they seek* the dead on behalf of the living? [20] <u>To the law and to the testimony!</u> If they do not speak according to this word, it is because there is no light in them (Isaiah 8:19-20).

(11) It is amazing to me how someone can be politically liberal but religiously conservative, which is serving two gods. They will claim to believe in the true God who says not to murder, but these same people will vote for a politician who supports the killing of the unborn. One who votes for a murderer partakes of their sins. "If professing Christians are unfaithful to the authority of their Lord in their capacity as citizens of the State, they cannot expect to be blessed by the indwelling of the Holy Spirit in their capacity as members of the Church."[7]

Conclusion

When we deny the only true God as our God, we make men to be gods over us, but here is what we were made for:

> "What is the chief end of man? Man's chief end is to glorify God, and to enjoy Him forever" (Shorter Catechism). **AMEN**.

---

[7] Archibald Alexander Hodge, *Evangelical Theology* (Edinburg: Banner of Truth, 1976, first published posthumously, 1890), p. 247.

Chapter 7—Second Commandment: Worship No Images

⁴ You shall not make for yourself a carved image, or any likeness *of anything* that is in heaven above, or that is in the earth beneath, or that is in the water under the earth; ⁵ **you shall not bow down to [worship] them nor serve them**. For I, the LORD your God, am a jealous God, visiting the iniquity of the fathers on the children to the third and fourth *generations* of those who hate Me, ⁶ but showing mercy to thousands, to those who love Me and keep My commandments (Exodus 20:4-6).

²² Professing to be wise, they became fools, ²³ and changed the glory of the incorruptible God into an image made like corruptible man—and birds and four-footed animals and creeping things. ²⁴ Therefore God also gave them up to uncleanness, in the lusts of their hearts, to dishonor their bodies among themselves, ²⁵ who exchanged the truth of God for the lie, and <u>worshiped and served the creature rather than the Creator</u>, who is blessed forever. Amen (Romans 1:22-25).

²³ "But the hour is coming, and now is, when the true worshipers will worship the Father in spirit and truth; for the Father is seeking such to worship Him. ²⁴ God is Spirit, and those who worship Him must worship in spirit and truth" (John 4:23-24).

My duty towards God is to put my whole trust in Him . . . (Book of Common Prayer).

Introduction

One news media person stated regarding the display of the Ten Commandments in Alabama's judicial building:

> This may sound especially blasphemous in the Bible Belt, but I don't get it. Wouldn't we do better to try to live the Commandments rather than bicker over mere symbols of them?

Is the symbol of the 5,300 pound monument of the Ten Commandments irrelevant?

Did you see the news story of a Christian high school girl who was suspended from her public school for wearing a chastity ring? She is committed not to have sex until she is married. The school allowed other kids to wear Islamic rings, satanic symbols, and other symbols. Why? Are symbols powerful, or are they just morally neutral physical objects? They can be either, but why does the world hate Christian symbols so much these days?

Images or symbols are very powerful. Ask the advertising media how powerful they are. They spend millions of dollars on ads for a few seconds to flash images in our faces. Think of how much money is spent on Super Bowl ads.

Remember the frogs in the beer ad: "Bud, Bud, Wise, Er." It was the image they wanted you to remember.

Finish this one: "Plop, plop, fizz, fizz . . . (O what a relief it is"). Alka Seltzer.

When you see a green Gecko with a Down Under accent, what do you think of? (Geico Car Insurance.)

"Head on, applied directly to the forehead." (I hate that ad.)

What do you think about when you see a swastika?

What does all this have to do with the Second Commandment? Symbols are all around us. They are both *reflective* of what a culture believes, and also *determinative* of what it believes. Does God want us to abandon all images and symbols in the Second Commandment? Should we just think about God and never use symbols? But can we think wrongly about God, and still violate this command by having wrong images in our minds?

Some think this commandment is opposed to all images or symbols. Some have even opposed pictures of Christ. I wonder if one could have taken a picture of Him if cameras had been invented then. Was it ok to see Him and have His image on one's retina? One allegedly cannot make anything that might remind us of God, for that would be an image. Is that what this commandment is saying? If so, we must go out of the world, for all creation reminds us of God (Romans 1:20).

The Hebrew word for "image" or "carved image" in Exodus 20:4 (*pésel*) means "idol." In other words, they were not to make an idol to worship it. That is clear enough, but that is not a prohibition to make anything physical that can be used in worship. Notice Deuteronomy 4:19:

> And *take heed*, lest you lift your eyes to heaven, and *when* you see the sun, the moon, and the stars, all the host of heaven, you feel driven to worship them and serve them, which the LORD your God has given to all the peoples under the whole heaven as a heritage.

The Lord God had given *everyone* the moon and stars as symbols of His authority, but they were not to worship them. In other words, it was legitimate to have these symbols, but sinful to worship them. God Himself had made these for all nations, but He would not allow them to be worshipped. If representations of the Lord were absolutely forbidden, then God violated His own law. Paul stated that we are not to worship physical things as if they were the divine nature:

> Therefore, since we are the offspring of God, we ought not to think that the Divine Nature is like gold or silver or stone, something shaped by art and man's devising (Acts 17:29).

If this Second Commandment is a prohibition against any images whatsoever, then why did God, in the same book that this command appears (Exodus), instruct Moses to build a tabernacle that would have images and all kinds of symbols in it? There were cherubim embroidered on the cloth inside the tabernacle, and in the Most Holy Place there was a box, the Ark of the Covenant, and on it was a lid made of gold with two golden cherubim facing one another, and there between the cherubim was where the Shekinah glory dwelt, the very presence of God Himself. How do we explain that if we must never use symbols?

But notice how I translated the Hebrew[1] word at the beginning of this chapter: not "bow down" but "worship." In the New Testament, the Apostle Paul gives us the divine interpretation of this commandment when he said that we must not "worship" or "serve" the creature rather than the Creator (Romans 1:25). Paul must have had this Old Testament passage in mind when he penned those words, for his text reads very similar to the commandment itself. (Read again Romans 1:22-25 at the beginning of this chapter.)

In fact, it is quite impossible not to have images that reflect God in some way, for all creation does that, such as the sun each morning. Each day when you look in the mirror, you see the image of God, for we are created in His image (Genesis 1:26-27). Also, the Son of God was the "image of the invisible God" (Colossians 1:15). During His incarnation, people who saw Him saw God, as it were, though God cannot be fully contained in human form. Jesus Himself said: "He who has seen Me has seen the Father" (John 14:9). As in the Old Testament when people saw the Shekinah glory, they saw something of God, likewise Christ is said to have been that Shekinah glory in His incarnation:

> And the Word became flesh and [tabernacled] among us, and we beheld His glory, the glory as of the only begotten of the Father, full of grace and truth (John 1:14, my translation based on the NKJ).

John says He *was* the tabernacle, and also the glory that dwelt in it, in bodily form.

A church that only has beige carpet, beige walls, and the preacher wears beige along with all the people, is very symbolic. You say, "Well no one really does that." But, have you heard of the Amish? They wear only black. But even those things are symbolic of something. Just look at creation and you'll see how much God loves color and beauty. He loved it in the tabernacle with all its silver, gold, incense, and cherubim.

---

[1] Not that my translation skills are infallible, but I teach both Greek and Hebrew in seminary.

But let us consider the Bible again. The same Hebrew verb can be used of both bowing and worshipping before the LORD and the king *at the same time*:

> Then David said to all the assembly, "Now bless the LORD your God." So all the assembly blessed the LORD God of their fathers, and *bowed their heads* and <u>prostrated themselves</u> before the LORD **and the king** (1 Chronicles 29:20).

The words in italics translate one verb that means "to bow," and the underlined words translate the word in the Second Commandment that we are not to do: worship created things. But the point is that they "bowed" and "prostrated" in one act — to God *and* to the king. It would seem obvious from the analogy of Scripture that they worshipped God not the king, but bowed in the presence of a *symbol* of God's authority, which was the king. Likewise, in Anglicanism, we bow in the presence of a symbol, a cross, but we worship God only. (See Appendix 3: Bowing and Worshipping.)

Here is another verse like 1 Chronicles 29:20:

> Exalt the LORD our God, and worship at His footstool — He is holy (Psalm 99:5).

The Hebrew word for "footstool" is used of the ark of the covenant (1 Chronicles 28:2), and in Psalm 132:7 David says, "Let us go into His <u>tabernacle</u>; let us worship at His <u>footstool</u>," which means to "worship" (the word in the Second Commandment) in the tabernacle in the presence of God's box that had the golden cherubim on the lid. If "worship" means bow sometimes, then it would certainly mean that here. Yet the box was not worshipped, but Yahweh was worshipped.

Do you recall the serpent on the pole in Numbers 21? The Israelites were being bitten by poisonous snakes under the judgment of God, and God told Moses to make a serpent, put it on a pole, and all those who looked at it in faith would be healed. Moses obeyed. No one worshipped the snake on the pole; it was a symbol of their sin and of God's grace. Jesus invoked it as a type of Himself (John 3:14).

But centuries later when the Israelites began worshipping the serpent on the pole, Hezekiah destroyed it with God's blessings (2 Kings 18:4). It was permissible to use the serpent on the pole as a symbol, but when they offered incense to it and worshipped it, when they thought the image incorporated the reality, they broke the Second Commandment. When the serpent was a *symbol* of God's grace, it functioned correctly. But when the people wanted to manipulate God with it, that was sinful. It could be used as an *aid* to worship but not as an *object* of worship, or we may say it could be used as a *tool* of worship but not an *object* of worship.

Moreover, God required His people to reverence the Ark of the Covenant, the box in the Most Holy Place, and only certain people, priests, were allowed to touch it. When some did touch it who were not supposed to, they died (1 Chronicles 13:10; 1 Samuel 6:19). Similarly, it is acceptable to have the cross as a symbol, and even to reverence it in the sense of worshipping Christ, but we must not worship it but Him. Some even oppose having a cross in the sanctuary, but is it permissible to think about a cross in the mind? If so, cannot we look at one on a table? Both a physical cross and a mental cross are created images. What are we to think of when we hear the word "cross"? Is it okay to wear a cross around the neck? One can even have theological images that he worships rather than God Himself. We should promote Christian symbols in our society to raise Christian awareness, to mold a Christian conscience.

Another aspect of this commandment is refraining from using images and symbols to control God. Consider the Ark of the Covenant again just mentioned. Israel thought the reason they were loosing a war with the Philistines was because they did not have God's box with them, the Ark of the Covenant (1 Samuel 4:3ff). So they went and got it, and again challenged the Philistines. They lost again, and the Philistines even captured the Ark. Then the Philistines thought they could control God with Israel's box, but their god fell on its face before the Ark, and God gave them plague. They could not wait to get rid of the box. God's symbol was used the wrong way. In each case, the Israelites and the Philistines tried to use magic to control God through some physical object. That was a violation of the Second Commandment. In other words, they had used God's gift to try to control God, using some created means to get God to bless them and do their will, but the only way to God is through His means. In the New Testament the only way to God is through the one Mediator, Christ (1 Timothy 2:5), not through Christ *and* something else, like Mary. She is not the mediator.

Jeroboam was judged for making two gold calves to go before the people for victory (1 Kings 12:28), and Israel was judged for making a golden calf that was their instrument to reach God and worshipped it (Exodus 32:8).

Also, we are not to make something that represents God Himself, to present His essence or person. Here is how the Apostle Paul put it:

> Therefore, since we are the offspring of God, we ought not to think that the Divine Nature is like gold or silver or stone, something shaped by art and man's devising (Acts 17:29).

Moreover, the Second Commandment forbids us to take glory from Him and give it to a created thing like one of the Herods did:

> 21 So on a set day Herod, arrayed in royal apparel, sat on his throne and gave an oration to them. 22 And the people kept shouting, "The voice of a god and not of a man!" 23 Then immediately an angel of the Lord struck him, because he did not give glory to God. And he was eaten by worms and died (Acts 12:21-23).

In sum, the Second Commandment does not forbid using symbols. As we've seen, the tabernacle had symbols, even images of the cherubim, the table of showbread with bread on it, the lampstand, the altar of incense, and so on. We see many of these also in the book of Revelation in worship in heaven. Indeed, we worship through Christ, the only acceptable worship, and He is the visible *image* of the invisible God (Colossians 1:15), having come to earth as a man whom people could see. And in the Gospels, people rightly worshipped Him since He was both God and man!

So what is the violation of the Second Commandment? *It is worshipping and serving the creature rather than the Creator.* (1) It is denying the Creator/creature distinction, making something in creation to be a god. It is to think of the infinite in terms of the finite, to liken the Creator to His creation, making God after our image instead of accepting that we are in His image, though sinful and marred. (2) And from the examples of the Ark being captured and the serpent on the pole being

128 Part 2—The Ten Commandments

allowed at one time and not at another, we can see that we must not consider that some created thing, an idol or image, is so connected with God that it can be used to control God. That would be magic. In other words, the connection of sign or image to what it represents is not a controlling connection, is not magic. (3) Moreover, the Second Commandment forbids making something to represent God Himself in some way. (4) Finally, the idol may be physical or mental. (See Appendix 3: Bowing and Worshipping.)

I. What We Get

The blessing is that the Creator is our God, that we are His creatures, that we get to enjoy Him and His creation to the fullest, that we can have His symbols to remind us of Him and His grace. How wonderful it is even in our worship services to be in His presence, to worship Him in spirit and truth!

We get to have bread that is set apart for Holy Communion that reminds of the body of Christ given for us, a channel of grace to us. This is a *required* symbol. We get to have wine that is a channel of grace to us of the blood of Christ. This is also a *required* symbol. The symbol itself is not grace,[2] but channels grace as we partake by faith.

We understand that the physical creation, especially the incarnation of God the Son, was such that *grace comes through His physical body*. If we were to see Him, we would all bow and worship Him, human body and soul and divine nature in one.

II. What We Must Do

(1) What is required is that we worship God as purely as possible, that we do not worship one another or physical objects, that we use His symbols in His way.

---

[2] We do not hold to transubstantiation, the Roman Catholic doctrine that says the bread and wine are literally turned into the human nature of Christ, while also containing the divine nature. In other words, one nature is now both divine and human, which is a contradiction and not what the Bible or the early church has taught. Rather, Christ has *two* natures, divine and human, separate and distinct but both joined to the one person, the Son of God.

Symbols are very powerful, whether physical symbols or symbols of the mind. Thus we must use *God's* symbols, not just anything, just as He had prescribed symbols in the tabernacle. Pornography is very symbolic and powerful, but that is using symbols the wrong way, causing one to worship his lusts, to worship the creature, and to invite the opportunity to break all of the other commandments, especially the Seventh Commandment on adultery or lusts.

(2) What is required is that we recognize that we are creatures, that we are dependent on Him for everything. We must not spend all our time acquiring money, for that is the worship of the creature rather than the Creator.

III. What We Should Avoid

(1) What is forbidden is the literal worship of manmade objects. We must not worship, serve, or be enslaved to physical objects, such as houses, cars, and money, to name a few. We must not treat man-made objects as links to God, as ways to get His attention, as somehow reminders of God so that we use them to get to Him. This would be the opposite of what took place in the tabernacle worship. We must not put our thoughts above God, requiring Him to give account to our "superior" insight.

Following St. Augustine, the Roman Catholic Church makes a distinction between worship for God (*latria*) and veneration for saints or images (*dulia*). Another way to say this is that worship is for God alone and veneration for something less, for some aspect of creation. The distinction is not so much the problem as is the practice. (See Appendix 3: Bowing and Worshipping.) Especially south of the USA border, Roman Catholics tend to practice virtual worship of relics and Mary. (They have a third distinction for the veneration of Mary, but that does not concern us here.) In the USA, Roman Catholics are more sophisticated, and perhaps most of their church members understand the distinction. We understand that we can venerate our cars, which means to take care of them, and if someone takes a hammer to them, we would rightly call the police. But we do not worship our cars; the thought never enters our minds.

As for the distinction between worship and veneration, it would seem to be biblical, for the Ark of the Covenant was highly venerated. Unauthorized touching of it or viewing its contents resulted in death (1 Samuel 6:19ff). It was set apart as especially holy. Only certain people were allowed to touch parts of the tabernacle, for they were holy, but this restriction showed only that the ark was venerated for the sake of the only One who is worthy of worship—God Almighty.

(2) What is forbidden is the worship of any human element or system, such as a government or its laws. No society can rise higher than its faith as expressed in its basic morality, and if its morality rises no higher than human government, it will lead the people into idol worship. The Second Commandment forbids worshipping and serving the creature rather then the Creator. One must not live and die only for something human, but for God. I don't want to be misunderstood; I shed my life's blood for the USA in Vietnam, but we must not terminate our standards on some human institution, even if it is the USA. We must die for God, not just for country, though maybe for God and country.

Which is more important in a country, treason or false worship? If the state puts itself above God, if it exalts its laws above God's laws, then it is requiring the people to worship the creature rather than the Creator. Once the state becomes the standard for idolatry, it will become tyrannical. It becomes the ultimate symbol.

(3) Earthly ambition alone must not be our goals, though productivity is good when done for God and His Church. But many live only for now, for storing up goods, for the "good" retirement. Another version of this is living for ease, despising any problems, thinking that the "good life" is owed to us.

(4) What about environmentalism? Certainly we don't want to waste the resources God has given to us, but to use the environment so that it has dominion over mankind is worshipping it. Man is to have dominion over the environment, as God said in Genesis 1:26, 28, not the reverse.

(5) The wrong use of symbols is forbidden, using them to hinder the worshipping and serving the true God. Here are a few things I've seen on TV to advertise Sunday worship: motor cycles jumping on

stage in the air, a giant globe behind the pulpit but no cross, people performing with swords. Moreover, other wrong symbols are witchcraft symbols, swastikas, Islamic symbols, pornography, which is the worship of the human body.

(6) What is forbidden is saint worship or using saints, creatures like us, to reach God. Notice what these people did when someone tried to worship them:

> 25 As Peter was coming in, Cornelius met him and fell down at his feet and worshiped *him*. 26 But Peter lifted him up, saying, "Stand up; I myself am also a man" (Acts 10:25-26).

> 8 Now I, John, saw and heard these things. And when I heard and saw, I fell down to worship before the feet of the angel who showed me these things. 9 Then he said to me, "See *that you do* not *do that*. For I am your fellow servant, and of your brethren the prophets, and of those who keep the words of this book. Worship God" (Revelation 22:8-9).

Then when Gentiles wanted to worship Barnabas and Paul, we read that they warned them not to do that:

> 14 But when the apostles Barnabas and Paul heard this, they tore their clothes and ran in among the multitude, crying out 15 and saying, "Men, why are you doing these things? We also are men with the same nature as you, and preach to you that you should turn from these useless things to the living God, who made the heaven, the earth, the sea, and all things that are in them" (Acts 14-14-15).

Worship and prayer go together so we should never engage in prayer to anyone but God Almighty:

> And the rest of it he makes into a god, his carved image. He falls down before it and worships *it*, prays to it and says, "Deliver me, for you are my god!" (Isaiah 44:15).

The virtually universal testimony of the early fathers of the church said that we should not pray to Christian martyrs, for that was worship.[3]

---

[3] Such fathers who condemned prayer to dead Christians were Justin Martyr, Tertullian, Origen, Lactantius, Athanasius, and though they believed that the saints in

(See Appendix 1: Worship of Images and Prayers to Saints where I discuss that prayer and worship go together so that if one prays to saints, one has crossed the line.)

Conclusion

The self-destruction of Western society is accelerating. All Christian symbols are being removed from our society. There is no culture without symbols, and the symbols it honors reveal the true god of that society. Symbols are very powerful. They not only reveal the faith of a people, but to a great extent they shape the faith of a people. Old Glory should conjure up pride and dedication, but the cross should conjure images of absolute glory to and worship of God, of forgiveness of sins, of our dedication to God to the death. The heart of the matter is the jealousy of God; He does not allow the worship of anything or anyone else.

The question is not whether we will have images and symbols, for that is a given. The question is whether we will have Christian ones or pagan ones, ones that honor God, or whether they will be representative of foreign gods. Moreover, we must not make anything that represents God Himself or that is used to try to manipulate God.

Again, "According to both the Ancient Near East and the Old Testament, an idol or image contained a god's presence, though that presence was not limited to the image."[4] Through the Incarnation of God the Son in human form, God's presence was indeed mediated to us, but He was also God. He was unique. A physical icon does not in itself mediate God to us, though it may remind us of God's presence. In

---

heaven prayed for those on earth, they strongly taught against invoking them to pray for us. The Council of Laodicea (AD 364), pronounced an anathema against those who would pray to angels, which would apply to dead saints as well, for both are creatures. Even the great St. Augustine refused prayers to and worship of dead Christians. See Harold Browne, *An Exposition of the Thirty-Nine Articles* (1865), Article 22, Section 1, History. The Roman Catholic Church wrongly encourages prayers to dead Christians and prayers to the Virgin Mary.

[4] Greg K. Beale, *We Become What We Worship* (Downers Grove, IL: Inter-Varsity Press, 2008), p. 17.

other words, we can take a cross and kiss it, but we have not kissed God, but if we kissed Jesus Christ, we have kissed God!

The animist worships his animals. The Buddhist worships his Buddha, or at least in the presence of his Buddha statue. But here in the USA we think we're more sophisticated. The miser worships his money. The atheist worships his mental images of reason, convincing himself that if a god exists, he must think like the atheist or not be god. But one thing they all have in common: They worship and serve the creation, not the Creator; they evaluate the infinite in light of the finite. But for us, let us worship and serve "God the Father Almighty, Creator of heaven and earth," let us honor the ultimate symbol of all time, the one most recognized in the history of the world, the cross, and let us live and die for the One who died for us, and raised Himself from the dead.

The word "altar" is used in Hebrews 13:10 of Holy Communion. In my denomination, the Reformed Episcopal Church, we place a cross on the altar, but we do not worship it. It is a reminder that our salvation is based only on the blood of Christ. That is Christian symbolism at its best, and it is honoring to the Second Commandment.

Finally, the first and second commandments are tied together, for the first one says to worship *only* the invisible God, and the second one commands us not to worship anything in creation. **AMEN**.

Chapter 8—Third Commandment: God's Name

You shall not take the <u>name</u> of the LORD your God in vain, for the LORD will not hold *him* guiltless who takes His <u>name</u> in vain (Exodus 20:7).

⁸ No human being can tame the tongue. It is a restless evil, full of deadly poison. ⁹ With it we bless our Lord and Father, and with it <u>we curse people who are made in the likeness of God</u> (James 3:8-9, ESV).

And you shall not swear by My <u>name</u> falsely, nor shall you profane the <u>name</u> of your God: I am the LORD (Leviticus 19:12).

Nor is there salvation in any other, for there is no other <u>name</u> under heaven given among men by which we must be saved (Acts 4:12).

Jesus said to him, "I am the way, the truth, and the life. No one comes to the Father except through Me" (John 14:6).

¹¹ And this is the testimony: that God has given us eternal life, and this life is in His Son. ¹² He who has the Son has life; he who does not have the Son of God does not have life (1 John 5:11-12).

⁹ Therefore God also has highly exalted Him and given Him the <u>name</u> which is above every <u>name</u>, ¹⁰ that at the <u>name</u> of **Jesus** every knee should bow, of those in heaven, and of those on earth, and of those under the earth, ¹¹ and *that* every tongue should confess that **Jesus Christ** is Lord, to the glory of God the Father (Philippians 2:9-11).

O LORD, who never failest to help and govern those whom
thou dost bring up in thy steadfast fear and love; Keep us, we
beseech thee, under the protection of thy good providence, and
make us to have a perpetual fear and love of thy holy Name;
through Jesus Christ our Lord. *Amen* (Book of Common Prayer).

Introduction

Have you noticed how easily people use God's name today, from "O
Jesus Christ" to "God da. ." to "O my God"? It is the "in thing" to use
God's name in a cavalier way. Here are some others: "I swear to God."
"I swear on my mother's grave."

But someone will object, "I don't mean anything by it." Then why
say it? God means something by those words, and we don't get to decide how to use them, for the Lord said:

Every idle word men may speak, they will give account of it in
the Day of Judgment (Matthew 12:36).

But we may object again that such is too harsh, but God has given
us the gift of speech, and He has given us words to honor Him with
them. If we don't use words His way, we are accountable to Him.
Every word a person says who has been given the power of speech invokes the Triune God, invokes His presence, not magically, but in the
sense that he imitates His ability for speech and depends on Him for
the immaterial laws of speech, logic, and grammar to make it work.
Conversely, every wrong word, especially in misusing God's names
(like "O Jesus Christ"), is an attack against Him personally. Thus every
wrong word will be judged (Matthew 12:36).

Notice from the James 3 passage above that it is just as wrong to
curse those made in God's image as it is to curse God Himself. It has
become fashionable on conservative talk radio and TV to make fun of
liberals, calling them all kinds of unbecoming names. However we may
disagree with the politics of others (and I've heard liberals call conservatives "as . . holes" and worse), God does not allow us either to murder His image in mankind or to disrespect it. To do so is a violation of
the Third Commandment.

The Hebrew behind the translation of "in vain" means that we must not use His name for any idle, insincere, or frivolous reason. The literal translation is "you shall not lift up the name of the Lord your God frivolously." The Third Commandment does not mean speech directly, but the idea of speech is rightly derived (Leviticus 19:12). The core idea is not to engage in perjury regarding God, who He is, His character, or to use His name in a frivolous manner. It condemns using God's name for any vain end, for false swearing, using it in every day life to buttress one's word.

Moreover, in the Third Commandment we see that we humans have the gift of speech, that with speech we are to honor God, to honor His character and His Name, and to have respect for godly authority and for those made in His image. Obeying the Third Commandment means that we speak with integrity, being consistent in what we say, not being double minded, not saying one thing to one person and another thing to someone else. When one is deliberately inconsistent in speaking, he is taking God's name in vain, thinking God does not take notice, that God will not require one to give an account. Perjury is more than lying in court; it is also saying we'll do something, even in private conversation, when we have no intention of following through.

The First Commandment stated that we must not worship anyone but God, and the Second Commandment forbade us to replace the Lord God with something manmade. Now the Third Commandment reinforces the first two by saying we must honor His name and character with our speech.

I. What We Get

The blessing of the Third Commandment is that we get to honor God, His name, His glory, and to bow in worship before Him. Can you imagine what a great privilege it is to be able to honor the one and only God of the universe?!

Moreover, we have God's written word given to us, which we are to honor as we honor Him, and this written word is a faithful deposit from God to His Church so that, as the Thirty-Nine Articles states, the "Church be a witness and keeper of Holy Writ" (Article 20).

Finally, names in Holy Scripture are often revelatory of character, and we know that God is infinitely holy, and the Third Commandment is designed to protect His holy name. We see that He is infinite in holiness, tender in mercy, consistent in justice, and we have the privilege to honor Him in all these areas of His being.

II. What We Must Do

We are to fear and reverence God above all else, especially above the fear of mankind. We must not be afraid to confess God or Christ publicly:

> [Jesus speaking] [32] "Therefore whoever confesses Me before men, him I will also confess before My Father who is in heaven. [33] But whoever denies Me before men, him I will also deny before My Father who is in heaven" (Matthew 10:32-33).

It is required that we honor God's names, attributes, character, written Word, His sacraments, and everything about God. We must not be frivolous or trite regarding Him in any way.

We cannot worship God without swearing by His Name, by invoking His Name, which is also to invoke the covenant we have with Him. The only way to invoke God's presence in worship is to invoke the name of Jesus. The reason I put so many passages about the name of Jesus at the beginning of this chapter is that *we come to God by the ultimate Name – Jesus!* (More on this in a moment.)

III. What We Should Avoid

(1) Refusing to honor God's name is to dishonor His character, but we can no more damage God, His name, or character than we can fly with our hands to the moon. Yet it is sinful not to honor God, His name, and His character.

(2) We are forbidden to use base speech. People use the most holy words they can think of to swear to demonstrate that they are in charge, even over God, or that they think little of Him. Thus they demonstrate a total lack of respect for God and for that which is holy, mock-

ing God. Like Satan who tempted Adam and Eve to fall into sin, like their father the devil, they seek to bring everything down. In vile speech against God, people are showing that they hate their circumstances, and therefore Him.

The gift of speech is part of being made in the image of God, and we are to use this gift to lift Him up, and to edify one another. *Degeneration of speech is one sign that a culture has left God.* Remember *Gone with the Wind* made in 1937 with that infamous line: "Frankly my dear, I don't give a da. . . ." When I was a boy, my mother would not let me see that movie because of that line. That is mild compared to today, especially with rap "music" and movies that use four-letter words as freely as breathing in and out. Here is what God says:

> Let no corrupt word proceed out of your mouth, but what
> is good for necessary edification, that it may impart grace to the
> hearers (Ephesians 4:29).

When the King James Version of the Bible was translated, it was not in the language of the people, but it was very exalted, majestic language, designed to bring the people up to the text of Holy Scripture, not to dumb down the text to the people. It did so for over 350 years. Today we have a new translation for every sector of society. Moreover, we have gutter language all throughout society with "Jesus Christ" being one of the most popular swear words and all manner of sexual slang words. But this commandment seeks to raise us up, to magnify speech, which is God's gift to us. He is holy and uses holy speech so we must do the same.

(3) Since this Commandment has to do with speech, theologians for centuries have understood that oaths are regulated by it. *We are forbidden to dishonor solemn oaths.* By an oath properly taken, we call God as witness to confirm our word. It is impossible to manage one's life, a business, or a country if there are not at least two things: oaths and penalties for violations of oaths. Without these, people do not trust one another, vice and wickedness increase, and the only thing that matters is what one wants.

God Himself swore an oath to be faithful to His covenant with us, so our oaths should honor Him in honoring our word and commitments just as He does:

> [13] For when God made a promise to Abraham, because He could swear by no one greater, He swore by Himself, [14] saying, "Surely blessing I will bless you, and multiplying I will multiply you" (Hebrews 6:13-14).

Indeed, taking an oath in the name of the Triune God points to Him as the center of meaning, the witness of one's conduct, and the object of one's dread at the Last Day. Therefore, oaths are legitimate, but let us consider some oaths.

First, there are the *wedding vows*, taken in the Name of the Triune God whether the person actually says "God" or not, for marriage is God's, not man's to remake. When marriages break down, the family breaks down and then all of society deteriorates.

Second, there is the *swearing in of a president* who vows to support the Constitution of the USA, *which is done with his hand on the Bible*, symbolizing that just as God is faithful and true to His word, so the President will be faithful to his word, that he will run the government by God's revelation in the Bible, not his own ideas. From 100 years ago and on back, this swearing in was recognized as coming under the Third Commandment. Now people take oaths on the Bible and cannot wait to violate both the Constitution and the Ten Commandments. This is disintegration in high places, and when the government is corrupt, so all the people will be the same, for mark it down that the people under authority take their example from those in authority. Now the government presumes to be a god, and thus it can do whatever it wishes.

In fact, not long ago a sitting president lied under oath, and his own party supported him. Who can respect something like that? So why do politicians go after others who do the same? This reveals the hypocrisy of those in authority.

Third, there are *oaths in court*. Because we have become a nation that dishonors the Third Commandment, we no longer fear God, so oaths are not considered important. Lawyers hire professional people to help choose a jury because it is assumed that people on the stand will lie, that there is no truth but only points of view, that the jury will not be objective because they don't fear God either.

In the 1830s, a Frenchman, Alexis de Tocqueville, toured the USA, and was astonished at the integrity of our court system. He observed this actual case:

> When I was in America, a witness who happened to be called at the Sessions of the county of Chester (state of New York) declared that he did not believe in the existence of God or in the immortality of the soul. The judge refused to admit his evidence, on the ground that the witness had destroyed beforehand all the confidence of the court in what he was about to say. The newspapers related the fact without any further comment.[1]
>
> [The year was 1831.]

If one did not fear the Last Day, there was no reason for him to tell the truth now, for often the only one who knows whether one is telling the truth is the person who testifies (and God, of course). Peter Hitchens, brother to atheist Christopher Hitchens, states a similar case:

> Without belief in God and the soul, where is the oath? Without the oath, where is the obligation or the pressure to fulfill it? Where is the law that even kings must obey? Where is the Magna Carta, Habeas Corpus, of the Bill of Rights, all of which arose out of attempts to rule by lawless tyranny? Where is the lifelong fidelity of husband and wife? Where is the safety of the innocent child growing in the womb? Where, in the end, is the safety of any of us from those currently bigger and stronger than we are?[2]

Fourth, *ministers in our denomination* (Reformed Episcopal Church) *take an oath* of office to be faithful to Holy Scripture, among other things. (See Book of Common Prayer of the Reformed Episcopal Church, p. 547ff for the oath.) We who teach at Cranmer Theological House (a

---

[1] Alexis de Tocqueville, *Democracy in America* (New York: Vintage Books, 1945), 1:317.
[2] Peter Hitchens, brother to atheist Christopher Hitchens, *The Rage Against God: How Atheism Led Me to Faith* (Grand Rapids: Zondervan, 2010), p. 147.

seminary in the Reformed Episcopal Church in the Houston area) and are in the Reformed Episcopal Church take an annual oath not to teach anything contrary to the Book of Common Prayer, to the three Creeds (Apostles', Nicene, Athanasian), to the Thirty-Nine Articles, and of course to Holy Scripture. Heresy is a violation of the Third Commandment, as well as the First one.

In fact, those modern ministers who speak in Jesus' name, claiming new revelations or just giving out heretical teaching, are taking God's name in vain, dishonoring Him, claiming something is from Him, and thereby attaching His Name to it. We see a lot of this today with TV ministers.

Fifth, the Lord Jesus said that we must be *truthful in everyday life*:

> "But let your 'Yes' be 'Yes,' and your 'No,' 'No.' For whatever is more than these is from the evil one" (Matthew 5:37).

No society or individual can exist very long when one's word means nothing. My grandfathers did business on handshakes for years. Today written contracts mean no more than the people behind them, and are easily broken with no thought of the matter. Today's politicians make a career out of lying and bearing false witness against one another, especially with negative ads during elections. Remember the false accusations against Supreme Court Justice Clarence Thomas during his confirmation hearings. Witnesses take the stand and lie as a matter of course. Indeed, fraud, which is lying, trickery, or deceit for one's own economic advantage, is still a crime in our culture, but if the government tried to prosecute all cases, it would shut down the court system from sea to shining sea.

I met a man once who was a home builder, and every few minutes he said, "I'll do what I say," which made me suspicious that he was a liar. When I checked on him with people who had done business with him, they confirmed that his word meant nothing.

By contrast, I witnessed a Christian friend take the stand in court, and he refused to swear an oath. The judge said, "You're under oath whether you swear or not." My friend stated, "Your honor, as a Christian man, I'm *always* under oath. It is not the oath that I object to but the swearing of it as if I were not always under oath." Now we may disagree with his reason, but it was refreshing to see a man take the Third Commandment seriously.

Not honoring God's Name in everyday matters leads to a complete breakdown of society because it only functions from day to day on truth, on implicit oath taking before Almighty God who will judge the hearts of all people at the Last Day.

(4) We are forbidden to take credit for the gifts God has given us, or to use them just for ourselves. We must use them to the glory of God's name and for others. Whom do movie stars serve with their talents? Many don't really have talents, just pretty bodies and graphics crews and stunt men to back them up. Now movies are not acting but action with graphics. Anyway, it dishonors God's name to pretend that we get credit for our gifts.

(5) We are forbidden to proclaim that something is from God when it is not, such as one preacher said, "God told me such and such," and his message contradicts God's written Word. Or a preacher may say God told Him something that has no basis in Holy Scripture, which is presumptuous, self-willed, from one's own authority, not from God, attaching something false to God's name, and contrary to 2 Peter 1:19-21. Old Testament prophets and New Testament preachers are to speak only truth in the name of God (Jeremiah 14:14; 23:25; Ezekiel 13:8) or be judged for taking His name in vain. We must be concerned to associate God's name only with truth, not with our imaginations.

(6) We are forbidden to give honor to mankind that is due to God alone, such as worship, unconditional obedience, and honor. (Yet we are to fear human government and its punishment, assuming it is godly, for God's authority is behind that authority (Romans 13:1ff).) Sometimes celebrities are virtually worshipped, especially when they die.

(7) We are forbidden to be frivolous in God's presence in worship. One reason people are rejecting worship and falling into entertainment is that they have forgotten that we enter the very presence of God in worship when the people of God come together. Many times in 1 Corinthians 11-14, Paul speaks of coming together "as a church" (11:17, 18, 20, 33, 34; 14:23, 26), and he did not allow nonsense, chaos, or anything that did not exalt the Lord. Consider that you are going to meet the

Queen of England, that you dress in motorcycle clothes, drive up on your bike, jump off and run up to the Queen, and say, "Gimme five, queeny baby."

Do you think the dignitaries would allow that? Multiply that over a billion times, that we gather into the very presence of God Himself, and that we can only come by confession of our sins and through the blood of Christ. Can you see the High Priest in the Old Testament entering the Most Holy Place with that attitude? One reason for the bells on his cloak was in case he messed up, the people would not hear the bells, and would drag his carcass out (Exodus 28:33).

IV. The Only Name for Salvation

There is only one name in which there is salvation and that is the name that our culture loves to hate. The only time this name is used in public is in a derogatory manner, some slang expression, some demeaning way, but it is the most exalted Name of all time. One who ignores this Name will be forced to bow before Him at the Last Day. Here is what God says about it:

> [9] God also has highly exalted Him and given Him the <u>name</u> which is above every <u>name</u>, [10] that at the <u>name</u> of Jesus every knee should bow, of those in heaven, and of those on earth, and of those under the earth, [11] and *that* every tongue should confess that <u>Jesus Christ</u> is Lord, to the glory of God the Father (Philippians 2:9-11).

The Lord Himself has said the same thing in another passage:

> Jesus said to him, "I am the way, the truth, and the life. No one comes to the Father except through Me" (John 14:6).

Then the Apostle Peter proclaimed about the name of Jesus:

> Nor is there salvation in any other, for there is no other <u>name</u> under heaven given among men by which we must be saved (Acts 4:12).

Here is the way one Gospel song put it:

> Won't be old Buddha who'll be sitting on that throne.
> Won't be Mohammed who'll call us home.

Won't be Haire Krishna who'll play that trumpet tune.

We're going to see the Son, not Rev. Moon.

No Jesus, no peace with God. Know Jesus, know peace with God. People become really outraged with the exclusive claims of Christ, but my response is that forgiveness of sins is a *free gift*. Would one turn down a billion dollars because Bill Gates gave it, saying that since it only came from him, that he would not take it? Jesus is the gracious Son of God who "who for the joy that was set before Him <u>endured the cross</u>, despising the shame, and has sat down at the right hand of the throne of God" (Hebrews 12:2). He had great joy in coming for us, to die on the cross for our sins, and He offers Himself as the free gift. Why would someone turn Him down? His name is the only approach to God, and those who use His Name in vain without repenting will meet Him in the Last Day judgment. But right now, one can come to God the Father through that Name and be forgiven. God the Father takes the same attitude toward us that we take toward His Son. If we reject the Lord Jesus, the Father rejects us.

Others use the name of Jesus, tacked on to the end of their prayers and often said several times, as if it were a magic word that will grant whatever they want. To ask for something in the name of Jesus means to ask according to God's revealed will in Holy Scriptures, not a blanket promise to make Jesus one's personal genie.

Conclusion

The only way we can come to God is by the NAME, the name of JESUS. We must swear by that name or we cannot worship Him, cannot come into His presence, and cannot have forgiveness of sins. Please say with me: "I honor the **Name of Jesus** above all names, that it is in this name alone that I boldly approach the throne, that I have forgiveness of sins. Jesus, I come to you with my sins, and I take your grace and forgiveness."

Honoring and worshipping the Name of Jesus is very much the Third Commandment. **AMEN**.

Chapter 9—Fourth Commandment: The Lord's Day

¹ Thus the heavens and the earth, and all the host of them, were finished. ² And on the seventh day God <u>ended</u> His work which He had done, and <u>He rested on the seventh day</u> from all His work which He had done. ³ Then God blessed the seventh day and sanctified it, because in it He rested from all His work which God had created and made (Genesis 2:1-3).

⁸ Remember the Sabbath day, to keep it holy. ⁹ Six days you shall labor and do all your work, ¹⁰ but the seventh day is the Sabbath of the LORD your God. In it you shall do no work: you, nor your son, nor your daughter, nor your male servant, nor your female servant, nor your cattle, nor your stranger who *is* within your gates. ¹¹ For <u>*in* six days the LORD made the heavens and the earth, the sea, and all that is in them, and rested the seventh day</u>. Therefore the LORD blessed the Sabbath day and hallowed it (Exodus 20:8-11).

¹² Observe the Sabbath day, to keep it holy, as the LORD your God commanded you. ¹³ Six days you shall labor and do all your work, ¹⁴ but the seventh day is the Sabbath of the LORD your God. *In it* you shall do no work: you, nor your son, nor your daughter, nor your male servant, nor your female servant, nor your ox, nor your donkey, nor any of your cattle, nor your stranger who *is* within your gates, that your male servant and your female servant may rest as well as you. ¹⁵ <u>And remember that you were a slave in the land of Egypt, and the LORD your God brought you out from there by a mighty hand and by an outstretched arm;</u> therefore the LORD

your God commanded you to keep the Sabbath day (Deuteronomy 5:12-15).

[16] Therefore let no one pass judgment on you in questions of food and drink, or with regard to a festival or a new moon or a Sabbath.[1] [17] These are a shadow of the things to come, but the substance belongs to Christ (Colossians 2:16-17, ESV).

One person esteems *one* day above another; another esteems every day *alike*. Let each be fully convinced in his own mind (Romans 14:5).

Let him who stole steal no longer, but <u>rather let him labor</u>, working with *his* hands what is good, that he may have something to give him who has need (Ephesians 4:28).

My duty towards God is to serve him truly all the days of my life (Book of Common Prayer).

Introduction

John was getting ready for the most important day of the year so he sent his wife and small children to her mother's house. He skipped church, and invited his buddies over. Each brought an offering for the occasion, beer, chips, pizza, candy, anything to make them bulge. The attire had to be rags with shirt tails out. During the program, they could scream at the screen, but during the commercials silence must be maintained with excommunication

---

[1] The Greek word for "Sabbath" here is plural, but often in the New Testament the plural is used for the singular. Thus the NKJ is wrong to translate this "sabbath days," as if this were not the weekly Sabbath but other high days. One could translate this "Sabbath days," with a capital first letter, thus indicating the weekly Sabbath. I'm aware that some take "festival or a new moon or a Sabbath" as all ceremonial terms and thus "Sabbath" is not the weekly Sabbath, but this is not the venue to go into this in detail. The Septuagint often translates the Hebrew singular "Sabbath" with a Greek plural noun, perhaps reflecting an Aramaic idiom. But the idea is still singular, which is the case here in Colossians 2. Indeed, in the New Testament "Sabbath" is usually plural in form but singular in meaning.

the penalty. After all, this holiest day of the year was Super Bowl.

People don't pay much attention to days anymore. Even Christmas has been secularized to the point that it has little meaning. Likewise, Thanksgiving means just food and getting off for work. The national holy days today are Super Bowl Sunday, New Year's Day, July Fourth, and a few other politically correct days. One can tell the faith of a culture by what it considers its holy days.

The Sabbath principle reminds us that God is to be the center of our lives and that we are to organize our time around Him, not around ourselves. "Idolizing our work by making it the center of value and meaning for our lives"[2] is really idolatry as well as a violation of the Fourth Commandment. Taking a day off to worship means that we define our lives by Him, not by our work. This day sets us free from the slavery of work and reminds us that our lives are defined by His redeeming grace.

From the verses quoted above, we can see three aspects to the Sabbath day. First, from the Genesis and Exodus passages, we are supposed to rest by faith on this day because God rested on the seventh day of His creation week. Since this is from the beginning of creation, this is for all people at all times, an acknowledgement of creation and creation's God.

Second, there is a redemptive aspect to the Sabbath, which is from the Deuteronomy passage above. We must acknowledge that God has redeemed us by the blood of the lamb. Thus on this special day, we must witness to the world regarding creation *but also* regarding redemption.

Third, we now have the Lord's Day, the first day of the week, as our holy day, not the Sabbath. Here we see all the aspects of the Sabbath coming together to form a new creation and a new people of God. The Lord's Day is the old creation recreated and the old covenant people of God made into new covenant people.

---

[2] Patrick D. Miller, *The Ten Commandments* (Louisville, KY: John Knox Press, 2009), p. 133.

These three "Sabbaths" are not three unrelated days, but actually the same thing in various ways, as I trust we shall see.

I. Rest and Work of the Creation Sabbath

The first major aspect to the Sabbath is creational. The above passage quoted from Exodus commands not only to rest for one day but also to work for six days. We often ignore the command to work six days. Before the fall into sin, the Sabbath was given, though the word "Sabbath" was not used in Genesis 2:1-3, but the words "seventh day." Yet since the command in Exodus to rest on the Sabbath is based on what God did in Genesis after He created for six days, we know by inference that the Sabbath was implemented at creation. Indeed, the reason God rested from creation was not that He was tired but that He was demonstrating that creation was done. If such a statement had not been given, we would be led to think that He was always creating, that He needed creation as much as it needed Him, and He was part of creation.[3] But the statement that He ceased made it clear that creation was once for all and that He was distinct from creation. A creator/creature distinction is introduced that runs through the whole Bible, thus denying pantheism, that we and "god" are the same.

Moreover, in Mark 2:27:

> The Sabbath was made for man, and not man for the Sabbath.

The word "made" would seem to imply the original creation and "man" would be Adam and mankind. Thus the Sabbath was given to mankind to remind him that one day his work would also be done, just as God's was.

Then again in Genesis 2:15 we read:

> Then the LORD God took the man and <u>put</u> him in the garden of Eden to tend and keep it.

It is significant that the Hebrew verb for "put" is the same as the word for "rest" in the Ten Commandments and is often translated "to give

---

[3] David Hazony, *The Ten Commandments* (New York, NJ: Scribner, 2010), p. 94. Book not recommended for most people; see the Annotated Bibliography at the end of the book.

rest."[4] In fact the verb is pregnant with various meanings throughout the Old Testament. It can mean the rest in death, or it can mean the rest God gives over His and our enemies. Similarly, it means our rest of salvation, especially our state of salvation as we enjoy God in the presence of worship.[5] The idea here is that in worship He prepares a banquet table for us in the presence of His and our enemies so that we rejoice in Him in the midst of them (Psalm 23:5). Here in Genesis 2:15 the "banquet" is before the fall into sin.

Moreover, after the verb "put," which carries the idea of being "set at rest, put in a place of rest" (not the same word for "put" as in verse 8), we have two infinitives in Hebrew: "to tend" the garden and "to keep it." The word for "tend" is a common verb, especially used in contexts of serving God (Deuteronomy 4:19), in priestly texts such as the Levites in the tabernacle (Numbers 3:7-8; 4:23-26, and so on). Similarly, "keep" carries the idea of "guarding" (Genesis 4:9; 30:31), and is used of the Levites for guarding the tabernacle from intruders (Numbers 1:53; 3:7-8), the two verbs sometimes used together, as here, for priestly duties (Numbers 3:7-8; 8:26; 18:56), all of which indicate that the garden and tabernacle are basically the same. The point is that the idea of rest is worship, even in the garden at creation.[6]

Adam was to till the garden (work), to exercise dominion, and then by implication to rest a day, as God did. Strictly speaking, the omnipotent God needed no rest. But the point of the rest for Adam was like God's day of rest, symbolic of satisfaction in His work, not the stopping of all bodily motion. Indeed, Adam's "rest" was to prepare for more work, for another assault on bringing creation under man's dominion. Before we proceed to the second major aspect, let us consider how sacred time is to God in light of creation.

Whatever time is, God created it. Moreover, He loves the cycles of time He has placed us in, such as the 24 hour cycle (days), the Lord's

---

[4] Allen P. Ross, *Holiness to the Lord* (Grand Rapids: Baker Academic, 2002), p. 397.

[5] Theological Wordbook of the Old Testament, under the verb for "rest," Bible Works 7.0 edition.

[6] Thoughts of this paragraph from Ross, *Holiness to the Lord*, pp. 105-108, and from Gordon J. Wenham, *Genesis 1-15* (Waco, Texas: Word Books, 1987), p. 67.

Day (weekly cycles), monthly cycles of the moon around the earth, and the yearly cycles of the earth around the sun with its seasons. Significantly, many of Israel's feasts were timed around the moon or the seasons, around the sun, and our days around the sun also, but the weekly cycle is revealed, not timed around some astral body. Anyway, the repetitions are constant reminders of the Creator's faithfulness to us and to remind us of our obligations to Him. In the Church calendar, we have Morning and Evening Prayer (daily), weekly worship (Lord's Day), and seasonal periods of concentration on matters of redemption, such as Christmas for the incarnation, Lent for our sins, and Easter for the bodily resurrection of Christ, just to name a few. One point to all these emphases is that all our time belongs to God and that we are accountable to Him for the use of it. He must be the center of all our thoughts.

A. God's Gift of Time

15 See then that you walk circumspectly, not as fools but as wise,

16 redeeming the time, because the days are evil (Ephesians 5:14-16).

In the context of Ephesians 5, Paul, under the inspiration of the Holy Spirit, commands us to "walk," that is, to live wisely, "redeeming the time." And why should we redeem the time? It is because the days are evil, because we have so little time to honor God, because we must not contribute to the evil around us by using His time wrongly.

The word for "redeem" means "make the most of," taking advantage of opportunities for godliness, or avoiding anything that interferes with godliness. "Redeem" also means to pay the price for something, and here it means to pay the price for godliness by giving up certain things and emphasizing others. Godliness *costs* us something, and that something that we must *spend* is time. It is not possible to gain godliness without spending this commodity called time, and we must especially teach our children to value time, to make the most of it, not to waste it in frivolous activities, although it is permissible to have fun.

What commodity does everyone on the planet have the same amount of? What is it that levels the playing field so that no one has an advantage? It is time: we all have 24 hours a day, 1440 minutes per day,

8,760 hours per year, and 24 more hours in leap years. God has given all of us the same amount of time in this respect, though we don't all live the same number of years. Perhaps if we knew when we would die, we would consider our time more valuable, not waste so much of it, but God does not tell us when we will die, which requires our trust of Him.

No amount of money can purchase more time on earth. We all have an appointed time to die (Hebrews 9:27), and there is nothing that will change that.[7] Once water is poured on the ground, we cannot get it back. Once time is wasted, it is gone forever. The only thing we can do about wasted time is to repent by using future time to better advantage.

Years ago when I was the pastor of another church in another city, I had a parishioner who was having financial problems with his business. He said he could not understand it because each Monday morning he would dedicate his business to God in prayer. I knew he was not attending worship. I make it a point not to keep up with who is giving how much in the churches I pastor, but he told me he was not tithing.

I then said, "Each Monday morning you're asking God to curse your business." He was taken back, but I explained that the biblical principle is that we sanctify the whole by giving the part. If he wanted his business blessed, he must give the part, the Lord's Day, to worship. Also, if he wanted his finances blessed, he must give to God the part, the tithe, the ten percent. He refused both, and God took his business.

B. Our Attitude to Time

Never did so much hinge on so little. A few years of life determine an everlasting destiny. Consider being in the afterlife for a million millennia, but that is a finite amount of time with an infinite amount of time to go! *There is infinite implication to every moment we spend in this life.*

The scarcity of any commodity causes people to set a high value on it, especially if it is necessary for life, such as potable water during a hurricane. So it is a contradiction that time is this commodity, but we do not value it as we should. A whole eternity depends on time, but we have so little of it now. We should value it greatly, but our tendency is

---

[7] The idea of dying before our time in Ecclesiastes 7:17 is looking at things from the human point of view.

to waste it. In our culture, we speak of "spending" time, a scarce resource.

Idleness is a great sin. When my son was still in school, even in grade school, I had him do projects out of the book of Proverbs each summer, along with enjoying his time off from school. I wanted to teach him that he did not get time off from the Lord, and to learn how to live. The Puritans used to say, "Idle hands are the devil's workshop." Too much idle time gives people opportunities to dream up corruption, such as gangs on the streets.

I hate the word "bored." I can honestly say that I have virtually never been bored, from childhood to now. When I go to the VA hospital for a checkup, patients are always cursing and getting angry over having to wait. I take a book to keep from wasting time. One reason people get so upset waiting is that they did not plan ahead to use the time wisely, which means they planned to waste it. Then they want the circumstances to conform to them, not them to the circumstances. When one is bored, he is really serving self, or wanting others to serve self. One who is bored with his work is just serving for a paycheck, not really serving the Lord through his job as he should be (Colossians 3:22-24).

The biblical principle is that we sanctify the whole by giving the part (money and time), giving the Lord's Day to God. If we think we don't have time for God on His day, we are not living by faith, thinking that if we don't spend all our time in whatever activity we are engaged in that things will not get done. But when God says to honor Him one day in seven, *He will assume the responsibility for our obedience*. He will bless six days as if seven. Things that don't get done were not important. God can fill up a week with many activities, and can take our time away from us, if we don't honor Him as He prescribes.

Get rid of or minimize time robbers, such as TV. TV is not wrong in itself, but it can be if abused. Moderation here is difficult. Do you know what "amusement" means? "Muse" means "to think," and "a-muse" means not thinking, which is the scourge of our age. People don't know how to meditate or to think.

There are few things more useless than Soap Operas. "As the Word Turns", we and "All My Children" must follow God's "Guiding

Light," considering "Another World" more important than this one, not worrying about being "Bold and Beautiful" or thinking that we are "Desperate Housewives" or that we are "Young and Restless," but develop our "Dynasty," that is God's children entrusted to us, lest we end up in God's "General Hospital." Seriously, don't stand before Christ on the Last Day having pilfered away God's gifts to you and say, "Lord, I spent *Your* time on soap operas, not in helping others."

Have you ever heard of the "tyranny of the urgent"? "The tyranny of the urgent lies in its distortion of priorities. One of the measures of good time management is the ability to distinguish the important from the urgent, to refuse to be tyrannized by the urgent, to refuse to manage by crisis" (Jim Clemmer). This is what I call bumper pool time management, just bumping from one crisis to another with no goals and no control. Sometimes this happens to all of us, but I'm not talking about the exceptions but the rule. The worst enemy of the best is often the better.

II. Rest, Redemption, & Dominion in the Old Covenant

The second major aspect to the Sabbath is redemptive. From Deuteronomy five quoted at the beginning of the chapter, we can see that the Old Testament Sabbath was a reminder of redemption from sin. Thus the Sabbath was as much about worship as rest. Moreover, as Deuteronomy stated, the people of God had dominion over Egypt when they were brought out by the Passover lamb. Therefore, on the Sabbath they were to remember not only the *creation* (Exodus 20:11) but also their *redemption* from Egypt (Deuteronomy 5:15), both of which would involve worship at the tabernacle for the priests and also for most of Israel who camped around the tabernacle.

Even the word "remember" (or "remembrance") refers to covenant renewal in worship, renewing our relationship with God (the covenant with Him). In other words, remembering is not just a mental action regarding the past, but a personal renewal with God in His presence in worship regarding the past and the future. "Remember" is used of keeping God's commandments,[8] and of activity, not just recalling the past.[9] Moreover, during the time the Ten Commandments were given, the tabernacle was in the midst of the people, symbolizing God in the midst of His people. On the Sabbath, God was celebrated as Creator and redeemer, which is what we see in Genesis 1-3.

Likewise, the word "keep" means to guard, watch over, fulfill, which is to be done regarding His day.

Moreover, mankind was given dominion over creation before the fall into sin, including dominion over the animals, and when he fell, redemption restored that original dominion, at least in principle. Therefore, the Fourth Commandment required that the masters of animals were to give them rest on the Old Testament Sabbath, which symbolized the original dominion Adam had over the animals at creation. Also, redemption gave redeemed man dominion over the one who caused his downfall, the devil, and over his seed:

> And I will put enmity between you and the woman, and
> between your seed and her Seed; He shall bruise your head, and
> you shall bruise His heel (Genesis 3:15; see also 1 John 3:10).

Genesis 3:15 spoke of the coming of Christ and His victory by crushing the head of the serpent, but that dominion also carries over to us under the new covenant:

> And the God of peace will crush Satan under your feet
> shortly (Romans 16:20).

Creation gave original man dominion over the earth and over the animals, and redemption restored fallen man to that place of dominion, both of which were to be celebrated on the old covenant Sabbath. Thus, *rest and dominion go together.*

We can see this especially in Joshua, which is the book of victory, but we must begin with Genesis to see the whole picture. We have the covenant seed beginning with Genesis 3:15, then going through Noah, Abraham, Isaac, Jacob, Joseph, all of whom were promised the land in Palestine, which was to be a beachhead to conquer the world. So the

---

[8] Numbers 15:39-40; Malachi 4:4.
[9] Joshua 1:13; Psalm 109:16; Isaiah 17:10; Amos 1:9.

godly seed began in Genesis but then ended in Egypt. While in Egypt (Exodus), they grew enormously in numbers, but they became slaves. Then the Lord brought them out of Egypt (a picture of sinful bondage) by the blood of the Passover lamb, thereby giving them victory (dominion) over Egypt. Israel took the wealth of Egypt with them, and saw their armies destroyed in the Red Sea. Next the book of Leviticus taught the people how to worship the Lord at the tabernacle on their way to the Promised Land and after they arrived. Much of this worship took place on the Sabbaths, both the seventh day and other high days. In the book of Numbers Israel was disobedient, and so God killed off that generation. Their disobedience was that they refused to rest in the Lord's sovereignty and refused to face their enemies, being cowards (Revelation 21:8), not believing that the Lord would give them the victory, even though they had already seen great deliverance out of Egypt and through the Red Sea. In the book of Deuteronomy, the people are at the edge of the Promised Land after wandering in the desert 40 years, and Moses again gives them the Ten Commandments, which was covenant renewal. Moreover, Moses commissioned Joshua to be the new leader of Israel to conquer the land, to destroy the seed of the serpent.

Now here is the point. The major theme in Joshua is rest, the people of God receiving God's rest over their enemies. Using the same Hebrew word for rest that is used of the Sabbath rest in the Ten Commandments, we read in the *beginning* of Joshua where the Lord promised them victory:

> Remember the word which Moses the servant of the LORD commanded you, saying, The LORD your God is giving you <u>rest</u> and is giving you this land. . . . until the LORD has given your brethren <u>rest</u>, as He *gave* you, and they also have taken possession of the land which the LORD your God is giving them (Joshua 1:13, 15).

Then as the people of Israel are preparing to engage in battle against God's and their enemies, the first thing they do is worship: they have covenant renewal with circumcision and Passover, the first time for Passover in 40 years (Joshua 5:1-12). Right after this worship the pre-incarnate Son of God appeared to Joshua, indicating it was time to conquer the land (Joshua 5:13ff). Thus by "resting" in the Lord through worship, they had victory, as we see at the *end* of the book:

> The LORD gave them <u>rest</u> all around, according to all that He had sworn to their fathers. And not a man of all their enemies stood against them; the LORD delivered all their enemies into their hand (Joshua 21:44).

> And now the LORD your God has given <u>rest</u> to your brethren, as He promised them; now therefore, return and go to your tents *and* to the land of your possession, which Moses the servant of the LORD gave you on the other side of the Jordan (Joshua 22:4).

> Now it came to pass, a long time after the LORD had given <u>rest</u> to Israel from all their enemies round about, that Joshua was old, advanced in age (Joshua 23:1).

The New Testament will make much of this rest that Joshua gave the people of God in Hebrews 3-4. The point now is that under the old covenant, the "rest" was not really so much the lack of bodily motion as it was the rest of worship, confessing their God as Lord of all, confessing Him as Creator and redeemer, and then conquering in light of that. Rest done properly *is* worship, for not working combined with not worshipping is to make idleness a god.

III. Rest, Work, and Redemption in the New Covenant

The third major aspect to the Sabbath is that it is fulfilled in the new covenant Lord's Day.

Please read the Colossians 2:16-17 verses again at the beginning of this chapter. The relationship of the Old Testament Sabbath to New Testament Sunday is bud to flower. Notice what Paul is saying: the Old Testament festivals, new moons, and Sabbaths were only shadows, copies of the real substance to come. Christ was the substance.

Here is what St. Augustine said about these verses:

> Here also, when he says, "Let no one judge you" in these things, he shows that we are no longer bound to observe them.

And when he says, "which are a shadow of things to come," he explains how these observances were binding at the time when the things fully disclosed to us were symbolized by these shadows of future things (Augustine, *Faustus*, Book IV).

Paul is clearly saying that the old covenant Sabbath pictured Christ, and thus no one should pass judgment on us for not observing the ceremonial Sabbath, or any of the old covenant rituals. They had their place as pictures of Christ, but when Christ came, the pictures were not needed anymore.

A. The Old Testament Sabbath Allowed Work and Emphasized Worship

16 For this reason the Jews persecuted Jesus, and sought to kill Him, because He had done these things on the <u>Sabbath</u>. 17 But Jesus answered them, "<u>My Father has been working until now, and I have been working</u>." 18 Therefore the Jews sought all the more to kill Him, because He not only broke the <u>Sabbath</u>, but also said that God was His Father, making Himself equal with God (John 5:16-18).

This passage was constantly referred to by the early fathers as proof that the Old Testament Sabbath was never an absolute prohibition against work, for God worked on the Sabbath. Though in Genesis 2:2-3 God had rested from His creation work, this was not a complete rest from all work whatsoever, for Jesus is saying that He healed on the Sabbath, meaning He and the Father are working together for our salvation.

Moreover, one was allowed to do good on the Sabbath, for that is really what the Sabbath was about, doing good to one another and obeying God, which is why Jesus healed so often on the Sabbath.

Also, the early fathers often spoke of the creation week, the seventh day that God blessed, and the new creation began on the eight day with the Lord's resurrection. Hear what St. Augustine said:

But there is not now space to treat of these ages; suffice it to say that the seventh shall be our Sabbath, which shall be brought to a close, not by an evening, but by the Lord's day, as an eighth and eternal day, consecrated by the resurrection of Christ, and prefiguring the eternal repose not only of the spirit, but also of the body. There we shall rest and see, see and love, love and praise. This is what shall be in the end without end. For what other end do we propose to ourselves than to attain to the kingdom of which there is no end? (Augustine, *City of God*, Book 22, Chapter 30)

What you call Sunday we call the Lord's Day, and on it we do not worship the sun, but the Lord's resurrection. And in the same way, the fathers observed the rest of the Sabbath, not because they worshipped Saturn, but because it was incumbent at that time, for it was a shadow of things to come, as the apostle testifies (*Faustus*, Book 18).

Socially, the Old Testament Sabbath was to give laborers a day off, reminding everyone that they were no longer slaves but belonged to God. God would bless them with seven days of productivity for six days of labor, which was a faith principle. The "no work" rule for any reason and all the picky rules were Pharisaic additions, but the main point was to do good, which the Lord demonstrated repeatedly by healing on the Sabbath. Moreover, theirs was an agrarian society, which worked much better than our modern industrial society where one cannot stop oil refineries or steel mills for a whole day.

Covenantally, the Old Testament Sabbath was a sign of Israel's relationship with God to the nations, just as now the Lord's Day is the Church's sign to our culture. Moreover, *the Old Testament Sabbath was about receiving from God while not working, which was a picture of the Gospel*. It was worship and covenant renewal. Just as we renew our relationships with our spouses by sending time with them, so we renew our covenant with God each Lord's Day. As we come together for worship, we are in His presence in a special way:

Not forsaking the assembling of ourselves together (Hebrews 10:25).

For where two or three are gathered together in My name, I am there in the midst of them (Matthew 18:20).

> You come together as a church (1 Corinthians 11:18, see also 11:20, 33, 34; 14:23, 26).

Moreover, the Lord Jesus worshipped on a regular basis each Sabbath in the synagogue, which included the reading of the old covenant scriptures. He attended faithfully "as His <u>custom</u> was" (Luke 4:16).

B. Temple and Sabbath Went Together (Matthew 11:25-12:8)

> ¹ At that time Jesus went through the grainfields on the <u>Sabbath</u>. And His disciples were hungry, and began to pluck heads of grain and to eat. ² And when the Pharisees saw *it,* they said to Him, "Look, Your disciples are doing what is not lawful to do on the <u>Sabbath</u>!" ³ But He said to them, "Have you not read what David did when he was hungry, he and those who were with him: ⁴ how he entered the house of God and ate the showbread which was not lawful for him to eat, nor for those who were with him, but only for the priests? ⁵ Or have you not read in the law that on the <u>Sabbath</u> the priests in the <u>temple</u> profane the <u>Sabbath</u>, and are blameless? ⁶ Yet I say to you that in this place there is *One* greater than the <u>temple</u>. ⁷ But if you had known what *this* means, 'I desire mercy and not sacrifice,' you would not have condemned the guiltless. ⁸ For **the Son of Man is Lord even of the <u>Sabbath</u>**" (Matthew 12:1-8).

Another reason the Old Testament Sabbath does not continue in its ritual form is that it was part of the ceremonial law. It was connected with the temple, as the Lord indicates here in Matthew 12.

- Temple = the sanctity of space
- Sabbath = the sanctity of time

The tabernacle (which became the temple) and the Sabbath were given by Moses in Exodus as part of the ceremonial law. The tabernacle and the temple pointed to Christ, and the Sabbath did also. When the temple was abolished, so was the ceremonial Sabbath. The Son of Man was Lord of the Sabbath, which meant that He controlled it, not it Him.

The Old Testament Sabbath was part of the ceremonial law, like the sacrifices, and thus there was prohibition against working, for that was a type of Gospel rest. But there were exceptions even to that since the priests worked, and God worked through His providence.

The ceremonial Sabbath was instituted when the tabernacle was instituted. In fact, when the Lord said, "If you knew what this meant: 'I desire mercy and not sacrifice,' you would not have condemned the guiltless," He meant that *mercy is the point of the Sabbath*, not ceremonial ritual and not wrangling over how far you can walk or how little you could do with your body.

Moreover, notice from the Matthew passage something that seems strange at first glance:

> Or have you not read in the law that on the <u>Sabbath</u> the priests in the <u>temple</u> profane the <u>Sabbath</u>, and are blameless? Yet I say to you that in this place there is One greater than the <u>temple</u>.

Christ is saying that **covenantally** the temple and the Sabbath went together. They were both types. Both pointed to Him. Read the Colossians passage again:

> "Therefore let no one pass judgment on you in questions of food and drink, or with regard to a festival or a **new moon or a** <u>Sabbath</u>. These are a shadow of the things to come, but the substance belongs to Christ" (Colossians 2:16-17, ESV).

What was a "festival"? It was part of the Old Covenant ceremony. What was the "new moon"? It was part of the sacrificial system when special offerings were made to God monthly. What was the "temple"? Every aspect of it was typical and pointed to Christ. What was the "Sabbath"? It was worship and doing good, pointing to the One to come who would cause all work to cease, who would cause all sinning to cease, and who would teach that we receive grace without working.

The Old Testament history of the ceremonial Sabbath indicates that tabernacle and Sabbath stand and fall together. The Sabbath was not formally given in the time of Abraham, was instituted by Moses as a type of Christ, and then was fulfilled by Christ. Likewise, the tabernacle/temple was not in the time of Abraham, was instituted by Moses as a type of Christ, and fulfilled in Christ. We cannot go back to the temple anymore, for Christ has caused it to cease. And we cannot go back to the old Sabbath, for it was tied to the temple, tied to the Old Testament people, and was fulfilled in Christ. We do not worship on Saturday anymore. The Sabbath and the temple were stages in history; they served their ceremonial purposes. They are not covenantal signs anymore. The Lord's Day, the day of resurrection and receiving without working, is our covenantal sign. Those who worship on the seventh day reveal their unbelief in Christ's resurrection (except for the Seventy Day Adventists, who are alone in their view).

C. Christ Rose on the First or Eighth Day

The first day of the week is the day of resurrection, according to all four Gospels, and we see worship on the first day in Acts 20:7 and 1 Corinthians 16:2.

Covenantally, why do we worship on Sunday? One reason is that it is the Lord's Day, as given in Revelation 1:10, and the early church, some of whom knew John who wrote Revelation 1:10, were unanimous that this was Sunday. It was the day of the resurrection of the Lord.

Moreover, was it just a coincidence that He rose on Sunday? No. He did not rise on the Sabbath or the seventh day, but He arose on the day *after* the seventh day. The Old Covenant was the old creation with its seven days. In Genesis one, we have creation in six days with God "resting" from creation on the seventh day (but not resting from all things, John 5:17). Now Christ inaugurates the New Covenant, which begins on the eighth day, a new beginning of the new creation week.

Covenantally, Israel had the temple and the Sabbath, and we have the new temple (Jesus) and a new Day, the Lord's Day on His resurrection. We have a new creation week that began with the Lord's resurrection. To bring the Old Testament Sabbath over to the New Covenant would be to take us back to the Old Covenant. Even Pentecost was on the 50th day, or seven weeks from the Sabbath plus one day, which was on Sunday, the first day of the new week, the beginning of the new people of God, the Church.

St. Athanasius, a fourth century father, stated:

> For the sabbath was the end of the former creation, but the Lord's Day is the beginning of the second, in which he renewed the old and made it afresh, and so, as he commanded them be-

fore to keep the sabbath day, the memorial of former things, so we honor the Lord's Day, being the memorial of the second creation.[10]

D. The Sabbath Was/Is Gospel Rest (Hebrews 3:18-4:11)

Hebrews 3-4 gives us tremendous insight into the Sabbath/Lord's Day issue throughout the Bible. Let us begin with a quote:

> [7] Therefore, as the Holy Spirit says: "Today, if you will hear His voice, [8] do not harden your hearts as in the rebellion, in the day of trial in the wilderness, [9] where your fathers tested Me, tried Me, and saw My works forty years. [10] Therefore I was angry with that generation, and said, 'They always go astray in *their* heart, and they have not known My ways.' [11] So I swore in My wrath, 'They shall not enter My <u>rest</u>.' " [12] Beware, brethren, lest there be in any of you an evil heart of unbelief in departing from the living God; [13] but exhort one another daily, while it is called "Today," lest any of you be hardened through the deceitfulness of sin (Hebrews 3:7-13).

Verses 7-11 are quoted from Psalm 95:7-11 where the Lord states that He did not allow the generation that came out of Egypt to enter into His rest in the Promised Land, but He made them wander 40 years. Then the generation of Joshua's day would enter the Lord God's rest. The others had not believed His word to conquer His and their enemies in Canaan when they first came out of Egypt, and so were denied true Sabbath rest, which obviously is by faith, not by the lack of bodily movement. As Hebrews goes on to say:

> [16] Who came out of Egypt, *led* by Moses? [17] Now with whom was He angry forty years? *Was it* not with those who sinned, whose corpses fell in the wilderness? [18] And to whom did He swear that they would not enter His <u>rest</u>, but to those who did not obey? (Hebrews 3:16-18).

By faith they should have entered God's Gospel rest.

---

[10] Roger T. Beckwith and Wilfrid Stott, *This Is the Day* (Greenwood, SC: Attic Press, 1978), pp. 105-106.

Moreover, God's rest began at the creation, and continued into the Promised Land:

> [1] Therefore, since a promise remains of entering His rest, let us fear lest any of you seem to have come short of it. [2] For indeed the gospel was preached to us as well as to them; but the word which they heard did not profit them, not being mixed with faith in those who heard *it*. [3] For we who have believed do enter that rest, as He has said: "So I swore in My wrath, 'They shall not enter My rest,' " although the works were finished from the foundation of the world. [4] For He has spoken in a certain place of the seventh *day* in this way: "And God rested on the seventh day from all His works" (Hebrews 4:1-4).

Notice that the creation "Sabbath" is combined with the redemptive Lord's Day and that we enter rest *by faith*.

As one author rightly summarizes:

> After the Fall, God's original intentions for humanity's enjoyment of the promised consummation rest are now worked out through God's acts of redemptive purpose. Now in Hebrews the final goal of salvation can be depicted in spatial terms. The consummation rest is pictured in terms of a heavenly resting place, the antitype of the resting place in the promised land referred to in Psalm 95:11. [11]

Therefore, our "Sabbath" rest is the Lord's Day as we worship the great King who by His resurrection has entered His rest. As we worship properly, we will conquer our "Canaanites" by the Gospel as we conquer *all* the earth, the new Promised Land. At the Last Day our rest will be complete. I have no doubt that the main reason Christians are so impotent in our culture is because on the Lord's Day we worship ourselves, emphasizing ourselves, not the great acts and works of redemption. Because we don't rest in worship and because we don't believe we can conquer God's enemies, we are being conquered.

---

[11] D. A. Carson, editor, *From Sabbath to Lord's Day* (Grand Rapids: Zondervan, 1982), p. 210.

If this "Sabbath rest" was still future when Joshua wrote, the Old
Covenant rest must have been future, meaning the rest from labor was
only a type of the final rest, further meaning the old covenant Sabbath
was not the real point, ceasing bodily motion was not the main point.
Thus spiritually, the Old Testament Sabbath was given to point to the
time of complete Gospel rest, when we will have complete dominion.

Moreover, some of the early fathers invoked Isaiah 1:13-20 to demonstrate that the point of the Sabbath was to do righteousness, not just
to stop the body from motion:

> [13] Bring no more futile sacrifices; incense is an abomination
> to Me. The New Moons, the **Sabbaths**, and the calling of assem-
> blies — I cannot endure iniquity and the sacred meeting. [14] Your
> **New Moons** and your appointed feasts My soul hates; they are a
> trouble to Me, I am weary of bearing *them*. [15] When you spread
> out your hands, I will hide My eyes from you; even though you
> make many prayers, I will not hear. Your hands are full of blood.
> [16] Wash yourselves, make yourselves clean; put away the evil of
> your doings from before My eyes. Cease to do evil, [17] learn to do
> good; seek justice, rebuke the oppressor; defend the fatherless,
> plead for the widow. [18] "Come now, and let us reason together,"
> Says the LORD, "though your sins are like scarlet, they shall be
> as white as snow; though they are red like crimson, they shall be
> as wool. [19] If you are willing and obedient, You shall eat the
> good of the land; [20] but if you refuse and rebel, you shall be de-
> voured by the sword"; for the mouth of the LORD has spoken.

This was confirmed by Jesus:

> Then Jesus said to them, "I will ask you one thing: Is it law-
> ful on the Sabbath to do good or to do evil, to save life or to de-
> stroy?" (Luke 6:9).

> [Jesus speaking:] "Of how much more value then is a
> man than a sheep? Therefore it is lawful to do good on the
> Sabbath" (Matthew 12:12).

The doing good aspect of the Sabbath anticipated the Gospel, especially the fulfillment of the Gospel in our lives — which means enter-

ing the kingdom of God and to cease from sinning at the Last Day. This is the final rest, the rest of the future, which the Lord Jesus said He would give a taste of now if anyone would come to Him:

> Come to Me, all *you* who labor and are heavy laden, and I will give you <u>rest</u> (Matthew 11:28).

Jesus made this statement just before He began his discourse on the Sabbath in the next few verses so that people would get the idea that He was the fulfillment of the Sabbath. Our rest is in Him.

Therefore, since there is yet the future and final rest to come, even the Lord's Day anticipates that, requiring us to rest and worship one day in seven. As one book well stated it:

> In the New Testament, there is held before us the prospect of entering into God's creation rest ourselves, in virtue of the saving work of Christ (Hebrews 3-4), so a symbolical rest, kept on the day which commemorates his saving resurrection and anticipates his glorious return, would have been no less meaningful to Christians.[12]

Both the Sabbath and the Lord's Day were holy days for praying, dedicated to God, not holidays just for playing.[13]

Conclusion

Israel's Sabbath was without parallel among the laws of the ancient Near East.[14] Israel had this special institution that distinguished them from other nations, and it has come over to the Church, being fulfilled in Christ. Now we have our day.

The original Sabbath was Genesis 2 and designed for creation. When man fell into sin, the original Sabbath was not only the basis for the Fourth Commandment in Exodus 20, but also it now had a redemptive aspect as well (Fourth Commandment in Deuteronomy 5). In other words, these are not parallel Sabbaths, but the Mosaic one is restorative

---

[12] Beckwith and Stott, *This is the Day*, p. 40.

[13] Allen P. Ross, *Recalling the Hope of Glory* (Grand Rapids, MI: Kregel Academic and Professional, 2006), p. 227.

[14] Mark F. Rooker, *The Ten Commandments: Ethics for the Twenty-First Century* (Nashville, TN: B&H Academic, 2010), p. 75.

of the creation one, and the new covenant Lord's Day is the fulfillment of the Moses Sabbath, taking us back to the original creation through redemption. On Sunday worship, we anticipate the final rest to come when creation will be restored to its pristine condition. Thus, the Sabbath concept is past (Christ's death on the cross), present (worship on the Lord's Day), and future (final restoration of all things).

What carries over? **Covenantally,** the Old Covenant *temple* ceased since all the sacrifices are complete in Him, so the typology of the temple is fulfilled in Christ, for Jesus said that He personally was the temple (John 2:19-22). We now have what the temple looked forward to: the once for all sacrifice of Christ. Also, the Old Covenant Sabbath typology finds its fulfillment in Christ, as Paul explicitly states in Colossians 2:16.

Spiritually, the point of rest means to find Gospel rest from our works, to stop trying to work our way into favor with God, to find Gospel rest in Jesus. We have it partially now, and we look for its completion in the future. We look forward to complete Gospel rest when we will sin no more. Today, for us to say that we have fulfilled the Lord's Day by not working is to miss the whole point. We enter Jesus' rest by trusting in Him. *He* is our rest.

What carries over is worship. We see in Hebrews 10:25, we are *not* to "forsake the assembling of ourselves together," and we know from the Lord's Day and the early church that worship was on Sunday. Worship was in the garden where Adam and Eve enjoyed the presence of God before they fell in to sin. Then worship was on the old covenant Sabbath day, and now it is on the new covenant Lord's Day. We must come together to cease from our labors, to cease sinning, to find Gospel rest in the ultimate "Sabbath," the substance of the Old Covenant Sabbath, even Christ. We do this on the eighth day, the first day of the new creation week, the resurrection of the true "Sabbath" rest, even our Lord Jesus Christ. When creation is fully restored (Romans 8:20-24), we will continue to worship the Triune God.

The change to the first day/eight day also signifies the new creation aspect of redemption, that God is now recreating the earth and a new people to be His own special people.

What carries over is the sanctity of time, meaning that Jesus is Lord over it, that it all belongs to Him, and that we are required to give part of our time to Him each week in worship. The biblical principle is that we sanctify the whole of our time by giving the part to God, which is worship on the Lord's Day.

What carries over is the creation rest of Genesis 2, which means physical rest is still with us. Just as we rest each 24 hours, so we do once a week. There are few if any rules for rest in the new covenant Lord's Day, though worship is certainly one rule, but Paul leaves the implementation mainly to us:

> ⁴ Who are you to judge another's servant? To his own master he stands or falls. Indeed, he will be made to stand, for God is able to make him stand. ⁵ <u>One person esteems *one* day above another; another esteems every day *alike*. Let each be fully convinced in his own mind.</u> ⁶ He who observes the day, observes *it* to the Lord; and he who does not observe the day, to the Lord he does not observe *it* (Romans 14:4-6a).

But whatever stance we take regarding how we rest, it must be in faith to the glory of God with a clear conscience: "Whatever is not of faith is sin" (Romans 14:23).

Yet it is sinful if one deliberately works on Sunday when he does not have to, thereby missing the worship of God. But I, as a minister of the Gospel, labor intensely on the Lord's Day to present the Gospel so those who hear can rest in that Gospel. Then the other six days we go forth under the banner of the cross and in the authority of the Lord's resurrection to conquer all His and our enemies. That is Sabbath/Lord's Day rest. Each Lord's Day the Church is proclaiming to the world the God of creation and the God of redemption. One day, when the Lord returns, we shall enter the never ending Sabbath, the Lord's Day, where there is no night, and the curse on creation will be forever lifted!

"Not forsaking the assembling of ourselves together" (Hebrews 10:25). **AMEN.**

Chapter 10—Fifth Commandment: Parents' Part

Parental Authority

Honor your father and your mother, that your days may be long upon the land which the LORD your God is giving you (Exodus 20:12).

[1] Children, obey your parents in the Lord, for this is right. [2] "Honor your father and mother," which is the first commandment with promise: [3] "that it may be well with you and you may live long on the earth." [4] And you, fathers, do not provoke your children to wrath, but bring them up in the training and admonition of the Lord (Ephesians 6:1-4).

[20] Children, obey your parents in all things, for this is well pleasing to the Lord. [21] Fathers, do not provoke your children, lest they become discouraged (Colossians 3:20-21).

To love, honor, and help my father and mother: To honor and obey the civil authority: To submit myself to all my governors, teachers, spiritual pastors and masters: And to order myself in that lowliness and reverence which becometh a servant of God (Book of Common Prayer).

Introduction

When I was drafted into the Army in February 1967, my grandfather, who had had 12 years of military experience, gave me excellent advice: "Boy, remember three things: Do as you're told, keep your mouth shut, and don't volunteer for anything." That proved to be excellent advice.

The first ten days we had orientation, and those days were very pleasant and slow paced. We had to send everything home (including underwear) but Bibles, got our heads shaved, had written tests of all kinds, and were introduced to one of our drill sergeants who would be training us for the next 10 weeks in basic training, who went out of his way to be nice to us.

At the end of orientation, we lined up with our duffle bags, went down an assembly line to get our shots in both arms with Army male nurses on both sides of us, and once having shots in both arms at the same time with air guns.

After our arms were loaded with shots and pain, they drove us to the other side of the base. Our drill sergeant had been very nice to us until this time, but when the bus stopped at what was to be our home for the next ten weeks, he began screaming at us to get off the bus—and I do mean screaming. Talk about a Dr. Jekyll transformation to a Mr. Hyde! My grandfather had prepared me, though.

Once off the bus, they had us on the ground doing pushups with shot-filled arms. After our arms were aching, one sergeant asked: "Are you tired trainees?" We all said, "Yes, sergeant." He responded: "Trainees don't get tired; do more pushups." Then after a while longer, he asked: "Are you tired trainees?" "No, sergeant." "Good, do pushups."

After several hours of our arms turning to rubber, it was time to go to the mess hall, which meant food. While we waited our turn to go inside, they made us do exercises, and between each exercise we had to run in place. For two months any time we were outside, we had to run between buildings or run in place. The exercises were the alligator crawl, dodge run and jump, sit ups at a huge angle, and then with our hands "walk" a horizontal ladder just before going into the mess hall. With my light weight, I did the bars like an orangutan. If you missed a bar, you had to start over.

Once inside, we had to eat *all* on our plates. Some were sick and could not do it. My stomach muscles hurt so badly that it was difficult to sit in the upright position they wanted us in, like a straight back chair, but I was hungry so I ate it all.

Now what was the point to all that? Were they just being mean? No, they had the **whole picture** of what it was like to be in war. Vietnam was hot, and they knew most of us would be going over there. They were training us to take orders, trying to save our lives when we got into combat and the shooting was for real. They had to break us like a wild horse. My grandfather had explained it all to me. When you're in combat, you don't have time to argue about what to do. Arguing would only cost lives, maybe our own, so we had to learn to obey *without knowing what the whole picture was*. Sometimes we would obey orders without knowing what the point was, trusting that someone up the chain of command knew.

Of course we didn't like the hard training. And do you think it bothered our sergeants that we didn't like it? Not on your life. Next time they would make sure we didn't like it more!

Guess who had the most difficult time in basic training? Those men who had not learned to obey at home, or who were used to being cut-ups at school. They would smart mouth the sergeants, curse everyone in sight, and rebel every chance they got, but guess who won? These rebellious guys had it three times more difficult than the rest of us. They were given extra duty, and sometimes made to carry heavy sand bags around a sawdust pit! On other occasions they had to do sit ups with logs on their chests. Guys who wanted to fight were given the opportunity to work out their hostilities against one another by getting into the sawdust pit with boxing gloves for all to see.

Likewise, God knows what is best for us because He **has the whole picture**, and He gave us parents to help us learn to take orders without griping to God or to others. *Learning obedience to godly authority is the first step to believing the Gospel.*

Moreover, *the principle of authority extends to every area of life.* If you want to know why our culture is perishing, it is because legitimate authority is not upholding God's law, and those under it are being rebellious. We slap murderers on the wrist and punish good people. But authority is the main principle God has given us both for evangelism and for restraint of those who will not be evangelized, and it is learned (or not learned) first in the home.

In government, God's authority is primarily for *punishment*, penal, for restitution of crimes, as we see in Romans 13:1ff. Therefore, we are not to think of rehabilitation, which does not work anyway, for one cannot change the hearts of criminals by putting them together 24/7 to share their problems. God's righteousness requires restitution, not relaxation of standards. Restitution must be made to those who were offended, such as paying back what was stolen and giving up the murderer's life for the one murdered.

In the Church and home, authority is primarily *remedial*, which means that it is designed to bring people back in line. The context here is the Gospel, or should be.

Moreover, some will say that they don't mind obeying God, but it is those sinful humans who irk them. Do we have to obey humans in order to obey God? Yes, for God has given His authority to humans in government, in business, in the Church, and especially in the family. Therefore, *God's authority is given to humans over other humans*. This principle of authority cannot be emphasized too much, for it is the key to eternal life itself. No one likes a rebellious person, and especially God Himself, who says:

> Rebellion is as the sin of witchcraft and stubbornness is as iniquity and idolatry. Because you have rejected the word of the LORD, He also has rejected you from being king (1 Samuel 15:23).

In this passage, God had commanded King Saul to do something, but he refused. Then Samuel said rebellion was like witchcraft. Witchcraft is magic, seeking to manipulate forces to get one's own way, rather than humble submission to God's way.

But what if the human authority tells us to do what is contrary to God's law? In that case, since God is the head of every chain of command, we must respectfully obey God rather than man (Acts 5:29), but we are never allowed to engage in anarchy.

Before we proceed with the Fifth Commandment, we must ask a stupid question: What is a child? The government and secular society say a child is a blob of chemicals who is a ward of the state to be trained by godless teachers who have been "certified" by the state to be able to teach. The Holy Scriptures present a child as one made in the image of God who belongs to the parents, who in turn have the right and obligation to train the child in righteousness. Thus, the former put the emphasis on the needs of the child to be made comfortable, to have his own way, which means to force a wedge between the children and the parents. The latter see children who need to be trained in righteousness, not just to have their own way.[1] "When the needs of the child are central, and a moral neutrality is asserted with regard to the new-born babe, then the basic responsibility and fault is the state's and society's. . . ."[2]

I. Children Are God's Gifts

Before we speak of the authority of parents in the home, we must recognize what a privilege it is to have children. It is a negative commentary on our society that we have to say that children are God's gifts to us, not a curse. Notice what God's word says about children:

> He seeks <u>godly offspring</u> (Malachi 2:15).
>
> [3] Behold, <u>children are a heritage from the LORD</u>, the fruit of the womb is a reward. [4] Like arrows in the hand of a warrior, so are the children of one's youth. [5] <u>Happy is the man who has his quiver full of them</u>; they shall not be ashamed, but shall speak with their enemies in the gate (Psalm 127:3-6).

With ever increasing rebellion, our culture sees children as a nuisance, but from the verses above we see that children are God's gift to us to raise for Him, not to be destroyed by abortion as an inconvenience. (If you have had an abortion, there is forgiveness at the cross of Christ, and then one day you shall be reunited with that child! Children who die in infancy go to heaven.)

What is the greatest gift ever given to mankind? It was a child, a baby, God's gift to the world, the incarnation of the Son of God. Even so, the greatest gift, except for eternal life, that God gives us is *His* children for us to raise to His glory. They are to be His lights in this dark world. The darker the world is the more "lights" we should have.

---

[1] Rousas J. Rushdoony, *Intellectual Schizophrenia* (Philipsberg, NJ: Presbyterian and Reformed, 1961), p. 69ff. Outstanding little book.
[2] Ibid.

Therefore, children are not a curse but a blessing. Some think children are vipers in diapers, only small bodies with a hole in each end that needs filling and emptying every few minutes, nasty urchins to be avoided except on weekends, organic material that makes the immediate air rather odiferous, sound machines that interrupt one's sleep with the ongoing "weh, weh."

But they are God's gift to His people, the blessing of God's seed wrapped in covenantal diapers, a new incarnation of the image of God, entrusted to us by the covenant Head to rear and place into His army, potentially mighty warriors for the faith, and slayers of Goliaths.

God has stated that part of the blessing of His covenant is to give us *His seed* for us to raise for His glory, His entrustment to us for the next generation, for the promotion of His covenant and kingdom down through the generations.

Moreover, if children are God's gifts to us, then motherhood is also a very high privilege. But those who want to redefine the family, such as Anna Quindlen, who as feminist elite stated that Andrea Yates drowned her five children in Houston because of the "insidious cult of motherhood."[3] Apparently it was morally acceptable, especially since the National Organized for Women said she had postpartum depression. But God places a very high value on being a mother. It is still true that "she who rocks the cradle rules the world." A mother's influence for good or evil cannot be over stated. One who is raised by a godly mother will owe a debt he can never repay.

II. Parents Must Teach Their Children to Obey

A. Evangelizing Our Children

The first step in knowing God is to submit to Him, to receive what He says about Himself and about us. A person who refuses God accepts his own ideas, loves his own authority more than God's revelation about Himself and thus rejects God's authority.

---

[3] Tammy Bruce, *The Death of Right and Wrong* (New York: Three Rivers Press, 2003), p. 64. (See my comments on this book in the Bibliography at the end of the book.)

Parents who do not take God seriously — as seen in seldom attending church, in not catechizing their children, in not teaching them the word of God, in having fits of anger, in not being submissive to God's commandments themselves, who consider God just an addition to their lives once in a while, when it's convenient — will find that their children do not take them seriously, will often end in rebellion, drugs, and often will not honor them in their old age. There is a one-to-one relationship between the parents' submission to God and the children's submission to their parents. *Whatever we do, we must teach our children obedience to godly authority*, with our words and our own obedience to Holy Scripture, and we must never let our children win in the struggle of who is the boss. If we lose this battle, we lose our children to the devil.

Consider this verse:

> Train up the child <u>according to his way</u>, and when he is old
> he will not depart from it (Proverbs 22:6).[4]

This is a warning that if we train them the way they want, they will reject the Lord. But who should train children? To whom is this verse addressed? Earlier in the Book of Proverbs, the book commanded youth to listen to their parents (Proverbs 1:8).

Furthermore, the passage in Ephesians 6:1-4 at the beginning of this chapter commands children to obey their parents, but guess who has to teach them that? Parents, of course. Parents must *make* their children obey them, or this command for children will result in rebellion and self-destruction.

God's discipline is not just directed to the mind, though that is included, but He directs discipline primarily to our wills by His authority

---

[4] This is a departure from the normal translation, but it seems correct. The word "should" in most translations must be justified since it does not occur in the Hebrew. Moreover, the word "way" occurs 25 times with a pronominal suffix in Proverbs, and none have the meaning "should." The unusual expression in Hebrew (עַל־פִּי) is used about 50 times in the Old Testament, and especially in narratives usually means "by the mouth" of someone, or "by the commandment" of someone. Here in Proverbs 22:6 it would seem to mean: "train the child by the mouth of his way," or "by the commandment" of his way. See the NASB in the margin, the New English Bible; Gary D. Pratico and Miles V. Van Pelt, *Basics of Biblical Hebrew* (Grand Rapids: Zondervan, 2001), p. 284.

to *make* us obey. Words are not enough. We must use our authority to make our children obey. Sometimes this is warfare, and parents want to give up; but we must persevere. Better they lose in this war with parents than in a war with Satan for their precious souls.

And notice the command is to fathers to teach, which would include the mothers, but the command is addressed to the covenant head, the fathers. Moreover, notice that this command is to the parents—not to the public schools.

This command in Ephesians 6 would not even be understood by small children, so they are completely dependent on their parents to teach them God's command to obey them, which is *the first principle of the Gospel: submission to godly authority.*

If children grow up bad, more times than not the parents are to blame. King David's son Adonijah rebelled against David his father and wanted to be king, and God says about David's rearing of Adonijah:

> [David] had not rebuked him at any time (1 Kings 1:6).

I had a relative who spoiled his son to death. Once my wife Ruth and I were swimming with him and his son, and his son behaved badly. His father promised to discipline him, and grounded him from some activity, but then he relented. His son grew up to be spoiled rotten, was too selfish to marry, is very loud mouthed and opinionated, and is now living off someone else's money.

In the neighborhood where I lived when in grade school, there was a bully, about five years older than me, who was the terror of the neighborhood. My grandmother went to his mother to tell about foul language he was using, how disrespectful he had been to her, and the damage he had done to a neighbor's porch. The mother called for Tommy, and he denied it all. This woman said, "See, he didn't do any of that." My grandmother was floored. That kind of thing did not happen in the 1950s. So she told the mother, "Do you think I made all this up just to have something to do?" The woman still defended her son.

Now what effect did that have on the boy? Did it help him to be a better person or a worse one? My grandmother told me later, and I was only about eight or nine, that he would grow up to be a criminal. Do you think that happened? Yes, it did. He went to prison for a long time, thanks to parents who would not make him obey. We do our children absolutely no good if we don't make them obey, and teach them this principle of authority.

Parents, have you taught your kids how to sin, or did they learn naturally? The answer is Yes; by example we teach them how to sin, but they also do it naturally. We have to work hard to teach them how *not* to sin, which is spiritual warfare, but the prize is their souls—we must never give up! We all enter the world as rebellious sinners; we have to be trained to pursue righteousness.

My paternal grandmother told this story for years. She was a masseuse, giving massages to rich ladies in Memphis, driving to their homes. She did that for 40 years. She used to tell about one 12 year old boy who was an unholy terror. Several times I saw him, and she was right. The parents hired a psychologist to work with him, and before one important function with many significant people coming to her house, she invited the psychologist over to talk to her son. He was an angel during the whole occasion. When all had left, she could not wait to ask the psychologist what he had said to the boy. He said: "I told him that I would beat the . . . out of him if he acted up." He told the mother that all he needed was authority and love. She did not listen, and her son committed suicide at age 17 with a shotgun.

Of course, part of evangelizing our children is *taking* them to church and Sunday School, not sending them. Moreover, we must require them to attend *our* church, not allow them to divide the family covenant by attending a different church. Disruption to authority from church to parents and then to children must not be compromised so that we have authority from two or more churches over a family. When one needs the church, which one do they go to? At one point in my home, our teens wanted to attend another church, but I would not allow it. Though my teens did not have this in mind, I've seen teens divide and conquer their parents by this division in the home. Very often they just want to get out from under the immediate authority of the parents, so they pretend how wonderful this other church is for their spiritual growth, but growth comes from submission to church authority, not in bypassing it. Moreover, they must obey the wishes of the parents in this, not seek their own authority. Continuity is very important.

B. How to Discipline Our Children

Parents, let me encourage you to discipline your kids, always out of love, (1) *but be sure to make it hurt. No pain, no gain.* We must not give them all they want, for that will spoil them. Give them chores to do, and do not remind them. If they don't follow through, discipline them either verbally or physically if they are young, or if older perhaps ground them. Sometimes words are not enough so God gives us commands to use physical discipline while they are young:

> He who spares his rod hates his son, but he who loves him disciplines him promptly (Proverbs 13:24).

> Foolishness is bound up in the heart of a child; the rod of correction will drive it far from him (Proverbs 22:15).

> [13] Do not withhold discipline from a child; if you strike him with a rod, he will not die. [14] If you strike him with the rod, you will save his soul from death (Proverbs 23:13-14, ESV).

> [15] The rod and rebuke give wisdom, but a child left *to himself* brings shame to his mother. [17] Correct your son, and he will give you rest; yes, he will give delight to your soul (Proverbs 23:15, 17).

Once my teenage son said, "Daddy, please ground me the next two or even three weekends, but not this weekend." My response was, "That tells me I made the right decision." It must hurt.

When they are on their own, if they have not learned at home how to deal with disappointment and to disciple themselves, how will they learn it? Here is more that God says about His discipline:

> [5] And you have forgotten the exhortation which speaks to you as to sons: "My son, do not despise the chastening of the LORD, nor be discouraged when you are rebuked by Him; [6] For whom the LORD loves He chastens, and scourges **every** son whom He receives." [7] If you endure chastening, God deals with you as with sons; for what son is there whom a father does not chasten? [8] But if you are without chastening, of which all have

become partakers, then you are illegitimate and not sons.
[9] Furthermore, we have had human fathers who corrected *us*,
and we paid *them* respect. Shall we not much more readily be in
subjection to the Father of spirits and live? [10] For they indeed for
a few days chastened *us* as seemed *best* to them, but He for *our*
profit, that *we* may be partakers of His holiness. [11] **Now no chastening seems to be joyful for the present, but painful**; nevertheless, **afterward** it yields the peaceable fruit of righteousness to
those who have been **trained** by it (Hebrews 12:5-11).

Notice from these verses several other aspects to discipline. (2) We
spiritual children must not *despise* the Lord's chastening, and we must
not get *discouraged*. Despising authority and becoming discouraged will
happen to any child who thinks he is not loved.

(3) We see in this passage that the Lord *loves* us so He chastens us.
We see His love in sending His Son to die for our sins (John 3:16; Hebrews 12:2). A child must feel loved by the parents spending time with
him, by having a genuine faith in God and walking with Him, by giving the child a lot of encouragement. Then a child will respond in loving obedience to the parent.

(4) Moreover, notice that God chastens *every* son He receives without exception, so we must discipline all our children as well. There is no
child who is so perfect that he does not need discipline verbally, perhaps a paddling when young, grounding, or what the parent thinks.

Here is the way my mother would discipline me:

> Son, you know I love you, that I would do anything for
> you, the Lord gave you to me, and I'm so glad. But what you did
> was wrong. Read here in the Bible what God says about what
> you did. Now here is what God requires you to do to correct this
> behavior. Now give me your belt.

Then some discipline would follow, always in love. I loved my mom. I
still love my mom. (She is 86 and still corrects me! Too often, she is
right!) She was an excellent mother, and I took the same approach with
my children. Even though my father had left us when I was too young
to remember, she was training me to relate to my heavenly Father.

(5) Finally, notice from the Hebrews passage above that *no discipline is joyful, but painful,* yet "afterward it yields the peaceable fruit of righteousness to those who have been trained by it." In 1977–78, I taught junior high students in a Christian day school. After the first two weeks, I did not know whether to resign, burn the school down, or commit suicide. They were very trying! But we had an outstanding Christian headmaster who helped us gain control of the students during those two weeks, and the rest of the year was very profitable.

I taught mostly Bible to those in the sixth through the ninth grades. One of the first things I taught them was the principles of discipline. I told the students I loved them, and demonstrated it by spending time after school with them in activities such as bowling. I had a rule if anyone broke, no matter who it was, that he would get one swat from my paddle. On one occasion a ninth grade girl, taller than I was, broke the rule. So I paddled her hard with one lick. Though all the parents had to sign an agreement for us to paddle, she was so spoiled that I just knew her parents would be at school the next day, so I told the principal what I had done. He stood with me. Later that day this ninth grade girl saw me in the hall, and with tears in her eyes, she said: "No one ever cared enough to do that." Now I had tears. We hugged. Apparently she never told her parents, and she responded to me with great respect and love the rest of the year.

C. Educating Our Children

Professor Bruce Ackerman, professor at Yale University, wrote the very liberal work, *Social Justice in the Liberal State.*[5] In chapter five titled "Liberal Education," he argues that a liberal education must not be authoritarian. Rather, the goal is to produce self-defining adults who choose their own values and lifestyles. Students should question everything, except for evolution and the government's right to impose its morality. Those two points are sacrosanct. He especially advocates

---

[5] Bruce A. Ackerman, *Social Justice in the Liberal State* (New Haven: Yale University Press, 1980); see also Philip E. Johnson, *Reason in the Balance: The Case Against Naturalism in Science, Law & Education* (Downers Grove, IL: InterVarsity, 1995), chapter eight. Ackerman believes that reason is primary and that neutrality is possible regarding education and morality.

teaching young students to question their parents' authority, and has a section on "The Decline of Parental Authority," (p. 146), which he thinks is good. Ackerman vehemently disapproves tuition vouchers where public money could be used to promote private schools, for these schools are not under government authority to brainwash the students. He says

> [Voucher plans] legitimate a series of petty tyrannies in which like-minded parents club together to force-feed their children without restraint. Such an education is a mockery of the liberal ideal.[6]

Christian scholar Samuel Blumenfeld wrote the excellent work *Is Public Education Necessary?*,[7] and in it he traces the origin of public education back to New England liberals and Unitarian Horace Mann who wanted to evangelize the nation for liberalism (beginning in the early 1800s and gaining force the rest of the century). One of their goals was to replace family education with liberal, public education, thereby supplanting parental authority with secular authority.

Then there is William Kilpatrick's *Why Johnny Can't Tell Right from Wrong*, in which he shows that public education leaders are training teachers to say repeatedly to their students that they are the only judges of right and wrong for themselves. He points out that classes on values clarification teach students that moral compromise is legitimate in certain cases, and then desensitizing sex classes teach students how to engage in "safe" sex. Girls practice putting condoms on cucumbers.

The conclusion students are reaching is that sex is casual, and that commitment in marriage does not matter since they are the moral judges. Society supports this with easy divorces. If sex is casual and open before marriage, why would it change after marriage?

Is it any wonder that we have so much rebellion from children against their parents? Without godly authority, you cannot educate properly. If you remove parental and godly authority from schools, you have the modern mess we now have with sexual promiscuity running

---

[6] Johnson, *Reason in the Balance*, p. 159.

[7] This is one of the most incredible books I've ever read, and the historical research is superb. Get this book! Try www.abebooks.com.

wild, with rebellion against parents, drugs, and the horrendous crime we have in schools with students shooting one another. In some schools, kids must enter through metal detectors. When I was in school, the worst thing that happened was an occasional fight (especially in Junior High), or getting caught smoking in the rest room (high school). Our culture is in moral free fall, especially because godly authority is ignored, or worse, denied. It is not only the schools, but also the parents—and government and churches—who allow this farce to continue.

Educating our children is what parents are required to do. It is not primarily the Church's responsibility to train children, and it is *not the government's responsibility to train our children at all*, but it is the parents' responsibility. The Church backs up the parents. One thing pastors endure is parents who will not train their children according to God's word, and when the children go astray, the parents want the pastor to wave a Bible over their disobedient children to make it all go away. It may take years for a rebellious child to come around.

It is a great failure for parents to abdicate their responsibility to teach their children, especially to teach them the Gospel. But parents today think nothing of sending their children off to public school to get their "normal" education and send them to church to learn the Gospel. So what is left for the parents to do? (There is nothing wrong with delegating the academic teaching of the children to schools as long as the schools are godly.)

We must never think that education is religiously neutral, for everyone approaches subjects either from God's view or from an anti-God view; there is nothing in the middle. Teaching facts that are left uninterpreted is not only impossible; it is really to teach that God is irrelevant. There is no moral neutrality in any area of life. The Lord said that the one who was not *for* Him was *against* Him (Matthew 12:30). Moreover, since God is the Creator, all knowledge must be learned with this assumption and from His point of view.

For example, one can study history by seeing God's providential hand in events and with the idea that God judges individuals and nations for their disobedience. Or one can study history by believing in random chance and that it does not matter what morality an individual or a nation chooses. One can say that history is going somewhere; that is, that history will end with the Second Coming of the Lord and the Last Day judgment. Or one can study history believing that history is going nowhere, that we are in endless cycles or just chaos. One can study math with the idea that math is consistent because God is infinitely logical and consequently math is the same, or one can say that numbers are what we make them. However, Jesus is the King over all knowledge. We must not capitulate to the devil or to the secular humanists in any area of knowledge. In summary, one can study subjects with faith in man (humanism) and chance (evolution) or with faith in the Triune God and creation.

Mankind is as constitutionally religious as he is rational, and to pretend that children can be educated in a religious vacuum is impossible. Since we are in the Triune God's image, we are necessarily oriented to some transcendent standard. For one to send his children to atheistic public schools, and then educate them at home to Christ, is reckless optimism. Generally, Churches are not able to counter the state with all its prestige and resources. "Theism and atheism cannot coalesce to make anything. All truth in all spheres is organically one and vitally inseparable."[8] There is no neutral knowledge to God and the atheist. Either God's intelligent design must be recognized everywhere or denied everywhere. As the former systematic theology professor at Princeton, A. A. Hodge (1823-1886), well stated:

> It is capable of exact demonstration that if every party in the State has the right of excluding from the public schools whatever he does not believe to be true, then he that believes most must give way to him that believes least, and then he that believes least must give way to him that believes absolutely nothing, no matter how small a minority the atheists or the agnostics be. It is self-evident on this scheme, if it is consistently and persistently carried out in all parts of the country, the United States system of national popular education will be the

---

[8] Archibald Alexander Hodge, *Evangelical Theology* (Edinburg: Banner of Truth, 1976, first published 1890, published posthumously), pp. 244-45.

most efficient and wide instrument for the propagation of atheism which the world has ever seen.[9]

I am as sure as I am of the fact of Christ's reign that a comprehensive and centralized system of national education, sepa-
rated from religion, as is now commonly proposed, will prove
the most appalling [engine] for the propagation of anti-Christian
and atheistic unbelief, and anti-social, nihilistic ethics, individual, social and political, which this sin-rent world has ever
seen.[10]

Indeed, *parental authority is expressed primarily through teaching,
through verbal instruction*, but it is also expressed by enforcement. If we
give our children over to ungodly teachers who will not honor God or
His authority in parents, children will rebel against their parents. Either
parental authority will be honored with peers conforming to that, or
peer authority will be the standard with rebellion against parents.
There are no other options. When our children spend seven hours a
day with peers at school and only an hour or so with parents at home,
whose moral authority will be the standard in learning?

Moreover, no one can properly instruct others without the authority to enforce knowledge, for knowledge alone will never change anyone. When we're born into the world, we all have a quest for autonomy, and without enforcement there will only be anarchy, which is
what we have in our public schools today, for virtually all authority is
removed. When the Triune God is left out of instruction, there is no objective knowledge, no goal of what life means, which in turn leads to
absorption with self. Welcome to the age of the psychological, to self, to
narcissism where all "values" are turned inward.

Consider this question. What standard is your child currently living by? When he makes a decision, is he using God's word, your authority, and godly input, or is your child just going along with the
crowd at school? How do you know what standard he is using? How
do you expect your children to obey this Fifth Commandment to honor

---

[9] Hodge, *Evangelical Theology*, pp. 242-43.
[10] Hodge, *Evangelical Theology*, p. 245.

parental and godly authority if you're not teaching them what it means and how to do it by being obedient to God yourself in church attendance and learning God's word?

And what is the cause of modern juvenile delinquency? It is parents not rearing their children to obey them and not teaching them the Gospel at home through Bible readings, catechizing, taking them to church. (The reader may order a catechism from me for $10.00. I have added memory cues and illustrations to make it easy to learn and verses to memorize. Send an email requesting *Keeping Covenant and Catechizing Our Children* as recommended in Dr. Crenshaw's book *Not Ten Suggestions,*" to: service@footstoolpublications.com. You will be contacted. You may also want to order for $5 each *Keeping Covenant and Educating Our Children*, and *Keeping Covenant and Disciplining Our Children*.)

The *generation gap* is a modern invention, created primarily by parents who refuse to take God seriously and by public schools that too often hate God and by design come between parents and their children. Thus kids pay more attention to peer pressure and encouragement to "do your own thing" than they do to parental authority. In other words, once the vertical standard for morality is gone (Triune God, parents, Ten Commandments), children will adopt the horizontal standard (peers). Consider how modern public schools work. Children are put into an environment with peers and peer pressure with little godly authority to compensate. In a Christian home, however, godly authority is the rule, and the peers are brothers and sisters, though even then they are rarely the same age. In a truly Christian school, parents' parental authority is upheld and the children taught to honor parents. One reason we have a generation gap is that the parents have a gap with God, which translates into a gap with their children. In other words, the vertical and horizontal are bound together. If the parents, who are made in God's image, are not walking with God, the children, who are in the image of the parents, will not walk with them. For a culture to endure, godly authority must be transmitted from the Triune God to parents and to children; otherwise, self-destruction ensues.[11] (One thing a totalitarian government will try to eliminate is parental authority; they want to take the place of God and parents.)

What is one sign of revival or of judgment? It is whether the hearts of the children are one with the hearts of the parents.

> [5] Behold, I will send you Elijah the prophet before the coming of the great and dreadful day of the LORD. [6] And he will turn the hearts of the fathers to the children, and the hearts of the children to their fathers, lest I come and strike the earth with a curse (Malachi 4:5-6).

These verses reveal that there should be no generation gap if children are brought up well. Conversely, it is a sign of judgment on society when children rebel against parents and that spills over to the culture (Micah 7:6; Matthew 10:21).

We parents are responsible for our children's education, not government. Here is the way one Christian teacher stated the problem with our modern public education:

> After being interviewed by the school administration, the prospective teacher said:
>
> "Let me see if I've got this right.
>
> "You want me to go into that room with all those kids, correct their disruptive behavior, observe them for signs of abuse, monitor their dress habits, censor their T-shirt messages, and instill in them a love for learning.
>
> "You want me to check their backpacks for weapons, wage war on drugs and sexually transmitted diseases, and raise their sense of self esteem and personal pride.
>
> "You want me to teach them patriotism and good citizenship, sportsmanship and fair play, and how to register to vote, balance a checkbook, and apply for a job.
>
> "You want me to check their heads for lice, recognize signs of antisocial behavior, and make sure that they all pass the final exams.

---

[11] Mark F. Rooker, *The Ten Commandments: Ethics for the Twenty-First Century* (Nashville, TN: B&H Academic, 2010), p. 119.

"You also want me to provide them with an equal education regardless of their handicaps, and communicate regularly with their parents in English, Spanish or any other language, by letter, telephone, newsletter, and report card.

"You want me to do all this with a piece of chalk, a blackboard, a bulletin board, a few books, a big smile, and a starting salary that qualifies me for food stamps.

"You want me to do all this and then you tell me that I CAN'T PRAY?"

When we leave the Triune God out, this is the mess we have.

III. Who Owns the Family?

Bishop Ray R. Sutton, Th.D., Ph.D., in the Reformed Episcopal Church wrote a book titled *Who Owns the Family?* He began with these words:

The family in America is under siege.

I know it.

You know it.

We all feel the truth of the words of a social scientist, "People are scared. They see relationships collapsing all around them, and they worry about whether theirs will last. But they don't know what to do about it."

Dr. Sutton wrote these words in 1986, and the issues are even clearer today. Sutton develops the book around these ideas. The family is a covenant with God, not with the state. God owns the family, the state does not. (In fact, God owns the state, for it is directly accountable to Him.) God makes a marriage, for Jesus said "what **God** has joined together, let not man separate" (Matthew 19:6).

Moreover, the standard for morality is God's Ten Commandments, not the government's laws, yet the public schools are increasingly taking over the moral instruction of our children, pushing the parents out. It is definitely not the school's responsibility to train children morally, and public schools are part of the problem. Parental authority should never be pushed aside as is too often the case in public schools. I heard one Christian who should know better say that when the child enters the doors of the public school, parental authority ends.

That is ungodly thinking, offering up the souls, minds, and bodies of our children to strange gods. We will never win this spiritual war if we give up God's covenant seed to that which is opposed to Him.

Indeed, public education is a modern invention, so how did cultures exist for centuries without them? I'm not saying we should abandon all education, but that the way the public schools are conducted today is undermining godly authority. They are teaching children that they evolved from a one cell "animal," that they will be extinct when they die, that there is no ethic except what they choose for themselves. Is it any wonder that our children are acting this out in sexual sins and murders? If we came from nothing and we going to nothing, what difference does the in between make?

Sutton develops his book by asking questions about the family:

- Who owns the discipline of children?
- Who owns the inheritance?
- Who owns the life of the children?
- Who owns the sexual privacy of the children?
- Who protects the family?

In each area, Dr. Sutton demonstrates from Scripture that the church and family have jurisdiction over their children, not the state, but we see public schools claiming ownership in some of these areas and government in others. A wedge is being forced between parents and children, creating a generation gap that normally does not exist, and children are given authority over parents that Holy Scripture reserves only for the parents, such as the right to sexual privacy and access to abortions without parental notification. Find Bishop Sutton's book, read it, and do what it says. Amazon.com may have some hard copies. (If you can't find it, send me an email requesting it, and I'll send you a free pdf copy: service@footstoolpublications.com.)

Now we have the USA Senate considering (June 2010) the U. N. Convention on the Rights of the Child, which would mean the government would be the caretaker and the guardian while the parents would be the babysitters. If the government thinks the parents are doing something not in the best interest of the child, such as home school, the children would be removed from the home. In Germany, home schools have been outlawed. The new law would at least require parents to give account of what they teach them and how they are reared.[12] Great Britain has ratified the treaty. When a 16 year old girl asked her parents to allow her boyfriend to move in with them and share her bedroom, they said No. She filed suit and won. Such are the rights of children.

All these observations are solid reasons either to home school our children or to put them in private Christian schools where biblical standards will be honored and parental authority upheld, at least as long as we can. Christian schools should be part of Christian churches to help rear children according to God's standard.

IV. What Are Parents Forbidden To Do?

(1) One thing forbidden in the Fifth Commandment is for the parents to use their authority in a demeaning manner:

> And you, fathers, do not provoke your children to wrath, but bring them up in the training and admonition of the Lord (Ephesians 6:4).

> Fathers, do not provoke your children, lest they become discouraged (Colossians 3:21).

God forbids that children be made fun of, demeaned, put on guilt trips, abused physically or sexually, constantly put down as being dumb, a klutz, a failure, or incompetent. Though harmful at any time, *these things are especially harmful in front of others.* Parents should function as priests to their kids in keeping confidences regarding their sins. It is very embarrassing for kids to have parents reveal their sins or even their failures and short comings.

Fathers are especially bad at demeaning their children, which must be the reason Paul addressed the above commands to fathers. They naturally want them to grow up to be responsible, godly adults, but the way to achieve that, according to God through Paul above, is not by

---

[12] http://www.onenewsnow.com/Culture/Default.aspx?id=1033838 accessed June 5, 2010.

constantly putting them down. I've seen children who would run from their father when he came home from work, rather than running to him. Or, they would close themselves off from their father in their room for fear of being abused either verbally or physically. Fathers who abuse their daughters (or sons) sexually commit the worst offense imaginable, (Leviticus chapters 18 and 20). In this case, no honor is due the father, but no personal revenge is allowed either.

I know a father who was full of anger against his children most of the time, and they could never seem to please him. Surprise! They rebelled against him and his Christian stance.

But being too easy is also a problem, for one will never rear godly children by letting them do what they please. If a child always gets his way, he will think the world owes him a living, and he will have a difficult time making marriage work if he thinks he is the center of attention.

(2) We are forbidden to make our children into idols. Some tie up their whole lives in their children and live for nothing else. We should live for God, and for our children in the right perspective. God may take what is an idol.

Conclusion

Parents, love your children enough to discipline them, and young people, love God enough to obey your parents. With proper love and discipline, our children will be *fun*, not *frenzy*. **AMEN**.

Chapter 11—Fifth Commandment: Children's Part

Children's Respect for Parents

Honor your father and your mother (Exodus 20:12).

[1] Children, obey your parents in the Lord, for this is right. [2] "Honor your father and mother," which is the first commandment with promise: [3] "that it may be well with you and you may live long on the earth." [4] And you, fathers, do not provoke your children to wrath, but bring them up in the training and admonition of the Lord (Ephesians 6:1-4).

[20] Children, obey your parents in all things, for this is well pleasing to the Lord. [21] Fathers, do not provoke your children, lest they become discouraged (Colossians 3:20-21).

Introduction

I'll never forget it. When I was about eight years old, my loving Christian grandmother was scolding me vehemently for something that I can't remember now. As soon as she turned her back, I stuck my tongue out at her. She must have suspected me because she whirled around and caught me. I was upgraded from a scolding to a whipping! Authority is God's gift not only to the parents but to the children, who would not be trained properly otherwise.

When I was in the sixth grade, I had a temper. On one occasion at lunch, a boy lobbed his corn bread into my soup, slightly splashing it out. I grabbed the corn bread, stood up, and threw it hard into his soup. From the side other of the lunch room Miss Hurt, the principal, was watching, and she lived up to her name, as the other boy and I discovered later when she got her paddle.

This commandment is the principle of authority, *but also of honor.* Authority leads to obedience, but honor is broader, requiring respect, reverent esteem. Yet one will never honor authority until he has learned to obey that authority.

Consider Jesus when He was only twelve years old (Luke 2:41-51). He lingered behind in the temple while His parents went three days journey back home before they discovered that He was missing. They were frantic until they found Him in the temple discussing matters with the Jewish leaders. They chastised Him for causing them to worry, but He stated: "Why did you seek Me? Did you not know that I must be about My Father's business?" Nevertheless, Luke reports that Jesus "was subject to them," which means He recognized their God-given authority. Here we see the first and fifth commandments coming together. The temple worship was the First Commandment, and obedience to His parents was the Fifth Commandment. Thus, to honor one's parents is to honor who He. God is the One who gave the parents His authority.

I. Children Must Honor Their Parents

The requirement to *obey* our parents extends only to those who are children at home (or still under parental authority such as away at school), but the Fifth Commandment is much broader. To *honor* is broader than obey. The Hebrew word for "honor" means to be heavy, weighty, and it often refers to persons in positions of responsibility and authority. It means giving honor or glory is to say that someone is deserving of respect, attention, and obedience.[1] Giving honor to God and to one's parents is tied together:

> A son honors *his* father, and a servant *his* master. If then I am the Father, Where is My honor? And if I am a Master, Where is My reverence? Says the LORD of hosts (Malachi 1:6).

---

[1] Theological Wordbook of the Old Testament, under the word for "heavy" (כָּבֵד), Bible Works 7 edition.

One example of honoring our parents long after we have become adults and obedience to them is no longer a factor is to help them financially when they are older and need help.

> ³ Honor widows who are really widows. ⁴ But if any widow has children or grandchildren, let them first learn to show piety at home and to repay their parents; for this is good and acceptable before God (1 Timothy 5:3-4).

> ³ [Jesus] answered and said to them, "Why do you also transgress the commandment of God because of your tradition? ⁴ For God commanded, saying, 'Honor your father and your mother'; and, 'He who curses father or mother, let him be put to death.' ⁵ But you say, 'Whoever says to his father or mother, "Whatever profit you might have received from me is a gift *to God*" — ⁶ then he need not honor his father or mother.' Thus you have made the commandment of God of no effect by your tradition" (Matthew 15:3-6).

This honor is not only financial support but also physical presence, being with them. My mother took care of her mother as long as she could, and my family and I took care of my paternal grandmother until the night she died in her sleep at age 95. I know that sometimes they don't want that, and sometimes we must divide the care with professional services to perform technical services we can't do, but as much as possible we should take an active part.

I've seen grown children take advantage of their parents' money they had saved up for retirement. Sometimes the children will take money that is needed for health care of the parents, put them in the Veterans Hospital or a government home so they can have the money when the parents die, or get advancements on their inheritance. They love money more than parents.

We can continue to honor our parents even when they are dead, for we can honor what they stood for, which hopefully was the Gospel. The Lord honored His mother even as He was dying on the cross, asking John to take care of her (John 19:26-27).

In the command to "honor" our parents, in the very word "honor," it springs back upon the parent and says, "Be honorable; because in your honorableness your child shall grow reverent" (Biblical Illustrator). I've seen parents who were immoral, full of verbal filth, blasphemed, and engaged in lying, deceit, not loving their own spouse, mean to their children, and so on, and yet they expected their children to honor them. This honor should be both ways.

I'm not suggesting that the children of such dishonorable parents be mean to their parents or treat them with disrespect, but I'm suggesting that their responsibility toward them once they are out of the home would be minimal. Just as parents should not enable an ungodly lifestyle of their children by allowing them to do whatever they wish while they are still at home, likewise godly children would not want to enable their parents to live ungodly by paying their way.

Yet we must not dishonor such ungodly parents, but seek to do them good, for God's command to honor them is not null and void by their conduct. I knew of a woman who married, and her husband turned out to be a drunk and an adulterer. Sometimes he beat his wife and kids. When the kids got older, they stopped the beatings, but until his death, this man was still honored by his two children. One of them took him in when he had a stroke and cared for him until his death, but did not allow him to drink. He did it out of love for God and honor for his sinner father. Perhaps this had some bearing on his father making a profession of faith in Christ late in life.

And this honor of parents means to treat them with respect with language and not call one's parents "my old man" or "my old lady." God said that "he who curses his father or his mother shall surely be put to death" (Exodus 21:17). This was not a one-time curse word or a slip into an occasional disobedience, but it was a rebellious posture, a steady state of hating parental authority by a child who was older and who knew better. The idea is that God has attached His authority to the family so that the one who continually curses his parents is really cursing God. We must be careful to teach our children proper respect for our parental authority and thereby to all godly authority.

I was recently told the following example. A man overheard a nine-year-old boy say to his mother, "*Cindy*, hand me that coke." The man said, "What did you call your mother?" The boy curtly said,

"Cindy." The man: "Why did you call her by her first name?" The father then chimed in to the boy's defense: "Well, that *is* her name." Here were parents who wanted to be cool rather than teach proper respect for authority, and honor for his mother. As my son has said, parents were given by God to make children holy, not happy.

II. What Are Blessings of the Fifth Commandment?

(1) One blessing is that we have parents, and according to this commandment, the parents are a man and a woman, not two men or two women. And they are not just living together, but have made a covenant to the death by vows in the presence of the appropriate witnesses.

Because God's family the Church and human families are related as cause (church) to effect (family), those who neglect God's family, the church, will neglect their own human families, which will often result in disintegration of that family, and even more in the next generation.

The reason we can't define a human family anymore is that the original family, the Church, can't define itself. Liberal churches have proclaimed a new Trinity: Mother, child, and womb. Then they have homosexual bishops and ministers. No wonder the families in those churches are confused. If the divine family, the Church, is messed up, the human family will be worse. *It is not human families that define the Church but the Church that defines the families.*

If a culture can't define a family, then it will quickly disintegrate into chaos. When the husband of a home functions as the godly head, he is teaching his children how to relate to authority. If he submits to the local church, assuming it is godly, he is teaching his children proper obedience. The children then do not get confused about gender roles. Christian psychologist James Dobson has stated, "In 15 years, I have spoken with hundreds of homosexual men. I have never met one who said he had a loving, respectful relationship with his father."[2] But if the wife overrules the husband and functions as the head, then the boys may think being feminine is acceptable, and the girls may identify with the effeminate husband.

---

[2] James Dobson, *Bringing Up Boys* (Carol Stream, IL: Tyndale House Publishers, Inc, 2001), p. 121.

But the Church is to obey God's definition of a family and to help determine the education, religion, and discipline of the children, and the parents must submit to God's authority in the Church regarding this. It is not that the Church is the primary teacher of the children, but that it guides and sets the standard for the parents who in turn teach their children. But practically we have handed over all these areas to the government, which should have handed them back to the Church. The government has become the parent to set the moral tone, to teach and to decide what to teach, and to define the roles of males and females, and it has usurped the Church's and family's role, giving us the mess we have today. We must take back control.

(2) Another blessing is having an inheritance, and by that I don't necessarily mean money, though that would be a blessing. Few things are uglier than family fights over the deceased's possessions. But there are several points to an inheritance we must note:

- If there are possessions, they are meant to continue the family covenant down through the generations. It is the godly seed who should receive these, not the government. For the government to make a prior claim on inheritance is tyranny, taking away the rights of the parents to continue God's covenant in their heirs, making the government the rightful heir, which potentially destroys the family.

- An economic inheritance is not for ungodly children, for to leave money to the ungodly is dishonoring to God. We must never promote wickedness, even if it is in our own household. The little saying we hear that "blood is thicker than water" means that family is closer than all other relationships, but that is false. Jesus said in Matthew 10:37 that one is to leave mother and father for Him. He takes the precedent in all relationships.

- The greatest inheritance that one can leave and that cannot be stolen by tyrants is the faith, the Gospel, knowing God and His Word. That is one of the points of the Fifth Commandment.

III. Dating

(See page 227, the paragraph beginning with "The problem today is that people engage. . . .")

IV. What Children Receive for Obedience

The Apostle Paul in Ephesians 6:2-3 introduces the command for children to obey parents with this promise: "that it may be well with you and you may live long on the earth." There are exceptions to this rule, but in general those who rebel against God's authority will die long before those who obey. Rebellion is death, but obedience is life. Those who rebel often get involved in crime, drugs, and other things that destroy life. The best way to have a long, wonderful life is to obey God's authorities He puts into our lives, beginning with parents, "which is the first commandment with promise, 'that it may be well with you and you may live long on the earth.' "

Conclusion

The Fifth Commandment (honor parents) goes with the Seventh Commandment (no adultery) to protect the family. Children are to honor parents, and parents are to honor God by honoring the sanctity of the marriage bond, being faithful to one another.

Finally, here is a true story. There was a four-year-old boy who had a single mom. She taught the boy about God and taught him some Bible verses. One day he was almost killed by a pickup truck when he ran into the street, but God spared him without injury. When the mother learned about it, she hugged her boy and told how much she loved him. She told him the story of Samuel, and said how like Hannah she had prayed for a son, that God had given her one. She said, "Now, like Hannah, I've given you back to God, and this is the verse you should always remember: God said: 'Those who honor Me, I will honor' " (1 Samuel 2:30).

Remember, we must honor godly human authority by respect and obedience, which is to honor God Himself. **AMEN.**

Chapter 12—Sixth Commandment: No Murder

You shall not murder (Exodus 20:13).

[Jesus speaking]: ²¹ "You have heard that it was said to those of old, 'You shall not murder, and whoever murders will be in danger of the judgment.' ²² But I say to you that <u>whoever is angry with his brother **without a cause** shall be in danger of the judgment</u>. And whoever says to his brother, 'Raca!' shall be in danger of the council. But whoever says, 'You fool!' shall be in danger of hell fire" (Matthew 5:21-22).

Whoever hates his brother is a murderer, and you know that no murderer has eternal life abiding in him (1 John 3:15).

So you shall not pollute the land where you are; for blood defiles the land, and no atonement can be made for the land, for the blood that is shed on it, except by the blood of him who shed it (Numbers 35:33).

But he who sins against Me wrongs his own soul; <u>all those who hate Me love death</u> (Proverbs 8:36).

My duty towards my neighbor is . . . to hurt nobody by word or deed: To bear no malice or hatred in my heart (Book of Common Prayer).

Introduction

One day when I was about 15, I was walking alone back to my grand-parents' house from rabbit hunting, and my grandfather and his brother saw me coming. As I got close, they saw the dead rabbit on my belt. My grandfather said,

"Hey boy, did you kill that rabbit?"

"Yes, sir."

"Doesn't the Bible say, "Thou shalt not kill"?

"I think that means people."

"That's not what it says. It says, "Thou shalt not *kill*, and you just killed a rabbit."

My grandfather was just making a joke, but I did not know then that there are a number of Hebrew words for "kill," and the one used here in the Ten Commandments in this context means not to murder another human. When no intrinsic value is seen in human life as being made in God's image, one can find any reason to take that life.

But I've killed people in war, and I don't know how many. Was it murder? On one occasion in Vietnam we dropped a 4.2 inch mortar round down the "back pocket" of two men running across a rice field. The forward observer said: "They just vanished into thin air." And there were other occasions where we did similar things. Is war murder?

Most everyone understands that war is the exception to this commandment. Even in the Bible itself, killing in war—at least one approved by God, such as self-defense—is not considered murder. Moreover, war is national, not individual, and this command is about one individual killing another.

But even as individuals don't we have the right to defend ourselves if attacked? If someone tried to rape or murder our wives, would we men not defend them even to taking of another person's life? I surely hope so; otherwise, the wives are in trouble (Exodus 22:2).

What is not forbidden is the taking of human life, for the commandment means not to commit murder, and not all killing is murder. Indeed, some killing is required:

> Whoever sheds man's blood, by man his blood shall be shed; for in the image of God He made man (Genesis 9:6).

> Whoever kills any man shall surely be put to death (Leviticus 24:17).

> If the thief is found breaking in, and he is struck so that he dies, there shall be no guilt for his bloodshed (Exodus 22:2).

> [3] For rulers are not a terror to good works, but to evil. Do you want to be unafraid of the authority? Do what is good, and you will have praise from the same. [4] For he is God's minister to you for good. But if you do evil, be afraid; <u>for he does not bear the sword in vain</u>; for he is God's minister, an avenger to *execute* wrath on him who practices evil (Romans 13:3-4).

Christians are pro-life, but that is under the broader rubric of pro-righteousness. In other words, we are *pro-justice*. That requires little babies to live and not be aborted and adults to die for capital offenses such as murder.

So what does the Sixth Commandment mean? It means that individually we are not to commit murder; just wars and self-defense are not murder. To restate this, one who takes life without God's approval is a murderer, but one who refuses to take life when God demands it is also a wrong, for he is approving murder.

Moreover, as with all the negative commands in the Ten Commandments, this command has a negative and a positive aspect to it. Negatively, on the individual level, we are not to engage in violence with one another, especially murder. Positively, we are to promote health and life among ourselves and others.

Since man has God's dignity in him in the form of God's image, we owe every person some measure of respect at least for the image in him, if not anything else. One reason murder is so heinous is that it is an assault on the image of God within us, which in turn means that it is an assault on God Himself. This is the main reason God requires the death penalty for murder. All the arguments about capital punishment not being a deterrent to crime are irrelevant (and not true for the one put to death never repeats the crime), because *the principle is restitution*. If someone kills another person's image (as it were), the murderer's image must be killed for the principle of justice to be met, as we see from Genesis 9:6 quoted above.

Therefore, His image must be honored in mankind. "There is a hierarchy of being from rocks to plants to animals and to humans. . . ."[1] Mankind is the apex of creation, who demonstrates God's image by his superior reason, by having morality, by having community, and so on. Every person has this image equally, though it is marred by sin. Those who are racists consider their own race to be superior to the general image of God in other humans. Slavery can be based on a denial of common humanity, that some are better than others, as if there were degrees of humanity or degrees of the image of God. The judgment of God is directed toward immorality, not toward lesser humans. It is not one's ethnicity that determines his destiny, but what he does with the image of God in him. In other words, the issue is moral, not physical.

But our society now has an orientation to death from abortion to murder to assisted suicide. What has brought this on us?

When a society (or an individual) turns from the Triune God, who is life, *there is only one alternative,* turning to death. I quoted this verse at the beginning of the chapter: "All those who hate me love death (Proverbs 8:36). We see the same two alternatives in John 3:19-20:

> [19] And this is the condemnation, that the light has come into the world, and men loved darkness rather than light, because their deeds were evil. [20] For everyone practicing evil hates the light and does not come to the light, lest his deeds should be exposed.

Since our society has turned away from God who is life, there is only one option: an orientation to death. (See Chapter 19.)

I heard one of the most ignorant statements recently by Dr. Kevorkian ("Dr. Death") in an interview on Fox News, when he said that Christians teach that we're all divine, being made in God's image. Gleefully, he challenged what that means when a baboon's heart is transplanted into a human or what that means when an appendix is removed and thrown away. Was part of the divine thrown away? What happens to the divine image then, he challenged. But no Christian theologian in the history of the world has taught that the image of God is

---

[1] Surrenda Gangadean, *Philosophical Foundation* (New York: University Press of America, 2008), p. 167.

physical, but it is in the immaterial soul of man. Even then we are not divine, just creatures. The body parts may be interchangeable between species due to a common intelligent design.

In gender wars, some place one gender over other genders, thus committing atrocities based on such. We see this in Islam where women are worth less then men, thus men can have four wives, and a woman's testimony means little in court. Women can be the subject of honor killings, but not the men, and so on. In the beginning, God made one male and one female, not one male and four females. There can be authority of males over females, such as the husband as the head of the woman in marriage, but this is not based on the alleged superiority of the image in males, but simply for good order as given by Christ (Ephesians 5:22ff).

Sometimes murder has been (and still is) justified based on racism, gender, and some sense of feeling superior to other humans. If one does not honor the image of God in mankind equally, if one places more value on some humans over others in disregard of our common creation, this is insipient murder, a demeaning of the common image of God in all humans.

The essence of the Sixth Commandment, therefore, is that we have life from God, that we are made in His image, and thus we must not destroy a human's life, for that is an attack against God who made the image, and we must equally honor God's image in all people.

I. Importance of the Sixth Commandment

The Sixth Commandment begins the second half of the Ten Commandments, and it is the most forceful one of the last five in the sense that death is final. Once one is dead, that cannot be reversed. Adultery (Seventh Commandment) can be repented of and the parties restored; restitution can be made for theft (Eighth Commandment); one can go make things right if he has borne false witness (Ninth Commandment); and only God knows if we covet (Tenth Commandment). It seems that the commandments become less destructive (in one sense) to others as we move from sixth to tenth. With the last four, one can fix it, but with the Sixth Commandment, the only way to satisfy justice is for the murderer to forfeit his own life.

One blessing of the Sixth Commandment is the right to life, a right that has been denied to the most innocent and helpless of our society — babies. Above all else, governing authorities are required by God to protect our lives both from thugs within and from thugs outside the nation. Government should be concerned about life, not about taking money from one citizen and giving it to another.

II. What We Must Do

(1) What is required is that we love our neighbor as ourselves, for hatred is murder in the heart (Deuteronomy 19:15-20; Leviticus 19:17). We must seek to live at peace with one another as much as is possible. (By the way, the Sermon on the Mount is not the intensification of the Old Testament law but the reinstitution of it, as the Lord specifically stated at the beginning of this sermon in Matthew 5:17-18.)

Love is the fulfilling of the law, for Paul stated in Romans 13:8-10:

> [8] Owe no one anything except to love one another, for he who loves another has fulfilled the law. [9] For the commandments, "You shall not commit adultery," "You shall not murder," "You shall not steal," "You shall not bear false witness," "You shall not covet," and if *there is* any other commandment, are *all* summed up in this saying, namely, "You shall love your neighbor as yourself." [10] **Love does no harm to a neighbor; therefore love is the fulfillment of the law**.

We see here that love is *defined* by God's law; it is not just a feeling or an agreement between two consenting adults regarding what is right or wrong. God's word defines love by making it an expression of law-keeping.

(2) What is required is that we protect one another. There is in Holy Scripture *the law of the bystander*. This means that we are required to be our neighbor's keeper, to help to watch over him. (I would say calling the police is usually the best solution.) Here is what God says:

> [11] Deliver those who are drawn toward death, and hold back those stumbling to the slaughter. [12] If you say, "Surely we

did not know this," Does not He who weighs the hearts consider it? He who keeps your soul, does He *not* know it? And will He *not* render to *each* man according to his deeds? (Proverbs 24:11-12).

> When you saw a thief, you consented with him, and have been a partaker with adulterers (Psalms 50:18).

If we see a crime being committed, and we do not report it to the police, we are guilty. This is both biblically and legally required. It is wrong to let someone die when we have the power to keep him alive.

Moreover, we must control ourselves in the protection of our neighbor's life, such as not driving and drinking alcohol, or getting behind the wheel when we may be dangerous, which could include being sleepy on legal drugs. If we kill someone under these circumstances, we could be required to forfeit our own life, especially if it is a repeat offense. (This is too complex for our purposes, but see the law of the ox in Exodus 21:28-32.)

Then there is the authority of police power in the ordinary citizen to make a citizen's arrest. My wife's brother did this once. He saw a drunk driver almost hit several cars on a Mississippi two-lane road, so he forced the man off the road with his pickup truck, went over to him, took his keys out of the ignition, and called the police. He was arrested for DUI. Later when the case went to court, the man tried to discredit her brother, and demanded his name and address. He refused to give personal information, and the judge agreed. Then the man's lawyer tried to get the case dismissed for false arrest, but the judge upheld that also, saying he wished more citizens would exercise their duty to enforce the law. And the judge told the young man that he should be grateful that only his license was going to be suspended and that he was not being buried.

Authority lies with the citizens to a great extent in the USA. (But don't try to be a hero. Know your state laws, and call the police.) The jury is the last hope for freedom, for upholding the federal Constitution. The jury has both the right and the responsibility to judge the law as well as the facts of the case. Most judges will not tell you this, but juries have the power of legal nullification. The state of Tennessee, for example, has in its Constitution a very clear provision for legal nullification. It works like this: if the jury does not think the law is right, even though the person on trial may be guilty according to that law, the jury has the duty to "nullify" the law, thereby providing the last Constitutional check against abuse of power. This is protecting life. Thus the defendant should be found not guilty. A "not guilty" verdict by a jury cannot be appealed in the USA.

(3) What is required is that we promote human life, and executing a murderer is doing just that—not allowing him to do it again! People say the death penalty is not a deterrent to murder, but execution is 100% effective against murderers; there is not a known case of one coming back to life to repeat the crime. Moreover, God says it is a deterrent to others not to commit crime (Deuteronomy 13:10-11).

The Sixth Commandment means that we preserve our own lives by healthy living, taking care of ourselves physically, mentally, and spiritually, not wanting to die but seeking to live. Thus one should watch his weight and diet to honor Christ with his body.

It used to be the case that medical doctors took an oath to save human life, but Dr. Kevorkian thinks he should help people take their own lives. He is not a hero. The courts agreed, and he served eight years for second-degree murder. When the Supreme Court ruled that abortion was legal in January 1973, some insightful Christians predicted that this would lead to an orientation to death in other areas, and Kevorkian has proved this prediction correct with his euthanasia.

Moreover, remember the Terri Schiavo case in Florida. She was taken off life support because she did not have "quality" of life, and was allowed to starve to death. She was considered less human than "normal" humans, which was a denial of God's image in her.

In 1984, Holland legalized euthanasia, and the *Journal of Medical Ethics* has reported that fully one fourth of the assisted suicides were involuntary. Doctors were murdering their patients. Now many elderly Dutch carry around "sanctuary certificates" that indicate they do not wish their doctors to assist them in suicide.[2] Holland is a death oriented society whereas once it was a bastion of the Gospel and therefore of life.

An emergency room doctor told me that she was ready to walk out because she was required to practice law more than medicine. She is required to protect the hospital from possible legal suits, even though her actions may not be best for the patient. She said sometimes a patient must be sent home even when he needs medical attention because the hospital's money is a higher priority than the patient's health, and that is in principle euthanasia.

Now we also have infanticide justified by Australian Peter Singer who teaches ethics at Princeton (originally founded by Presbyterians who loved the Lord!). He states regarding humans who are long-term patients in a coma or who are barely functional:

> In most respects, these human beings do not differ importantly from disabled infants. They are not self-conscious, rational, or autonomous, and so considerations of a right to life or of respecting autonomy do not apply. If they have no experiences at all, and can never have any again, their lives have no intrinsic value. Their life's journey has come to an end. They are biologically alive, but not biographically.[3]

Singer applies this line of reasoning to infants who have been born, and adults who cannot function according to his definition of what it means to be a viable human (self-aware, intelligent, can respond to their environment). But he is also for death for adults who do not meet his definition of a viable life:

> We have seen that it is possible to justify ending the life of a human being who lacks the capacity to consent.
>
> Now suppose we have a situation in which a person suffering from a painful and incurable disease wishes to die. If the individual were not a person—not rational or self-conscious—euthanasia would, as I have said, be justifiable.

---

[2] David Berlinski, *The Devil's Delusion* (Philadelphia: Basic Books, division of Random House, 2009), p. 32.

[3] Peter Singer, *Practical Ethics*, 2nd edition, Cambridge, 1993, pp. 175-217, accessed from http://www.utilitarian.net/singer/by/1993----.htm, accessed 17 Dec 2008.

Of course, a wealthy person could hire two doctors to declare another person "not rational or self-conscious" and have him/her legally killed. One source reports on Singer's ethics:[4]

> Singer's response came to Dublin reader Karen Meade's question: "Would you kill a disabled baby?"
>
> "Yes, if that was in the best interests of the baby and of the family as a whole. Many people find this shocking, yet they support a woman's right to have an abortion," he said.
>
> He added that one point on which he agrees with the pro-life movement is that, "from the point of view of ethics rather than the law, there is no sharp distinction between the foetus and the newborn baby."
>
> The statement furthers the arguments that Singer's position is just an extension of the culture of death that has developed in the world, with euthanasia legal in some locations, abortion legal in many and even charges that in some repressive societies there's an active business in harvesting healthy organs from victims in order to provide transplants for the wealthy.
>
> Singer holds that man is no different from other forms of life, and therefore man's life is not worth more than, for example, a cow.
>
> He told readers he'd kill 10 cows before killing one human, but that's not because they are of less value, only that humans would mourn.
>
> "I've written that it is much worse to kill a being who is aware of having a past and a future, and who plans for the future. Normal humans have such plans, but I don't think cows do," he said.
>
> However, he did qualify his description with the word, "normal."

---

[4] http://www.worldnetdaily.com/news/article.asp?ARTICLE_ID=51963, accessed 17 December 2008.

"Once again Singer is making distinctions between human beings he would consider normal and those he would consider not normal, thus he is deciding who is a person and who is not," Schadenberg told Life Site News.

"Non-persons are allowed to be killed," under Singer's theology, he said.

Dinesh D'Souza, who is a Christian and a former White House domestic policy adviser, and has debated Singer publicly, states regarding Singer:

He cheerfully advocates infanticide and euthanasia and, in almost the same breath, favors animal rights. Even most liberals would have qualms about third-trimester abortions; Singer does not hesitate to advocate what may be termed fourth-trimester abortions, i.e., *the killing of infants after they are born.*

Singer writes, "My colleague Helga Kuhse and I suggest that a period of 28 days after birth might be allowed before an infant is accepted as having the same right to live as others." Singer argues that even pigs, chickens, and fish have more signs of consciousness and rationality—and, consequently, a greater claim to rights—than do fetuses, newborn infants, and people with mental disabilities.[5]

Singer's "signs of consciousness" may just be instinct, and those animals that do not have a high intelligence to learn behavior are born with instincts. Humans, made in the image of God, are born with the capacity to learn what they need to know, which means they must be taught, which in turn means they come into the world with few skills, yet enormous potential. But we can see that Singer denies that humans have the divine image of God and so he can make such discriminations between humans—this one dies, that one lives.

Singer's whole position assumes that mankind is not created in God's image but that we evolved from a common life. Evolution leads to death and cheap human life, but creation leads to life and infinite value to each human being.

---

[5] *Christianity Today*, March 2009, p. 60.

Also, one wonders about Senator Barbara Boxer of California who will not take a strong stand against infanticide as seen in the dialogue between her and Senator Rick Santorum in the Senate in which he could not get Senator Boxer to oppose infanticide.[6] She basically kept saying she was in favor of *Roe vs. Wade.*

Moreover, on the one hand, Living Wills often do little more than give the doctors the right to kill you if they see fit, especially if it is going to cost the hospital a lot of money to keep you alive. On the other hand, some Living Wills will protect life, if the patient has stated that he wants others to make efforts to save his life.

According to one pro-life lady who is an R.N., President Obama supported live birth abortions, even when the Senate voted 98 to zero not to support it. An African American man says this is infanticide. See this video: http://media.causes.com/543421?p_id=16203881, which is on www.youtube.com.

And once the dominoes begin to fall regarding death, there is little stopping more deaths for all kinds of people. Consider this possible scenario as written by Focus on the Family.

> Suppose Diane is a 16-year-old high school student who is loved greatly by her family. One day, she fails to come home from school when expected. By six-thirty that evening, her mother is starting to worry. When eight o'clock rolls around, her father calls the police. There has been no report of an accident, he is told. None of the local hospitals have a patient named Diane. Mom then begins making frantic telephone calls and finally reaches Diane's best friend, Rene. "Oh, Mrs. Johnson," Rene says with compassion. She begins to cry. "I wanted so much to call you, but I promised Diane I would let the clinic tell you."
>
> "Clinic? What clinic?!" says Mrs. Johnson.
>
> "You know," says Rene. "The Life Choice Clinic downtown. I think you'd better call them."

---

[6] See http://www.nrlc.org/news/1999/NRL1199/boxsan.html, accessed December 18, 2008.

Diane's mother gets the clinic administrator on the line, who says, "I'm terribly sorry, Mrs. Johnson, we were just getting ready to call you. I know this will be hard for you, but please sit down. Diane came in this afternoon and asked to be assisted in her passing. You may know that she had been very depressed about her grades and because of the rejection letter she received from the state university. Then when her boyfriend let her down . . . well, she just didn't want to go on living. And as you know, 'right to die' laws now apply to every one 16 years old or older. We do not have to notify the parents before assisting one to pass."

I've changed very little of the words. Do you say this could never happen in the USA? Is that what they said in Hitler's Germany about the six million Jews and who knows how many Christians? Is not this happening right now when our daughters can put to death their unborn babies without their parents' consent? What voice do the babies have? Have we not surpassed six million Jews and Christians to 50 million babies and *counting*? What is the difference between Hitler and us?

(We can't have "free will" without suffering. When someone dies in a plane crash, an atheist will charge God with being at fault, deciding who will die and who will live. But when someone decides to kill her child by abortion, that is deemed "personal choice" and allowed. What is the difference? If humans can kill the innocent and not be wrong, why can't God kill those who are sinful (no human is sinless) and not be wrong?)

(4) If we are not to take life, the flip side is that we should enjoy life to its fullest, as the book of Ecclesiastes instructs. I especially love to be out in God's creation, for it reveals the beauty of God. Fishing, swimming, sports, are activities that we can enjoy.

III. What We Must Not Do

(1) Obviously murder is forbidden, but also what is forbidden is allowing a murderer to live, for this exalts human life above God's righteousness. Once human life is placed above righteousness, society degenerates quickly into chaos. Then the criminal is given rights and the

victims are condemned. Society becomes the one to blame rather than the offender. It is a liberal principle that death is worse than immorality.

So what is forbidden is allowing a murderer to live, and especially to go back into society. The unofficial moratorium against the death penalty back in the 1960s substituted medicine for morals, rehabilitation for righteousness, denying individual responsibility and placing responsibility on society for one's crimes. Soon, most states began again to practice the death penalty to curb crime.

(2) Violence is also forbidden in the Sixth Commandment, for in principle it also can be detrimental to life. This includes violence at home, and even verbal violence. When the stores opened after Thanksgiving Day 2008, a crowd was eager to rush into a Wal-Mart on Long Island at five in the morning. They forced open the doors, trampled an employee to death, and then stepped right over the body to get into the store. The mob ran over other employees trying to help the downed man, and anybody else in its way, including a 28-year-old pregnant woman. The shoppers could not be bothered; they were on a mission to find a bargain. Life means little in 21st century USA.

(3) What is forbidden is abortion, and this is *the* political issue of our nation. If a politician is for abortion, I do not vote for him. It is a single issue. If a politician cannot clearly and with conviction support life for his most innocent and helpless citizens, the unborn, then we must not support him. If the most helpless do not have the right to life, then in principle all lesser rights are likewise negotiable. But notice in elections that money is nearly always the main issue, not morality. People will vote for the politician who will give them the most benefits, bypassing the most important issue of all—life.

And recall the compromises we get from politicians: "I'm personally opposed to abortion, but this is a difficult issue. We must allow for differences of conscience; also, abortion is not required, only allowed."

Now let's take out the euphemism to see how completely ridiculous this is. "I'm personally opposed to murder, but this is a difficult issue. We must allow for differences of conscience, and also murder is not required, only allowed." And make no mistake, abortion is murder, and murder for hire. (But there is forgiveness through the cross of Christ for those who confess their sins to Him.)

Two objections arise, one of rape and the other of the case in which the mother's life is in danger. Sarah Palin was asked in an interview:

> Do you still support life when a father has raped his daughter, and she becomes pregnant?

In the first place, this is very rare. But if it happens, our answer should be, "Does the crime of rape justify the crime of murder?" Adoption is always a good alternative, and here is what God says about those who may be born with defects:

> So the LORD said to him, "Who has made man's mouth? Or who makes the mute, the deaf, the seeing, or the blind? Have not I, the LORD?" (Exodus 4:11).

One very good statement about rape was given by one lady who was raped and became pregnant: "It's not the baby that needs killing."

Of course, we all recognize that if the life of the mother is endangered that we must save the mother, for there is a covenant with her prior to the child to save her life. Moreover, often the choice is not between woman or child but between the woman or the death of both.

Conclusion

Modern man stands helpless before a coffin with no hope, no assurance, just darkness ahead. If one is not prepared to die with meaning, he is not prepared to live with meaning. And one can only be prepared to die if he trusts in the One who was dead and has risen from the grave.

Unlike other cultures in Israel's day when the Ten Commandments were given, there was no capital punishment for stealing. Islam today cuts off a person's hand if they steal, but the Triune God is more merciful, not requiring any physical punishment for theft, but restitution is required. (See Chapter 15 on the Eighth Commandment.)

God created us in His image. Let us honor this image by protecting the life of the innocent and by executing the guilty. **AMEN.**

Chapter 13—Seventh Commandment: What Is Marriage?

You shall not commit adultery (Exodus 20:14).

Therefore a man shall leave his father and mother and be joined to his wife, and they shall become one flesh (Genesis 2:24).

[Jesus speaking:] [4] And He answered and said to them, "Have you not read that He who made *them* at the beginning 'made them male and female,' [5] and said, 'For this reason a man shall leave his father and mother and be joined to his wife, and the two shall become one flesh'? [6] So then, they are no longer two but one flesh. Therefore **what God has joined together**, let not man separate" (Matthew 19:4-6).

[28] If a man finds a young woman who is a virgin, who is not betrothed, and he seizes her and lies with her, and they are found out, [29] then the man who lay with her shall give to the young woman's father fifty *shekels* of silver, and she shall be his wife because he has humbled her; he shall not be permitted to divorce her all his days (Deuteronomy 22:28-29).

Marriage is honorable among all, and the bed undefiled; but fornicators and adulterers God will judge (Hebrews 13:4).

My duty towards my neighbor is . . . To keep my body in temperance, soberness, and chastity (Book of Common Prayer).

Introduction

Someone has said:

> I learned that there is little difference in husbands. You might as well keep the first one.

Consider another witticism.

> A woman accompanied her husband to the doctor's office for a checkup. Afterwards, the doctor took the wife aside and said, "Unless you do the following things, your husband will surely die. Every morning make sure he gets a good healthy breakfast. Have him come home for lunch each day so you can feed him a well-balanced meal. Make sure you feed him a good, hot dinner every night. Don't overburden him with any household chores. Also, keep the house spotless and clean so he doesn't get exposed to any unnecessary germs." On the way home, the husband asked his wife what the doctor said in private. She replied, "You're going to die, and there is nothing that can be done about it."

Our culture is fighting for a definition of marriage. Who gets to define it? Is just living together marriage? If two people keep house together and pretend marriage, is that it? Can any two consenting adults do what they wish in private, and everyone else is required to honor the relationship? Who is sovereign in this world? Whose word counts?

This article was sent to me by email:

NY recognizes Canadian same-sex marriages

Kelly Patterson, Ottawa Citizen

> In a landmark case, an American court has ruled that gay couples who tie the knot in Canada can be treated as legally married in the state of New York.
>
> Justice Joan Lefkowitz of the New York Supreme Court ruled last week that same-sex marriages performed outside the country are valid, even though gay New Yorkers cannot be legally married in their home state.

This is the first time Canadian same-sex marriage laws have triumphed in U.S. court, according to Alphonso David, a lawyer for the gay rights group Lambda Legal, which intervened in the case.

"Couples can *go to sleep at night* without worrying about the security of their status," says David.

"I feel vindicated," his client, Robert Voorheis, told reporters after the March 12 ruling. "When I say, 'I'm married,' I'm married."

Voorheis and his *partner*, both of Yonkers, N.Y., were married in Niagara Falls, Ont., four years ago.

"This is extremely important," says Andrew Koppelman, a Northwestern University law professor and expert on the issue.

If the ruling holds up on appeal, "it will mean for all practical purposes, same-sex marriage is legal in the state of New York," because people can easily cross the border to get married, said Koppelman.

While the lower-court ruling is not technically binding on other state courts, it's significant in that "it says you can recognize a (same-sex marriage) even if locally you can't perform it," and lays out historical examples of that recognition, explains Mark Strasser, a law professor at Capital University in Columbus, Ohio, who has written extensively on same-sex marriage.

The case centered on a 2006 order by Westchester County Executive Andrew Spano that county officials must recognize same-sex marriages from other jurisdictions.

A conservative Arizona-based group called the Alliance Defense Fund took Spano to court, arguing his order violated the state's constitution and municipal laws.

Last summer, the New York Court of Appeal upheld the state's century-old definition of marriage as a union between a man and a woman.

But Lefkowitz found that ruling did not address the issue of marriages performed outside the state.

She then applied the legal test of comity, the principle that
countries should recognize each other's laws on marriage and
other such issues as long as they don't offend community values
or run strongly against public policy.

With the ever increasing Islamic presence in the USA, it won't be
long until polygamy is also recognized. Perhaps the Mormons will re-
adopt their view on polygamy. When you don't have a bottom line to
morality except what is popular, anything goes.

My wife and I were in Manitou Springs, Colorado to go up Pikes
Peak, and while there we saw two men walking on the streets holding
hands. What is the definition of marriage?

One cannot define adultery until one knows what marriage is? Is it
wrong for a homosexual to cheat on his civil union partner? Is that
adultery?

That is not adultery; it is sinful just to be in that relationship in the
first place. Yet God through Christ will forgive all those who repent.
Adultery is cheating on your heterosexual spouse that you've married
by covenant vows, or it may be serial marriages where one marries one
person after another without biblical divorce. (See the next chapter.)

The point of this Seventh Commandment on sexuality in marriage
is that all sex outside heterosexual marriage of one male and one female
is wrong. I've been giving you the flip side of each commandment each
time we've looked at one of the Ten Commandments, such as the commandment not to murder means to support life as well as to condemn
murderers to death. Now this Seventh Commandment means that sexual relations can only be practiced in a heterosexual marriage; all else is
sin.

The essence of this commandment among humans is that God
gave us families, one male and one female, who are to be in covenant
with one another for life, which includes sexual intimacy. This close-
ness is not to be violated — ever.

What Is Marriage?

Notice the two passages printed first in this chapter: Genesis 2:24, and
the Lord's interpretation of that passage in Matthew 19:4-6. We know

that marriage is a covenant, which means a commitment to one another by vows in the presence of the appropriate witnesses. (More on this below.)

Often when something is first mentioned in Scripture, especially in Genesis where all begins, we can derive a definition of that doctrine. But this is even truer in the case of marriage since the Lord Jesus Himself used this Genesis passage to derive His definition of marriage.

(1) The *condition* for entering the marriage covenant is that there must be a man and a woman, for God created Adam and Eve, one male and one female. Moreover, He created only two to make a family. One of the reasons for this one male and one female is that God commanded the first couple to "be fruitful and multiply" (Genesis 1:27-28), which meant to have many children. Through many children the earth would be subdued:

> "Be fruitful and multiply; <u>fill the earth and subdue it</u>; have
> dominion over the fish of the sea, over the birds of the air, and
> over every living thing that moves on the earth" (Genesis 1:28).

It is a fact that homosexuals cannot reproduce, so how can they spread their views except by converting others to their ways? If all "marriages" were two of the same sex, it would mean the end of the human race, for no children would be produced. If the first two humans had been gay, we would not have a human race.

And if cloning is ever possible for humans and catches on so that gays can "reproduce," the gay rights movement will gain more momentum. However, the child will only be the product of one partner, not both, and perhaps there will be a degenerative gene weakness from one generation to the next. And if they "divorce," will not the child belong to the one from whom he was cloned? What will that child grow up with? God threatens diseases for those who violate His sexual commands (Exodus 15:26; Deuteronomy 7:15; 28:60). Indeed, sexually transmitted diseases ensure that sex is no longer a private matter.

According to the Lord Jesus, two people, one male and one female, is what constitutes a marriage. Two *complement* one another while three *complicate* the matter exceedingly. For example, if you have one husband and four wives as in Islam, the man is the father of all the children. What kinds of rivalries will this produce between the wives to promote their offspring as the favored one? Who will get the inheritance? For an answer to this, just see what happened to Jacob in the Old Testament with his wives, Solomon and his wives who led him into idolatry, or David and his wives.

We see that the son cleaves to his wife and becomes one flesh with her (Genesis 2:24), which is more than just sexuality. So what do we say of a son who cleaves to four wives? Are they all one flesh? That is not possible. The *two* have become one, not the three or five have become one.

In Genesis 2:18 God says:

> And the LORD God said, "It is not good that man should be alone; I will make him a helper comparable to him."

From this we can see that the woman was made to complete the man. The "not good" of the *one* man alone was made good by the *one* woman. The one woman completed the one man; that is, she was to be his "helper," which in Hebrew is often used of God helping His people but here means that man was created in such a way that it is unnatural to be alone, that he can do more with his wife than he can do without her. Someone said that woman was not taken from man's head to rule over him, nor from his feet to be walked on, but from his side to complete him.

Also, the idea in the words "comparable to him" means corresponding to him, essential to him, suitable for him. In this case, since neither is complete without the other, one plus one equals one, not two. They are like two halves that form a whole. Thus, marriage is one male and one female that make one new covenant, one new family. (In so doing, they are to reflect the unconditional love of Christ for His Church (Ephesians 5:22ff). Moreover, we are not dealing with those who have the gift to remain single (Matthew 19:11; 1 Corinthians 7:7), and who are still complete in Christ.)

God made all the things that reproduce, the whole animal kingdom, to have a male and a female. There is distinction here along with sameness. The distinction is male and female, and the sameness is the same species. We can see why the first three chapters of Genesis have been so vehemently attacked, for if these are true, those who "marry" as same sex unions are in serious trouble with God.

To have one husband and many wives implies that females are worth less than males, that females are worth less as created beings than males, which explains why women are treated so terribly in Islam, as for example in Saudi Arabia. Moreover, in polygamy full person-hood is denied to the women, who often have less rights than men, not to mention less place in the marriages.

To put this another way, there are to be two parents, not more than two since the two become one. But there can be many children, for they are not joined as one. Moreover, since children are not joined as one, their relationship to parents and to one another is temporary, but the relationship of husband to wife is permanent.

(2) The *basis* for human marriage is Christ's love for the Church, Christ as groom and the Church as bride, as St. Paul says in Ephesians 5:25-27. We learn about human marriage from the divine marriage of Christ with the Church. To put this another way, God deliberately has made the human marriage to be a reflection of the divine marriage. Christ as male has one bride who is female, the Church.

Even those who are not Christians still seek love in marriage, not knowing they are doing so because God is love and they are made in God's image. Hollywood presents romantic love as the meaning to love, but this love makes another creature the highest good. Therefore, this love self-destructs, for Christ must be the highest good. When we love Him more than all else, human marriage will be fulfilling; other-wise, we will be disappointed. We humans *always* disappoint. More-over, Christ's love for His Church is the standard for marriage, and no one can find true fulfillment until they know God. Yet they seek Him in human relationships, which by themselves do not satisfy the longing heart to know full pardon for sin, to have unconditional love, and to rest in the arms of one whom to know means a relationship that never ends, going beyond death.

How is a husband to love His wife? Paul commands that we do so like Christ has loved the Church, which is an *unconditional* love, a love that is not conditioned on what the object of that loves does. Christ did not love us because we were lovely; indeed, we were (are) sinful. But

He loves us because of what is in Him, not in us. If His love for us depended on us, He would love us one day and not the next. There would be no security in the relationship. Human marriages that are not grounded in Christ tend to fall apart because the object of love (spouse) is so flawed.

Moreover, a husband is to love His wife *self-sacrificially*, as Christ did the Church and gave Himself for her. A husband must spend his life in serving his wife, and be willing to die for her. This means he provides for her in every way, financially, emotionally, spiritually, and supports her with his time and care.

Also, when a husband marries, he must set a *goal* of making his wife and his family *holy*, that she "should be holy and without blemish." In other words, the Ten Commandments are God's terms of marriage, the standard, and the husband must run his home in humble obedience to these. If he does not adopt God's standard, his home will self-destruct.

The oneness in marriage should be because of their oneness in Christ; otherwise, the marriage loses perspective. Thus most Anglican marriage ceremonies do not use the unity candle, for it tends to put the unity in the couple rather than in Christ and His Church. It is a recent invention, perhaps 50 years old, and used mostly in the USA.

(3) A marriage is *created by covenant*:

> . . . the LORD has been witness between you and the wife of your youth, with whom you have dealt treacherously; yet she is your companion and your wife by **covenant** (Malachi 2:14).

The ideas of "leaving," "cleaving" or "joining" are covenantal language (Deuteronomy 4:4; 10:10; Joshua 23:8). In other words, a *new covenant is made*, and a new home is created (see Hosea 2:14-23; Ephesians 5:22-32). If the son leaves parents and cleaves to his wife, the parents should be witnesses.

So what is a marriage covenant? This is an agreement between a man and a woman to be faithful to one another to death. The agreement is not a loose one, but solemn vows before the Triune God who is the One making the covenant ("What *God* has joined together") and before all the human witnesses present, vowing to be faithful to death. They are vowing never to look for another spouse while the original one is alive, and are vowing never to question whether they have married the right person or not, for they have vowed that they have married the right one. After the vows of both the groom and the bride are pledged, the couple is declared married, *for the vows made to God, to the witnesses, and to one another constitute the marriage.* This is the solemn covenant to one another.

How can a person keep such a covenant? How can a person know that he will still love this person a few years down the road? Don't people "fall in love" and then "fall out of love"? Love is not in our control, is it? Does not the other person control it?

Remember that marriage is based on Christ's love for the Church, and His love for us was in *His* control. Remember also what we said in Chapter 3, that love is primarily a function of the will, which means we can even love our enemies. We can never use as an excuse that we cannot control our love, saying that if we fall out of love we cannot help it; we can help it! Love is controlled by the will, not by emotions.

So how does this parallel Christ's marriage to the Church? We enter that relationship with Him by covenant in baptism, which covenant is a vow. This is an unconditional commitment to God through Christ by the vow of baptism, either as adults or as children who are represented by their parents or god-parents.

How does this work out in marriage? A man leaves his father and mother; and ideally in the presence of at least the two original families (the mom and dad of each person) and God's representative (minister), he and his engaged bride make an unconditional commitment to one another for life. In other words, this is a witnessed ceremony, not the private "commitment" of consenting adults who just live together. God requires the commitment of "baptism" as it were by witnessed vows before there can be "Holy Communion" (consummation of marriage). And by "witnessed," we mean the marriage covenant is made at least in the presence of other humans, especially the Church. Vows, to be valid, must not be taken in private, for they can easily be denied later. Public vows bind the couple, keeping them accountable.

Marriage is not an experiment to see if the couple is compatible but the giving of oneself to another by vows and by commitment for life to make the relationship work. If we can love our parents and siblings without experimentation, without trying them out, why can't we do the same with our marriages? We can, by God's grace! It is the soul of the other person we love, not just the body, and the relationship must be grounded in our spiritual relationship with Christ. Of course, the body is very important and we cannot have marriage without it, but the point we're making is that physical union is a reflection of spiritual union, not the reverse.

From the passages at the beginning of this chapter (Deuteronomy 22:28-29 and Hebrews 13:4), we can see what God says about the consenting adults' model (read these again). In Deuteronomy, if a single man takes advantage of a single woman, and if the father approves to give her to him (assumed from other passages), the man must marry her and *may never divorce her*, which obviously meant that the sex they had was not marriage. They both consented, but that was not marriage.

Notice again what God says in the Hebrews passage quoted at the beginning of this chapter:

> Marriage is honorable among all, and the bed undefiled;
> but fornicators and adulterers God will judge (Hebrews 13:4).

Those who are consenting adults who have sex outside marriage (fornicators) fall under the judgment of God unless they repent. Those just living together are said to be fornicators. They cannot say that they are married because they said so, but marriage is God's for *Him* to join two people: "What *God* has joined together. . . ." This requires a covenant before other human witnesses, which means a covenant must be witnessed not only by the couple *but also by a third human party*, without which there is no covenant. The covenant justifies sexual union, not that sexual union makes the covenant.

Parallel adultery is condemned very strongly in the Old Testament, even to the death penalty in some cases (Leviticus 20:10; Deuteronomy 22:22), but fornication, sex between those who are single and who are not engaged, is also condemned, but not to the death (Deuteronomy 22:28-29). Often today couples are just living together, have made economic commitments they cannot easily get out of, want to get married and for whatever reason have not married. The best cure for this type of sin is to get them married as soon as possible.

The problem today is that people engage in casual dating that leads to emotional and physical involvement without boundaries. In other words, physical involvement, such as kissing and then fondling, leads to living together, if not in an apartment somewhere, then in the car on a regular basis. Parents who let their teens date unsupervised are asking for trouble, for this circumnavigates the authority of parents and of the church. Scripture presents a courting model where the boundaries are established by the parents and the church, where the young man asks permission of the parents to court a young lady, or if she is on her own, he would see her under the authority of the church. Then they see one another in a controlled environment, honoring God's authorities and determining if they want to marry one another. (This is too complex to consider all the details here.)

The point of these passages is that a couple by themselves cannot constitute a marriage covenant without the approval of others. One cannot enjoy the fruit of marriage (one flesh) and call that marriage. Marriage is a covenant where the couple commit themselves to one another by vows *with witnesses.*

In the case of Christians, the Church must seal the marriage with an ordained minister under the authority of the Church, for marriage is a sacrament. We do not mean that it is one of the two main sacraments (baptism and Holy Communion), but that it partakes of sacramental properties as a means of grace when done under the authority and blessing of Christ in His Church. St. Paul specifically states that human marriage is a reflection of Christ's relationship with His Church.[1] Moreover, this covenant implicitly involves a commitment to rear children when they come along, not to destroy them by abortion. I know of no culture that does not have some way to publicly seal the commitment of a man and woman. See the First Helvetic Confession (A.D. 1536) that says a marriage is to be "confirmed in the presence of the church by a public exhortation and vow in keeping with its dignity." Though we Anglicans do not consider marriage a sacrament like Baptism and the

---

[1] Ephesians 5:22ff. This is too involved for this book.

Lord's Supper, nevertheless it is sacramental, and thus must be performed by the Church.

Moreover, the father is required to give his daughter in marriage, not that someone can sneak around and take her away from him privately. We see half a long chapter committed to the father giving his daughter in 1 Corinthians 7:25-40 where Paul says a father can give or not give his virgin daughter in marriage. Thus the idea is that the father (as the head but obviously the mother also) is the protector of his daughter. The custom we have in the USA of a father walking down the aisle to give away his daughter reflects this biblical idea. Often the minister says, "Who gives this woman to this man?" and the good answer is, "Her mother and I." In the case of a Christian lady who has been living by herself, supporting herself, the Church can be the covenant head to help her marry the right person.

Giving away is part of the covenant commitment. The parents of the bride are agreeing to transfer the care of their daughter to a new head; they are implicitly making a vow to let her go to someone else to continue what they had begun—the making of a godly woman. This is not a light commitment, not a meaningless ceremony. The parents also take an implicit oath to support the new family, not to take their child's side when problems arise.

Then both bride and groom take the vows. Traditionally, the man takes the vow first, for he has just received her hand from her father, and like Christ's love for the Church, the groom is the initiator of their love relationship, so he vows to her first. Then like the Church that loves Christ *because* He first loved her (1 John 4:19), she responds to his love with her vows. Once the vows are made, the minister of the Gospel, the one who represents God and His marriage covenant with the Church, pronounces that they are married in the name of the Holy Trinity. *The covenant is now ratified; the couple are married.*

Moreover, the vows are *unconditional*, which means one commits himself or herself to the other person with no reservations. In other words, there are no prenuptial agreements.[2] A prenuptial agreement

---

[2] As a general rule, there are no prenuptial agreements. But for a marriage later in life where there are grown children, perhaps there could be prenuptial conditions to

says: "I love you almost as much as my money, but not quite. I'll try you out, and if you don't do what I like, I'll take my money and throw you away." It is an escape clause in case we want out for whatever reason. It is difficult to think of this as a marriage but rather a selfish experiment. When we come to Christ for forgiveness of sins, we come without reservation, not trying Him out to see if things work out.

The man says to the woman in the Reformed Episcopal Book of Common Prayer for a wedding (p. 493):

> With this ring I thee wed, with my body I thee worship, and with all my worldly goods I thee endow. . . .

There is no financial reservation, no prenuptial qualification. One throws the dice as it were and puts all his eggs in one basket, to love this one person no matter what, to say to God and the world that by His grace, we'll make the relationship work to God's glory. That is the intent of the vows.

Since God requires that marriage be done with vows and witnesses, we can see that marriage does not belong to us to invent, change, redefine, or just do with as we please, but that *marriage belongs to God*. What did the Lord Jesus say in the Matthew passage quoted at the beginning of this chapter?

> Therefore what **God** has joined together, let not man separate.

In other words, there is no marriage except God's marriage, and anyone who tries to change it, to nullify it with easy divorces, or just mock it by living together, is asking for judgment. And we have plenty of judgment today on families.

It is *God* who joins a couple together, and He loves the idea of marriage so much that He often refers to His relationship to His people as a marriage. God made the marriage between the Church and His Son, and He makes the marriage between one male and one female who humbly submit to His covenant model. He will bless such a union.

---

protect an inheritance, but there should be financial commitments between the new couple, not living as two separate, financial institutions, so to speak. This is too complex to handle here.

Conclusion

In Christian marriage, two people grow increasingly one with every passing year. They are "fellow heirs of the grace of life." *Each is helping the other on the way to eternity.*

Someone asked, "Is there anything more beautiful than a young man and young woman clasping clean hands and pure hearts in the path of marriage?"

The answer is, "Yes, there is a more beautiful thing: it is the spectacle of an old man and an old woman finishing their journey on that path. Their hands are gnarled, but still clasped; their faces are seamed but still radiant; their hearts are tired and bowed down but still strong. They have proved the happiness of marriage and vindicated it from the jeers of cynics. Their covenant is complete." **AMEN**.

Chapter 14—Seventh Commandment: What Is Adultery?

You shall not commit adultery (Exodus 20:14).

Therefore a man shall leave his father and mother and be joined to his wife, and they shall become one flesh (Genesis 2:24).

Do not lust after her beauty in your heart, nor let her allure you with her eyelids (Proverbs 6:25; see also Job 31:1, 9-12).

[Jesus speaking:] 27 You have heard that it was said to those of old, "You shall not commit adultery." 28 But I say to you that whoever looks at a woman to lust for her has already committed adultery with her in his heart (Matthew 5:27-28).

3 Let the husband render to his wife the affection due her, and likewise also the wife to her husband. 4 The wife does not have authority over her own body, but the husband *does*. And likewise the husband does not have authority over his own body, but the wife *does*. 5 Do not deprive one another except with consent for a time, that you may give yourselves to fasting and prayer; and come together again so that Satan does not tempt you because of your lack of self-control (1 Corinthians 7:3-5).

Marriage is honorable among all, and the bed undefiled; but fornicators and adulterers God will judge (Hebrews 13:4).

And I say to you, whoever divorces his wife, except for sexual immorality, and marries another, commits adultery; and whoever marries her who is divorced commits adultery (Matthew 19:9).

Introduction

A woman had just gotten married, and she wanted to emphasize to her husband to stay faithful to her. So she decided they should go to Grand Canyon and take a tour of it on donkeys. Knowing the propensity of donkeys to stumble, she thought it would be a good object lesson for her new husband.

Not long into the trip, the donkey stumbled, and the wife said: "That's once." A mile later the donkey stumbled again, and the wife said "That's twice." When the donkey later stumbled badly the third time, she said: "That's three times." She dismounted the donkey, produced a hefty revolver from her purse, and shot the animal dead.

Naturally the husband was horrified, so he proceeded to rebuke his wife, at which point she said: "That's once."

Well there are better ways to keep our spouses in line, and the best way to keep ourselves is by honoring our spiritual marriage to Christ.

One of the treasures that I value most is a stain glassed window that was dedicated to me as a lover of Holy Scripture, and there is a verse quoted at the bottom of the plaque:

Teach me thy law . . . that I may delight in obeying it with all my heart (Psalm 119:33-34).

What does this have to do with the Seventh Commandment? As I've been saying that our relationship with God determines everything else in our lives—everything. I can guarantee you that *no one commits physical adultery without having committed spiritual adultery first.* Never happens. This Seventh Commandment in regard to God is not so much about the physical act of adultery as it is about faithfulness to God.

Moreover, adultery begins in the heart with lust. The Lord Jesus said:

I say to you that whoever looks at a woman to lust for her has already committed adultery with her in his heart (Matthew 5:28).

Once lust has conceived, it leads to physical adultery. We see that the soul and the body work together to commit adultery. If we are only a product of nature, there is no lust, for we are only chemicals, but we know better. We know what goes on in our hearts. Man is not just a product of material from below, but he is also a product from above, made in God's image with an immortal soul. We are soul and body. The soul lusts, and the body commits the adultery.

I. Spiritual Adultery

What is adultery? It is spiritual idolatry, every time, without exception. The reason one falls into adultery is that he is not pursuing his spiritual spouse, Christ.

God reveals that His relationship with His people is a marriage. As we saw last chapter, our commitment to Christ is an unconditional covenantal commitment by vows in the presence of witnesses, and we call that baptism. The same definition applies to our human marriages. We are not allowed just to take secret vows, live together, and call that marriage. We saw in the previous chapter that God calls that fornication: "Marriage is honorable among all, and the bed undefiled; but fornicators and adulterers God will judge" (Hebrews 13:4).

Our marriages to Christ are sacred, the most sacred thing we have on earth, and our human marriages are to be a reflection of our divine marriages to Christ: faithful to our spouse to death.

The Book of Hosea is a visual object lesson of God's marriage to Israel. God commanded Hosea to marry a woman who had been a harlot (not that she was at the point of the marriage), but God said that she would be unfaithful to him. And when that occurred, he was to take her back.

That is a picture of God's love for us: we were spiritual harlots, but God sought us out; and even when we're unfaithful, He brings us back to his clean and pure home. Ideally, our commitment to our spouses is to be like God's commitment to us — unconditional.

Christ came to be our spiritual spouse: "To seek and to save that which was lost" (Luke 19:10). Before the world was created, the Father gave the Son a bride (John 17:6, 9, 11), and then in the fullness of time

God sent forth His Son born of a woman, born under the law (Galatians 4:4), to claim this bride for Himself.

Now we belong to Him. He is our spouse. We maintain that relationship by spending time with Him in worship each week, by honoring our vows by obeying the terms of our commitment, which terms are the Ten Commandments, and by private prayer. I say again that it is only when someone is first unfaithful to his faithful Savior Christ that he will act out that unfaithfulness by committing physical adultery.

We must, if at all possible, renew our vows weekly to Christ in the worship service. One who does not spend time with his spiritual spouse cannot maintain the relationship. One who finds excuses to miss this time with God each week will suffer for it spiritually, just like one who does not spend time with his human spouse cannot maintain the relationship. No relationship can be maintained by physical absence. Just look at all the celebrities who divorce because they do not spend time with one another, who are seeking their respective careers rather than one another. An absentee husband or wife, for whatever reason, will destroy a marriage.

So what is adultery, whether spiritual or physical? *It is the giving of one's time and affection to someone other than one's spouse.* That's it. Often, those who are unbelievers are just fornicators, not committed to any spiritual spouse, and not generally committed to their human spouses. They are committed to themselves. Having sex apart from marital commitment separates sex from true love, and treats the other person as an object to be used

But when a professing Christian finds reasons to miss worship over and over, he is being unfaithful to Christ. It won't take long for that to result in being unfaithful to the human spouse, to have rebellious children, like the parents who are rebellious to Christ.

So how does one maintain his relationship with his human spouse? He does so by being faithful to his divine spouse, Jesus Christ. There really is no other way. Our physical marriages are a reflection of our divine "marriage" to Christ in the Church. The oneness we have with Him should be reflected in our human marriages. Sex is the sacrament of marriage. "It is the outward, bodily sign of the spiritual union of two lives into one flesh."[1]

We have to learn how to recognize this spiritual adultery in our children and to protect them from it. When my son was small, there were times when he was not listening to dad, but being rather rebellious and stubborn. I would take inventory and sometimes realized that I was not spending enough time with him, so we would go on a trip, such as hunting for a couple of days. I never said anything to him about his behavior, but just spent time with him having fun. Each time we returned from such, he was a different boy, obedient and listening to dad again. But that took time commitment to my son.

Spousal love is found first in the Triune God, then in the soul of the spouse through absolute commitment. *The other person is not an object for one's own pleasure, but a person to be cherished.* The physical side of marriage is a result of all these things, not the cause, and for one to pursue it as the cause always leads to compromised fulfillment and despair.

II. Human Adultery

There are at least two ways of giving one's affection to someone other than one's current spouse and thus committing adultery: sexual unfaithfulness to one's current spouse (parallel adultery), or constantly "divorcing" and marrying new spouses (serial adultery). The Seventh Commandment forbids both. The first type of adultery is clear to most people: the married person is not to have sex with someone not his spouse, not even to give that person the time and affection that belongs to one's current spouse.

The second type of adultery is not generally recognized. We think that if we "divorce" someone in the civil courts that God accepts that, but read again Matthew 19:9 just quoted above. The Lord said that if we divorce someone for a reason that *God* does not accept and remarry that we commit adultery. A civil divorce is not necessarily a biblical divorce. In fact, today most civil divorces are not biblical. It has become common for people to jump in and out of bed with one another under

---

[1] Carroll E. Simcox, *Living the Ten Commandments* (New York: Morehouse-Graham, 1953), p. 90.

the guise of marriage. In other words, they use "marriage" to hide their sexual promiscuity. They think that "marriage" gives them a license to change spouses every few years, but the Lord's point is that such is not marriage at all, just adultery. Marriage is to be for life to one person, and it is not to be used as a license to have free sex. In those rare instances where one can divorce and remarry, it is by God's laws, not ours, for marriage belongs to Him, not to us to redefine as we go along. *He* defines both marriage and divorce, not the civil courts. Suffice it to say that God divorced Israel and then took her back (see Jeremiah 3:8; Hosea 1:9), but this was a rare exception. It is amazing to me how Christians are always trying to find the loophole in God's law so they can do what they want. (There is not enough room in this work to go into divorce and remarriage. The best work I know, having read quite a few of these over the years, is Rt. Rev. Ray R. Sutton, Th.D., Ph.D., *Second Chance*, if you can find a copy. Email me at service@footstool-publications.com, and I'll send you a free pdf copy.)

This commandment essentially says that one can have a physical relationship *only* with one's *heterosexual* spouse in the covenant of an unconditional relationship, marriage. Everything else is forbidden. Human adultery is covenantal treason to God first and also to one's spouse. Let's consider some examples of how this works out.

We are forbidden to give our time and affections to another person besides our spouse. A wife called me to meet with her and her husband. She was very upset because her husband was meeting another woman for lunch and even calling her from home. He assured me that nothing physical had happened, but he admitted what his wife said, justifying that it was all very innocent, that she had nothing to worry about. He was a Christian and loved his wife, but they just did not communicate like he did with this other woman. I told him that he was committing adultery, and he adamantly resisted the idea. He kept saying nothing physical had happened. I said that he was giving his time and communication to another woman that belonged to his wife, which he admitted, and that was in principle adultery. In other words, adultery was more than the physical act but was initiated by sin in the heart (Matthew 5:27-28).

Moreover, I explained to him that he had started the dominoes to fall, and though it was not presently sexual adultery, that was the logical conclusion. The other woman was bonding with him. He saw the point and repented.

But spiritual adultery is also revealed in the new sin for which our culture is being evangelized, which is a same sex relation. This is a classic case of the vertical (God) not defining the horizontal (marriage), or the lack of a spiritual marriage distorting the human marriage. And in Holy Scripture Christ the male is spiritually married to the Church, His female bride. Earlier I quoted James Dobson's book *Bringing up Boys* where he states that it is virtually unknown that a young man will take up homosexuality if he has had a healthy relationship with his father. Why is this so?

In Romans 1:22-23 we see that those who go into that lifestyle have first rejected God. Here is what Romans 1 says:

> 22 Professing to be wise, they became fools, 23 and changed the glory of the incorruptible God into an image made like corruptible man—and birds and four-footed animals and creeping things.

From these verses we see that the vertical (God) defines the horizontal (man). When the vertical is rejected, when idolatry is accepted, they lose definition of the horizontal so that human relationships become distorted. If you reject God and His Holy Scripture, you have no standard by which to define humanity. And the Apostle Paul goes on to describe what often happens to those who reject the Triune God:

> 26 For this reason God gave them up to vile passions. For even their women exchanged the natural use for what is against nature. 27 Likewise also the men, leaving the natural use of the woman, burned in their lust for one another, men with men committing what is shameful, and receiving in themselves the penalty of their error which was due (Romans 1:26-27).[2]

---

[2] Recall earlier (Chapter 2, V, B) that we quoted Robert Gagnon that "natural use" and "against nature" were set phrases that referred to heterosexual and homosexual behavior respectively with no known exceptions.[2] See Robert A. J. Gagnon, *The Bible and Homosexual Practice* (Nashville: Abington Press, 2001), chapter four.

But these same sex relationships do not work even on the human level because our strengths and weaknesses are completed in the opposite gender. For these relationships to exist at all, one person often has to become "feminine," revealing once again that this is God's world, and the only way to live in it is to assume His categories, even if they are distorted.

In a home, an absent father means a son does not learn how to relate to the opposite sex; and without the vertical standard of a father, the son does not understand his proper role as a male. God the Father will make the difference if He is brought into the picture in the life of a boy without a father. I know, for I was reared without a dad in the home.

Am I an exception to the study Dobson footnoted? Yes, and why am I an exception? It was not something good in me, but my mother had me in a good church all those years. I learned to relate to God as Father in church. Also, I had a relationship with her brother, my uncle, for the early period of my life. But it was the consistent mother-enforced faithfulness to our heavenly Father that developed me. And we did not jump around from church to church, but I had the security of being in one church for many years.

Suppose God is feminized, as is often done today by feminists, and suppose there are women ministers? The feminine minister relates to the feminine church, which is spiritual lesbianism. That turns things on its head, and now the vertical is misconstrued, so that it is no wonder that feminist churches or churches with women ministers have a tendency to attract homosexuals and lesbians. The male-female roles, as defined by creation and by who God is, are distorted.

Though God is not male or female,[3] He reveals Himself as "He," and it is in that authority context that children learn their proper roles,

---

[3] Both the man and the woman were originally and equally created in the image of God. It does not take both of them to make the image. Genesis is clear that each person, Adam and Eve, were not half human, but each fully human and each fully in God's image. Here is Genesis 1:27:

God <u>created</u> **mankind** in His image,
In the image of God He <u>created</u> **him**;
Male and female He <u>created</u> **them**.

to define themselves. God also defines marriage, for the Father gave His divine Son a *feminine* bride, the church.

So how can a homosexual overcome his sin? It will be by consistently, persistently, attending divine worship where the Triune God is honored as the only God, relating to God as Father, seeking to have good friends in that local parish who will love him spiritually in Christ; thus, he can learn what a biblical, human relationship truly is. This will take time, a lot of time, but persistence will pay off. I've seen it happen.

Husbands, *here is a good prescription for adultery.* You are not spending time with your wife, ministering to her, and someone where she works does. She bonds with him emotionally as he tells her how wonderful she is and spends time with her. Then she runs off with him. You must guard your relationship with your wife, learn her ways, and then seek to love her, to spend time with her.

III. Sins Forbidden

About the only evil recognized today is censorship. Porn is considered free speech, and Christians are increasingly castigated as engaging in hate speech when they quote the Bible that God forbids sexual sins. The only two sexual acts considered wrong today are rape and pedophilia, but the dominoes are falling regarding pedophilia, and there is a movement to legalize that. Apparently, what makes rape and pedophilia wrong (at the moment) is that the innocent parties do not consent.

In other words, the fact that they are wrong allegedly has nothing to do with God's law or that they are destructive of the family. Once

---

The repetition of the word "create" three times is for emphasis. The word "him" in line two is synonymous to "mankind" in line one. But "them" in line three emphasizes two distinct beings made in His image, each *equally* in that image. In other words, the "them" explains the "him" and the "mankind." The conclusion to be drawn is that there is one mankind, but two aspects to this mankind, male and female, each equally made in the image of God.

To deny each as fully in God's image is to make Christ not fully in the image of God because He did not have a human wife. As God-man, He has a *spiritual* wife, but He was fully in the image of God as Incarnate (Colossians 1:15). (Most commentators and exegetes agree with my analysis.)

again, mankind is setting his own standard, like Adam and Eve wanted to do in the garden. It is also interesting that committing sexual sins is really laughing at death and at the God who has imposed the death sentence on us all for sin. Mankind wants to proclaim that he can sin without consequences; he'll show who the real god around this world is. But let us consider the sins in this commandment.

(1) We are required to render conjugal rights to our spouses, as St. Paul stated in the passage at the beginning of this chapter in 1 Corinthians 7:3-5. I'm not going to elaborate on this but only to say that it is preventative of adultery, though not the only preventative. Also men, do not demand this as some kind of sovereign right from your wife, but be kind to your wives. And wives, do not use this as a weapon, for that is a prescription for disaster.

(2) *We husbands are not to commit adultery with our jobs.* This is one of the greatest dangers of the ministry. Once I had been dealing with a couple for some time. He brought home (this was in the late 1980s) $2,400 a week, and was also supplied with room and board. They had three kids. However, he was not spending time with his wife, but was a workaholic. He was also on cocaine from time to time. I warned him that he must quit the cocaine immediately, and we set up 24/7 accountability for him. But I also warned him to spend time with his wife. One Saturday morning he called me in tears. She had left him and the kids for a convicted felon who could barely make minimum wage. He could not understand it, but it was obvious to me. The felon spent time with his wife and cherished her. The husband cherished his job. One cannot make a marriage work when he does not give his spouse time, time to be together, time to support one another, time to listen. Time says "I love you" more than anything else. We call this the incarnational principle, for just as God came to be with us in the person of His Son, Christ, so we must spend time with our spouses also.

(3) Sex change surgery is the rage today, especially in foreign countries. A male wants to become a female, and a female submits to becoming a male. God requires us to be satisfied with who we are, and to function within our born sexuality. A male who "becomes" female is really just a man without the proper plumbing, like one who was in a car wreck and lost his masculinity. He is still the same person, with the

same personality and orientation. Suppressing the truth with a sex change won't change the basic person.

(4) Not only is adultery forbidden, but we are forbidden all other sexual sins. Scripture has quite a list of prohibitions besides the ones we've already mentioned:

- Incest (Leviticus 20:11-12, 14)
- Bestiality (Exodus 22:19; Leviticus 20:15-16)
- Pornography (Matthew 5:27-28)

Pornography has become the plague of modern culture with easy access over the Internet. At the beginning of this chapter, I quoted the Lord as saying that "whoever looks at a woman to lust for her has already committed adultery with her in his heart." Porn is the incitement of the imagination, inducing lust that the Lord Jesus forbids (Matthew 5:27-28), and is a great evil, and one that is difficult to get over. It seems to be innocuous, not hurting anyone, but these are illusions. It makes one dissatisfied with one's spouse and makes one want to engage in bizarre sex. This will destroy a marriage quickly.

Pornography involves an extreme hatred of Christian morality, often indulging in long and highly emotional attacks on Christians, the sanctity of marriage, having children, and monogamy. Those in the porn industry have given themselves over to evil, and dare anyone to challenge them.

I've seen men who've said they need to know what is out there so they can help their children or help others so they begin to gaze at porn on the internet. I had a man in a church once who wanted to "minister" to strippers, so he frequented a strip joint. I did not know what he was doing or the rationalization for it until he wanted to leave his wife for a stripper. The stripper did not want him, and he repented.

Some cannot even define pornography so they do not make laws against it and declare that it comes under the First Amendment for free speech. In Genesis 9:22-23 we have the story of Noah's son Ham who voyeuristically looked on his father's nakedness. Ham's two brothers, Japheth and Shem, took a blanket, walked backwards not to see their father asleep naked, and covered him. God judged Ham for his actions.

How much worse is it for those filled with lust not to respect the nakedness of others outside the family (exceptions would be married couples, babies, doctors, etc). Before the fall, Adam and Eve were naked and not ashamed, but part of the fall into sin is to be ashamed at nudity, with the exceptions just mentioned. The first thing God did with Adam and Eve when they fell into sin was to clothe them, not only to cover their sin, but also to establish proper, discreet, chaste morality, *to establish boundaries*. Now clothes are a large part of our makeup, every culture has them, and are to be worn in modesty, to honor others by not showing our nudity. Just as our sinfulness must be clothed in the righteousness of Christ (see Zechariah 3:1ff; Isaiah 64:6; Matthew 22:11-13, the wedding garment; Revelation 7:13-14; 19:8), so our bodies must be clothed. One of the sins of the porn industry is to show nudity, which not only plays on lust, but is also an attack on God who requires modesty (1 Peter 3:3-4), and an attack on the dignity of one another. Those who cannot blush at sin are cursed by God:

> "Were they ashamed when they had committed abomination? No! They were <u>not at all ashamed</u>; nor did they know how to blush. Therefore they shall fall among those who fall; at the time I punish them, they shall be cast down," says the LORD (Jeremiah 6:15; see also Jeremiah 8:12).

In short, the only sexual relationship allowed is between one man and one woman who are biblically married. We must wear clothes to keep proper boundaries between those who are not spouses, and to help control lust. All through scripture, shame is associated with nakedness and wrongful sexuality, but today people make fun of those who can be shamed, "men with men committing what is <u>shameful</u>" (Romans 1:27). To keep from having shame from sin, one must work hard at self-deception, inventing reasons to cover the wrong.

Thus pornography may be described as the display of one's nakedness to incite lust from someone who is not one's spouse. Some want to know how much nakedness must be displayed before it can be considered lewd. This is the logical fallacy called the "argument of the beard," which goes like this: if you can't tell me how many whiskers it takes to make a beard, there are no beards. Yet it is obvious when one person has a beard and when another does not. Because there are times when it is difficult to tell does not mean beards do not exist.

Consider the hypocrisy of NOW (National Organization of Women). When Tammy Bruce was working with them at the national and local levels, she said that they refused to engage in action against pornography or prostitution. Pornography was said to be a "free speech" issue and prostitution a "career choice."[4]

Conclusion

Here is the sum of the matter. Marriage is a spiritual institution, a reflection of Christ's love for His Church. His love is original, and our love is reflective. We are to honor Him by being faithful to our spiritual marriages. If we are faithful to our heavenly spouse, we will not commit adultery but will be faithful to our husbands and wives. Young ladies and young men, you have a very precious gift to give so save it for your husbands and wives. God will greatly bless you. **AMEN**.

---

[4] Tammy Bruce, *The Death of Right and Wrong* (New York: Three Rivers Press, 2003), p. 73. (See my comments on this book in the Bibliography at the end of the book.)

Chapter 15—Eighth Commandment: You Shall Not Steal

You shall not steal (Exodus 20:15).

But seek ye first the kingdom of God, and his righteousness; and all these things shall be added unto you (KJV, Matthew 6:33).

Will a man rob God? Yet you have robbed Me! But you say, "In what way have we robbed You?" In tithes and offerings (Malachi 3:8).

Let him who stole steal no longer, but rather let him labor, working with *his* hands what is good, that he may have something to give him who has need (Ephesians 4:28).

For even when we were with you, we commanded you this: If anyone will not work, neither shall he eat (2 Thessalonians 3:10).

Therefore if you have not been faithful in the unrighteous mammon, who will commit to your trust **the true *riches*?** (Luke 16:11).

[7] Two *things* I request of You (Deprive me not before I die): [8] Remove falsehood and lies far from me; give me neither poverty nor riches—Feed me with the food allotted to me; [9] lest I be full and deny *You,* and say, "Who is the LORD?" Or lest I be poor and steal, and profane the name of my God (Proverbs 30:7-9).

A faithful man will abound with blessings, but he who hastens to be rich will not go unpunished (Proverbs 28:20).

The soul of the sluggard craves and gets nothing, while the soul of the diligent is richly supplied (ESV, Proverbs 13:4).

The plans of the diligent *lead* surely to plenty, but *those of* everyone *who is* hasty, surely to poverty (Proverbs 21:5).

ALMIGHTY God, who by thy blessed Son didst call Matthew from the receipt of custom to be an Apostle and Evangelist; Grant us grace to forsake all covetous desires, and inordinate love of riches, and to follow the same thy Son Jesus Christ, who liveth and reigneth with thee and the Holy Ghost, one God, world without end. *Amen* (Book of Common Prayer).

Introduction

Say what you will, inveigh as indignantly as any prophet against the "unjust distribution" of things, the fact remains that your neighbor possesses certain material goods that you do not possess. It seems that God wills it to be so; if He did not, there would be no point in His Eight Commandment.[1]

Indeed, God has not ordained the equal distribution of wealth, and the government that commits to redistribution of wealth is both tyrannical and a thief. Liberty not only allows for inequality of wealth as people accumulate it by hard work and thrift, being rewarded according to their efforts, but it also should protect those who have honestly gained more. (See the parable of the talents where the Lord rewarded more to the one who had worked hard. See Matthew 25:14-18.)

Equality of wealth is a myth, according to this commandment, and the government that tries to enforce such is tyrannical. Such a government steals from the productive to give to the non-productive, which means perpetual compromise to force equality, and thus perpetual conflict.

---

[1] Carroll E. Simcox, *Living the Ten Commandments* (New York: Morehouse-Graham, 1953), p. 100.

But what is theft? It is taking something that does not belong to you without permission from the owner. This can be the theft of property, fraud, extortion, selling inferior goods, moving the boundaries of property (Deuteronomy 19:14), charging interest to a poor brother (Exodus 22:25), and many other ways.

Fraud is especially egregious. Though outright theft is bad enough, yet with fraud a person's trust is assaulted, and he feels violated, that he does not have a brain and cannot make up his own mind. I recently went to a local car dealership to price some specific cars I had in mind, and the salesman had to take me through their "game" of introducing me to the sales manager, who proceeded to lower the price each time I was ready to leave, and even said he was losing $3,000 on the car because he just wanted to reduce inventory. A third man followed me to my car, analyzing my voice pitch! I felt raped, and told them I would never buy a car there.

People who steal do not want to work; they want to get rich quickly. But one thing required in this command is that a person must work for his living, unless of course one's health is so bad he can't work. Work helps to keep us from sin. But consider this.

A little old lady enters a bank with $100,000 in cash. The cautious banker asks where she got the money. "Gambling," she replies. Then she adds: "I'll bet you $25,000 that by noon tomorrow you'll have a tattoo of the sun on your right buttock."

The banker says that he could not take such easy money from a sweet elderly lady, to which she replies: "If you don't take the bet, I'll find another bank." So the banker opens her an account.

The next day the old lady walks in with her attorney. The banker takes them to his private office and shows them that he has no tattoo on his right buttock. Then the woman counted out $25,000 in cash to the banker, while the lawyer held his face in his hands.

"What's wrong with him?" asked the banker.

"Aw, he's upset because I bet him $100,000 that by noon today you would moon us in your office."

There are better ways to make money!

The Eighth Commandment not to steal deals with the rule of property, and the Tenth Commandment not to covet speaks to the rule of desire. In this chapter, we address the rule of property. Theft is also devaluing property, not taking care of property, or that our property owns us. The last three commandments (8-10) have to do with greed. One might not think that bearing false witness concerns greed, but it is virtually impossible to steal (8th) or covet (10th) without bearing false witness (9th). With stealing, one bears false witness about a product or service, and with coveting one bears false witness to himself, engaging in self-deception. Moreover, one who bears false witness steals the truth from others and does so because he covets something.

But especially notice Ephesians 4:28 quoted above, which is the flip side of "You shall not steal," for it says to work so we can give to others. In the other words, the opposite of stealing is working, developing some talent we have so we can help others. If we don't work (assuming we're able), we rob others of the benefits of our talents.

The Eighth Commandment means we have the right to own property, to have part of the earth, as it were, to be God's faithful stewards in managing His property that He lends us for a while, to respect it and to protect it, both for ourselves and for others. This eliminates communal ownership of property, for if others are not to steal what we have, we must have the right to own it. This further means that God owns it all if He regulates it and that He can take back what is His any time.

Finally, the Eighth Commandment is opposite the Seventh Commandment. The Seventh commands us to love only one person in marriage, our heterosexual spouse, but the Eight means that we are to extend love to all people. In other words, only one person has access to your spouse — you, but all of us must be accountable to enforce against theft, at the very least by not doing it but also by blowing the whistle when we see violations.

I. Right to Own Property

It should be obvious that this commandment gives us the blessing of owning personal property, both real estate and things necessary for this life, as well as things that are nice for this life. There is nothing wrong with being rich in itself, such as Abraham, David, and Solomon were in the Bible, as long as things do not own us, and as long as we do not hoard things, never sharing with others.

"Biblical faith is land-oriented. . . ."[2] One can be free internally when he has a redeemed soul, and one is free externally when he can own property. Evolution denies the soul, saying that we are just chemicals, and the state that denies its citizens property makes the citizens dependent on the state, and thus enslaved. If a man has no soul, he cannot allege to have a personal relationship with some transcendent person (like the Triune God), and if he can own no property, he does not even have external freedom. The freedom to acquire property necessarily means inequality in wealth, and God protects that with this commandment. Liberty means inequality in wealth; equality in wealth means no liberty.

This does not mean we should be greedy and not help the poor. The Bible is full of exhortations to help the poor, and the Church is usually the first one to do so. But this is voluntary, not forced transfer of wealth by government theft.

Some of the doctrinal standards in the Protestant Reformation spoke against the Anabaptists of their day who held to communal property, having all things in common. Some went so far as to have their wives in common. Our own Article 38 of the Thirty-Nine Articles speaks against this:

> The Riches and Goods of Christians are not common, as touching the right, title, and possession of the same; as certain Anabaptists do falsely boast. Notwithstanding, every man ought, of such things as he possesseth, liberally to give alms to the poor, according to his ability.

Since Communism is unbiblical, it does not work, as seen in the former USSR that self-destructed when they stole from their people for many decades. Governments try to be the ultimate owner of all things and to regulate who owns what.

---

[2] Rousas J. Rushdoony, *This Independent Republic* (Fairfax, VA: Thoburn Press, 1978), p. 52.

But this Commandment speaks to the right of each person to own things. Does the USA honor this right? It is very mixed. To some extent it does, for we seemingly own houses, cars, furniture, and so forth, but taxation is the power to own. What is taxed is presumed to be owned by the government. Don't pay the tax, and the government will sell *their* property. What it does not own it should not tax, especially real estate. One can never be secure in his property these days, though in times past it was possible, but now each state assumes ultimate ownership of real property by taxing it.

John Locke (1632-1704) was the man that Jefferson, Franklin, and others around the time of 1776 had been reading, and he presented the idea that we have rights to "life, liberty, and *property*," which Jefferson replaced in the Declaration of Independence as "life, liberty, and the *pursuit of happiness.*" (Locke, however, had used the same expression as Jefferson at one time.) Happiness is rather subjective; property is objective. One wonders if that replacement had not taken place if we would have a different USA today with better rights to own personal property. Jean-Jacques Rousseau (1712-1778), whom many fathers of our country were reading, did not think it was a right to own property. Thomas Jefferson (1743-1826) and Benjamin Franklin (1706-1790) thought that property was a creation of society, and real property should be taxed as a way to finance government. But what the government controls the government can take away. Robert Owen (1771-1858), as we saw in Chapter 2, VIII, thought that he could create a harmonious society by the elimination of private property. But the Eighth Commandment gives us the right to own private property, and it should be the government's job to see that we keep it, not help others to steal if from us.

There was a time when a man owned his labor, but today that is not true either, for the IRS presumes to own it and thus to tax it. The government has assumed divine status, claiming to own everything in our lives, including our very lives, which it may claim by abortion, infanticide, or euthanasia.

One of the worst taxes imaginable is the inheritance tax, for this comes between parents and their covenant children, with the government assuming to be the rightful heir of every estate. The government is under God also, and does not have the right to keep the next generation from its rightful inheritance, to take away the future of a family, to destroy covenantal continuity. Government theft from its citizens is God's judgment on the culture.

II. Devaluing Property

A. Counterfeiting

One of the most subtle thefts is counterfeiting, which is the printing of money that is not backed by real money, such as issuing paper money that is not backed by silver or gold, which in turn devalues the purchasing power of our money. When the money supply is increased, goods cost more because there is more paper money to compete for the same amount of goods, which means our money is devalued. This is the true cause of inflation, not big businesses raising prices. But the Constitution is ignored regarding this, and we are now given money that is not backed and counterfeited. Who changed the Constitution to overturn its clear statement that only specie—silver and gold—was to be the basis for our money? Here is what the Constitution says:

> "No state shall enter into any treaty, alliance, or confederation; grant letters of marque and reprisal; coin money; emit bills of credit; *make anything but gold and silver coin a tender in payment of debts*" (emphasis added, Article 1, #10, clause 1).

If there were no amendment overturning this—and I don't know of any—US money is illegal. If we don't think a country can behave illegally, we think there is no law higher than it, making the country a god, but one reason the Constitution stated this was to bind the country to law so it would not become a god to make up its own laws.

The fact is that politicians love to print up money for their pork barrel projects for their constituents, for that keeps the constituents dependent and keeps the politicians in office with paid for votes. It is a power move. They promise more goodies to the poor people, print up money to cover these projects, sell the debt to foreign investors, who in turn will be paid in the future with more paper money that has also been devalued, thereby stealing from them also. At some point, this carousel will have to end, and a crash of huge proportions will ensue.

Of course, part of the problem is that those who receive these "benefits" from the government have come to expect them. Now many of them are just as guilty as the government, for they vote other people's money into their pockets by voting in politicians who will give them a free ride.

In the past, our paper silver certificates had on them: "Five dollars in silver payable to the bearer on demand." This was an acknowledgement that the note was not lawful money but that it was backed by such. The legal money was silver and gold. A five dollar bill, for example, had on it: "Silver Certificate," and also on the bill were these words: "This certificate is legal tender for all debts public and private." One word has now been changed, the former "certificate" now reads "note." A "certificate" was *certification* that real money existed, but now we just have a note with nothing behind it. Legal tender laws force us to take worthless notes, but no law is needed for people to take silver and gold.

A "dollar" was a standard of weight, 371 ¼ grains of pure silver, as construed in the U.S. Constitution and in the Coinage Act of 1792. Now a "dollar" is a piece of paper that costs a few cents to print, the same as it cost to print a hundred dollar bill.

Someone will say that our currency is backed by "the full faith and credit of the United States Government." So was the Confederate dollar. But if the Confederate dollar had been backed by silver and gold, no proclamation of the Union could have made it worthless. Can you see someone making a proclamation that on a set date that all gold and silver will be worthless? Do you think anyone would care? The only that would accomplish is to drive good money (silver and gold) out of circulation, to create a "black" market. A government can outlaw precious metals, but it cannot make them worthless. God indicted Israel for diluting the silver money with dross, such as our coinage today has had the silver removed (Isaiah 1:22). In A.D. 301 Diocletian, a Roman emperor, issued price controls over the people, but he did that to hide that the real problem was he was issuing coins that were debased, thereby causing inflation. Of course, like politicians today, he blamed big business.

And our Congress is passing a trillion dollar stimulus package, which means they think they are greater than world markets, that debt (lending to other nations) can lead to prosperity. Here is what God has said about debt: "The borrower is <u>servant</u> to the lender" (Proverbs 22:7). If we do not repent of spending like there is no tomorrow, our whole economy will come down, and the politicians will blame one another, that enemy *they created* called inflation, and those "greedy" big businesses who make "too much" profit. They promote envy of those who are productive. But they will have created the whole debacle, and they make profit by printing money, which is fraud, theft by devaluation, counterfeiting, and stealing our children's futures. Who can plan for retirement when the government is devaluating our money? One cannot save fast enough to cover the devaluations.

How much is a trillion dollars? Consider that a trillion is one thousand times a billion. If you had a billion dollars when Christ was born, spent a thousand dollars a day from then to now (January 2009), never earned a penny on your money, today you would still have approximately 270 million dollars left. Now multiply that by one thousand, and you have one trillion.

Philip Johnson insightfully states:

> . . . government has increasingly to finance its expenditures with borrowed money and to conceal its real costs with ever more elaborate financial gimmickry. A financial crisis is inevitable. By sometime not far into the twenty-first century, all the revenues available to the government will be consumed by entitlements and interest on the federal debt. To try to solve the budgetary crisis with economic policy measures is about as realistic as treating cancer with painkillers. *The financial deficit is merely a reflection of the underlying moral deficit, which is incurable unless there is a moral revival.*[3]

---

[3] Philip E. Johnson, *Reason in the Balance: The Case Against Naturalism in Science, Law & Education* (Downers Grove, IL: InterVarsity, 1995), p. 149. Emphasis added. Excellent book.

B. Ponzi Schemes

Wikipedia online encyclopedia defines a Ponzi scheme: "A Ponzi scheme is a fraudulent investment operation that pays returns to investors from their own money or money paid by subsequent investors rather than from profit." In other words, people enter an agreement to invest and make a return on their money, but they are not paid from returns on investment. Instead, they are paid when others invest in the scheme. Original investors are paid by later investors. Meanwhile, expenses are accrued; and to keep the scheme going, percentages of "return" are paid out when there was no return. Now there is less money than has been invested. What happens when everyone wants his money? The scheme collapses. What is the difference between this and a government stimulus package in the trillions of dollars being paid out with no return? This devalues all the money in the system; it is theft.

C. Taking Care of Our Property

We must take care of the things God has given us, not allowing them to be destroyed. If we squander what He blesses us with, we are stealing His blessings, taken them and Him for granted. So let us take care of our homes, cars, and other possessions, for all things are His.

Moreover, we are required to help others keep their property, which is one very legitimate function of our underpaid and often overworked police officers. If we witness theft, we must report it.

> When you saw a thief, you consented with him, and have
> been a partaker with adulterers (Psalm 58:18).

III. Property Owning Us

Do you remember the Gospel passage where the rich man built bigger barns to store all his goods (Luke 12:19-20)? It was not the productivity that was the reason for his judgment by God, but the enjoyment of the world while refusing God. This man's problem was not his riches *per se* but leaving God out. Thus he was poor toward God.

We often teach our children by example that true wealth is the accumulation of toys. And of course there is nothing wrong with being responsible and getting ahead. We all want that for our children, but if we do this at the expense of leaving God out, or just adding Him on when it's convenient, we are robbing our children of the faith, which is the true wealth.

Now I have a confession to make. I did not encourage my children to go to college right out of high school. Why? Because I wanted them prepared for life, to have a good future. I did not want them robbed of their future by some college professor who thinks it his duty to relieve incoming high school grads of their Christian faith. I wanted them to live some first, to get grounded in life and more in the Christian faith. I did not want their lives ruled by materialism. I did not want them to have it better than I did, but to struggle, to learn to live by faith, to love God above all else so they can have the best retirement — to be at home with the Lord! (2 Corinthians 5:8).

What do we live for? What we do with our time and money, regardless what our words say, demonstrates whether we are thieves or not. Those who claim to be Christians and who do not give to God His tithe and His time are severely compromising their profession of faith. Consider the man who won the largest lottery in US history, and what the property did to him:

> MOUNT HOPE, W.VA. — In his darkest moments, Jack Whittaker has sometimes wondered if winning the nearly $315 million Powerball game was really worth it. He was left with $93 million after taxes.
>
> The jackpot that was the stuff of dreams turned into a nightmare: His wife left him, and his drug-addicted granddaughter — his protégé and heir — died. He endured constant requests for money.
>
> Almost five years later, Whittaker is left with things money can't cure: His daughter's cancer, a long list of indiscretions documented in newspapers and court records, and an inability to trust others.
>
> "I don't have any friends," he said. "Every friend that I've had, practically, has wanted to borrow money or something and, of course, once they borrow money from you, you can't be friends anymore."

He still has plenty of money. And instead of retiring, the 59-year-old starts his day at 5 a.m., juggling ventures in construction, real estate, used cars, even movies. Work is the last remnant of his old life.

Winning the Powerball was a different kind of wealth that brought instant celebrity status.

Whittaker's struggles with drinking, gambling and philandering became public, and tales of his transgressions were retold with relish.

His home and car were repeatedly burglarized. At a strip club, thieves broke into his Lincoln Navigator and stole a briefcase stuffed with $245,000 and three $100,000 cashiers checks. The briefcase was later found, with the money.

Whittaker was charged twice with driving while under the influence and sued repeatedly, once by three female casino employees who accused him of assault.

In all, Whittaker says, he's been involved in 460 legal actions since winning.

His daughter, Ginger McMahan, has battled cancer for years. The disease is in remission, though she remains in poor health.

Whittaker says he hasn't been stingy. The Jack Whittaker Foundation has spent $23 million building two churches. His family donates food, clothing and college scholarships to local students, "but all the big work with the foundation is completed," he said.

Whittaker is also done with boozing—which, on his worst days, involved a fifth of vodka. He says he drank in part because he was worried about granddaughter Brandi Bragg, who shared his independent, headstrong personality and knew from a young age she wanted to run her Paw Paw's businesses.

"She was going to inherit everything," Whittaker said. "Everything that we have was built in a way that it went to her on her 21st birthday."

She never saw that day, dying at 17 after struggling with drug addiction.

He says he hired sheriff's deputies to track Bragg who hunted her down and reported her drug dealers, and he repeatedly sent her to rehab.

He remembers their last conversation, when she was packing up to move to his home. "I told her, 'I'll come and get ya. I'll come and get ya right now if you're ready to come.' "

But she wasn't. Her body was found two weeks later wrapped in a sheet and plastic tarp, hidden by a boyfriend who panicked when he found her dead.

Whittaker has little doubt as to his legacy:

"I'm only going to be remembered as the lunatic who won the lottery. I'm not proud of that. I wanted to be remembered as someone who helped a lot of people."[4]

Few people can survive riches, and so far in the history of the world since Adam and Eve, no country has survived prosperity. The Church has not done better. It survived the persecution of the Roman government, of many governments both ancient and modern, but we have abused prosperity, the blessing of God, to our detriment. So we are doing it today in the West, and nothing will change our materialism except a great revival or a great judgment, and most likely the latter.

It is the mercy of God that the Lord Jesus, that Great Shepherd of the sheep, does not give us what we ask for—instant riches. It is a rare person who can handle it. For the rest of us, we must pray "Give us this *day*, our *daily* bread," not our monthly, yearly, or lifetime bread.

Money is not the root of all kinds of evil, but the *love* of it, the *desire* to be rich. The seeming godly but actually self-deceptive desire to be instantly rich is where the problem is.

---

[4] http://209.160.2.83/photos/webarticles/lottery_blues.txt . Accessed 7/30/09.

IV. Stealing from God and Others

Consider again what stealing is. It is the *taking* from someone that which is theirs, such as stealing from a store, or the *withholding* of something that is due them, such as withholding the tithe from God, or not using our talents to work so we can help others.

I've been saying that the sins in the Ten Commandments have their vertical dimension first. It is stealing from God when we don't give to His Church, for He said that we have robbed Him in not giving our tithes and offerings (Malachi 3:8). This is where it begins, with God and the vertical.

The biblical principle is that *we sanctify our whole lives by giving the part*, the tenth, the tithe. Our Book of Common Prayer has an especially good place for giving to God in our liturgy after the sermon, after the Creed, after the reading of the Bible, and after our singing the word. At that point, it is the dedication of all our lives by giving the tenth.

When the usher brings forward the offering after the people have given and we sing the doxology, we are giving ourselves back to God by giving the part. The doxology we sing is not just a hum-drum automatic response that is a nice ritual we grew up with, but it is very significant:

> Praise God, from whom all blessings flow;
> Praise Him, all creatures here below;
> Praise Him above, ye heavenly host;
> Praise Father, Son, and Holy Ghost.

This is an acknowledgement that what we just collected is from God's bounty. And our Book of Common Prayer even makes it clearer with a verse from 1 Chronicles 29:14, which we break in half for each to say their part:

> Minister: All things come from thee, O Lord,
> People: And of thine own have we given thee.

We owe all we have and are to God, and we give our lives back to Him each Lord's Day by giving time to Him, and by giving our tenth back in money. Those who do not so give, for whatever reason they invent, indicate that they do not believe that He will supply their needs. They cannot bear to give up a tenth for fear they will not have enough for themselves. In other words, they steal from God because they do not believe He will supply. These people need Matthew 6:33 quoted at the beginning of this chapter. Here are some other things we must do to honor God by keeping the commandment not to steal.

- Misleading people to purchase items at a price that is supposed to be the sale price when they never were sold at the higher price (double tagging).
- Car salesmen steal by representing a car to be better than it is.
- We must not hoard something when others need it to survive.
- We must avoid unnecessary law suits.
- We must watch a neighbor's property and report any wrong doing to steal or destroy it.
- We must not engage in extortion, usury, bribery, illegal drug dealing, or loving things more than God.
- Some people steal time from their employer. I knew a situation in seminary where a student was promoted to be head of a department in a savings and loan because he wrote down his time honestly while all the others wrote down they left at 4:30 but really left at 4:15. The boss of that department was immediately fired and the seminary student given the department.

V. Fraud

If we stand by while watching theft or fraud taking place, that is also theft. My third major trial in my life happened in my mid-thirties when I was working at an insurance and investment firm while helping to start a church. I had checked out the firm with some older Christian business men who said it was over 100 years old and was very reliable. But I had only been there a couple of months when I discovered a fraud scheme.

I had a wife, two small children, a new home with monthly notes, and tuition for my son to pay. I had no other means of support. It would have been easy just to look the other way as the salary was good, at least at first, or just as easy to walk away without saying anything, but . . .

> When you saw a thief, you consented with him, and have
> been a partaker with adulterers (Psalm 50:18).

I apprised the other Christians who were working there what I had discovered, that some of our clients had been defrauded, that we had a moral obligation before God to try to get their money back and to stop the fraud.

Being young and naïve, I thought the hierarchy of the business would want to know and would stop it, so we went to them, but they were part of the problem. I went to an attorney general who said those kinds of things were very difficult to prove and that his plate was already full. I went to the FBI because the fraud was interstate, but they said they would get back with me, and that it was very difficult to prove. I went to the fraud division of the police and received the same answer.

I discovered that the scheme went from Memphis, TN, back to New York City, and the big boss from NY flew down personally just to meet with me and a good friend, privately, in a hotel room. Like naïve young men, we went, even though we thought we were dealing with organized crime, and perhaps we were. But we demanded to get the money back for our clients, which to my surprise he agreed to do but only over time. He came through, slowly, wanting to delay so he could continue the scheme, but we kept pushing for quicker resolution.

My immediate boss, who claimed to be a Christian, was defrauding the people in his conservative Southern Baptist church. I and two others went to the pastor and told him about the deception, that he should immediately place the man under discipline because by the mouth of two or more witnesses every fact was established, that we were three witnesses, that he should find out to whom he had sold the fraudulent investment and apprise them. But he had about 700 members in his church, the con man was liked a lot (his method of operation was to join Southern Baptist churches by walking the aisle and to use his winning personality to gain people's confidence), and he did not want to upset anyone but to "love." I told him love was defined by God's law. I got rather angry and quoted to him the above verse from the Psalm about watching a thief and doing nothing made one an accomplice. He did nothing so we left in disgust.

It seemed that nothing we did legally or morally would stop it. Then I got a brain storm. I had a friend who knew an investigative reporter for one of the local TV stations, so I went to him. It was difficult for the reporter, at first, to believe my story, but I had documentation and eyewitnesses so he decided to do a one-night story on the 6 pm news. Then as he got into the story, he would do a three-night piece, but finally as I uncovered the whole scheme, he did five consecutive nights on the 6 pm news, interviewing me.

On the Monday before the first part of the story aired, I called the Southern Baptist pastor at home and told him to watch the news, that the man in his church would be named, that it would be brought out that he as the pastor had been apprised of the situation only to do nothing. He was speechless, utterly hunting for words. Shortly after that, he lost his position as pastor. He should have been required to help pay for those who lost money in his church. Many law suits were filed against the company, and the fraud scheme was shut down. The moral light that was shown on the scheme caused the crooks to run for darkness. I think I was followed by some thugs for a while, but nothing ever happened. The Lord protected me.

(The last I knew of my immediate boss, he was serving 15 years for armed bank robbery, and his boss was in jail for failure to pay alimony, and then went to jail for a more serious crime later. I don't know what happened to the company long term. Of course, there was the finger pointing back and forth as the thieves tried to blame one another.)

VI. Defrauding the Poor

It is terrible to defraud the poor, and God will take vengeance on those who do. The worst offender of this in the USA is the government with its taxation laws that penalize the poor by keeping them poor with handouts. No one objects to helping those who really need it, but we have created a whole class of poor who have learned how to work the system and avoid gainful employment. As it has been said, if you give a man a handout who does not really need it, you feed him for a day, but if you teach him how to work, you feed him for life.

Conclusion

Commandments six through eight are especially about one's personal life. Murder is the violation of one's life. Adultery is the violation of one's family. Theft is the violation of one's property.

Here is the solution to theft. What is our retirement like? What will we say when we stand before Christ at the Last Day? Here is what we should take with us: **"Godliness with contentment is great gain"** (1 Timothy 6:6).
AMEN.

Chapter 16—The Ninth Commandment: No False Witness

You shall not bear false witness against your neighbor (Exodus 20:16).

You shall not steal, nor deal falsely, nor lie to one another (Leviticus 19:11).

You shall not go about as a talebearer among your people; nor shall you take a stand against the life of your neighbor: I am the LORD (Leviticus 19:16).

You shall not circulate a false report. Do not put your hand with the wicked to be an unrighteous witness (Exodus 23:1).

16 If a false witness rises against any man to testify against him of wrongdoing, 17 then both men in the controversy shall stand before the LORD, before the priests and the judges who serve in those days. 18 And the judges shall make careful inquiry, and indeed, *if* the witness is a false witness, who has testified falsely against his brother, 19 then you shall do to him as he thought to have done to his brother; so you shall put away the evil from among you (Deuteronomy 19:16-19).

16 These six things the LORD hates, Yes, seven are an abomination to Him: 17 a proud look, a lying tongue, hands that shed innocent blood, 18 a heart that devises wicked plans, feet that are swift in running to evil, 19 a false witness who speaks lies, and one who sows discord among brethren (Proverbs 6:15-19).

A talebearer reveals secrets, but he who is of a faithful spirit conceals a matter (Leviticus 11:13).

Let no corrupt word proceed out of your mouth, but what is good for necessary edification, that it may impart grace to the hearers (Ephesians 4:29).

A *good* name is to be chosen rather than great riches, loving favor rather than silver and gold (Proverbs 22:1).

A false witness will not go unpunished, and *he who* speaks lies will not escape (Proverbs 19:5).

From all blindness of heart; from pride, vainglory, and hypocrisy; from envy, hatred, and malice, and all uncharitableness, *Good Lord, deliver us* (Book of Common Prayer).

Introduction

Mark Twain once said: "None of us could live with an habitual truth-teller, but thank goodness none of us has to."[1]

A police officer pulls a man over for speeding and has the following exchange:

Officer: "May I see your driver's license?"

Driver: "I don't have one. I had it suspended when I got my 5th DUI."

Officer: "May I see the owner's card for this vehicle?"

Driver: "It's not my car. I stole it."

Officer: "The car is stolen?"

Driver: "That's right. But come to think of it, I think I saw the owner's card in the glove box when I was putting my gun in there."

Officer: "There's a gun in the glove box?"

Driver: "Yes sir. That's where I put it after I shot and killed the woman who owns this car and stuffed her in the trunk."

Officer: "There's a BODY in the TRUNK?!?!?"

---

[1] David Hazony, *The Ten Commandments* (New York, NJ: Scribner, 2010), p. 78. Book not recommended for most people; see the Annotated Bibliography at the end of the book.

Driver: "Yes, sir."

Hearing this, the officer immediately called his captain.

The car was quickly surrounded by police, and the captain approached the driver to handle the tense situation:

Captain: "Sir, can I see your license?"

Driver: "Sure. Here it is."

It was valid.

Captain: "Who's car is this?"

Driver: "It's mine, officer. Here's the owner' card."

The driver owned the car.

Captain: "Could you slowly open your glove box so I can see if there's a gun in it?"

Driver: "Yes, sir, but there's no gun in it."

Sure enough, there was nothing in the glove box.

Captain: "Would you mind opening your trunk? I was told you said there's a body in it."

Driver: "No problem."

Trunk is opened; no body.

Captain: "I don't understand it. The officer who stopped you said you told him you didn't have a license, stole the car, had a gun in the glove box, and that there was a dead body in the trunk."

Driver: "Yeah, I'll bet the liar told you I was speeding, too."

John Calvin said:

> The reason why I am prohibited from bearing false witness against my neighbor is because God intends for friendship to be established between men and for no one to be tormented with regard to his honor.[2]

Sometimes people disguise their false witness with pious phrases: "I'll tell you this so you can pray for him." But if we're not part of the problem or part of the immediate solution, we have no need to know,

---

[2] David Hazony, *The Ten Commandments* (New York, NJ: Scribner, 2010), p. 214. Book not recommended for most people; see the Annotated Bibliography at the end of the book.

even to pray for such a person. Gossip is cowardly, back stabbing, rejoicing in someone else's sin or ruin.

The Ninth Commandment not to bear false witness deals with the rule of speech, of justice, of reputations, of our attitudes towards others.

Let me ask you a question: When O. J. Simpson was arrested again in 2008, was he guilty? How could we answer definitively without bearing false witness since he had not been tried?

Bishop Morse and I were defendants (along with 16 others) in federal court, and we expected the government to lie against us, but one discouraging thing about our trial was not the government lying against us, it was a fellow Christian. One former disgruntled member took the stand and lied against me and others. During a break, a lady in our church asked him how many pieces of silver he got for those lies against Bishop Morse, me, and others. It was a good question. (Remember that Judas betrayed Jesus for 30 pieces of silver.) One member of our presbytery said before the whole presbytery after our arrest that the government had better things to do than to arrest innocent people. (We were all found innocent at the end of the trial.)

Opinion polls often want us to render a judgment without knowing the facts, and even if we knew the facts, it may not be our jurisdiction to judge. In other contexts (such as on a jury), we must judge. Judging is not wrong in itself. (The prohibition not to judge that everyone quotes in Matthew 7:1 is followed by other verses that tell us how to judge rightly.) The Ninth Commandment does not say don't witness, but don't bear *false* witness. Indeed, in this Ninth Commandment the importance of the moral judgments we make against one another is taken very seriously, so seriously that we must be careful not to bear false witness in saying things about one another or else we are liable to God.

Notice that this commandment is *against one's neighbor,* for we are members of one another. Every time we bear false witness, we hurt one another in the covenants of which we are members: family, church, society. Remember the poem by John Donne *For Whom the Bell Tolls?* He said that no man was an island, and his point was that when someone died in his day, the church bell would toll (ring), and people would ask who died. Donne was saying that it tolls for each of us, for a little of us dies when anyone else dies. Likewise, when we damage someone's reputation, we are damaged.

So what is bearing false witness? The Ninth Commandment has to do with truth, giving others the benefit of the doubt, guarding their reputations, and seeking to honor the God of truth. People lie usually because they have sinned or because they do not trust God with their future, so they have to manipulate matters to "predestinate" a future they don't trust God to deliver. Moreover, integrity and consistency will lead one to tell the truth. Politicians who promise one thing when candidating for office and do another after elected reveal that they have no integrity and no godly character. Finally, those who are silent in the face of injustice violate the Ninth Commandment. The silent majority is an immoral majority.

I. What Is Bearing False Witness?

The scorpion carries poison in his tail; we carry it in our tongues. One minister asked a little girl what bearing false witness was, and she said: "It is when nobody does nothing and somebody goes and tells it." That's not bad.

St. Augustine said that a lie was the voluntary speaking of something false to deceive someone.[3] This fits well with bearing false witness also. Moreover, the Hebrew means to witness falsely against *someone*, especially in court (we saw this in the Third Commandment), but it also means that one can speak falsely against *truth*.

The Ninth Commandment, like all the others, has two sides, and is stated in the negative fashion, but the positive is to be inferred by long history of interpretation.

On the *negative side*, it is straightforward: do not misconstrue the facts about someone or something. Moreover, do not use the facts to injure someone. Do not lie. Do not make up things about them that are wrong. Do not exaggerate the truth, especially with the intent to harm. One of the most consistent and worst ways to bear false witness is to draw inferences to someone's motive in a negative way, not giving

---

[3] *Biblical Illustrator* on Exodus 20:16.

them the benefit of the doubt. We do this often, thinking we know why someone did something. How can we possibly read someone's heart?

I've seen churches destroyed when people attack one another, bearing false witness, hating each other, wanting to hurt one another. This is not only destructive, but also a terrible testimony to the world. The Lord said, "By this all will know that you are My disciples, if you have love for one another" (John 13:35), but we bite and devour one another.

Then there was the young man who said to Mr. Jones that Mr. Smith was a hypocrite because he slept through the preaching while pretending to be such a religious person. Mr. Jones asked the young man what the text was, but he could not produce it, but persistently stated that Mr. Smith had his eyes closed. Mr. Jones replied that Mr. Smith had stated to him the text and the points of the sermon, that Mr. Smith had an eye condition that prevented him from keeping his eyes open in the bright light of the sanctuary. The young man had the fact correct (Mr. Smith's eyes were closed), but the reason for it went to motive, and he bore false witness.

Have you played the game Scandal where people sit in a circle? The first person is told something, who whispers it to the next person, and that one to the next, and the last person tells what came to him. It is nearly always skewed. The temptation we all face is to pass along skewed information, and to embellish it just a little each time.

We tend to jump to conclusions without sufficient evidence. William Wilberforce, who worked for years in Parliament in England to get slavery outlawed, had to endure slander in the newspapers of his day, calling him hyper-Saint Wilberforce, and worse. But he endured it, and eventually got slavery outlawed. What makes things like that so bad is that hardly one in a thousand has the discipline not to listen to media gossip, or not to gossip about one another. It takes two to slander: one to say it and one to listen. If no one listened, it could not happen. Think of all the negative ads that run during election campaigns.

Have you noticed how politicians answer questions from the media? Often, they don't; they answer something else. Or, they give an answer that is slippery, one that can be interpreted various ways. Liberal theologians have been terrible at giving lay people straightforward answers. For example, if asked about their belief regarding the Virgin Birth of Christ, they might say something like this: "Well that is a good question, and the Church over the centuries has considered this important. Yet, it is only mentioned twice in the New Testament, and there are various ways to interpret those passages. But the Christian faith is very important, and I think each person should carefully weigh the issues." Mark it down that a politician or theologian who will not answer a question in a clear manner is either incompetent or bearing false witness against the truth.

On the *positive side*, we are required to guard and support our neighbor's reputation and character. We must give one another the benefit of the doubt. We can also bear false witness by withholding some pertinent facts, or tell the partial truth that leads someone to believe the negative about someone.

To put this another way, the positive side means that all things being equal we believe one another when someone tells us why he did something. It is not enough not to bear false witness, but *we must actually believe one another* (Ephesians 4:25), especially in the body of Christ. This means that we presume one another's innocence until proved guilty. When our big trial began that I mentioned earlier, our judge said to the jury that each of the 18 defendants was presumed innocent until proved guilty beyond a reasonable doubt. And she went on to state that no defendant had to take the stand, and that no guilt was to be presumed because of that. In the beginning, it was a good display of the Ninth Commandment; in the end, she revealed extreme bias against us and helped to try the case. (But the Lord delivered us anyway.)

Someone will say that our whole culture is given to lying and bearing false witness, and unfortunately this is true. My grandfather used to say you can tell when a politician is lying if his lips are moving. Lying is a way of life with some politicians; they make a career of bearing false witness. Again, as my grandfather would say, "If you tell the truth, you don't have to remember anything."

But it is not wrong to defend oneself against false accusations. Our reputations are one of the most important things we have (Proverbs 22:1). When the early Christians were falsely accused of incest and killing their children, Tertullian responded to their defense in a treaty he wrote. Paul the Apostle defended his apostleship in the last four chapters of 2 Corinthians, and the Lord defended Himself at His mock trial (John 18:22-23).

Moreover, in a legal setting, telling the truth is paramount or society cannot function. The courts were designed to hand out justice, not to engage in social engineering with the ACLU leading the charge to reinterpret (by false witness?) virtually everything in the Constitution and in society. Courts were designed to enforce the law, not legislate it.

II. Applications of Bearing False Witness

A. False Preachers

The worst case of bearing false witness is against God, as Satan did in the Garden of Eden when he told Eve she would not die if she followed her own ethic because God was holding out on her. But continuing in the devil's practice, preachers are making a career doing just that with all the special revelation they claim to have from God, much of which is contrary to God's written word. How many times do we hear them say, "God told me," yet what they say is contrary to Holy Scripture. Can you imagine the judgment of those preachers who claim to have had a private interview with Jesus in the flesh? In one example I read, Jesus allegedly knocked on the door, came in, and while watching TV He had a private conversation with the preacher. This is bearing false witness against God and His written Word. False prophets are strongly condemned all through the Bible.

> [30] "An astonishing and horrible thing has been committed in the land: [31] The prophets prophesy falsely, and the priests rule by their *own* power; and <u>My people love to have it so</u>. But what will you do in the end? (Jeremiah 5:29-31).

So today, the pew loves to have the pulpit tickle their ears, especially with false prophecies. People will flock by the tens of thousands to be told how wonderful they are and how much money they can get if they only have enough faith.

With others today, the Bible has been turned into a psychology manual for personal success rather than a witness to the great historical acts of redemption, such as creation, fall into sin, incarnation, redemption by the cross of Christ, His bodily resurrection, and glorious ascension. Sermons have become motivational pep-talks for self-improvement, but this is not the faith. Worship services must not be about affirming *us* but affirming *God*. When we behold *Him*, we are changed (2 Corinthians 3); but when we behold ourselves, we become warped and self-centered.

One problem today is that so many preachers on the airwaves, especially mega-churches on TV, are not telling the truth; they do not preach the Gospel of the death and resurrection of the Son of God, but they proclaim health, wealth, relationships, and other cultural niceties that our culture wants to hear. The culture is trying to change the Church instead of the Church changing the culture.

B. Society

The whole fabric of society depends on its citizens telling the truth, especially in the courts. Once this breaks down, society self-destructs.

The public prosecutor is supposed to be the agent of God's justice, and the personal and forensic witnesses the supporters of the same (Romans 13:1). In the Old Testament, the witnesses had to be the first ones to cast the stones for capital crimes (Deuteronomy 17:7), so in our society the witnesses must be willing to tell the truth, even if it means someone's death.

But in a trial, we are witnesses only to what we've seen and can testify to, not to conclusions, interpretations, and personal bias. This is the way it should be with us in everyday life with one another and with those in society. We can draw no opinion without the facts.

One Christian scholar has stated that Texas had on the books at one time (still valid in the 1960s) that if a witness deliberately lied to get a man convicted for murder, the witness was to be charged with the crime. That is precisely what God said to do, for the crime of a false witness is very great.

If a society does not punish those who bear false witness, whether politically or especially in the courts, it will disintegrate, for all societies exist only by truth. What a society punishes or fails to punish reveals the real god behind that society, the morality, or lack of it.

C. Free Speech

A society that allows anything to be promoted under the guise of "free speech" is idolatrous, assuming many gods behind the many competing systems of morality. Freedom of speech is not the right of expression without consequences.

Consider an example of bad speech causing a death. Remember your history. Alexander Hamilton had denounced Aaron Burr repeatedly, and this led to the infamous duel on July 11, 1804, in which they settled their differences with guns. Did Hamilton bear false witness against Burr that caused the problem? Anyway, over the years Hamilton had become an ever increasing pious Christian after his son had been killed in a duel, and he deliberately missed Burr when he shot, not wanting to harm him. (Perhaps if we brought duels back, politicians would be less likely to make a career out of negative ads and lying against one another! Just kidding.)

III. Proclaiming the Truth

The flip side of lying or of not bearing false witness is speaking (and writing) the truth. To elaborate, all Christians, but especially Christian preachers, are required by God to present His truth, the truth of the Gospel. These verses in Romans 10:14-15 state:

> [14] How then shall they call on Him in whom they have not believed? And how shall they believe in Him of whom they have not heard? And how shall they hear without a preacher? [15] And how shall they preach unless they are sent? As it is written: "How beautiful are the feet of those who preach the gospel of peace, who bring glad tidings of good things!"

Notice the words I've put a line through so that it reads "how shall they believe **Him whom** they have not heard." It seems to me (I teach Greek and Greek scholars generally agree with me) that when the Gospel is truly preached, it is *Jesus Himself* who is speaking through such preachers. Moreover, we have a strong statement that King Jesus the omnipotent *requires* His preachers to proclaim His truth; otherwise, people are not converted. Remember the watchman of Ezekiel 33 who was required to proclaim God's warnings or be judged. This means a nation should have laws encouraging such proclamation.

But even if there are laws against proclaiming the truth of the Gospel, Christian preachers, those duly called by Him and trained, have the divine command to do so anyway.

> [18] And Jesus came and spoke to them, saying, "All authority has been given to Me in heaven <u>and on earth</u>. [19] Go therefore and make disciples of <u>all the nations</u>, baptizing them in the name of the Father and of the Son and of the Holy Spirit, [20] teaching them to observe all things that I have commanded you; and lo, I am with you always, *even* to the end of the age" (Matthew 28:18-20).

In the USA and in the West in general, for the past several hundred years we have had legal authority to proclaim the truth of God's written word, but today things are changing. The Fairness Doctrine is trying to make a come back in the USA so that if one teaches a particular point of view publicly, they must pay for the opposing view to be presented. In modern newspeak that means Christians and conservative radio talk shows would have to pay but not non-Christians. (The predictions of George Orwell's book *1984* are here, only 25 years later.) Also, Christians are increasingly coming under attack by government officials and judges saying that if we say anything against Islam or sexual sins, we are engaging in hate speech, which is bearing false witness against us. Moreover, to oppose God's truth is to be a false witness against Him, proclaiming that He is a lie while the ungodly are allegedly proclaiming truth.

Persecution of Christians in ungodly nations usually begins with regulating and then forbidding the dissemination of Christian truth. We are now at that point, which is a violation of the Ninth Commandment to hinder the proclamation of God's truth. It is bearing false witness against God and His people.

Mark it down that when a government regulates free speech against Christians that this is a frontal assault against Christians, not to mention against Christ Himself, and usually the beginning of wholesale persecution. The dominoes do not stop falling with silencing Christians, but end with full scale persecution. Such tyrannical laws are saying in effect that other points of view are legitimate but that Christianity is not. With increasing velocity, we see Christians discriminated against in the USA, while Islam, ACLU, promoters of porn and other sexual sins, especially the homosexual community, are given the right to say whatever they want. They demean Christians with impunity, calling us filthy names in public, but we must not say a word in response or face legal prosecution. There is rage against Christians, which is actually rage against Christ Himself who said:

> [18] If the world hates you, you know that it hated Me before *it hated* you. [19] If you were of the world, the world would love its own. Yet because you are not of the world, but I chose you out of the world, therefore the world hates you (John 15:18-19).

The Lord in the next verse also stated: "If they persecuted Me, they will also persecute you." In other words, it is becoming increasingly clear that saying homosexuality is legitimate is free speech, but saying it is sin, forgivable sin we must add, is considered hate speech. This is a new development in the West. But we as Christians owe them the love of Christ, not to respond to them with malice or hatred, even though they often do such to us.

When government attacks Christianity and seeks to regulate the churches, it is a direct assault against the King of kings. If they succeed for a while in silencing the Gospel (at His pleasure, not theirs), the cultural decline will overwhelm us in the USA.

Conclusion

"Truth and justice are opposed to restrictions on freedom of speech."[4] The more tyrannical a government becomes, the more it restricts free speech, for it cannot stand up to close scrutiny. Such a government does not want its lies revealed.

---

[4] Surrenda Gangadean, *Philosophical Foundation* (New York: University Press of America, 2008), p. 199.

Once a woman told her priest that she had been very bad about slandering people. For penance, he told her to go scatter some flower seeds in the grass at the four corners of the church, and then return. She thought that strange, but she did it. When she returned, he said to go back and get them. When she said that was impossible, he said that was the point. Words are like water: once poured out, they cannot be taken back again. Make them count.

What can we do if we've injured someone with our words, whether said or written? We can apologize for them, offer to make some kind of restitution, such as going back to people we've talked to and make an apology. And the offended person is required by God to accept that, to "forgive us our trespasses *as we forgive those who trespass against us."*

There is mercy at the cross of our Lord Jesus Christ. He is the One who guards our reputations and who will forgive our sins by His grace. He was lied against during most of His ministry and especially in His trials just before His crucifixion. Think of how many times you and I have stated rash words about others, and if we were to consider each word the size of a brick, how tall would the pile be? I suggest that it would be taller than the Empire State Building. But where sin abounds, grace abounds more (Romans 5:20), if we repent. It is always right to speak the Gospel to others. Be encouraged that the Lord Jesus knows what it's like to be on this planet and among us sinners:

> For we do not have a High Priest who cannot sympathize with our weaknesses, but was in all *points* tempted as *we are, yet* without sin (Hebrews 4:15).

And especially remember these verses:

> Preach the word! Be ready in season *and* out of season. Convince, rebuke, exhort, with all longsuffering and teaching (2 Timothy 4:2).
>
> Let no corrupt word proceed out of your mouth, but what is good for necessary edification, that it may impart grace to the hearers (Ephesians 4:29). **AMEN.**

Chapter 17—The Tenth Commandment: Do Not Covet

You shall not covet (Exodus 20:17).

⁴ Do not overwork to be rich; because of your own understanding, cease! ⁵ Will you set your eyes on that which is not? For *riches* certainly make themselves wings; they fly away like an eagle *toward* heaven (Proverbs 23:4-5).

¹⁹ He who tills his land will have plenty of bread, but he who follows frivolity will have poverty enough! ²⁰ A faithful man will abound with blessings, but he who hastens to be rich will not go unpunished (Proverbs 28:19-20).

Covetousness is idolatry (Colossians 3:5).

[JESUS]: And He said to them, "Take heed and beware of covetousness, for one's life does not consist in the abundance of the things he possesses" (Luke 12:15).

ENVY:

Where do wars and fights *come* from among you? Do *they* not *come* from your *desires for* pleasure that war in your members? ² You lust and do not have. You murder and [envy] and cannot obtain. You fight and war. Yet you do not have because you do not ask (James 4:1-2).

¹¹ For this is the message that you heard from the beginning, that we should love one another, ¹² not as Cain *who* was of the wicked one and murdered his brother. And why did he murder him? Because his works were evil and his brother's righteous (1 John 3:11-12).

CONTENTMENT:

Keep your life free from love of money, and be <u>content</u> with what you have, for he has said, "I will never leave you nor forsake you" (Hebrews 13:5, ESV).

[6] Now godliness with <u>contentment</u> is great gain. [7] For we brought nothing into *this* world, *and it is* certain we can carry nothing out. [8] And having food and clothing, with these we shall be <u>content</u>. [9] But those who <u>desire to be rich</u> fall into temptation and a snare, and *into* many foolish and harmful lusts which drown men in destruction and perdition. [10] For <u>the love of money</u> is a root of all *kinds of* evil, for which some have strayed from the faith in their greediness, and pierced themselves through with many sorrows (1 Timothy 6:6-10).

[11] Not that I speak in regard to need, for I have learned in whatever state I am, to be <u>content</u>: [12] I know how to be abased, and I know how to abound. Everywhere and in all things I have learned both to be full and to be hungry, both to abound and to suffer need. [13] I can do all things through Christ who strengthens me (Philippians 4:11-13).

Do not overwork to be rich; because of your own understanding, cease! (Proverbs 23:4).

My duty towards my neighbor is . . . Not to covet nor desire other men's goods; But to learn and labor truly to earn mine own living, And to do my duty in that state of life unto which it shall please God to call me (Book of Common Prayer).

Introduction

Two young brothers were at the breakfast table, and were arguing over who would get the first pancake. Their mother saw the opportunity for a moral lesson. She said,

"If Jesus were sitting here, He would say, 'Let my brother have the first pancake, I can wait.'"

Kevin turned to his younger brother and said, "Ryan, you be Jesus."

If you'll notice, the Ten Commandments begin with idolatry ("no other gods") and end with idolatry, for "<u>covetousness is **idolatry**</u>" (Colossians 3:5). Like bookends, the first and tenth commandments speak more to how we think than do the other commandments. These are commandments that governments cannot legislate against, for these are thought crimes against God; only He can read the heart. Also, they are dominating sins, ruling one's life.

Covetousness has consumed the West in general and the USA in particular, being materialistic to the core. One reason the Islamic people do not fear us is that they see we are materialists, consumed by the passion to have more toys, and consequently they know that there is virtually nothing we'll die for, no principle that is above our personal comfort. They know that like Rome of old, we'll crumble internally, and they have a long-term view. Our long-term view is the next market swing. Materialism in our society may be seen by:

- Most people in our society want to be materially rich, not rich in prodigy. So they have few children while piling up more toys. With God, riches are exactly the reverse—many children with or without money. (Islamic people are encouraged to have many children.)

- We pay our sports players millions of dollars and our teachers very little.

- Even preachers are helping their people covet with their prosperity "gospel."

The Tenth Commandment is about integrity with God, being content with what He gives us, believing that *God Himself* is all we need for life. One who covets does not value God, but values things above God. One who worries all the time is filled with covetousness, for if he were satisfied with the Triune God, he would not need to worry.

This sin especially emphasizes the sin of insecurity, for the one who covets is not secure in what he possesses (see Matthew 6:33 for the cure). Those who complain against their circumstances, which is complaining against God, are very odious to Him, for they are saying that though He planned their providence, they hate Him for it and will not be satisfied. We see this especially with the children of Israel in the wilderness wanderings, where they coveted various things that God would have been pleased to give them for the asking.

I. What Is Covetousness?

Covetousness is the *demand* to have more, more things, more fame, more sex, more power, and so forth. How much does it take to satisfy a covetous person? Just a little more. One person can desire a new car and not covet, for he leaves it in God's hands. Another person will fret, connive, and do all in his power to get a new car, even if he can't afford it; he *must* have it. One is a healthy desire, but the other is a consuming passion. It comes down to attitude, faith, and trust in God's providence. The covetous person is *not satisfied* with what he has — that is covetousness. (For a free pdf file on gambling, please send an email to: service@footstoolpublications.com)

Covetousness is idolatry, and idolatry consumes a person as he lives for his god, and covetousness rules him. He is controlled by possessions. But "what profit is it to a man if he gains the whole world, and loses his own soul?" (Matthew 16:26). This person is a materialist, living for the "good life," the life of ease. This person has nothing that he will die for, for nothing matters but things, or power, or fame. In other words, the person is consumed *in* himself, *for* himself, and not for others. His one passion in life is to have more, and he will stop at nothing to get it. But death is the great leveler, and all will go to the grave. What will we have to show for our lives? My grandmother used to work for rich ladies, and one of her ladies died. Someone asked my grandmother how much she left, and she replied: "All of it." We all leave the same amount.

Covetousness is like the cartoon someone sent me of a man calling his wife from work, saying, "Honey, would you raise the kids, I'm trying to get ahead."

Covetousness is when Achan wanted the spoils of war for himself and his family when Joshua took the people into the Promised Land, and he took and hid some valuables in his tent that God had forbidden them to have (Joshua 7:21). Covetousness is a sin that we think cannot be found out, for it is a sin of the heart, but Achan's sin was revealed.

His covetousness gradually worked his death as he tried to harbor it. "Those that would be kept from sinful actions must mortify and check in themselves sinful desires" (Matthew Henry). O what a world of evil is the love money! We convince ourselves that we are pursuing money for our family so that our children can have it better than we did. But our children need to have their faith developed, not their pockets filled.

The covetous person agrees with Malcolm Forbes:

> "He who dies with the most toys wins."

II. What Is Envy?

Envy is covetousness on steroids. Covetousness says, "You have something, and I'll take it from you." But envy says, "You have something, I can't have it, so I'll destroy it or you." Covetousness is the lesser evil, but only by degree, as it is not seeking to destroy but to obtain. Covetousness says, "I'll get yours," but envy says, "I'll smash yours."

When King Ahab wanted Naboth's vineyard in 1 Kings 21, he coveted it. And when Naboth refused to sell it to him, he was very upset. According to God's law, it was to be Naboth's property for all his generations. But Jezebel, Ahab's wife, "upgraded" the covetousness to envy when she had false witnesses testify against Naboth and had him murdered. This was destructive envy.

In 1959 when Stephen Nash was executed for killing eleven people, some who were young boys, he said before he died: "I never got more than the leavings of life, and when I couldn't even get those any more, I started taking something out of other people's lives." That's envy.

Envy is destructive:

> [11] For this is the message that you heard from the beginning, that we should love one another, [12] not as Cain *who* was of the wicked one and murdered his brother. And why did he murder him? Because his works were evil and his brother's righteous (1 John 3:11-12).
>
> Where do wars and fights *come* from among you? Do *they* not *come* from your *desires for* pleasure that war in your mem-

282 Part 2—The Ten Commandments

bers? [2] You lust and do not have. You murder and [envy] and cannot obtain. You fight and war. Yet you do not have because you do not ask (James 4:1-2).

There have been large studies written on envy, and I have one in my library. One of the reasons other countries want to destroy the USA is because we have what they don't. In the 1960s when riots took place around the country, it was because they could not have what they wanted so they would destroy, even if it meant destroying their own neighborhoods. Cain would not have Abel's righteousness so he murdered him. Murder is often envy taken to its logical conclusion.

In the James passage above, one murders and fights when he cannot have. The New King James version translates it "coveting," but from the context it is highly intensified, and I would say to the point of envy, and some of the translations have "envy." That truly fits the context.

On a national level, one person said, "Socialism is nationalized envy."[1] It is the religion of destruction (and it is a religion), wanting to rule the details of everyone's lives, thinking the government is a god, and so it will make everything equal by force. Spend, tax, and transfer payments are the order of the day, based on destructive envy, which is ruining our economy. Socialism is very militant, like envy, and is intent on the abolition of godly authority, especially in the family, destruction of private property, and especially of Christianity, which it correctly perceives is the only thing that can block its path. The movement is not new, but goes back for centuries, and tends toward self-destruction.[2] Confiscation and destruction are the hallmarks of socialism.

III. What Is the Cure?

The cure is given in the passages at the beginning of this chapter under the heading "Contentment."

---

[1] Do not recall the source of the quote.

[2] David Chilton, *Productive Christians in an Age of Guilt Manipulators*, p. 341, 1981 edition, published no longer at old address. There is an earlier edition. One of the best books on wealth and helping the poor without confiscation that I've ever read.

The cure is relaxing in God's providence for our every need, being content with what He gives us, or with what He takes away. The tongue is silent, the soul is restful, and the mind gives God thanks for all things. We pray "give us this day our daily bread," and we must believe it.

Now let's briefly look at each passage at the beginning of this chapter under **CONTENTMENT.**

From Hebrews 13, we see that we must be free from the love of money because God never leaves us or forsakes us. *He Himself* is our "exceeding great reward" (Genesis 15:1).

From 1 Timothy 6, we must not pursue riches for their own sakes; we must not love them above God, "for the one who <u>desires</u> to be rich will fall into temptation and a snare, and into many foolish and harmful lusts which drown men in destruction." It is the all consuming passion for things that will destroy us, and they lead to nowhere. We must "not overwork to be rich"! Be content with the work of the day, come home to be with your family, and the Lord will take care of your needs.

Here is the theme verse for my wife and me when we first began to date: "Seek ye first the kingdom of God and His righteousness, and all these [material] things shall be added unto you" (Matthew 6:33 KJV).

In the Philippians verse, Paul stated that he had to *learn* to be content, for this is not a natural trait. The Holy Spirit must give us opportunities to learn this, and we must seek by His grace to adjust to His loving providence.

The longer I live the more I'm convinced that we must *learn* to trust God's providence, especially for our "daily bread." We're so self-sufficient in the USA that we give very little thought to providence. We tend to think that we are self-made, that the government god will take care of us, or that we can take care of ourselves. And though we should do all in our power provide for ourselves ("He who gives you power to get wealth," Deuteronomy 8:18), yet when we've done all we can, it is God's providence that rules the day. Our problem too often is that we don't really trust His providence, or we don't like His providence.

We have so little understanding of God's providence. We may think that we or someone else is at fault, and that God consequently has nothing to do with the stressful situation in our lives. Of course it is true that God cannot be the author of sin, but in some mysterious way, He still brings good—in the long run—out of our sins and the sins of others so that "all things work together for good" in our lives (Romans 8:28).

Just think of the life of Joseph in the Old Testament. His brothers sold him into bondage. Then the boss' wife made advances to him, and when he refused her, she claimed he tried to rape her. Thus he was sent to prison. But in time God exalted him next to the king, and many years later when his brothers realized how badly they had sinned, Joseph forgave them, saying, "But as for you, you meant evil against me; *but God meant it for good*, in order to bring it about as it is this day, to save many people alive" (Genesis 50:20). He trusted God's providence.

Daniel was taken to Babylon probably in his late teens, and he refused to eat the king's food because it was contrary to the law of God. He trusted God's providence to make him and the other young Hebrew men as healthy as those who ate the delicacies from the king's table.

Christian contentment comes to us, in other words, not by raising our circumstances to meet our expectations, for that is really the satisfying of covetousness. It comes to us not by addition, by adding things to us, but it comes by subtraction, lowering the desires to meet God's circumstances. In other words, we are happy with what God does for us and with what He gives us and not angry at Him for what He does not do, knowing that He knows us better than anyone and knows what is best for each one of us. He loves us more than we love ourselves.

If you have had a nice financial estate suddenly reduced, either by the market's sudden turn, by some thief, by some unusual turn of circumstances, know that God is in it. It may be that God wants *you*, not your money, so He is seeking to remove the idol in your life. Money is not the slightest problem for God for any need, and He can cash in some of those cattle on a thousand hills that He owns, but he seeks to develop us—it is *us* He wants! Some people think that God does not want us happy, that He will hold out on them as if He were envious of their estate. But though God delights to gives us things, He is more concerned that we be holy than happy, and sometimes that means that we will be without to learn to trust Him. Charles Swindoll once said:

> I'll never forget a conversation I had with the late Corrie ten Boom. She said to me, in her broken English, "Chuck, I've learned that we must hold everything loosely, because when I grip it tightly, it hurts when the Father pries my fingers loose and takes it from me! "[3]

What value do we really put on life and what is important?

> During World War II, Eddie Rickenbacker, American's most famous army aviator in W.W. I, was appointed special consultant to Secretary of War, Henry L. Stimson. It was Rickenbacker's task to inspect the various theaters of war.

> During one tour in 1942, Rickenbacker and seven companions made a forced landing in the Pacific Ocean. There they experienced 24 terrifying days drifting in a lifeboat until they were rescued by a navy plane. After his recovery from the ordeal, Rickenbacker said: "Let the moment come when nothing is left but life, and you will find that you do not hesitate over the fate of material possessions."

So it happened to me in Vietnam. It was the Tet Offensive. Once we were being severely attacked next to the Laotian border, and many of my friends had died or had been taken out injured. I thought I would not survive. I was ordered to run for the airstrip in the middle of the jungle. We were being hit very hard by the North Vietnamese Army, and all the men in my squad had been injured and evacuated. As I went for the air strip, I had to duck under some equipment that had been blown up, and wait for it to clear. As I sat there, I thought:

> All my Army buddies have been airlifted out, and I don't know how many have survived. All my lifetime friends and family are on the other side of the world. I've had to leave behind what few possessions I have. Lord, all I have left is You . . . and, well, that is enough.

---

[3] Charles Swindoll, *Living Above the Level of Mediocrity*, p. 114.

Martin Luther stated: "I have held many things in my hands and I have lost them all; but whatever I have placed in God's hands, that I still possess."

My favorite American Patriot, Patrick Henry, declared:

> "I have now disposed of all my property to my family. There is one thing more I wish I could give them and that is faith in Jesus Christ. If they had that and I had not given them a single shilling, they would have been rich; and if they had not that, and I had given them all the world, they would be poor indeed."

But let us understand that not all coveting is bad. It is right to covet spiritual growth, to covet knowing God better, to covet one's wife or husband, and anything that is revealed in God's word that is designed for us. Indeed, Paul stated that the Corinthians were to covet the best spiritual gifts (1 Corinthians 12:31).

Conclusion

We must be content with God's providence, not complaining that we deserve more things. I don't know about you, but I want to be rich, rich toward God, and those riches I can take with me, being the *true* riches (Luke 16:11). We must covet these riches with every fiber of our beings, seeking to develop our souls for God, to serve others, to rear our children in the faith, for these are the true riches. Houses, cars, furniture, and clothes will perish, but spiritual riches cannot be taken away. Jesus said:

> [19] "Do not lay up for yourselves treasures on earth, where moth and rust destroy and where thieves break in and steal; [20] but lay up for yourselves treasures in heaven, where neither moth nor rust destroys and where thieves do not break in and steal" (Matthew 6:19-20).

Have you heard of Horatio Spafford? Here is a quick summary of some trials he faced.

First tragedy: The Great Chicago Fire

In 1871 Horatio and his wife Anna were still grieving over the death of their son. Moreover, Horatio was a prominent lawyer in Chicago, and had invested heavily in real estate. On October 8, the Great Chicago Fire swept through the city, and destroyed almost everything he owned. There was not much insurance in those days so he was financially devastated.

Second tragedy: The wreck of the Ville Du Havre

Two years later, in 1873, Spafford decided his family should take a holiday somewhere in Europe, and chose England, knowing that his friend D. L. Moody would be preaching there in the fall. Delayed because of business, he sent his family ahead of him: his wife Anna, and his four remaining children, daughters Tanetta, Maggie, Annie, and Bessie. On November 21, 1873, while crossing the Atlantic on the *S.S. Ville Du Havre*, their ship was struck by an iron sailing vessel and two hundred and twenty-six people lost their lives, including all four of Spafford's daughters.

Spafford himself then took a ship to England, going past the place in the ocean where his daughters had died. According to Bertha Spafford, a daughter born after the tragedy, the following hymn was written in mid-Atlantic.

When peace, like a river, attendeth my way,
When sorrows like sea billows roll;
Whatever my lot, Thou has taught me to say,
It is well, it is well, with my soul.

Though Satan should buffet, though trials should come,
Let this blest assurance control,
That Christ has regarded my helpless estate,
And hath shed His own blood for my soul.

My sin, oh, the bliss of this glorious thought!
My sin, not in part but the whole,
Is nailed to the cross, and I bear it no more,
Praise the Lord, praise the Lord, O my soul! **AMEN.**

PART THREE: IMPLICATIONS—God's Judgment Now

Our theme verse for nations has been:

> Righteousness exalts a nation, but sin is a reproach to *any* people (Proverbs 14:34).

I'm always hearing people say that if the USA does not repent that the Triune God will judge us in the future, but God's judgment on America is *now* . . . and increasing daily. It is all around us if we only have eyes to see. Some think of God's judgment as only cataclysmic, such as the events of 9/11/01, an epidemic, a nation destroying us, some natural disaster (earthquake, hurricane), oil spill, or financial ruin. And those can be His judgments. But what is more devastating is the increasing judgment that destroys us slowly, like the frog that gradually boiled in the water as the temperature was incrementally increased.

I have tried to present the idea in this book that there are only two alternatives, God's law or man's law, God's law or judgment. God's law is the only moral law; it is already imposed on us, and we either obey it or rebel against it. There is no neutrality.

Sometimes the patience of God is very longsuffering, but at other times He judges severely when the sin has run its course:

> But in the fourth generation they shall return here, for <u>the iniquity of the Amorites is not yet **complete**</u> (Genesis 15:16; see also Matthew 23:32; 1 Thessalonians 2:16).

God just waits for the iniquity to saturate the land, and that in itself is part of His judgment. In other words, the judgment for sin is more sin. The more a nation sins, the more it sinks into the quagmire of its own self-destruction, and everyone becomes miserable. But then God sometimes will bring a climactic judgment that will virtually destroy the nation. The same is true of individuals. The choice of the kind of judgment is His. One thing is clear:

> "To whom much is given, from him much will be required"
> (Luke 12:48).

God has blessed the USA more than any nation in the history of the world, and so He requires much from us. At one time, we sent Christian missionaries all over the world, and now African nations are sending missionaries to us — and we need them!

But since God is incredibly patient, we tend to think that we can pursue our own way with no consequences:

> Because the sentence against an evil deed is not executed
> speedily, the heart of the children of man is fully set to do evil
> (Ecclesiastes 8:11 ESV).

God's patience is like the man who kept seeing boys who were stealing his apples from his orchard. He saw them but let it go for a while. Then one day he went to their parents with pictures of what they had been doing, and then he went to the police. They paid dearly. We mistake God's patience for indifference. But His judgment is *already here* in one form, and that is the consequences of our sins, as we shall now see in Part 3. (You really cannot understand this section without Part 1, and Part 2 would be very helpful.)

Chapter 18—Judgments & Blessings

Introduction

As we consider the implications of this study, there are various ways to respond to the Lord's Ten Commandments. First, we should be grateful to God for His love and care for us to be so concerned that we "grow up" to be responsible and God-loving creatures, made in His image. When I read them, I know that a loving God has given them to me for my good, just as my wife and I taught our children.

Second, we must understand that apart from God's grace, we cannot keep His commandments, and even with His grace, we cannot keep them perfectly. This means we must run, not walk, to Christ, who had the *penalty of the law* nailed to Him on the cross for our forgiveness (Romans 6:23; Colossians 2:13-14). Once we receive His grace of forgiveness, we will receive His grace to love Him through obedience to His law.

R. L. Dabney, writing in the late 1800s, gave this illustration (from *Christ Our Penal Substitute*).[1] But some do not understand what we mean when we say that Jesus took the "penalty" of the law. Consider an illustration. Mr. Smith is hired as a salesman for ABC Company. Mr. Smith has to collect large sums of money in cash for the ABC Company, so they want a bond issued to protect them in case Mr. Smith runs off with the money. Thus, Reliable Bonding Firm signs an agreement to cover Mr. Smith. In time, Mr. Smith cannot resist the temptation so he runs off with $10,000. ABC Company then goes to Reliable

---

[1] Send email to order ($10): service@footstoolpublications.com.

Bonding Firm, who in turn pays ABC the $10,000. This was a legal agreement, Reliable Bonding Firm having agreed to assume the liability, the penalty, of Mr. Smith's sin, but the Firm would never be charged with the crime of theft. This was purely a legal transaction, not one of moral liability.

Likewise, Jesus took the penalty of the law in our place, which was death, but He was not polluted by our sins. He paid the "bond," but He was not guilty for our sins personally.

Third, the Lord Jesus spoke of His people as the salt of the earth (Matthew 5:13). We Christians have allowed our culture to nullify Christian influence to virtually nothing; there is very little "salt" to keep the USA from decaying, and like rotten meat exposed to a hot summer day, we are rotting quickly.

Now we will consider the Ten Commandments more topically, and how we violate many of the Ten Commandments each time we violate one of them.

As we noted under the First Commandment, the mother of all sins is idolatry. At every point, our culture is out of sync with God's Ten Commandments because the culture wants to make its own laws in rebellion to God's commandments. *Our culture wants to be god.*

- First Commandment: We want to be our own gods, thinking we can disobey God with impunity, but we are at spiritual war with one another and each person's gods.

- Second Commandment: We worship the creature and its images, not God, so we place undue emphasis on things, hating those who get in our way.

- Third Commandment: We debase speech and violate our word so there is no honor to God or respect to those made in His image.

- Fourth Commandment: We think we can master time and make it serve us by throwing it away, but we are judged with less time to do those things that are necessary, such as worship God and honor our families with our time.

- Fifth Commandment: We are destroying the family with lack of godly authority, and with redefinitions of what constitutes a family.

- Sixth Commandment: People are destroying their prodigy and yet hope to have a future. Abortion, infanticide, euthanasia, and murder orient us to death, not life.

- Seventh Commandment: People exploit one another with sexual disobedience and then are surprised when society is selfish and life is cheap.

- Eighth Commandment: We are given to stealing, from the least person to the highest people in the land, politicians who deceive, and take bribes, business men who promote Ponzi schemes, executives who promote false companies—and we wonder why no one can be trusted.

- Ninth Commandment: Politicians make a living out of bearing false witness, promoting negative ads against one another; hustlers with small businesses defraud everyone, and the courts are disintegrating as no one tells the truth.

- Tenth Commandment: Society thinks it is owed a living. If there is not enough money, just have the government print more of it, and call it a stimulus package. No one is content with his state in life, so people expect the government god to print them more benefits, and so our money is debased with each new printing.

We are at war, spiritual war, and we Christians **must** wake up, or we'll be the ones going to the Gulag if not the next Auschwitz, and that is not an over statement; it is the logical conclusion. Slaughter of Christians has happened in Germany, in the U.S.S.R., in China, in Vietnam, Cambodia, North Korea, and many other countries, far beyond what the Jews experienced, with numbers around 60 to 100 million being consistently cited. Christians are becoming the worldwide persecuted minority, and no one is saying anything. We must attend churches faithful to God's word and to His Gospel, then we must be faithful to God, faithful to our spouses, and faithful to our children. The line in the sand has been drawn by those who hate us, and we must stand for

Christ. We must not hate in return, but love our enemies for Christ's sake. Adding hate to hate only produces more hate, but countering with His love will stem the tide.

I. Judgment Itself

CNN reported regarding Judge Moore's refusal to remove the Ten Commandments from Alabama's state judicial building:[2]

> The nine-member Court of the Judiciary issued its unanimous decision after a one-day trial Wednesday.
>
> The panel, which includes judges, lawyers and non-lawyers, could have reprimanded Moore, continued his suspension, or cleared him.
>
> The ethics [!] panel said Moore put himself above the law by "willfully and publicly" flouting the order to remove the 2.6-ton monument from the state judicial building's rotunda in August.
>
> U.S. District Judge Myron Thompson ruled the granite carving was an unconstitutional endorsement of religion. Moore refused to obey the order but was overruled by his eight colleagues on the state Supreme Court.
>
> On November 3, the U.S. Supreme Court refused to hear Moore's appeal of Thompson's ruling.
>
> Moore "showed no signs of contrition for his actions," the Court of the Judiciary found.
>
> Moore's critics said they were *not yet satisfied*.
>
> Richard Cohen, a lawyer for the Southern Poverty Law Center—one of the groups that sued Moore over the monument—said the organization would seek to have Moore disbarred.

This is the spiritual warfare I've talked about.

---

[2] http://www.cnn.com/2003/LAW/11/13/moore.tencommandments/ (emphasis added, accessed January 2009)

I've also said that worship is *always* exclusive, which means it will not tolerate competition. There really is no tolerance by any religious person, and every person is religious. The other judges were intolerant of Moore's religion, even though there was historical precedent for the Ten Commandments, and they insisted that *their humanistic religion* be the one in public. If Moore wanted to believe the Ten Commandments in private, that would be fine, *for now*, but paganism must rule in public. The God-haters attacked a Christian man, an Alabama Supreme Court judge. They hate him and want a pound of flesh for refusing to bow to their humanist god. They wanted him disbarred. How dare a judge not consider humanistic law to be the supreme standard!

We are glad that Moore "showed no signs of contrition for his actions," for he was confessing the Triune God as Lord in the public arena, as we are required to do (Matthew 10:32-33). The other judges made a direct, frontal assault against the LORD and His Messiah, which is what God said they would do:

> ² The kings of the earth set themselves, and the rulers take counsel together, against the LORD and against His Anointed [Messiah], *saying,* ³ "Let us break **Their** bonds in pieces and cast away **Their** cords from us" (Psalm 2:2-3).

The word "their" refers to the LORD *and* His Messiah (the Father and the Son), for They are equal, revealed as one God. The word for "bonds" means God's law in Jeremiah 5:5, but in most places it means some kind of rule or binding statement. Likewise "cords" carries the idea of restraint, rulership. They don't want to be ruled, even by one who is omni-benevolent. According to Milton in *Paradise Lost*, when Lucifer was banished from Heaven, he said, "It is better to rule in Hell than serve in Heaven."

And notice the hatred for Moore and wanting a pound of flesh to have him disbarred. This is what the Lord Jesus said would happen:

> ¹⁸ "If the world hates you, you know that it hated Me before *it hated* you. ¹⁹ If you were of the world, the world would love its own. Yet because you are not of the world, but I chose you out of the world, therefore the world hates you" (John 15:18-19).

As we indicated in the Chapter 3, God's commandments are for both individuals and groups, including the family, churches, and governments. In other words, there are no loopholes in God's law that allow some special interest groups to escape His sovereignty.

But let us consider a more direct event like 9/11. Was that God's judgment? There are various ways this must be answered. First, we must consider it individually. For those individuals who died in the twin towers, it could be either a judgment or a blessing. If a person was a believer in Christ, then he went to heaven to be with Christ. Thus it was a blessing. For the individual who was not a Christian, it ended all hope of ever coming to know God through Christ; it was a judgment.

Second, for those individuals who were injured but did not die, it could be either a blessing or a curse. For Christians, in the long run God promises that "all things will work together for good to those who love God" (Romans 8:28). The verse does not say that all things are good, or that each individual thing is good, but that all things, *together*, will work out in the end for the good of God's people. If they bear these pains patiently, God will bless them with inner peace, and He may use their quiet confidence to convert others.

For non-Christians who have suffered, we have to wait to see if God will use the 9/11 events to bring them to Himself, or if they will blame God, never coming to know Him through Christ.

Third, for the nation as a whole, it could be either a blessing or a judgment. If people would wake up, realize how short life is and that we have turned from God, confess their sins to Him, trust in the death and resurrection of Christ who died for our sins, then it would become a blessing. But if the nation hardens itself against God, then we will continue to slide increasingly into more judgment. But it is at least a wakeup call for the USA to get right with God, and the number of prayer services in the week after the event was phenomenal. Consider what the Lord said about such events:

> [4] "Or those eighteen on whom the tower in Siloam fell and killed them, do you think that they were worse sinners than all *other* men who dwelt in Jerusalem? [5] I tell you, no;

but unless you repent you will all likewise perish" (Luke 13:4-5).

But we forget too soon. In this chapter, therefore, we shall consider both individual and national judgment, but especially national.

II. Who Is Lord, Caesar or Christ?

In Chapter Three we saw that God's law was for the nations, for the ungodly, and for Christians. Let us take a closer look at the nations.

In Psalm two, we see the nations rebelling against the LORD and His Messiah, but God rules over them through His Messiah. Notice that the Psalm is in four stanzas, and reveals that *God's law is for the nations* of the world. In the first stanza, the nations rebel against the Lord and against His Messiah. In the second stanza, God laughs at such rebellion, for He is absolutely sovereign, and has installed His Messiah as King of the world. In stanza three, the Messiah speaks, saying that the Father has given Him the nations to rule. In the final stanza, the nations and leaders are commanded to repent, to kiss the Son, less they perish. Remember that this Psalm was written by King David almost 1,000 years before Christ came.

> [1] Why do the nations rage, and the people plot a vain thing? [2] The kings of the earth set themselves, and the rulers take counsel together, against the LORD and against His Anointed [Messiah], *saying,* [3] "Let us break Their bonds in pieces and cast away Their cords from us."
>
> [4] He who sits in the heavens shall laugh; the LORD shall hold them in derision. [5] Then He shall speak to them in His wrath, and distress them in His deep displeasure: [6] "Yet I have set My King on My holy hill of Zion."
>
> [7] "I will declare the decree: The LORD has said to Me, 'You are My Son, today I have begotten You. [8] Ask of Me, and I will give *You* the nations *for* Your inheritance, and the ends of the earth *for* Your possession. [9] You shall break them with a rod of iron; You shall dash them to pieces like a potter's vessel."

¹⁰ Now therefore, be wise, O kings; be instructed, you judges of the earth. ¹¹ Serve the LORD with fear, and rejoice with trembling. ¹² Kiss the Son, lest He be angry, and you perish in the way, when His wrath is kindled but a little. Blessed are all those who put their trust in Him. (Psalm 2)

This Psalm shows there is spiritual warfare regarding who rules the world. The nations of the earth claim that they will rule, and so they rebel against God the Father and His Son, but the Father responds that He has installed His King, the Son, and that the nations must repent or be destroyed. Repent means to turn from sin, and in this Psalm, written about 900 years before Christ came, sin is rebellion against the Lord and His Messiah, which in the Psalm is the Father and the Son.

We see the same Messiah as Lord in the New Testament. Consider Romans 10:9:

> If you confess with your mouth <u>Jesus as Lord</u> and believe in your heart that God has raised Him from the dead, you will be saved.

Why did the Apostle Paul choose the expression "Jesus as Lord"? Was there something in Paul's culture that needed to be addressed? The history of the expression "Jesus as Lord" is very enlightening.[3] The Roman emperors Augustus (31 B.C.-A.D. 14) and Tiberius (A.D. 14-37) rejected the expression "Lord." But Caligula (A.D. 37-41) accepted it. The Roman Caesar, Nero (A.D. 54-68), under whom Paul was executed, is described in an inscription as "Lord of all the world." The title "Lord" was very common both of Nero and of many Roman emperors subsequent to him. In fact *the same Greek grammatical construction* "Nero as Lord" is used in writing on the papyri (paper) and on ostraca (pottery) of Nero's time. Once a year, all people under Rome's authority were required to offer a sacrifice and confess "Nero as Lord." "It was

---

[3] The history is from: Adolph Deismann, *Light from the Ancient East* (Grand Rapids: Baker Book House, 1978), pp. 350-357; Colin Brown, *The New International Dictionary of New Testament Theology* (Grand Rapids: Zondervan, 1971), 2:511-515; C. E. B. Cranfield, *The International Critical Commentary: The Epistle to the Romans* (Edinburgh: T. & T. Clark, 1979), 2:526ff.

against such a religious claim, which demanded so much of the burdened conscience, that the Christians turned and rejected the totalitarian attitudes of the state."[4]

Here is the point. The Roman emperors did not mind its citizens worshipping any god they chose as long as *once a year they proclaimed the Caesar as the ultimate Lord,* meaning that Caesar was the Lord of lords. And the emperors did not think of the divine title Lord without the implication of obedience, for if this had been so, why did they murder so many Christians for refusing to worship them? The ultimate lawgiver had the right to demand obedience over all other lawgivers. Caesar claimed ultimate lordship, ultimate obedience, and thus the right of absolute obedience, which directly conflicted with the authority of Jesus. Many centuries before Christ came, Daniel wrote:

> [20] Daniel answered and said: "Blessed be the name of God forever and ever, for wisdom and might are His. [21] and He changes the times and the seasons; He removes kings and raises up kings; He gives wisdom to the wise and knowledge to those who have understanding" (Daniel 2:20-21).

Our own government is making the same claim today, not caring what god one worships as long as its citizens give ultimate allegiance and confession to the federal government. Thus Jesus has no place in the public arena, in political elections, in government, in our schools, in the officials we elect, in the laws of sexuality and abortion, or in the forced redistribution of wealth through taxation. It is allegedly a confusion of Church and state for the Church or for Christians to "force" their morality on society, but it is acceptable for the secularists to force their morality on the Church. Jesus must be confined to an ever decreasing private Church. It is politically correct to be religiously "neutral" about all religions except Christianity. One can bash Christians and Christianity with approval. The reason Christians are hated is still the same: We recognize no ultimate King but Jesus, which means the government and the public ethics of abortion, sexual disobedience, etc, can be judged, which is intolerable today. The ACLU insists that the

---

[4] *New International Dictionary of the New Testament Theology*, 2:511.

Jesus God stay out of the public arena under the mistaken guise of separation of Church and state, misinterpreting the Constitution to mean freedom *from* religion rather than freedom *for* religion. But the Constitution itself is under, not over, King Jesus and His law. Christians are allowed, for now, to confess Jesus as Lord privately but not publicly. "There is nothing new under the sun." England is considering legislation to criminalize Christian practice in public while they have appointed a Muslim as the head of religion in a government post in England.[5] This is all out spiritual warfare as given in Psalm two above. Recall what we said in Chapter 4 that Christ is the head of all chains of authority. Only He is Lord of lords.

One thing the world hates about Christianity is that there is a God over the government who holds it accountable. We proclaim the one and only true God, the Father and the Son and the Holy Spirit, and this transcendence is not tolerated. It would be fine if we stated that Jesus was Lord to *us*, that we believe it for *us*, that others can with equal assurance confess some other god, that sincerity is all that is required.

The issue, however, is not sincerity but *truth*. The media who challenge Christians that others are just as sincere in their beliefs as we are in ours so why aren't we tolerant, completely miss the point. We are tolerant personally, and we are non-violent, loving our enemies, but we are lovingly intolerant regarding the truth of Holy Scripture. Jesus is the only way to God because He said so: "Jesus said to him, 'I am the way, the truth, and the life. No one comes to the Father except through Me' " (John 14:6). And this salvation is free for the asking, so why would one turn down a free gift of such magnitude just because it is the only gift that brings salvation. It is unimaginable to say, "I reject the gift because it is the only one."

III. What Composes a Nation's Soul?

The answer is easy:

> Righteousness exalts a nation, but sin is a reproach to *any* people (Proverbs 14:34).

---

[5] http://downloads.cbn.com/cbnnewsplayer/cbnplayer.swf?aid=9425

Righteousness is from God Himself and His law. Righteousness is also the Gospel of Christ. Recall we have said that a nation's (or individual's) law reveals its true God. We have had a complete change in the USA from an orientation to the Triune God and His law to paganism and our own law. Consider now our culture's religious beliefs. (Remember there is no sacred/secular distinction with God; Christ is Lord of both.)

The one true *creator* is evolution, which is the god of chance. The god of chaos rules.

The *goddess* we are to worship is the earth, as Nietzsche stated,[6] for she brought us forth. Thus we have extreme environmentalism offered as a sacrifice to her.

The *moral law* is whatever the pseudo-intellectuals force on us through the ACLU in the courts, and whatever the power mongers in Washington decide is politically correct.

The *churches* are the public schools where the new citizens learn to worship chaos, learn the new morality, and learn about the latest messiah image, to sing his praises (as was done recently in New Jersey by grade school children to Obama), but biblical morality is forbidden. These new citizens are turned into "sheeple," people who are sheep to be sheared. They can't read and write, but they can take orders.

The *sacraments* are abortion and sexual promiscuity. Nothing is more sacred to many than the right to kill their unborn babies (or born babies), and like baptism can only be performed once per individual who receives it. You can only die once. Unlimited sexual promiscuity is the other sacrament, and like Holy Communion in the Church it may be practiced repeatedly.

Worship is directed toward the politicians who have the "divine" power to give us new revelation about new morality, and who give us "this day, our daily bread" by printing money into existence. Many politicians exist for power.

The *preachers* are the trend setters, such as the media who promote politically correct gods, Hollywood, terrible music that engulfs our young, and the high profile pseudo-intellectuals whose personal life

---

[6] Alistar Kee, *Nietzsche Against the Crucified*, p. 102.

styles are atrocious. University professors think it is their duty to rob young people of their reasoned Christian faith, only to give them an irrational, blind faith. Moreover, there is nothing so decadent that we can't find some professor to justify it—even cannibalism.

The *message* is science, for it is the only truth, but it must be guarded from "false prophets," such as intelligent design scientists. Science is inerrant.

Purpose or meaning in life is given up as death is now the orientation of society, not life.

The *message* is eat, drink, and be merry for tomorrow we die.

As I said above, the preachers are the media that have a voyeuristic preoccupation with evil. It seems as if the media are in competition to see who can report the most filth, with the liberal media attacking Christians and Christianity, seeking to crucify us before all, revealing their true hatred toward Christ and the righteousness of God's written Word. Notice how National Geographic will blast Christianity at sacred days, such as Christmas and Easter. Now "reality TV" is presenting news as it is being made and thus fulfills one's desire for sin without having to wait for what little censorship remains. One can see it as it happens.

You can have sex in public. You can masturbate in public. You can cross dress in public. You can engage in verbal filth in public. But you can't pray in public because it is too offensive! You can't even say Merry *Christ*mas in public! How utterly ridiculous! Our culture is consumed with little antichrists. Indeed, the more the logical conclusion of denying the Triune God is pursued, the more man is devalued.

As a result of this new society of Nietzsche, our churches are caving in to what our culture wants, giving up belief for behavior modification; our families are being redefined as mobs; no one knows what true morality is or cares; our children are given to drugs and death since they have no hope; the Triune God is scorned; and God's judgment hangs over us like the sword of Damocles. When will the thread break?

This self-destruction is not a haphazard, accidental conversion of the USA from Christian to pagan, but it is planned, thought out, systematic deconstruction of the greatest country in the history of the world. I do not believe in conspiracy theories, at least not sustained over centuries, but there is a mind behind this, a dark, ungodly, very powerful mind that hates the Triune God, that is orchestrating this destruction, and thus his human minions hate this true God as seen in their outspokenness against Him. Like father, like son. That mind is Satan, for how else can we explain so many different people pursuing the same goal at the same time who do not know one another? How is it that Islam is mobilizing against Christians worldwide? How can we explain the internal hostility toward anything holy and righteous in our country, in other words, anything Christian? How is it that Jesus is being attacked so vehemently as not the only way to God, as Oprah Winfrey (and others) has done on national TV? Why is it that she (and others) has especially attacked the cross of the Lord Jesus as being nonsense, or just a symbol of each one of us, rather than the only way to have forgiveness of sins? At each point, a vital part of the Gospel itself is being attacked. Who is directing these common attacks at the heart of the Gospel? They are being directed by the devil, "having been held captive by him to do his will" (2 Timothy 2:26). It is not so much the USA that is the problem, but God is seeking to discipline the Church within the USA (and the West). *We Christians are the problem*, for we have allowed the darkness to come in. We must repent:

> If My people who are called by My name will humble themselves, and pray and seek My face, and turn from their wicked ways, then I will hear from heaven, and will forgive their sin and heal their land (2 Chronicles 7:14).

The answer is the Gospel, for only Christ can overcome this rebellion. Satan is the dumbest creature of all, for here is essentially what he has thought from the beginning:

> "Christ is omnipotent. He has created all things. I cannot hurt Him. . . . Yes, I think I can take Him."

Amen.

Chapter 19—God's Judgment is Now . . . Death Wish

Introduction

Why does the West in general and the USA in particular have such a fascination with death? It is difficult to estimate the moral evil that was unleashed on the West with the publishing of Charles Darwin's *Origin of Species*. Though evolution was not a novel idea, having been around in some form for a couple of millennia or so, yet the way Darwin presented it, and with the West already in decline and looking for a way to deny the Triune God, the book gave the world its excuse to deny God.

This book you are reading is not about the scientific evidence of creation versus evolution, and the details of technical areas are beyond my expertise. Yet I studied electrical engineering for three years in college (1963-66), and I dearly love technical matters. I'm a geek, fixing my own computer and doing hardware and software maintenance on it. I used to program in dBase 4 for small, stand alone businesses. At times, I read a lot in the area of science and the Bible, from both Christians and non-Christians, but I'm not a fundamentalist, whatever that may mean. In college I almost lost my faith to evolution, but once I read a book by an evolutionist admitting to many evolutionary assumptions that could not be proved (written in 1960 and quoted in Chapter 1, "I. Origin of All Things"), and read creation works that did prove their points, I've never looked back. (See the Annotated Bibliography at the end of this book for a few works in this area.) I also pursued (but did not finish) a master's degree in philosophy after my seminary days, so I like to read it also. I've read the most in Nietzsche, but I also read Christians in philosophy. My point is that I will give you reasons (hopefully good ones) why we are in such a mess in the West.

I. Orientation to Death

A. Can't Define Evil

As we saw earlier, when a nation loses its vertical orientation to the Triune God, it loses the definition of evil. Part of man's rebellion is pretended deity, that we can define ourselves and define our own ethics apart from God. We are now like those in the book of Judges where the people were being defeated by enemies from outside Israel and also had civil war internally. The last verse of the book truly describes their degeneracy: "Everyone did what was right in his own eyes" (Judges 21:25).

B. The Only Alternative

So what happens when a nation can't define evil? It turns from God who is life to the only alternative—*death*. Would you think that a nation today would be too civilized to make child sacrifices? In Ancient Israel before they entered the Promised Land, God warned them not to offer their children to Molech or other false gods:

> Any one of the people of Israel or of the strangers who sojourn in Israel who gives any of his children to Molech shall surely be put to death (Leviticus 20:2).

> And you shall not let any of your descendants pass through *the fire* to Molech, nor shall you profane the name of your God: I am the LORD (Leviticus 18:21).

The god Molech was represented by an iron statue that stood vertically with fire in its belly, it had arms and hands that extended out, and the head of a bull. A father would burn his child to death in honor of this god.

Then after Israel had been in their Promised Land for some generations, they began to offer their children to a false god, "to burn their sons and their daughters in the fire" (Jeremiah 7:31).

But this is precisely what we're doing here in the USA. We offer our children in the abortion death mills to the gods of personal convenience (not right time to have a baby, and I have a career), embarrassment (what would others think of getting pregnant when not married), and money (I don't have the money to raise a child). We kill our most innocent citizens for the flimsiest moral reasons, but we don't have enough moral principle to die for a cause in a war. In other words, we kill our babies but do not want to defend our nation against aggression. This is masochism, God's judgment, and orientation to death. Sin always leads to self-destruction (Proverbs 11:5).

We make Hitler look like a saint because he "only" killed six million Jews (besides the Christians and handicapped that we don't hear much about and besides the millions in his war on both sides), but we've now (2010) killed over 50 million babies and counting since *Roe v. Wade* in January 1973. And when we murder a person made in God's image, it is striking out at God Himself (Genesis 9:6). Each time we kill a child we lose the blessing of productivity and talent of that child. This is judgment.

And make no mistake that there is a sense in which we're all guilty, for we have elected officials who have approved this genocide. And when we see people being led to slaughter, and we do nothing, we partake of their deeds:

> [11] Rescue those who are being taken away to death; hold back those who are stumbling to the slaughter. [12] If you say, "Behold, we did not know this," does not he who weighs the heart perceive it? Does not he who keeps watch over your soul know it, and will he not repay man according to his work? (Proverbs 24:11-12 ESV).

This passage is part of the *law of bystander* in Holy Scripture, which says that if we do nothing regarding evil, we are actually supporting it. This is sin of omission. Inaction is action,[1] and God will require us to give account for inaction. We participate in this guilt if we help to elect those who will continue the baby killing, considering money and economic benefits more important than the lives of babies. All it takes for

---

[1] I got this from a young man who gave a speech on abortion. I don't recall his name.

evil to triumph is for godly people to do nothing. God help us. This is judgment.

The consequences are already having their toll on us, such as fewer people who populate the USA to grow our nation. The more people we have, the more productive we can be, and now we're facing the consequences of baby boomers reaching their retirement with few to take their place in the market. God said to fill up the earth with people, but we are destroying people at the rate of one and a half million per year, not counting the generations they would have produced in turn.

Moreover, this orientation toward death is seen in the huge illegal drug industry that has infected our nation. This is the message of the movie *No Country for Old Men*. It shows how the entrance of the drug trade has unleashed an evil that we are incapable of managing. No one cares for anyone else so we exploit one another to get what we can. Human lives take a back seat to making money by selling drugs. The only way to cleanse the land of this death is to come to God through Christ, and to repent of our sins, but public schools are teaching our children the ethic that makes them vulnerable to drugs. The illegal drug problem will not be solved until the hearts of the people are not oriented to living for now and for pleasure, but to the future and to God.

Judgment is also seen in the morning-after pill that kills the baby. Thus one can have sex and kill the baby (murder), all in 24 hours.

We see death in infanticide with the killing of babies after birth, such as some death mills aborting children alive, only to allow them to die alone without treatment as they gasp for air. Then we have euthanasia with the killing of adults, such as Terri Schiavo, and only God knows how many others. Ten years ago Oregon was the first state to legalize physician-assisted suicide. Here is another state to do so:

> On Election Day 2008, 58 percent of Washington voters approved a measure allowing terminally ill adults to obtain lethal prescriptions if they are deemed competent. Just two states away, a judge in Montana ruled in early December [2008] that physician-assisted suicides are legal in the state.[2]

---

[2] *Christianity Today*, March 2009, p. 16.

Some countries allow physician-assisted suicides, such as the Netherlands, Belgium, and Quebec. One problem with these suicides, besides the inherent immorality, is that relatives and "friends" will manipulate the process to have someone killed (murdered) to get their money.

II. Moral Decline

This is not a detailed book on ethics to the non-Christian but is designed to awaken Christians to their obligation to God, to one another, and to obey God's law. I've not delved into ethical theory[3] in detail, just enough to make some points. But now we must ask how we have come into an orientation to death and to such a despising of God's Ten Commandments.

A. Darwin and Eugenics

When Charles Darwin published his *Origin of Species*, the West was ready to be rid of the Christian God, for reasons that we shall not consider in this book.[4] But consider the beginning point of Darwinism: everything began with molecules in motion. From pure matter, just raw physical material, everything else has come. Life came from non-life; order came from chaos; humans came from animals, and so on. There is no God, no intelligence, no design, just blind, random chance. (See Chapter 1, "I. The Origin of All Things.") Once this theory was accepted, here is what has followed.

The Christian ethic was completely rejected for evolutionary ethics. This further meant that metaphysical (or transcendent, or any person outside creation, or any standard of morality from outside the physical) implications were summarily denied. There is only the physical, naturalistic materialism. If everything is nature, whatever exists is the way it

---

[3] Such theory would be deontological ethics, utilitarian ethics, and so on. See books in the Bibliography at the end of this book.

[4] Read Alister McGrath, *The Twilight of Atheism*, and see my annotated bibliography. Moreover, I would strongly urge you to read Francis Schaeffer's trilogy: *The God Who Is There, Escape from Reason, He Is There and He Is Not Silent*, and Schaeffer has said to read them in that order. I would especially recommend C. Gregg Singer, *A Theological Interpretation of American History*.

ought to be, which means homosexuals are born that way. (This is, of course, a metaphysical/religious statement.)

This in turn meant that Darwinists were monists, which meant the rejection of mankind as body and soul, but he was only body, chemicals, nothing more. The mind of man was just chemicals in some kind of reaction to one another. Moreover, those who would improve mankind by moral persuasion or by the gospel were beating a dead horse, as they assumed that something was transcendent over mankind, that man had a soul and character that could be improved, but that is wrong. In this view, humans are only a vertical column of chemicals.

Next was the idea that "morality" was a product of these chemicals, and that "bad" morality was a product of the wrong chemicals. The only way to "improve" the race was to change the chemicals, and one could only do that by breeding. If one could get superior people with superior genetic code to breed, that would produce "better" people with the "right" ethic. In other words, whatever genetically improved the race was "good," and whatever would not promote the species was "bad." One must eliminate the inferior from reproducing. Thus, one could be born an alcoholic, a murderer, drug addict, homosexual, or whatever. Those undesired would be eliminated by a eugenics program, for ethics was only genetic. Change the genetic breeding stock, and you change the ethics.

This is where eugenics came in, the study of reproduction. In the late 1800s and early 1900s, eugenics was being widely studied by the intellectuals in the USA and in Europe, especially in Germany. (One must read Richard Weikart's excellent historical treatment of this movement in his revealing book, *From Darwin to Hitler*.) Books and papers were being written by the hundreds on eugenics. There needed to be some way to control those who reproduced, and several ways were proposed.

One way was by birth control, which was fairly new at the time. Another way was by sterilizing the "inferior" people of the population, which was done in Germany to some extent. Then Margaret Sanger in the USA founded Planned Parenthood with the idea of eliminating minorities through abortion. She said: "More children from the fit; less from the unfit—that is the chief issue of birth control."[5] It is no wonder that many abortion mills are located in minority neighborhoods.

Who would control all this: the elite, of course, the self-appointed intellectuals, those who were the "fittest" and had the money to make things happen. This is the way it always is. You know the golden rule, don't you? Those who have the gold make the rules.

We can see the great change that took place in the West and in the USA with the rise of Darwinism. Not all humans have the same value. Those with Down Syndrome are less valuable that those without it, for only the survival of the fittest should be allowed. In this view, people are not created equally in God's image, but there are degrees of humanity, some worthy to live, others worthless to die. Peter Singer who teaches ethics at Princeton even states that people with brain problems or in a coma should be eliminated, like Terri Schiavo. Those less fit must be eliminated or the progression of the human race by eugenics will be hindered, and why not help evolution along, now that we have the intelligence to do so, by breeding good stock with good stock. Ernst Haeckel, an intellectual who wrote prolifically about eugenics in the early 1900s in Germany, said:

> The value of our human life appears to us today, on the firm foundation of evolutionary theory, in an entirely different light, than it did fifty years ago. . . . Personal individual existence appears to me so horribly miserable, petty, and worthless, that I see it as intended for nothing but for destruction.[6]

Moreover, since mankind was deemed to come from animals by evolution, there is no qualitative difference between man and animals; the value is the same. Sometimes I hear Christians ask why the abortionists are not convinced that life begins at conception and therefore should be protected, but perhaps from this summary of what has happened to us in the West we can see that they don't care. Human life has no value to them. We could (and have) given sufficient proof that life

---

[5] Richard Weikart, *From Darwin to Hitler*, p. 135. For an excellent work on Margaret Sanger and Planned Parenthood, you must read George Grant, *Grand Illusions: The Legacy of Planned Parenthood*.

[6] Ibid., p. 76.

begins at conception, but to these barbarians human life has no value. We are just another animal, being related to animals as ancestor to prodigy, one chemical soup giving rise to another chemical soup.

Science is considered their god, but not objective science, just science as a religion. They speak of evolution as the sure results of science, but though there is microevolution (variation within a species such as Chihuahua to Great Dane), yet macroevolution (the creating of new species) is a myth. There is no such thing as *the* missing link; there are millions of them. There are no "dats" around, a cross between a dog and a cat. (See my bibliography for good books refuting evolution.)

Evolution is not science; it is religion with all the zeal of any fanatic. The adherents will persecute any who deny their faith. For a prime example of this, see two sources. (1) Ben Stein put out *Expelled: No Intelligence Allowed*, which is a documentary demonstrating how much bias and hate there is toward Christian academics who do not sign off on the confession of evolutionary faith. They are not being hired, or if already hired, then fired. (2) Atheist Richard Dawkins is the current evangelist for atheism, his latest installment being *The God Delusion*, which is a pseudo-intellectual work that has almost no scientific argument in it but is mostly name calling. Alister McGrath (who has Ph.D. in molecular biophysics and another in historical theology, formerly an atheist) calls Dawkins's work atheist fundamentalism. He quotes a senior atheist scientific colleague at Oxford regarding Dawkins: "Don't judge the rest of us by this pseudo-intellectual drivel."[7] Here is one example of Dawkins fundamentalism and outlandish name calling:

> The God of the Old Testament is arguably the most unpleasant character in all fiction: jealous and proud of it; a petty, unjust, unforgiving control freak; a vindictive, blood thirsty ethnic cleanser; a misogynistic, homophobic, racist, infanticidal,

[7] Alister McGrath, *The Dawkins Delusion* (Downers Grove, IL: IVP Books, 2007), p. 51.

genocidal, filicidal, pestilential, megalomaniacal, sadomasochis-
tic, capriciously malevolent bully.[8]

If that is the best that atheism can do, I can rest in the secure knowledge of creation and of the resurrection of my Lord and Savior, Jesus Christ.

Did you ever wonder why those in political power have such a fixation on abortion, why they support it as if it were a god? The fact is that it is a god, the eugenics god that can change who breeds and what the human species will look like in the future. Some have even gone so far to say that the right eugenics, the right breeding, would eradicate crime from society. If we are just genes, then the "crimes" we do are a product of our breeding. Straighten out the reproduction, and crime will go away. Thus, controlled evolution is viewed as an alternative form of salvation. One way to eliminate bad genes, so the theory goes, is by putting abortion mills in minority neighborhoods.

B. Nietzsche and Death

Moreover, consider the contribution of Nietzsche at this juncture, who died in 1900. Nietzsche wanted to take evolution very seriously so he said we should be able to kill with no conscience, just as nature does. There is nothing transcendent to nature; death is a large part of what nature is about, improving species by death and reproduction through the survival of the fittest; thus we should understand the implications of these things. There is no Christian God; He is now dead. There is no morality, just interpretations. Now that God is gone, there is no truth, so we must have "the revaluation of all values." We must eliminate all Christian vestiges from our societies, to stop fooling ourselves that there is something when there is nothing. Each individual is his own god, his own morality, and whatever promotes this is good, and whatever challenges this is bad. Nietzsche wanted to rid us of the idea of morality as submission or obedience, for there is nothing above us. We should embrace our animal instincts to survive, such as aggression, which is what we see the animals doing.

---

[8] Richard Dawkins, *The God Delusion* (New York, NY: First Mariner Books, 2006), p. 51.

Think how evolution and death go together. Evolution speaks of the survival of the "fittest," which means the weak must be eliminated. Thus abortion has always been aimed at the "inferior" minorities to eliminate them. Nietzsche[9] drew the conclusion from evolution that the weak should be eliminated, and especially that they should not be pitied, for pity is weakness. Christianity supports the weak and has mercy or pity on them, which Nietzsche despised and found contemptible.

In fact, the law of the survival of the fittest demands that we do not have pity or exercise compassion on the weak, such as those with handicaps. Evolution eliminates these in nature, and so should we. If we did not spend so much time and money on helping the weak but in promoting the strong, mankind could advance much faster, and who knows what kind of super-race that we will become. Nietzsche saw hope in evolution to bring about a Superman, a superhuman who could advance mankind to another level.

It is well known that Hitler revered Nietzsche, and several times visited Nietzsche's home where he died. How much Hitler read Nietzsche is debated, but he absorbed some of his ideas. Hitler especially adopted ideas of eugenics from various sources, and when he instituted the "final solution" for the Jews, his idea was that they were "unfit," not good for breeding, in fact that they were very poor specimens. The best thing was to eliminate them, as animals, without conscience, as Nietzsche taught. So Hitler murdered six million Jews and numerous Christians.

If we are just animals, there is nothing special about Christian sexual morality or about the family. We are free to redefine these, and to be told that is wrong, enrages modern "Nietzsches" (read: modern intellectual elite) as a challenge that there is a God, that there are no private moral worlds where they can be their own gods and create their own standards. To be told they are accountable to the Triune God who made them is a challenge to their whole system. Therefore, they hate Christians with an unholy passion. Like Adam and Eve, they believe they can be as God Almighty, determining their own ethics. To be told they will be judged infuriates the god of this world who energizes

[9] Alistar Kee, *Nietzsche Against the Crucified*, ch. 7, "The Will to Power."

them, and in turn they attack all who remind them of this. There is no tolerance.

These differences in value regarding life, sexuality, and the family all stem from a difference in where one begins his thinking: denying creation, one begins with molecules in motion. Only creation gives us what was said in the Declaration of Independence: "endowed by their *Creator* with certain unalienable Rights." (Glen Beck reported recently [May 2010] that some public school texts leave out the word "Creator" in their version of the Declaration. Apart from Him, no one has any rights, not even the right to life, for the elite will control everything. In place of creation, they promote evolution. In place of life, they promote death. In place of the one male and one female family, they promote anything goes.

> Thus Hitler perpetrated one of the most evil programs the world has even witnessed under the delusion that Darwinism could help us discover how to make the world better.[10]

The Soviet Union did even worse, killing an estimated 62 million of its citizens, with the world looking the other way. China has slaughtered approximately 34 million, and counting, and Hitler killed 21 million total,[11] and the other Communist nations, in the name of evolution and atheism, have added many more millions. If we count abortions in all these countries, we could easily double the numbers. In the USA, we are up to 50 million babies and still going strong. In all, since Darwin, estimates run as high as 250 to 300 million people slaughtered, counting wars begun by evolutionists and all the babies killed, based on their theory that we are just animals, nothing more—and the slaughter of the unborn worldwide is ongoing. A tree is known by its fruit, and atheistic evolution the last 100 years has produced little more than death and destruction. (Muslims don't abort their babies, and just with their current birth rate they will win the world in another 100 years or less by sheer numbers alone.)

---

[10] Weikart, *From Darwin to Hitler*, p. 227.

[11] These numbers (62 million, 34 million, and 21 million) were reported (October 19, 2009) on Bill O'Reilly Fox News from a study done.

Conclusion

So what is the fruit of all this in the USA? Once we reject the Triune God and accept only materialism, we have absurdities that I mentioned in Chapter 1, "I. The Origin of All Things." Rejecting God who is life necessarily leads to an orientation to death. If we are not made in the image of God but are only animals, we have no intrinsic value. Then it makes sense to breed for the future of the race, which leads to abortion, infanticide, voluntary euthanasia, and then to involuntary euthanasia. All these atrocities are promoted by euphemisms: abortion is *pro-choice* or *Planned Parenthood* (which is really planned baby killing); suicide is doctor assisted *mercy killing*; infanticide is keeping the unfit babies from having *no quality of life*; and on it goes.

Consider this scenario. A woman goes to her doctor to discuss her pregnancy. She has just had a baby a few months ago, and she is not ready for another one so she asks for an abortion. The doctor gives her an alternative: kill the one you gave birth to, for this provides no risk to her body. The other baby will be born normally, and this will give her more time to prepare for the new baby. With evolutionary ethics, this will be another "choice" available in our culture. One will have the choice to kill a baby say up to one year of age. Truly we have an orientation to death, and this is the judgment of God on our culture.

All those who hate me love death (Proverbs 8:36).

Lord Jesus, have mercy on us. **Amen.**

Chapter 20—God's Judgment Is Now . . . Our Families

Introduction

In this chapter, I must be candid, but I don't want to be misunderstood. I have no righteousness to present to God to accept me. I'm not so holy to be able to cast judgment on others; we are all subject to the judgment of God, including myself. My only hope in life and in death is my Lord Jesus Christ. I love those who are opposed to me and what I say in this book, and truly hope and pray to the Father by the merits of the Son that they will come to a better mind, be converted, and have their sins forgiven. It is not my intention to offend anyone, but I must tell the truth and give the implications of errant sexual behavior and its consequences to the family. I am required by God to sound a warning (Ezekiel 33:2-6).

But I criticize my own world also. Christianity today is hypocritical, for it condemns substance abuse in being hooked on drugs while overlooking substance abuse of obesity. We look down our long noses on same sex unions, and then overlook the rampant divorce rate in our own backyards. We proclaim that adultery is wrong, but we conveniently overlook living together before marriage, or we think that a couple can create their own marriage privately without public vows in the Church. But let us consider how the culture is destroying families.

I. Family Disintegration

There is the continued increase in divorce rates (though some divorces may be biblical, for God divorced Israel (Jeremiah 3:8)), and continued increase in violence in the home. In some minorities, most of the children are born out of wedlock, not knowing who their fathers are. This in turn produces children who grow up to have even less morals. No one even considers this abnormal.

In each case, the children suffer innocently, and then they carry these scars into their own marriages, if they ever marry, and at an increased rate of abuse. We have become like some animals where the male has many females and produces offspring only to leave them. The spiral continues downward to the next generation, but becomes worse. This is self-destruction for not obeying God's Ten Commandments, and it is God's judgment built in, as it were, to His commandments. One cannot live life successfully without assuming His loving commands.

Then the Fifth Commandment is sorely compromised when parents kill one another or their own children, which is becoming increasingly more common. Our children are sent to public schools where they are taught not to honor their parents' authority. As they enter their teens, they rebel. Then parents wonder why.

II. Education of Our Children

God gives parents the command and authority to educate their own children (Deuteronomy 6:1ff; Ephesians 6:1-4; Colossians 3:21-22), but we send them off to public schools where they are not allowed even to talk about the Triune God! Yet we have many Christian schools available. The most common excuse I hear for not putting one's child in a Christian school is that the parents can't afford it, but I would say we can't afford not to do so, especially in this environment. I also struggled greatly financially to give my children a thoroughly Christian education, but we did it. Most of the time we had hand-me-down furniture, rented a small house, and only had one used vehicle. And when we could no longer afford tuition, we home schooled. There are many more resources available now to help Christian parents home school than when we did it, with co-ops to help teach the more technical subjects.

Those who don't believe they can afford tuition should take stock of their possessions — cars, home, electronics — to see if they have their priorities straight. There is nothing wrong with these if one can truly afford them, but we're here on planet earth to conquer it for Christ, to rear *His* children *His* way, not to collect toys. (Please contact

service@footstoolpublications.com

to order the booklet, *Keeping Covenant and Educating Our Children* for much more on this. Send an email requesting it, and you will be contacted. We will not give your email to others.)

III. Consequences of Sex Sins

LifeSite News is reporting that parents in the United Kingdom could face criminal charges for removing their children from programs held at George Tomlinson Primary School that promoted the homosexual lifestyle. School officials have apparently announced they will prosecute parents of approximately 30 children who did not attend a week's worth of lessons coinciding with "Lesbian, Gay, Bisexual and Transgender History Month."[1]

A. Pornography

If elite people want to institute totalitarianism, they must destroy the family; and one way to do that is to allow porn.[2] The family is a stronghold with its independent, private moral stance, with the children loyal to parents. The loyalty to parents can be broken by public education that teaches children they can make up their own minds about morality so that they self-consciously drive a wedge between parents and children. Then if the state allows porn, that means the state is the institution that defines morality, not parents or anyone else. The children are taught that self is to liberated from God, from any restraints, except those imposed by the new god, the state.

Our whole nation has given itself over to sexual sins of all kinds, as seen in the huge rise of the pornography industry that is reportedly on the internet. These predators deceive the unwary that what they are presenting will satisfy. They hawk their wares to enslave men, women, boys, and girls to bizarre practices. As a pastor I have to deal with those

---

[1] http://www.onenewsnow.com/Blog/Default.aspx?id=447414, accessed March 2009.

[2] Rousas J. Rushdoony, *This Independent Republic* (Fairfax, VA: Thoburn Press, 1978), p. 121.

who have been snared by these sexual predators, and it is destroying marriages and teens. And it is not just men who are viewing the internet, but also women in their 40s as reported by one Christian psychologist to our diocese in 2002. The predators do it for money and for the temporary thrill. Fathers assault their daughters, those in gay bathhouses prey on others and have anonymous sex, pedophiles attack children and promote child porn on the internet, and the list is endless.

Some of these pedophiles are in high government places, as witness one man appointed for a position in one president's administration who has argued in favor of pedophiles to have "free speech" on the internet. Also, it is most amazing to me that a father can sexually abuse his daughter (Seventh Commandment), or a mother can throw away her child in the garbage (Sixth Commandment). This demonstrates no natural affection that we all should have in our families. All this destroys the family and is the indirect judgment of God for not keeping His Ten Commandments. It is not possible to live life profitably without embracing His morality.

When Tammy Bruce, a pro-choice lesbian, was involved with certain gay communities, they used the mass media to "brainwash the public into believing that certain sexual practices are merely 'alternative lifestyles.'" They wanted to inform the public about AIDS, but some others in the movement wanted to show support for those involved in sadomasochism, the inflicting of pain during sex. The fetish for pain and violence that two lesbians shared were a shock even for Tammy.[3] Yet masochism is the logical product of degeneracy.

B. Same Sex Consequences on the Family

Then there are consequences of same sex unions on the family. One is that such unions cannot reproduce, which means that they will pressure others to have children for them or seek to dominate the adoption agencies once these unions are legal. Will affirmative action apply here? Vermont, Connecticut, Massachusetts, and Iowa have given gays

---

[3] Tammy Bruce, *The Death of Right and Wrong* (New York: Three Rivers Press, 2003), p. 89. (See my comments on this book in the Bibliography at the end of the book.)

the right to "marry" so far in early 2009. Will these unions be recognized in the other states?

During the early history of this country, many settlers took their families west to settle. They were often given land by the government. With their families, they reproduced and grew to large numbers; but if they had been same sex "unions," they would have become extinct.

With heterosexual couples, a new person can be created in the image of both parents. This is one of the most profound acts of love God has given us. With homosexual couples, we only have reciprocal masturbation with no possibility of reproducing. Thus from nature itself we learn that same sex unions are not right since the species cannot be propagated. If all were gay, the human race would become extinct.

Then will male gay couples pay others to have someone's seed implanted into some woman to have a child for them? Will female gay couples have someone's seed implanted into them, perhaps simultaneously, to have children? In either case, if they "divorce," whose children are they?

Lutzer reports:

> Because gay couples cannot produce children on their own, James Skillen of the Center for Public Justice predicts that hopeful parents may seek to rent wombs and deny children to know their biological parents. "It is going to be increasingly possible to produce, buy, and sell children, because in addition to adoption, that is the only way homosexual couples can 'have' children." *Whether raised by lesbians or two homosexual men, these children will be denied either a mother or a father.*[4]

And if children are adopted, which person will be the mother and which the father? What kind of confusion will that produce when they are shopping at Kroger, and the child in the same sex union sees another child call his female parent "Mom" and his male parent "Dad"? Will he ask his "parents" why he has two men as parents or two moms? Will there be laws made to change the speech to accommodate the gays? George Orwell's *1984* is here with newspeak. Same sex un-

---

[4] Erwin W. Lutzer, *The Truth about Same-Sex Marriage* (Chicago: Moody Press, 2004), p. 62. Emphasis his.

322 *Part 3—Implications*

ions generally seek to erase the distinction between male and female, and that just can't be done. It is interesting that one of the partners often takes a female or male role, for we cannot live life without assuming God's categories. Besides the emotional differences, the "plumbing" is different. One cannot permanently alter the definition of marriage as one male and one female, for it not only violates God's command, but it also violates the way we were created. Once marriage is redefined, other groups will want even looser definitions of marriage, such as group marriages. It is not really new definitions of marriage that is wanted, but the *destruction* of marriage.

Another argument from nature is that it should be obvious, without getting too graphic, that women are made to receive the male organ whereas men are not. The female vagina receives the male penis, sperm is deposited, egg is fertilized, and in nine months a human baby is born. That is natural and how everyone comes into the world. The anatomical difference and complementary nature of male and female is too obvious to need detailed explanation.

Moreover, we must not think that giving in to homosexuals to marry will appease them. They and others will only demand more liberties. Sin is never satisfied, and the sinner, given what he demands, will only demand more to try to reach the same thrills. (Chamberlain thought he could appease Hitler but only discovered that he demanded even more.) The punishment for deviant behavior is for God to give them over to even more bazaar behavior (Romans 1:24-28). The only way to stop this freefall is to confront them with righteousness, and to press the claims of Christ, His love, and forgiveness on them, for only He can stop the dominoes from falling.

Moreover, these unions do not usually remain monogamous, which can mean the spread of AIDS, and if there are children, they will adopt the same lifestyles. Tammy Bruce, a former gay insider, reports that male homosexuals "have hundreds of sex partners a year while spreading an incurable disease or two."[5] (Blood banks will not allow

---

[5] Tammy Bruce, *The Death of Right and Wrong* (New York: Three Rivers Press, 2003), p. 25. (See my comments on this book in the Bibliography at the end of the book.)

male homosexuals to give blood because of the high risk of diseases.) This adds to the instability of home life for those involved and especially for the innocent children. From rectal and oral sex, there is infectious hepatitis, which increases the risk of liver cancer, fatal rectal cancer, not to mention HIV and AIDS, and a 30 year decrease in life expectancy.[6] "The American Psychiatric Association Press reports that '30% of all 20-year old gay men will be HIV positive or dead of AIDS by the time they are age 30.' "[7] Add to this the demand that the government pays for all these diseases, and we have an economic meltdown, not only from the medical bills but also from the decreased productivity in the market of those who cannot work.

Moreover, whom will the children "marry"? Where will they find "spouses" since their "parents" cannot reproduce, and others they associate with cannot reproduce? "Love" does not justify these relationships, for love is not subjectively defined, as we saw in Chapter 2, VI, but is defined by God's law. Will these children adopted by gays want to find out who their natural parents are? Will that be deemed unconstitutional? It irks them that every child that comes into the world is the product of one man and one woman, which is a constant reminder that they are wrong. Will there be a push to have human cloning so gays can have children?

But *only* one male and one female can reproduce *both* their images in the new offspring. Cloning *one* parent will not do so. Adopting will not do so. Planting male sperm into a female egg of a lesbian partner will not do so, for the other "parent" contributed nothing. Only the one impregnated will have a relationship with the "father," the child being in the image of the donor father and receptor mother, but not the other female partner. The female partner will have no biological relationship at all with the child. Two (or more) males won't be able to receive any implanting. They will be left to cloning or adopting.

This will be devastating to the children and family as they fight over who has the right to rear the child, to make rules, and when "di-

---

[6] John Stott, *Same-Sex Partnerships?* (Grand Rapids: Fleming H. Revell, 1998), p. 53.

[7] Stott, *Same-Sex Partnerships*, p. 63.

vorces" inevitably occur, who will have the right to the children? As it stands now, when a man and woman marry, and if one had children before the marriage and the other one did not adopt them, if they divorce, the childless parent does not have the right to visit the child. How will this work out in people of the same sex when males "marry" and one has a child or when lesbians "marry," and only one gives birth, or "marries" with a child? In all cases, the children will be the victims.

Then there will be a move to legitimize unions between three or more of both sexes, group marriages. Do *not* think that the radical sexual movement will stop with gay unions of two partners; they want complete sexual anarchy—pan sexuality. Have you heard of LGBT: Lesbian, Gay, Bisexual, and Transgender? The dominoes are falling, and one sin inevitably leads to another; the *only* way to stop these dominoes is to come to Christ and to His law-word. "Triad" marriages are already being put forward, according to Fox News host Bill O'Reilly. There is no one who has a stop-gap morality by the grace of God and the Gospel to stop the disintegration except Christians.

On the Phil Donahue talk show some years ago, I saw three who were living together, two men, and a woman. The men were homosexuals and the woman a lesbian who had her various partners visit her. But once in a while one of the men would go to the other part of the house to have sex with the woman so they could have a child, which they did, a little girl. They did not care which man was the father. All of them claimed to be her parents. When the audience asked the three what sexual orientation they wanted for their daughter, they all said together, "happy." That meant she was being taught complete license in her sex life; all options were on the table.

Then it becomes more bizarre with four or five having legal status as a "union." What happens when one wants to "divorce" the others? Who will pay what, and who will get what children? Then we will have a completely permissive society with God knows how many children who don't have a clue who their real parents are, and who will be taught that it does not matter. They will truly be the victims. We will be a jungle, mating like animals with no accountability. How can children honor father and mother if they don't know who they are? With no real commitment to anyone but ourselves, we'll sink into total narcissism (and are sinking now) and sexual "freedom" (read: "enslavement") with the motto that "anything goes." Pedophilia will seem mild.

Such legal group "marriages" will essentially be farms to raise children on, with multiple partners, like farm animals that breed with one another, producing many offspring, but with no direction, no morality. Because we have lost the vertical standard with God, we have lost the ability to define right and wrong between ourselves. As soon as the Triune God is removed as the standard for morality, there is no objective way to define human relationships. There will be no families, just individuals seeking their own interests, not the well being of others in a family. And who in the world will be the in-laws to all these people? Who will be the grandparents? Millions of motherless and fatherless kids will be produced.

Within "families" there will be horrendous confrontation built in between parents, between children, and between parents and children. To make matters worse, if that is possible, a straight couple marry and have their own children. Then one of them leaves the marriage for a person of the same sex, and gets divorced from the original marriage to "marry" the same sex partner. Now who gets the children? Judges' hands will be tied, for the children, even of an innocent Christian parent, will have to live in a gay situation, or at the least to have visitation rights. The souls of the children will be in jeopardy, for God says that those who practice sinful sex will perish unless they repent (1 Corinthians 6:9-11).

Then the public schools will be full of gay people, and students are already being primed to accept that orientation and to castigate any who disagree, especially Christians. What will this do to those children who come from godly homes, or just from homes who do not want their children exposed to sexual promiscuity? Since God's Ten Commandments have to be rejected to promote this errant lifestyle, what will this do to the children's morals in general? As an increasing number of Christians take their children out of such schools to put them in private schools, those who promote such a lifestyle will seek to pass laws to prevent such, or to make it financially difficult, if not impossible. Don't forget that those who promote such lifestyles are *not* neutral — they hate those who oppose them, as evidenced by the recent gay riots in California when the gay marriage law did not pass. The anger on their faces said it all.

I just heard on the national news (Fox News April 2009) that some gays are claiming discrimination against Knoxville and Nashville, TN, public schools that block their students from gay sites on school computers.

> The ACLU, in a tersely worded letter, told the schools Wednesday it would sue them if the sites don't come back online. The blocked sites include the Human Rights Campaign, Marriage Equality USA, the Gay Lesbian Straight Education Network, the Lesbian Alliance Against Defamation and Dignity USA.[8]

Of course, the opponents say they are not in favor of the gay porn sites (for now), just the "regular" gay sites. Is it possible to have a gay site that is not porn? That means that all the kids will have access to such sites, which in turn means more children convinced that God's morality is obsolete. Indeed, this means gays are targeting our children, right now, using the ACLU to place children into their hands. They must convert others to their cause since they cannot reproduce, and they will go after the most vulnerable of society. Perhaps some of them have no interest in children. Perhaps some of them are very sincere about their relationship with another of the same sex, but as we've explained many times in this book, sincerity is not the issue; truth is the issue. Some will resent it, but how is this new pursuit of gay web sites in public schools not some form of pedophilia? Should I not warn regarding the moral safety of our children, as God requires (Ezekiel 33)? Moreover, I'm not aware of any instance of a country giving itself over to a homosexual lifestyle that did not also embrace pedophilia. Another reason is that they demand complete sexual freedom of any kind, and will stop at nothing to get it. Accepting sinful behavior breaks down barriers, leading them further from the truth, their consciences having become seared (1 Timothy 4:2).

---

[8] From http://blog.wired.com/27bstroke6/2009/04/pro-gay-sites-f.html. Accessed April, 2009.

But whose morality is defining porn, and how long will it be before any site will be legally open to public school children because it can't be defined, or because of alleged free speech? *Once the vertical goes, anything goes.* Recall what I said in Part 1: once God is removed, morality will be reduced to its lowest common denominator with the government moderating. The dominoes are falling, right now. **Christians must get their children out of the public schools, and put them in Christian schools, and then monitor them closely, or home school them.** Remember that sin does not stand still, but like water it always seeks it lowest level.

Then there is GLSEN (Gay Lesbian Straight Education Network) that has a workshop for those ages 14-21 in some public schools to teach children how lesbians have sex, and other practices too awful even to describe in this book.[9] Then President Obama appointed Kevin Jenkins as the Safe School Czar who is the founder of GLSEN. Do you think your children will be safe with him? Notice the word "safe," which is another euphemism.

It gets worse, if possible. Peter Singer has been teaching relativism at Princeton University. He has been hailed as a brilliant scholar. He has written on the positive aspects of bestiality, describing a dog and a human, to which Bruce said "he has made Princeton unsafe both for your child *and* your beagle."[10]

How would you like your children taught by people who had been trained by Judith Levine, highly respected in academia, who wrote *Harmful to Minors: The Perils of Protecting Children From Sex*?[11] Levine has the audacity to state that Christians who protect their children from sex until they are married "are more harmful to minors than sex itself."[12] Our families are being targeted for destruction, and the public schools are the means to bring this about.

Lutzer reports in his book:

---

[9] Tammy Bruce, *The Death of Right and Wrong* (New York: Three Rivers Press, 2003), p. 104ff.

[10] Bruce, *The Death of Right and Wrong*, p. 191.

[11] Bruce, *The Death of Right and Wrong*, p. 194.

[12] Bruce, *The Death of Right and Wrong*, p. 200-201.

The San Francisco Unified School District has a lesson plan for teaching kindergarteners and first graders about homosexuality. It defines a family as a "unit of two or more persons, related either by birth or by choice, who may or may not live together. . . ."[13]

But with one man and one woman committed to one another for life, they can have their own children; and no one loves children like the original parents, for they are created in the image of *both* parents, even looking like them. This godly relationship produces stability, security, knowing who they are and who their parents are and what morality is.

IV. Other Attacks against Christian Families

Moreover, abortion is also destroying the families, but if Christians will get their priorities right, have many children, not aborting them, then we can make progress. The ungodly are aborting their children. But those who hate us may seek to pass laws to keep us from having many children, making abortion mandatory if a couple has over one child, like in China today. Already President Obama is threatening to *require* all hospitals in the USA to perform abortions; even Christian doctors will be required to do so. Several Catholic bishops have said that if that happens they will shut down all their hospitals, which is about 30 percent of all hospitals in the country. Then the government would take them over and nationalize the hospitals, as they are nationalizing big businesses, such as Obama firing the CEO of GM.

The complete destruction of the family is the judgment of God on our land, for no country can survive without stable homes, families with one man and one woman who have godly children to rear for the good of society and for the glory of God.

Charles Colson reported these attacks against Christians and against the family.[14]

---

[13] Lutzer, *The Truth about Same-Sex Marriage*, p. 26.
[14] http://mail.google.com/mail/?shva=1#inbox/12135ef105ba2b20, accessed April 2009.

- Two women wanted to be married at a New Jersey pavilion owned by the Ocean Grove Camp Meeting Association, a Methodist group, who denied the request based on their religious beliefs. The women won a lawsuit, and the Methodists lost their tax exempt status, costing them $20,000.

- Christian physicians who refused to provide *in vitro* fertilization treatment to a woman in a lesbian relationship were sued, the California Supreme Court said their religious beliefs did not give them the right to refuse her.

- In Massachusetts, Catholic Charities was told they had to accept homosexual couples in their adoption service, or get out of the adoption business. They chose correctly—they got out of the business.

- In Mississippi, a mental health counselor was sued for refusing to provide therapy to a woman looking to improve her lesbian relationship. The counselor's employers fired her—a move that was backed up by the U.S. Fifth Circuit Court of Appeals.

- In New York, the Albert Einstein College of Medicine at Yeshiva University refused to allow same-sex couples to live in married student housing, in keeping with the school's orthodox Jewish teachings. But in 2001, the New York State Supreme Court forced them to do so anyway—even though New York has no same-sex "marriage" law.

- In Albuquerque, a same-sex couple asked a Christian wedding photographer to film their commitment ceremony—and sued the photographer when she declined. An online adoption service was forced to stop doing business in California when a same-sex couple sued the service for refusing, on religious grounds, to assist them.

Perhaps you see that we're in a religious war with the religion of Christianity being discriminated against and persecuted while the religion of the secularists is being upheld. Private business and private religion have extreme intolerance displayed against them. May God grant us the courage lovingly to stand for Him. **AMEN.**

Chapter 21—God's Judgment Now . . . National Judgment

Introduction

There is not only individual judgment, family judgment, and judgment on businesses, but all through Holy Scripture we see nations judged for their sins. In other words, *there is a national righteousness*, or lack of it, just as there is individual righteousness. God takes note of both, and a whole nation can and will be judged, including those who would seem to be innocent. But by allowing wickedness to prevail, we all contribute to national righteousness.

> Righteousness exalts a nation, but sin is a reproach to *any* people (Proverbs 14:34).

Part of our judgment is wicked politicians. As John Adams (1735 – 1836), a founding father of this great nation, once noted:

> "In my many years I have come to a conclusion that one useless man is a shame, two is a law firm, and three or more is a Congress."

Or, another person rightly noted:

> The real reason we can't have the Ten Commandments posted in a courthouse or Congress is that you can't post "Thou Shall Not Steal," "Thou Shalt Not Commit Adultery," and "Thou Shall Not Bear False Witness" in a building full of lawyers, judges and politicians; it creates a hostile work environment.

Seriously, politically we are a nation of idolaters, and when a nation turns away from the Triune God, we have either totalitarianism or anarchy. No one can live with anarchy so people cry out for order, which leads to tyrants who will give order, at a price of enslavement. We are quickly heading in the direction of totalitarianism. When a people lose the vertical, the transcendent God, they become a law to themselves. The political environment leads the people to be their own god, their own law-giver. They become politically pantheistic, for then the state becomes the god for morality, with each citizen as part of the answer. Those who will not be absorbed into the "machine" must be destroyed, which is why Christians have been attacked so vehemently and why the Intelligent Design movement is so hated.

An intellectual and moral vacuum is then created into which ignorance, refusal to think, and concentration on accumulating toys consumes one's time. Such individualism "isolates [people] from one another, to concentrate every man's attention upon himself; and it lays the soul open to an inordinate love of material gratification."[1] Now the individual lives by such mottoes as "to thine own self be true." We go within to find god, plumbing the depths of our own depravity to find a rudder that will guide us, only to end in despair, like the lesbian lover of Tammy Bruce, Brenda Benét, TV actress of *Days of Our Lives*, who ended her life with a gun. We believe we are not to blame for our faults, such as murder, stealing, adultery, but it is society. We claim for ourselves divine authority so we reject individual responsibility.

When godly authority goes, tyrants enter, for people fear anarchy as this would take away their toys. Those without any principle to die for will compromise anything to survive. There is never a lack of tyrants. Thus, when God goes, the only authority to maintain order, people are frightened. People will then surrender their liberties when there is no godly authority under the illusion that now any authority will do. Being dominated by a society that rejects the Triune God, people will accept substitute gods, for worship is inevitable, being part of the image of God within us. The illusion then becomes that politicians will grant liberty, but Christ will bring bondage. At this point the whole culture has come under His judgment, which is basically were we are.

---

[1] Alexis de Tocqueville, *Democracy in America* (New York: Vintage Books, 1945), 2:23. This set is one of the most insightful books I have ever read. This quoted material was written in 1840!

The only thing that can successfully oppose run away public opinion, the only thing that can keep people from surrendering their minds and souls to be absorbed by the pantheistic state, is His Sovereign majesty, the King of kings and Lord of lords, Jesus the Christ, who even now holds all accountable to Himself. It is the Church who can and will oppose false worship, and we as individuals have identity and meaning within this body, not apart from it. We will never win as individuals, but only as the Church will we storm the gates of hell and prevail (Matthew 16:18). It is easy for Satan to conquer a lone sheep, but together, under the Great Shepherd, we are safe. We must remember that though we rightly think of Romans 8:28 as applying to individuals, yet its major application is to the corporate Church:

> And we know that all things work together for good to those who love God, to those who are the called according to *His* purpose.

Everything that happens in the whole world is ultimately for the good of Christ's Church, for He is in charge, not unholy tyrants. If ungodly tyrants rebel, they will self-destruct, or Christ will judge them directly. If they convert to Him, Christ wins. Either way Christ wins.

In short, a democracy without Christ will quickly become a hell-hole with tyrants; it cannot be otherwise. Remove Him from society, and we are left with radical individualism (tyranny of the one), radical egalitarianism (tyranny of the many), materialism (toys are gods), unholy tyrants, moral relativism (emphasis on illicit sex and death), which in turn leads to messiah images to bring us "change" by rearranging things, not by leading us back to the Triune God. As one former atheist stated, who has traveled widely in communist countries:

> And in all my experience of life, I have seldom seen a more powerful argument for the fallen nature of man, and his inability to achieve perfection, than those countries in which man set himself up to replace God with the state.[2]

---

[2] Peter Hitchens, *The Rage Against God: How Atheism Led Me to Faith* (Grand Rapids: Zondervan, 2010), p. 152.

In light of these concepts, let us consider a few areas of national judgment.

I. Financial Judgment (Economic Suicide)

Just recently (2008-09) we've heard of major financial institutions in the USA (and worldwide) going under because of bad debt. The USA government has bailed out some of the financial institutions and large businesses, which means more printing of money, more inflation, and more problems with paying our national bills. We've already seen that printing money is theft (Eighth Commandment), but also debt is not a blessing but a curse. God says that it was a blessing for Israel to lend to other nations (Deuteronomy 28:12) but a curse to borrow from other nations (Deuteronomy 28:44). Now the USA is the largest debtor nation in the world with trillions of our national debt held by other countries, like China and Japan, and still growing. A nation can be destroyed by bad currency and bad debt, such as the USSR that came apart in 1991.

Because of covetousness, which is idolatry (Colossians 3:5), our finances are in shambles, both nationally and individually. Nationally, we give everyone what he wants (covets) with fiat money. Individually, we purchase new houses, new cars, new furniture, and new clothes, new entertainment centers — all by debt, hocking up our futures and our children's futures. That in turn puts enormous pressure on families and finances. We take the lead from the government and overspend, but unlike the government we are not allowed to print money. All this is the judgment of God.

The American dollar used to be the world's currency because it was backed by silver and gold and by a thriving economy, but because someone (without Constitutional authority) took us off the silver and gold standard, the dollar is becoming weaker all the time. This is the judgment of God.

So the government steals (Eighth Commandment) from its citizens by inflating the dollar and thereby taking away its purchasing power. The citizens covet (Tenth Commandment) what others have and vote for politicians who will transfer it to them. People seek to gain wealth by deception (Ninth Commandment). Many are in debt beyond their capacity to pay, which destroys lives and homes. Both parents must work to keep up with the demand for government taxes and the American Dream, and credit card debt is sinking many families. (In Memphis, TN, homeowners have to pay a tax for rain water rolling off their roofs!) Thus we see many politicians' agenda is tax, spend, lie, fornicate, kill babies, and make us weak militarily. They make a career out of bearing false witness. This is the judgment of God.

Many years ago I used to be in the floor covering business. I took a credit application from an airplane pilot who (in the mid-1980s) was bringing home $8,800 a month. He had to juggle bills to qualify for $2,000 worth of carpet. He lived in a plush house in an upscale neighborhood. He was a slave to toys.

I knew another man who worked for a company whose employees tended to go on long strikes. After being on strike for several months, some elders in his church approached him to see if he needed any financial help. He was surprised, but not offended, and said: "My cars are paid for. My house is paid for. I have money in the bank, but thank you for asking." He lived in a moderate house and neighborhood, but owned his property. Which man was free? Which man had wealth? The pilot did not own anything, but his things owned him. We cannot live with blessing without assuming the Ten Commandments.

CEOs of large corporations deceive their employees that everything is fine with the company so they should put money in the company stock (Enron). CFOs tell Wall Street that all is well. Everyone is out to line his own pocket, such as Bernie Madoff who made off with many billions with his Ponzi Scheme. Banks ride the real estate boom and speculate, only to pay for it later. The whole savings and loan industry went under. It seems to me that the whole USA economy is teetering on the brink of major disaster, and few pay any attention. They just say "pass the salt." Apathy is destroying us.

There are whole industries that have a bad reputation, such as home improvement companies, car salesmen, and others. Here is what once characterized apostate Israel:

> Therefore I will give their wives to others, and their fields to
> those who will inherit *them;* because from the least even to the

greatest <u>everyone is given to</u> **covetousness**<u>; from the prophet</u>
<u>even to the priest everyone</u> **deals falsely** (Jeremiah 8:10; see also
Jeremiah 6:13).

The wealth of the USA is being transferred to other countries, such
as cheap labor we employ from China and India, countries who have
bought our debt (such as Japan and China), purchasing oil from other
countries when we could drill at home, allowing other countries to purchase huge amounts of our real estate, and many other transfers. God is
judging us financially, both nationally and individually.

II. Lack of Justice (Moral Suicide)

A. Murders

As incredible as it seems, we slaughter the unborn and allow murderers not only to live, but also to go free again after being incarcerated
at our expense (violation of the Sixth Commandment). What kind of
justice is that? Consider Abu-Jamal who murdered Daniel Faulkner for
a few dollars, who wanted to make a difference so he taught in the inner school system. The Left embraced Abu-Jamal, even had him speak
at a commencement address from jail, and he was eventually moved
from death row to a lighter sentence. Where is the justice?

Holly Joshi, spokeswoman for the Oakland police, said recently:
"If you come home to find your house burglarized and you call, we're
not coming."[3] Because of government over spending, the city of Oakland does not have the money to pursue these "minor" crimes. Take
away the Second Amendment right to keep and bear arms, and one is
not safe in his home.

Consider one who murders a baby that is one week old, and then
walks away from it without even being charged. Is that justice? What if
the baby is one day old, or one hour old? Now suppose the baby is nine
months old, and as the child comes down the birth canal, the head
comes first. Just before the head comes out, it is punctured, the brains
sucked out with a vacuum, and the skull crushed, then the whole baby

---

[3] http://www.usatoday.com/news/nation/2010-08-25-1Anresponsecops-25_ST_-
N.htm (accessed August 26, 2010).

is pulled out. Does the murderer still get to walk away? Where is justice? (First and Sixth Commandments) That is of course the euphemism "partial birth abortion."

B. Courts

The slaughter of babies came about because of the horrible *Roe v. Wade* decision in 1973 where the Supreme Court stopped being a court and became a legislative body, changing the law of the land to allow abortions that were illegal since the beginning of this great nation. Habakkuk speaks to such "justice":

> Therefore the law is powerless, and justice never goes forth.
> For the wicked surround the righteous; therefore perverse judgment proceeds (Habakkuk 1:4).

Moreover, politicians are sworn in with their left hand on the Bible only to break their oath at the first opportunity. No one's word means much anymore (Ninth Commandment). I've seen a "Christian" man lie against his fellow believers in federal court after putting his hand on the Bible to tell the truth. Everyone lies in court, and the judges rarely enforce the perjury laws.

Widows are robbed of their inheritance by the IRS, which is one of the most insidious sins of our culture. It is double taxation, for the father paid the tax on the money when he earned it, and now the widow must pay again, simply because her husband died. This is an attack on the family to keep them from becoming strong. Tyrannical régimes know they cannot take over unless they neutralize the family. Notice what God says:

> [1] Woe to those who decree unrighteous decrees, who write misfortune, which they have prescribed [2] to rob the needy of justice, and to take what is right from the poor of My people, that <u>widows</u> may be their prey, and *that* they may rob the fatherless. [3] What will you do in the day of punishment, and in the desolation *which* will come from afar? To whom will you flee for help? And where will you leave your glory? (Isaiah 10:1-3).

Politicians and judges have no fear of God and so do whatever will get them the most personal benefits, and then dare to use the name "God" in public as if God favored all this:

> [9] Now hear this, you heads of the house of Jacob and rulers of the house of Israel, <u>who abhor justice and pervert all equity,</u> [10] who build up Zion with bloodshed and Jerusalem with iniquity: [11] Her heads judge for a bribe, her priests teach for pay, and her prophets divine for money. Yet they lean on the LORD, and say, "<u>Is not the LORD among us? No harm can come upon us.</u>" [12] Therefore because of you Zion shall be plowed *like* a field, Jerusalem shall become heaps of ruins, and the mountain of the temple Like the bare hills of the forest (Micah 3:9-11).

Even the justices and law makers are corrupt:

> Who justify the wicked for a bribe, and take away justice from the righteous man (Isaiah 5:23).

Power and money are the politicians' gods, with illicit sex as a perk. Truth and righteousness are only words, and *management* of the public is more important than being moral. Morality is valued by these white washed tombs according to how it will contribute to elections, to money, and especially to power. Expediency is the only sacred moral principle. Thank God there are some fine exceptions to what I've just described, but unfortunately they are *exceptions*.

Tammy Bruce insightfully states regarding the lack of justice:[4]

- Murdering your children isn't murder if you're a woman — it's post-partum depression.
- Sex addiction, compulsion, and promiscuity aren't problems if you're gay — they're part of an "alternative lifestyle."
- Degrading symbols is off limits if you're Muslim but fair game if you're Christian.

---

[4] Tammy Bruce, *The Death of Right and Wrong* (New York: Three Rivers Press, 2003), p. 18ff. (See my comments on this book in the Bibliography at the end of the book.)

- Being unfaithful to one's wife isn't sin unless you get caught.

C. Supreme Court

The Supreme Court has done more harm to our country than any other one institution, for they have become law makers instead of law interpreters, and they are appointed for life—like federal judges—and they are not accountable to anyone. There is not one word in the Constitution about abortion, and yet they have found a way to interpret it to say such. The Constitution has not one word about prayer in the schools, but they managed to remove that. We came within one vote of having a new definition of marriage that would include gays. The reason Judge Bork's nomination was so strongly opposed is that he did not believe in reinterpreting the Constitution but in its original intent. The Supreme Court has become the magisterium, the official interpreter of our most basic founding document, and no one can say anything. This is incredible tyranny. To see anyone as the official interpreter of any document without recourse will introduce new doctrines.[5] The states should be able to reject decisions of the high court if they think it is wrong. As it stands, there are no checks on their novel interpretations.

III. Other Nations Judging Us (National Suicide)

One sure sign of God's judgment on a nation is how other nations treat that nation. The West in general and the USA in particular are being attacked in various ways by other countries. It is no secret that China and Russia hate the USA. Moreover, many of the nations in the Mid-East, which are primarily the Islamic nations, are attacking us. We are not only speaking of 9/11, which was perhaps the very first frontal assault on the USA on our own land, but also the bombings that have taken place against our citizens and military around the world by suicide bombers. Osama bin Laden has stated that the West is decadent, especially the USA, and he is right. Therefore, he thinks that we must be

---

[5] This is not the place to deal with the magisterium of the Roman Catholic Church, but the issue is the same.

judged, but that is the Triune God's jurisdiction, not his. But Osama has a long term view so he is willing to outwait us, and to encourage all Muslims to have numerous babies while waiting for us to self-destruct.

The Lord has stated that a nation that forgets him will be judged by other nations. In fact, the little book of Habakkuk is about a more unholy nation judging ancient Israel. That led Habakkuk to ask how God could allow such a thing, but His answer is that when He's done using that wicked nation to judge Israel, He will judge it also.

> You are of purer eyes than to behold evil, and cannot look on wickedness. Why do You look on those who deal treacherously, *and* hold Your tongue when the wicked devours a person more righteous than he? (Habakkuk 1:13).

God Himself raises up such nations (Habakkuk 1:6) to judge other nations. Nations think they are doing what they want (and they are), not realizing that God has raised them up as His instrument of judgment (mystery of providence).

Other nations begin to devastate the nation being judged, devouring their livelihood and speaking another language:

> 15 "Behold, I will bring a nation against you from afar, O house of Israel," says the LORD. "It is a mighty nation, it is an ancient nation, a nation whose language you do not know, nor can you understand what they say. 16 Their quiver is like an open tomb; they are all mighty men. 17 And they shall eat up your harvest and your bread, *which* your sons and daughters should eat. They shall eat up your flocks and your herds; they shall eat up your vines and your fig trees; they shall destroy your fortified cities, in which you trust, with the sword" (Jeremiah 5:15-17).

Isn't it interesting that most of the world's oil reserves are in Islamic nations or other nations hostile to the USA? Why, at this time in our history, has that happened? It could be God's pressure on us to repent.

We're so willfully blind in the USA that we don't understand that our battle with Islam is not just over oil, 9/11, or car bombs. It is spiritual. There is no separation of religion and state in Islamic countries because they see Allah as lord over both areas. We try to separate the two areas, thereby proclaiming a religious god over religions and a secular god over politics. Islam will never adopt such idolatry; we adopt it wholesale.

We try to export our modern Democracy, which is now basically mob rule with elites moderating, and it does not work. It requires a secular state, and Islam does not believe in such. The USA was established as a Republic, which was rule by law, thus the written Constitution to keep from having tyrannical government, and that only works if the hearts of the people are free by faith in the Triune God. The Constitution was written to chain down runaway government and to maintain the rights of the people as the Declaration says, "endowed by their *Creator*," not as arbitrarily given by Washington. What Washington giveth Washington taketh away. (The Constitution should have invoked the Ten Commandments, but that is another story for another time.) We must not have democracy but submit to God's law.

Moreover, we have the huge immigration problem from Mexicans from the south to Muslims from the north. Islam has a long term view to take over nations of the West by taking advantage of our non-discrimination laws and our laws of freedom regarding religious worship. Mexican and Islamic immigrants are taking advantage of our anti-discrimination laws. We have become so paranoid about the "d" word (discrimination) that we have now compromised ourselves beyond repair. France and the United Kingdom are being invaded by Muslims demanding their rights and wanting Sharia law. Current immigration adds another language to weaken our ability to conduct business internally and weakens our ability for the military to defend us. What language will the soldiers speak in combat? Borderless globalism, the imagined dream of the socialists, would introduce lowest common denominator morality, economics, and military defense, with the elite controlling everything, of course. Yet the lordship of Christ through His law "is the most coherent and potent obstacle to secular utopianism."[6] As Peter Hitchens, the brother of the atheist Christopher Hitchens, says:

---

[6] Hitchens, *Rage Against God: How Atheism Led Me to Faith*, p. 134.

> The concepts of sin, of conscience, of eternal life, and of divine
> justice under an unalterable law are the ultimate defense against
> the utopian's belief that ends justify means and that morality is
> relative. The concepts are safeguards against the worship of hu-
> man power.[7]

We pride ourselves with our pluralism, but no nation has ever survived it. Pluralism is just a euphemism for polytheism, many gods,
many competing moralities with built in antagonism, all of which are
self-destructive. If all the Mexicans coming to the USA were conservative Roman Catholics, it might help us to some extent with the abortion
problem. But Roman Catholicism in general has not withstood tyranny
in most countries. Moreover, those south of the border were not instructed properly in the Roman Catholic faith when they converted
from their paganism centuries ago, and they bring a mixture of paganism, prayers to dead people, Mariolatry, and immorality, not to mention another language to complicate things.

Financially, the USA will be stressed to handle the real estate crash
we're facing, the price of oil, if we can get it, the counterfeit money
we're printing all the time that weakens the purchasing power of the
dollar, the baby boomers retiring, wanting Social Security, the influx of
poor people from south of the border who demand welfare, the banks
and other financial institutions that are crashing, financing wars and
health care, public schools pushing their various student tests so they
can get more federal money (but students graduating who cannot
read), and on it goes. All these projects will mean the printing of more
money, which in turn will devalue the dollar even more, making retirement plans worthless. This is judgment.

But discrimination is not a dirty word, and we must be discrimina-
tory about many things, such as the basis for morality, the Ten Commandments. I can guarantee you that if we keep removing every ves-
tige of Christian morality and the Gospel from our society that things
will only get worse, for Christianity is the *only* hope of resisting these
false gods and false moralities and their resultant judgments.

---

[7] Hitchens, *Rage*, p. 135.

Combine all the above with the feminization of our culture, and we can see God's judgment all around us:

> As for My people, <u>children are their oppressors, and women rule over them</u>. O My people! Those who lead you cause *you* to err, and destroy the way of your paths (Isaiah 3:12).

IV. Electing Corrupt Politicians (Political Suicide)

What do you think of Delaware's law that required its elected political representatives to take this oath?

> "I, . . ., do profess faith in God the Father, and in Jesus Christ His only Son, and in the Holy Ghost, one God, blessed for evermore; and I do acknowledge the holy scriptures of the Old and New Testament to be given by divine inspiration."

Or here was Massachusetts's Constitution, Article I, with their oath for elected officials:

> "I, . . . do declare, that I believe in the Christian religion, and have a firm persuasion of its truth. . . .

Delaware's law was in 1777, and Massachusetts's law in 1780. What has happened to the USA?

Every four years in the USA someone presents himself as the new messiah, the one who has all the answers, the one who will give us *change*. Roosevelt had his New Deal; Johnson proclaimed the Great Society, and Obama launched his campaign on Change. Just elect this one as President, and all our problems will be solved. However, the only problems the electorate recognize are economic ones. The *lack* of money is presented as the root of all evil so the printing presses are cranked up. Politicians promise what they can't deliver—unending prosperity. Few think that our problems are sin, but just political, economic, social, so all we allegedly need is better *management*. Get rid of the present management, and everything will be fine. Move the chess pieces on the board differently, but don't replace the chess board.

Or, perhaps what we need is less involvement in world affairs so bring home our military, and other countries will love us; all will be well. The lack of military involvement is the root of all good.

Are people sick and lack healthcare? Then get them healthcare at any cost, and make it "free," even though the quality may be such that it takes weeks or months to see a doctor, or one can only see a doctor approved by some bureaucrat, like my friend in England whose wife was in dire need of a physician, but is on a waiting list. The lack of universal healthcare is the root of all evil. As euthanasia spreads, people will be regularly euthanized to save the government health care money.

So at every point, *management*, not morality, is the perceived problem. But will we manage God Almighty who has imposed His Ten Commandments on us? It is our sins that are the problem, but we stubbornly refuse to believe that. There is no judgment, because we say so, and our word is final, not God's.

To restate this, the Ten Commandments remind us that we owe God a debt. For every sin, restitution must be made. On the human level, a thief must repay what he stole, a murderer must forfeit his life, but on the divine level, the debt is infinite. There is only one who was both God and man in one person, our Lord Jesus Christ, who as one person functioned as God and man simultaneously, identifying with us and God, making restitution for us. (See Appendix 2: The Incarnation.)

But we Christians are now a persecuted minority in the USA, being discriminated against with malice and forethought. We are surrendering our Christian heritage to politicians who hate God, who want to have death as an option open to all citizens at any age, who do not want God's law in society. The euphemistic Freedom of Choice Act, if it passes, will set us back decades in the abortion fight. It will also enhance the march toward full acceptance of euthanasia. The euphemistic Fairness Doctrine will take away Christians' right of free speech to proclaim God's Gospel and His law. We will not be able to use radio, TV, or the Internet to disseminate anything about the Triune God. This will mean government control over the airwaves, over the internet, and even over the pulpits of America. Already, liberals who cannot compete with conservatives on talk radio and TV are calling for the regulation of conservative radio and TV. But this will be a loss not just for Christians but also for all people's rights to life and to free speech. Only the political left will have rights. As Samuel Adams, one of the founding fathers of our country, so well expressed it:

> "No people will tamely surrender their Liberties, nor can any be easily subdued, when knowledge is diffused and virtue is preserved. On the Contrary, when People are universally ignorant, and debauched in their [morals], they will sink under their own weight without the Aid of foreign Invaders." (Letter to James Warren, 1775)

Then we think that our mighty military weapons will protect us from the national judgment of the sovereign Christ. Ancient Israel thought they were safe from their political and national enemies because they had many military weapons. The USA military is very advanced with many new ways to kill people with bombs that guide themselves to their targets, planes without pilots, but that means nothing to the Creator. One retired high ranking military officer said recently that our next Pearl Harbor will be in cyberspace. Christ could take us out in one day.

> Woe to those who go down to Egypt for help, and rely on horses, who trust in chariots because they are many, and in horsemen because they are very strong, but who do not look to the Holy One of Israel, nor seek the LORD! (Isaiah 31:1).

We are ignorant, both of basic morality and of our own history as a nation. We can regain what we have had if we stand for Christ. The place to begin is in our churches, and then in our homes. Homes by themselves will not be able to stand against the tidal wave of immorality that is sweeping our nation, but strong churches, composed of many families, can, especially if all Christians ban together.

V. Ignorance (Intellectual Suicide)

I'm not going to write much here as there are other works that cover this. (See Samuel Blumenfeld, Robert Bork, Alister McGrath, and Dinesh D'Souza in the Annotated Bibliography at the end of this book for excellent works on this). Suffice it to say that our public schools are a disaster, and that we are producing basically ignorant citizens who do not know math, science, how to think, history, even of our own country, but they know how to feel good about themselves. Our future generations are being lobotomized by computer games, TV (especially sitcoms), MTV, and sick, morally degenerate movies.

Rudolph Flesch wrote a very insightful book, *Why Johnny Can't Read*, followed by *Why Johnny Still Can't Read*, demonstrating that the abandonment of phonics for the look-say method was producing a generation of functionally illiterate people. As a pastor, I've seen many high school graduates, especially young men, who were promoted without making the grade ("no child left behind"), who can't read well enough to fill out an employment application.

Also, many public schools do not teach American history but distort it, leaving out either altogether George Washington or pertinent facts about him. The brilliant "Give me liberty or give me death" speech of Patrick Henry to convince people to sign the Declaration of Independence is not taught. Many don't even know who Patrick Henry was, and have never read this speech. We had students memorize this in high school in the early 1960s. But many today are taught to hate our culture, that the USA is evil, and so they are embarrassed by the founding fathers of the USA, especially of their Christianity.

To see how bad things have gotten, just watch a political debate, which is not a debate, but usually name calling, playing race cards, posturing, marginalizing, and so on. It is a sad commentary on how terribly we have been educated that we allow such a farce to continue. Moreover, just watch the news when a liberal and conservative go at it. The liberal will be rude, dominating the conversation, butting in. The conservative will try to make a few points from some statistics. Both will use arguments that are utilitarian, the ends justifying the means. Liberals want to forget the Constitution, appealing to the wants of the people, and conservatives won't force the issues of the Constitution. If just the Tenth Amendment were enforced, we could confine federal government to their listed powers.

Then on the campuses thought police make sure that no one will deny the current politically correct agenda: evolution, moral relativism, socialism, and killing babies. I'm wondering if some college student will kill dozens of fellow students, then proclaim he was taught moral relativism so why is everyone so upset.

Now William K. Kilpatrick has written *Why Johnny Can't Tell Right from Wrong.* Kilpatrick teaches education courses at Boston College. He says these are being pushed in the public schools:

- "Forty percent of today's fourteen-year-old girls will become pregnant by the time they are nineteen" (p. 14).
- Not only is morality not taught in the public schools, but parents are routinely marginalized and students taught to derive their own "values." There is no one above the students, not parents, and especially not God. Two approaches to ethics are used in the classrooms: (1) Values Clarification, where the student is taught that whatever he thinks is right and wrong is ok for him, and (2) decision making according to reason. But whatever conclusion the student reaches is ok. Is it any wonder that students are killing one another, having sex all the time, getting pregnant without two parents to raise the children, and using drugs? Since there is no right or wrong, getting drunk, having sex, taking drugs are just things to do (p. 14).
- There were exercises in an elementary school in St. Louis: use four-letter words for intercourse, drawing mother and father making love (p. 20).
- One junior high school administrator in a junior high school in Missoula, MT gives out valentines with condoms inside (p. 20).
- In one text book of sex education, the authors state: "Moral values cannot be taught and people must learn to use what works for them. . . . The essence of civilization is not moral codes but individualism . . . The only way to know when your values are getting sounder is when they please you more" (p. 22).
- The National Council for Self-Esteem and the Foundation of Self-Esteem are dedicated to teaching children to feel good about themselves, but pursing such in itself is teaching children to feel good about anything they do, even

drugs and murder. Self-esteem is a by-product of obedience to God's law, never to be pursued in itself (p. 41).

- Quest is a program designed to help students make decisions based on feelings (p. 47).

In other words, public schools are engaging in social engineering according to the latest academic fad, and nearly always in opposition to the standards of parents. This is not a book on the state of public schools, but the colleges are even worse. (Send for my booklet titled *Keeping Covenant and Educating Our Children* from service@footstool-publications.com.

VI. Gays in the Military (Self-Defense Suicide)

If Obama opens the military to gays, our defense shall be weakened enormously. Many who have been thinking of making a career of the military will now change their minds. Who would want to bring his heterosexual family into such an environment? Others who are making a career of it will take an early retirement. If the draft is restored, ninety percent of men are straight, and who will want to be subject to such pressure? Many of these potential draftees will go to places like Canada. Moreover, considering that homosexuality is such a dominating lifestyle, with many men having hundreds of "partners" each year, how will they be able to maintain focus? Can you imagine having a group of homosexuals in a submarine for a few months? The diseases that will ensue among the soldiers and the continual fights over lovers will hamper military efforts. This is the judgment of God.

VII. National Media (Character Assassination)

S. E. Cupp, an atheist lady, has written a very well documented book titled, *Losing Our Religion*, and the sub-title is *The Liberal Media's Attack on Christianity*. She repeatedly demonstrates how the media are extremely biased against Christians, documenting it with many footnotes. Though she is not a Christian, by her own admission, yet this dear lady has the temerity to face the lions, whom I'm sure are attacking her as well. She names people, times, incidents, and proves her case quite well. My book is already long enough, but I will give you one quote from her, which she makes as a summary after pages of documentation:

> For Kristof, apparently, teaching children that perhaps they should wait until they're older to have sex is frothing and going crazy — the kind of thing that should land you in a psych ward.
>
> But the idea that proponents of abstinence education are crazy (literally and figuratively) is hardly uncommon in the liberal media, which decided long ago that abstinence is silly and doesn't work, that everyone who matters agrees on that, and that those who don't are crazy Christians ignoring the enthusiastic stampede of progress — which includes, apparently, an upswing in sex.
>
> This isn't because they really care all that much if you're morally opposed to abortion or premarital sex, or whether you're encouraging your kids to make responsible decisions about sex. They paint pro-life and pro-abstinence Christians as crazy because they don't want to have to live up to those standards.[8] And they don't want Christians making them feel guilty about it. To put it even more bluntly, it's not that they don't think abortion and premarital sex are sins — it's that they don't want to be called sinners.[9]

Ms. Cupp is a media insider, having been interviewed by too many media to mention and is a nationally published political columnist. She wrote the book to wake up Christians, for she realizes that if our rights are trampled, everyone else's will be next. I'm grateful for this work.

AMEN.

---

[8] This is precisely what Romans 1:18ff says!

[9] S. E. Cupp, *Losing Our Religion: The Liberal Media's Attack on Christianity* (New York, NY: Threshold Editions, 2010), pp. 136-37.

Chapter 22—God's Judgment is Now . . . Religious

Introduction

Our culture at one time was very supportive of Christianity. But like most cultures, we have given over our religion to the culture. As Edward Gibbon said of the last days of Rome in his *Decline and Fall of the Roman Empire*:

> The various modes of worship which prevailed in the Roman world were all considered by the people as equally true; by the philosopher as equally false; and by the [politician] as equally useful.[1]

I. Modern Christianity

Suppose you visit a church. The sermon is about how to succeed in life. Point one is to be kind to yourself, for Jesus said that we must love our neighbors "as *ourselves*." It is negative not to love ourselves. Point two is to think positive thoughts and confess them verbally, for how can you achieve success with negativism? Thus, believe in yourself. The next three points are how to achieve financial success.[2] After all, God wants to bless His children, doesn't He?

If someone who knew nothing about Christianity were to visit this church a dozen times, hearing basically the same things, would he un-

---

[1] Jaroslav Pelikan, *The Excellent Empire: The Fall of Rome and the Triumph of the Church* (San Francisco: Harper and Row, 1987), p. 106-07.

[2] Yes, the Bible has a lot to say about finances, and there is a proper time to teach on these matters, but not when we come to worship God and proclaim His Gospel.

derstand what Christianity is all about? Does this sort of teaching help us to know Christ?

Now suppose you enter a Mosque. You hear: "There is no God but Allah, and Mohammed is his prophet." "God is one, he has no son." You attend a dozen times, and always hear that creed and the Koran explained. The speaker calls for you to commit to Allah to the death. Would you know what Islam is about?

What is wrong with this picture? Can we win spiritual battles with materialistic mantras about personal success while Islam teaches their people the essence of their faith, and are willing to die for it? This new Christianity is *consumerism*, which is obvious from the ads that churches run. They are catering to the *wants* of the consumer, not to the sovereignty of Almighty God. We deserve judgment.

At the Christian church mentioned above (actual church), there is no mention of sin, no mention of the Triune God, no mention of the Incarnation, no mention of the death of Christ on the cross for our sins, no mention of His bodily resurrection or ascension, indeed, no mention of anything that is distinctively Christian. One could go to a rock concert and get the same kind of entertainment. At too many local churches, the Bible has been turned into a popular psychological manual, and Christ-centered preaching has been traded for motivational pep-talks designed for self-improvement. God may not be glorified, but worshipers go home happy, and that seems to be all that matters. Moreover, worshippers are taught that they are sovereign, not God. God does their bidding and exists to make them happy, like a genie in a bottle, just waiting to jump out to grant us wishes if we perform correctly.

The contemporary church has become enslaved to self-worship, and not to pleasing God. Christians are given over to narcissism. My heart breaks as I write this, and it would appear that the only thing that will get our attention is severe judgment. Nothing short of repentance and giving ourselves totally to Christ can spare His wrath, but repentance will not be taken seriously *until we have pain*. We have transformed the faith from creeds to candy, from serving the Lord Christ in His army to demanding that He serve us. We should be serving the world, loving the people in the world to point them to the Savior, which requires an orientation to truth, such as the Holy Trinity and the Incarnation of the Son of God, but we want our play pretties. Now Christianity is market driven, from all the incredible number of Bible translations and study Bibles to all the TV ads to get people in the door with our latest slick slogans to cater to the "consumers." One slogan a mega-church in Houston promoted was "Find the champion in you." People in our churches want quick fixes for their problems, not repentance from sin over time. We want ditties, not doctrines; spiritual junk food, not banquets over the Lord's Supper; sweet Jesus, not the One who is final Judge and Lord of all the world, not the One who has predestined the world to His glory. God forbid that we are not in charge. The emphasis is on the "consumer," not on God, and we are so pleased with ourselves.

> What is uppermost on [their] minds is not the moral fabric of life but how to cope with their wayward personalities, self-doubt, the stages of life, marital stress, as well as calamities like job losses and the soaring cost of college tuition. . . . However, while these are not inconsequential matters, they are not burning moral issues with which the Bible is concerned. What is central to the Bible is . . . sin and grace, God's wrath and Christ's death; what is central to so many people today is simply what offers internal relief.[3]

In 1992 I met the famous pastor in Romania, Laszlo Tokes (pronounced toe-kesh), who made a stand against the dictator Ceausescu. He wrote about this in his book, *The Fall of Tyrants*. Christians from all over Romania stood with Tokes, and quickly the anti-Christian dictator was overthrown, tried, and executed. Tokes came to the USA for a conference, and I had the privilege to meet and talk with him for extended periods. After he spoke at a conference, there were questions and answers in a public forum. One American Christian wanted to know what we could do for them. Politely he responded that we were too weak to help them, but perhaps they could help us. What he meant is that we were too morally compromised.

---

[3] David Wells in Greg K. Beale, *We Become What We Worship* (Downers Grove, IL: Inter-Varsity Press, 2008), p. 294.

Last night (September 19, 2010), I heard an interview with the new president of Focus on the Family, Jim Daly, on Mike Huckabee show. He had recently returned from China. As he was being told goodbye at the Beijing airport, the Chinese Christians said they would be praying for American Christians. Out of curiosity, Daly asked what they would pray for. They said, "American Christians have it too good and are weak. Therefore, we pray for your persecution." While we should not be masochists, the Chinese Christians are right about us.

We American Christians are whoring after false gods, and because we don't know our Bibles, we think we are doing quite well with God—but we are not. Our gods of self-comfort and self-absorption have us blinded. We are in a moral free fall in the USA, especially after this last presidential election (2008) with so many god-haters in power. The churches are asleep, and the ministers hold their people's hands while whispering sweet ditties as they perish together. Christians have become cafeteria Christians, picking and choosing according to personal likes what parts of Christianity they want. Roman Catholics engage in abortion and Protestants take God for granted in worship.

The Baal religion of the Old Testament that so captivated God's people three thousand years ago was an exciting religion. It had sexual freedom (Judges 2:17; Jeremiah 7:9), sacrificing their children by burning (Jeremiah 19:5), burning incense to false gods (Jeremiah 19:4), and all these have now entered the churches in the West. Baal religion was all about feeling good; it was total immersion in "what's in it for me." God have mercy on us.

Whatever happened to dying for Christ, taking up our cross daily (Luke 9:23) to sacrifice our lives in service to Him? And in obedience to our spiritual marriage vows, our commitment should be "until death do we part," but even then we really don't part from Him; we just go home to be with Him forever!

The psychological pep-talk approach to preaching really makes Christianity just another *natural* religion, not a *supernatural* one, and eviscerates its power in confronting people with God Almighty. The power of God for salvation is the cross, as St. Paul specifically says, not our so-called wisdom (1 Corinthians 1:18ff). *It is precisely in the offenses of Christianity, such as the cross and sin, where the power of God resides to con-*

vert people. Pep-talk preaching is basically a liberal approach, making Christianity just another moralistic religion that can be molded into what the hearer wants. The church will not solve its problems with moral compromise, business management, and pop-psychology.

We are changed by viewing *God*, not ourselves. The modern approach to preaching tends to focus on *ourselves, our* needs, *our* wants, *our* successes, how *we* can live a wonderful, fulfilled, and happy life. It's all about *me*. But *we become like that which we worship*. Thus we are twisted and ugly, being transformed by material things and worldly success. But God has revealed Himself in the great works of redemption, and Paul states in clear terms in 2 Corinthians 3 that as we behold *Him* we are changed:

> But we all, with unveiled face, beholding as in a mirror the
> glory of the Lord, are being transformed into the same image
> from glory to glory, just as by the Spirit of the Lord (v. 18).

We Christians are now earth dwellers, those who are at home in this ungodly world, and who do not want to leave it for Christ. We have forgotten—or don't want to know—that "our citizenship is in heaven" (Philippians 3:20). We are ambassadors of Christ as in a far country (2 Corinthians 5:20), and then when we die we shall go *home*. Sometimes I ask my congregation if they are planning for retirement, and our tendency is to think of age 65, but I'm speaking of 100 years from now, indeed, 1,000 years from now.

When we worship false gods, we give authority to those false gods over us, and we seek to protect our idols with statements that only reveal our hearts, not what God thinks. We hear such things as "the service does not keep me awake," usually with a chuckle, or, "I feel more comfortable at this new church," as if that mattered. Christianity has nothing to do with "feeling comfortable," whatever that means. We don't care what God thinks or if the worship is biblical. "This other church is very informal, and we can drink coffee during the service." Can you imagine at the tabernacle worship in the Old Testament, expecting God to conform to our demands, not us to His, and entering His presence with coffee and doughnuts?

II. A Better Way

There is a better way. Do we want to be successful in our marriages? We must preach Jesus' love for His bride and the bride's submission to Him (Ephesians 5:22ff). Do we want to know how to forgive and how to be forgiven? We must see how God for Christ's sake has forgiven us at the cross (Ephesians 4:32). Do we want success in life? We must see how God defines success and pursue that (Psalm 1), which is doing His will, not our will ("Thy will be done"). Do we want our people to change and be conformed to the moral image of Christ? We must hold Him up so people can see Him, for if He is lifted up, He will draw all people to Himself (John 12:32). Anything else is just playing church games to be popular. We are not in a popularity contest with other ministers, but in a judgment contest to please Him who is "the blessed and only Potentate, the King of kings and Lord of lords, who alone has immortality, dwelling in unapproachable light, whom no man has seen or can see" (1 Timothy 6:15-16), whom to know is life eternal and whom to reject is death eternal.

By the way, sometimes I hear people jokingly say that if they go to hell at least they will have a lot of company with their friends and that God will not be there. Both statements are wrong. The Gospel is reconciliation between people, while hell is alienation, and in hell there will only be enemies; no friends there. Moreover, what makes hell so scary is being in the presence of the holy God without any grace to ameliorate the situation. One must face God and His wrath forever with no solution, no mediator, not even one drop of common grace that everyone has while on earth.

Moreover, the answer to Islam and the need for our culture is the Gospel as revealed in the Creeds (Apostles', Nicene, or Athanasian) that grounds the local church in the faith. Notice how the Nicene Creed, which is held by *all* branches of Christendom, is designed around the Holy Trinity and around the great historical acts of redemption in Christ. I quoted this in the Preface: How to Read This Book, but let us see it again.[4]

I believe in one God,
the Father Almighty,
> Maker of heaven and earth,
> And of all things visible and invisible:

And in one Lord Jesus Christ,
> The only-begotten Son of God;
> Begotten of his Father before all worlds,
> God of God,
> Light of Light,
> Very God of very God;
> Begotten, not made,
> Being of one substance with the Father,
> By whom all things were made:
> Who for us men and for our salvation came down from heaven,
> And was incarnate by the Holy Ghost of the Virgin Mary,
> And was made man,
> And was crucified also for us under Pontius Pilate.
> He suffered and was buried,
> And the third day he rose again according to the Scriptures,
> And ascended into heaven,
> And sitteth on the right hand of the Father.
> And he shall come again with glory to judge both the quick and

the dead:
> Whose kingdom shall have no end.

And I believe in the Holy Ghost,
> The Lord and Giver of life,
> Who proceedeth from the Father [and the Son,][5]
> Who with the Father and the Son together is worshipped and

glorified,
> Who spake by the prophets.

---

[4] Also, this Part 3 will be printed separately so some will not have access to the Preface.

[5] "And the Son" can be dropped without damage, as Eastern Orthodoxy does.

And I believe one holy Catholic and Apostolic Church.
I acknowledge one baptism for the remission of sins.
And I look for the resurrection of the dead,
And the life of the world to come. *Amen.*

Now when people come into our churches and hear this, they will know what Christianity is about, which is the Holy Trinity, creation, the person of Christ who was incarnate by the Virgin, died on the cross for our sins, was raised from the dead, the Church and sacraments as God's way of worshipping Him, and Christ is coming again to judge the world. It is this faith that will overcome the world, overpower Islam, overcome the new gods of our society, and save the soul. This Creed is the wonderful combination of the historical revelation from God to us and of theological meaning of those historical events as revealed in Holy Scripture. This Creed is the core of Christianity, and even the Ten Commandments are secondary. The "virtues" of Christianity are meaningless apart from knowing this God personally.

Virtually all Christianity has said this Nicene Creed for 1,500 years. Moreover, the Christian Church for many centuries has said that three things are necessary to be a Christian: (1) the Apostles' Creed, which is shorter than the Nicene above but in essence the same, (2) the Ten Commandments, and (3) the Lord's Prayer, and (4) of course one must do these in the context of a local church that preaches the Gospel. That is the minimum, but how many churches do you know that ever mention these things? Too many churches consider end time prophecy more important than the Holy Trinity, so when one seeks to join, they are asked virtually no questions about God, Christ, the Church, or the sacraments but are asked their view of the rapture or antichrist. No wonder we are so weak culturally when we are more concerned with leaving (the rapture) the culture than confronting it with the Gospel.

III. Worst Sin in America?

It is difficult to say what is the worse sin in America without direct access to the mind of God, but surely one of them is *Christian apathy.* If Christian pastors had been preaching the Gospel the way we did 100 years ago, we would not be in the moral decline we're in nationally or personally, but too many Christian pastors are compromisers. They will do anything to get numbers for an outward show of success. There are few ministers on national TV who seek to honor the Triune God, to preach Jesus and His bodily resurrection, to preach and teach his Ten Commandments. Instead, they affirm their members and thereby deny God. It is saccharin Christianity, sickly sweet and artificial. Even Christians in their retirements don't seek to advance the kingdom of God but seek their own kingdoms as they pursue the stock market, quilting, dancing, gardening, and so forth. There is nothing wrong with these last things in themselves, but we're at war spiritually. It is time to lay aside the good things and pursue the best—God, His written word, and His Church.

When the Gospel is preached consistently, many are converted to Christ, and the whole culture is affected by Christian morality. We call this the cultural effect of the Gospel. This is the way it was in 1776 when the Declaration of Independence was signed. Not everyone at that time was a Christian (Thomas Jefferson was a deist who denied the Virgin Birth, the Holy Trinity, etc.), but the *culture* basically received the Bible as God's word, the Ten Commandments as God's morality, Jesus Christ as the Son of God, and believed in the Holy Trinity. Christian morality was assumed in society. Even most of those who did not embrace these publicly at least gave lip service to them. In fact, as we have seen, some states required belief in the Holy Trinity before anyone could serve in office.

IV. Good Bye to Judgment

The first things to go when liberal preachers gain dominance are sin and judgment. You can't build a mega-church by preaching sin and judgment, or the Ten Commandments, so these ministers, often untrained in good seminaries, promise not to preach on sin. I heard one such preacher in Texas say on TV that he would never preach on sin but always affirm his people. Another one in California stated that Jesus never mentioned sin, which is incredibly false, and this minister built a large glass church. More than ever, "Christians" today want to have their ears tickled, to be told they are fine, that God does not judge. Here is the way Jeremiah put it in his day:

> ³⁰ "An appalling and horrible thing has happened in the land: ³¹ the prophets prophesy falsely, and the priests rule at their direction; **my people love to have it so**, but what will you do when the end comes?" (Jeremiah 5:30-31, ESV).

Notice the bold, underlined words: "My people love to have it so." False prophets are characterized by giving the people what they want to hear. Similarly, we read:

> ⁹ They are a rebellious people, lying children, children unwilling to hear the law of the LORD; ¹⁰ who say to the seers, "Do not see," and to the prophets, "Do not prophesy to us what is right; speak to us smooth things, prophesy illusions, ¹¹ leave the way, turn aside from the path, let us hear no more about the Holy One of Israel" (Isaiah 30:9-11, ESV).

When the Twin Towers were destroyed on 9/11/2001, do you remember how the liberal news media interviewed liberal preachers who stated that it was not the judgment of God? At all costs, they wanted God, His Ten Commandments, and His judgment removed from the picture. There are many ministers who are for hire ("Have Preacher Will Travel"), who will say what the people want to hear.

> ¹⁶ Thus says the LORD of hosts: "Do not listen to the words of the prophets who prophesy to you. They make you worthless; they speak a vision of their own heart, not from the mouth of the LORD. ¹⁷ They continually say to those who despise Me, 'The LORD has said, "You shall have peace" '; and *to* everyone who walks according to the dictates of his own heart, they say, 'No evil shall come upon you' " (Jeremiah 23:16-17).

There comes a point in time when the Triune God will not want to hear our dead worship services anymore:

> ¹⁰ Hear the word of the LORD, you rulers of Sodom; give ear to the law of our God, You people of Gomorrah: ¹¹ "To what purpose is the multitude of your sacrifices to Me?" Says the LORD. "I have had enough of burnt offerings of rams and the fat

of fed cattle. I do not delight in the blood of bulls, or of lambs or goats. [12] When you come to appear before Me, who has required this from your hand, to trample My courts? [13] Bring no more futile sacrifices; incense is an abomination to Me. The New Moons, the Sabbaths, and the calling of assemblies — I cannot endure iniquity and the sacred meeting. [14] Your New Moons and your appointed feasts My soul hates; they are a trouble to Me, I am weary of bearing *them*. [15] When you spread out your hands, I will hide My eyes from you; even though you make many prayers, I will not hear. Your hands are full of blood (Isaiah 1:10-15).

Surely the Triune God is sick of our "worship" services here in the USA. We come into His presence with sin that we have no intension of repenting of and expect Him to bless us. People take God for granted, or else don't take Him at all, but He is the holy God who will not tolerate people claiming to know Him while not repenting of their sins:

[8] Behold, you trust in lying words that cannot profit. [9] Will you steal, murder, commit adultery, swear falsely, burn incense to Baal, and walk after other gods whom you do not know, [10] and *then* come and stand before Me in this house which is called by My name, and say, "We are delivered to do all these abominations"? (Jeremiah 7:8-10).

There is one Episcopal denomination that has consecrated bishops who are gay, one priest elected to be bishop who is Buddhist, another priest who is Druid, another who is (or was) a priestess and at the same time Islamic, and clergy who deny the bodily resurrection of Christ. The first commandment says we are to worship "only" the one God, not Him *and* false gods. If the pulpit is so unreliable, what can we expect of the pew?

One of the worst sins today among Christians is either denying what God says in His holy and infallible written word, or adding to it with "God told me this." People, Christian people, are inventing things that God allegedly says to them. But listen to what God says about this:

[19] And when they say to you, "Seek those who are mediums and wizards, who whisper and mutter," should not a

people seek their God? *Should they seek* the dead on behalf of the living? [20] <u>To the law and to the testimony! If they do not speak according to this word, it is because there is no light in them</u> (Isaiah 8:19-20).

[16] All Scripture is given by inspiration of God, and is profitable for doctrine, for reproof, for correction, for instruction in righteousness, [17] that the man of God may be complete, thoroughly equipped for every good work (2 Timothy 3:16-17).

These passages could be repeated many times, but we see that God says His written word is all we need from Him for the content of our faith and for godliness. In other words, the Bible is not only *necessary*, it is *enough*. I've always used the following as a plumb line for the extra revelation that allegedly comes from God apart from the Bible: if it contradicts the Bible, it is wrong; if it says the same thing as the Bible, it is not needed; if it goes beyond the Bible's statements, it has no authority.

Indeed, *there are two ways to apostatize*: (1) formally in what one believes and (2) morally in what one practices. Formally, there are so many heresies today that we need another Reformation more than the first one under Martin Luther in the 1500s. Ministers and parishioners deny the Holy Trinity, the Virgin Birth, the deity of Christ, His death on the cross for our sins, His bodily resurrection, and His coming again in judgment at the Last Day. And now there are two revisited beliefs that have been consistently condemned by the Church over the centuries: that God is not omniscient (called the openness of God movement), and that all will be saved (universalism). Those who deny eternal punishment especially hate the Athanasian Creed with its doctrine of hell, even saying it is not a creed. In the days of the Protestant Reformation in the 1500s, these truths were believed by all major parties. But today we need a new Reformation of all Christianity—Roman Catholic Church, Eastern Orthodoxy, and Protestant.

Also, we know of the terrible immoral problems among the clergy, such as the pedophilia of the Roman Catholic priests, the adultery among Protestant ministers, and I'm sure Eastern Orthodoxy has not been spared. The Episcopal Church consecrates homosexual bishops. Many ministers and members have given themselves over to ungodliness, such as sexual sins, covetousness, exploiting others for money, and so forth. Just read what the Apostle Peter wrote not long before the Lord took Him home:

> ¹ But there were also <u>false prophets</u> among the people, even as there will be false teachers among you, who will secretly bring in destructive heresies, even denying the Lord who bought them, *and* bring on themselves swift destruction. ² And many will follow their destructive ways, because of whom the way of truth will be blasphemed. ³ By covetousness they will exploit you with deceptive words; for a long time their judgment has not been idle, and their destruction does not slumber. ⁴ For if God did not spare the angels who sinned, but cast *them* down to hell and delivered *them* into chains of darkness, to be reserved for judgment; ⁵ and did not spare the ancient world, but saved Noah, *one of* eight *people,* a preacher of righteousness, bringing in the flood on the world of the ungodly; ⁶ and turning the cities of Sodom and Gomorrah into ashes, condemned *them* to destruction, making *them* an example to those who afterward would live ungodly; ⁷ and delivered righteous Lot, *who was* oppressed by the filthy conduct of the wicked ⁸ (for that righteous man, dwelling among them, tormented *his* righteous soul from day to day by seeing and hearing *their* lawless deeds) — ⁹ *then* the Lord knows how to deliver the godly out of temptations and to reserve the unjust under punishment for the day of judgment, ¹⁰ and especially those who walk according to the flesh in the lust of uncleanness and despise authority (2 Peter 2:1-10).

In 1958 when I was 13, I had a step-father who was a preacher. He tried to murder my mother, who was pregnant with his son, so he could marry another woman in his congregation who had suddenly come into a lot of money. He began having sex with this woman. Unknown to my mother, he had gotten into sexual problems in another state in a former church before they were married. His murderous plot did not work, but he was never prosecuted. He broke the entire law of God and never repented, revealing that he was not the minister of Christ, but of the devil:

[13] For such are false apostles, deceitful workers, transforming themselves into apostles of Christ. [14] And no wonder! For Satan himself transforms himself into an angel of light. [15] Therefore it is no great thing if <u>his ministers</u> also transform themselves into ministers of righteousness, whose end will be according to their works (2 Corinthians 11:13-15).

And the Lord Himself stated regarding those who pretend to be ministers but who hate His commandments:

[21] "Not everyone who says to Me, 'Lord, Lord,' shall enter the kingdom of heaven, but he who does the will of My Father in heaven. [22] Many will say to Me in that day, 'Lord, Lord, have we not prophesied in Your name, cast out demons in Your name, and done many wonders in Your name?' [23] And then I will declare to them, '<u>I never knew you</u>; depart from Me, <u>you who practice lawlessness</u>!' " (Matthew 7:21-23).

But all true Christians know that they are sinful, that God's law reveals the holiness of God, and that they fall short of His standard. We know that since God is infinite, sin has infinite implications. We know that we cannot offer anything to God to make Him accept us, which is where Christ comes in. Christ, as the infinite Son of God, has obeyed the law for us and has died on the cross to take our penalty for breaking God's law. He is our only hope, and He is acceptable to the Father!

V. Standing for the Triune God

One other matter. *Christians today are cowards.* God says cowards will perish. (Read Revelation 21:8.) Even some ministers will not stand publicly for God's word, like one couple who pastor a large church. (How in the world did couples in our day suddenly become called together to co-pastor?) When they were interviewed recently by Larry King, they weaseled about gay marriages, saying the postmodern thing that "for them" it was wrong, and that it was "better" to have one man and one woman for marriages. They agreed with Larry that gays are good people, when the Bible clearly says none are good, not anyone, not me, not you (Romans 3:9-18). Moreover, the Bible says that what they do is wrong and they need to repent, like I need to repent of my sins. The

Lord warned regarding those who want to be liked by people rather than pleasing to God:

> "Woe to you when all men speak well of you, for so did
> their fathers to the false prophets" (Luke 6:26).

It is a sign of a false prophet when one wants to be accepted by all, rather than be accepted by God. We can only win this culture back by confrontation, by polarization, so our culture will know where the boundary lines of truth are, not by compromise. When Christians compromise, those engaged in wickedness love it, for it means we do not take seriously our beliefs, and that does not threaten the ungodly. It is well defined faith that Satan and his seed fear, not compromise.

AMEN.

Chapter 23—Conclusion: The Way Back

Introduction

So what is so wrong with the Ten Commandments? What is so horrible with being faithful to one's spouse, with not killing the unborn, with telling the truth, with being obedient to godly authority, with not stealing, with not coveting? What is so wrong with using speech in a respectful way, not gutter language? What is so wrong with taking one day a week off for worship?

I can tell you why people hate these things, which I've said multiple times in this book. It is the first five commandments that present the Triune God as the *only* God; that is the problem. People don't want *Him*. Since we are born in sin, we humans naturally hate Him. Remember the very insightful lines from the movie *Tombstone* where Val Kilmer played Doc Holliday (his best performance of all his movies, in my humble opinion). Wyatt Earp (Kurt Russell) asks Holliday questions, as Holliday lies sick in bed. They are fighting the cowboys, and their new leader is Ringo. Earp has to face Ringo soon in a shoot out.

Wyatt Earp: "What makes a man like Ringo, Doc? What makes him do the things he does?"

Doc Holliday: "A man like Ringo has got a great big hole, right in the middle of him. He can never kill enough, or steal enough, or inflict enough pain to ever fill it."

Wyatt Earp: "What does he need?"

Doc Holliday: "Revenge."

Wyatt Earp: "For what?" (The camera closes in on Doc, and he pauses to emphasize his answer.)

Doc Holliday: "Bein' born."

That's it. As we're born into the world, we hate righteousness and therefore hate God. We are sinful at birth, and the political God-haters hate that idea with an unholy passion. We want our own way, not *His* way. We want to commit sexual sins, murder babies and others, steal, lie, and so on *because we love it*. Moreover, we're at war with God, and rebellion is the only way we can attack Him. Here is what the Lord said, which I've quoted before:

> [19] And this is the condemnation, that the light has come into the world, and men loved darkness rather than light, because their deeds were evil. [20] For everyone practicing evil hates the light and does not come to the light, lest his deeds should be exposed. [21] But he who does the truth comes to the light, that his deeds may be clearly seen, that they have been done in God (John 3:19-21).

I have not made a major issue of liberal versus conservative politics, for rebellion against God is from both sides of the aisle. We must not be concerned about the right or the left but about right and wrong. There are people of principle in both parties but no party of principle.

There is no political solution for our nation, except that of repentance, confession of our sins, and coming to the Triune God through the Son of God. Anything short of this adds more fuel to the fire of our judgment. Both sides of the aisle are given to idolatry. Both believe that a few tweaks of the political process will cure our problems. Both believe that new management is what we need, not a radical confession of sin, and turning to God through Christ.

Some will call what I'm saying a religious solution, and as a result they will easily dismiss this book. My response is that any solution is necessarily all these: political, religious, and moral. It is impossible not to have a religious solution, for every solution either invokes God (religious) or rejects Him (religious). Every solution assumes some view of some god, some view of morality with some authority behind that morality, either by might or by votes. Some of the most religious people I know are atheists who are very committed to their faith and world view. (Read the very insightful book by Christian philosopher and scholars, Norman Geisler and Frank Turek, *I Don't Have Enough Faith to be an Atheist*.)

Others will object that we'll never get enough people to agree with that. In other words, the answer is allegedly how many people will sign off on God. But that is precisely the problem; they don't believe that God is the answer but people. We don't need millions of Christians to turn the nation back, though that would be ideal, but we need a few who believe God. Remember Gideon in the Bible who defeated 120,000 men with only 300 (Judges 6-8), but the Triune God was on his side. It is not that the Triune God and one are a majority; God is the majority — period. But He normally uses humans to accomplish His will, so we just need a few people who have faith in Him. Will you be one of them?

But political conservatives think that conservative politics is the answer to our moral decline. Some otherwise conservative Christians make the USA and its Constitution their religion with liberals and those in power (conspiracy theories) as their enemy. The religion of politics will not save our country, not even conservative politics. Christ is the *only* answer.

Here is what Glenn Beck had on his web site, and many think that he has a grassroots movement to unite Americans concerned about the current path of our government:[1]

9 Principles	12 Values
1. America is good.	Honesty
2. I believe in God and He is the center of my life.	Reverence
	Hope
3. I must always try to be a more honest person than I was yesterday.	Thrift
	Humility
4. The family is sacred. My spouse and I are the ultimate authority, not the government.	Charity
	Sincerity
	Moderation
	Hard Work
5. If you break the law you pay	Courage

---

[1] http://www.glennbeck.com/content/articles/article/198/21018/ , accessed October 21, 2009.

the penalty. Justice is blind and no one is above it. 6. I have a right to life, liberty and pursuit of happiness, but there is no guarantee of equal results. 7. I work hard for what I have and I will share it with who I want to. Government cannot force me to be charitable. 8. It is not un-American for me to disagree with authority or to share my personal opinion. 9. The government works for me. I do not answer to them, they answer to me.	Personal Responsibility Gratitude

While I can cooperate with anyone, even an atheist, on some level regarding social issues, such as abortion, theft, unjust taxes, and while I especially admire Glenn Beck and his courageous stand for our country, we cannot turn this nation back to the Triune God by adding idolatry to our list of sins. While I don't mean to be unkind, Mormonism is part of the problem. My heart really goes out to Mr. Beck, and I've sent him a free copy of this book (who knows if he will personally get it as I'm sure he receives such gifts continually and there are only 24 hours in a day).

But he is doing to Christianity and its founding documents what he is rightly pointing out that liberals are doing to the founding documents of the USA—especially the Constitution—reinterpreting it according to some new standard. There are three branches of Christianity, Eastern Orthodoxy, Roman Catholic, and Protestant, and *all three interpret the New Testament the same way* in the basics: according to the Nicene Creed. All three branches can trace their history and interpretation back through the first form of the Nicene Creed in A.D. 325, back through the Apostles' Creed, and back through the early fathers to the New Testament itself. Moreover, all three branches agree that Mormonism is not Christian. Though we Christians have our differences among ourselves, when it comes to the basics, we all believe the Nicene Creed, and all agree that Mormonism is outside the faith. In other words, Joseph Smith was equivalent to a modern day liberal who takes the Constitution and twists it, for he said that only he had restored the true faith and the true interpretation of the New Testament after 1800 years of heresy. (For an astonishing comparison of Mormons and Muslims in free pdf file, please send an email to service@footstoolpublications.com.)

It is very ironic that Glen Beck proclaimed George Whitefield a great preacher to the Colonies on his TV program, but he preceded Joseph Smith, the founder of Mormonism, by 75 years, and would have been appalled at Mormonism and its departure from the Bible. Even more to the point, there was not one Mormon among the founding fathers of this great country, not one. Most of them were Trinitarian, by which we mean one God as Father, Son, and Holy Spirit. He is not just one in *purpose*, as the Mormons say, with the Father existing before the Son, but one in *essence*. In other words, the reason there is only one God is that there is only one divine essence, not three distinct essences and three independent individuals who cooperate with one another in purpose, as the Mormons say. Mormons teach that the Father has a body, the Son has a body, but the Holy Spirit is spirit. Moreover, they teach that Father and Son are completely distinct from one another as different entities, different bodies, different essences, and thus separate beings. In other words, there are two gods with the Father over the Son. Thus, in Mormonism there are three distinct gods, each with his own essence and distinct personhood. As one Mormon scholar said to me as we engaged in Instant Messaging on the official Mormon site, the Mormon gods are like the President and his cabinet: one (the Father) over the others, but the others are gods as well.

The nine principles and twelve values on Beck's site are just what I've been trying to refute this whole book. First, where is the Triune God in all this? This is a so-called political solution that leaves God out of the picture. It is to make a religion of America. Both political liberals and conservatives believe in a civil religion and a generic God. Both have their politically correct values. Both say your view of "God" and your relationship with Him is only a private matter, even though Jesus make it a public matter also so that the one who does not confess Him in public, He will not confess to His Father (Matthew 10:32-33). The liberals fight for "their commandments" to be public policy: sexual immorality, redefinition of the family, transfer of wealth, death orientation through abortion, infanticide, and euthanasia, and the disarming of its citizens, which would make it easier to take over. Many political conservatives have their own public commandments or "values": obedience to "God" (whoever that may be), both for and against the "traditional" family (some are pro-gay), generally pro-life, wink at sex outside marriage, porn is not something to worry about, and so on. The difference between the parties is degree, not kind. Both sides tend to agree that economic matters are the problems rather than a symptom of the problem, and both agree that the Triune God and His law are not for the public arena. Some political conservatives understand the issues and are self-consciously seeking to turn people to the Triune God, like Bryan Fischer with American Family Association, Jim Daly and James Dobson with Focus on the Family, Franklin Graham, but these are exceptions.

Neither political liberals nor political conservatives dare think of Jesus as Lord in public as well as in private. Yet this is a violation of the First Commandment regarding idolatry, the Second Commandment in worshipping the creature state rather than the Creator, the Third Commandment by taking Jesus' Name in vain, and so on. Will we really defeat Satan without the Triune God? Will God be pleased with private worship and public rebellion?

He is not a house god who takes sides, who waits for people to invoke Him so He can bless them. Joshua asked the pre-incarnate Christ: "Are you for us or for our adversaries," to which He responded: "No, but as Commander of the army of the LORD I have now come." Our response must be that of Joshua's: "And Joshua fell on his face to the earth and worshiped, and said to Him, *What does my Lord say to His servant?*" (Joshua 5:13-15). The question is not whether the sovereign King is on our side; the question is whether we are on His side. He is not the Lord of liberalism or of conservatives, but the Lord over the nations who rules directly, sovereignly, and especially through His law word, the Ten Commandments.

Furthermore, the idea behind these principles and values mentioned on Beck's web site above dethrones government and enthrones the individual, moving from the tyrannical solution of the one to the tyrannical solution of the many. Freedom does not lie in government or in the individual but in the gospel of the grace of the Triune God as one believes in the Son of God who died on the cross for our sins and raised Himself from the dead. Freedom does not lie anywhere else. We must pursue the conversions of millions of people in the USA, and pursue bringing our institutions under the lordship of the one and only King, Jesus the sovereign Lord. Only then will He turn back the tsunami of Islam and other false religions, death, economic oppression, destruction of the family, and other evils.

And what is wrong with using the Ten Commandments for our "values," especially since God has already imposed them on us, and it is not possible to live profitably without assuming them? Recall what we said earlier: every moral law enacted is either obedience to God's law or rebellion against God's law. Every law system implies *someone* behind that system, and the many gods of Mormonism will not turn this nation around, for they do not exit. There is no other alternative than the Ten Commandments, and that holds true individually and nationally. We either embrace the Triune God or reject Him, as seen in how one treats His character in His law. Thus for one to claim to have moral principles apart from God is rubbish, and to think that we will be blessed by the Triune God when we embrace some of His moral laws while rejecting others, therefore rejecting Him personally, is rebellion.

And what is the definition of the twelve "values" listed above? Who will define them? Most political liberals would agree with those "values" so what does the political conservative hope to accomplish?

Then there are "principles" on Beck's site that do not have the Triune God attached to them, but just abstract moral ditties, implying no judgment. In other words, each person chooses what morality he *wants*.

And many of the things listed under principles are just plain wrong. America is not good; we are wicked. If we are good, there is nothing we need to repent of.

And what "God" does one believe in? Here once again is the generic "god" that is politically correct, but not the one and only Triune God who said to worship no one but Him.

"My spouse and I" are not the ultimate authority over the family, the King of kings is the head of every godly chain of command. Moreover, the government does have jurisdiction over the family when a crime against the family is committed, crime being defined by God's law, and the Church is also over Christian families. It is moral anarchy to say there is no authority over the family.

To say that one must be more honest each day is nice, but how does one define honesty? The Ten Commandments define it, but they are conspicuous by their absence.

Finally, to say that one does not answer to government is also anarchy, which is contrary to God in Romans 13 where God through Paul says that God has given the government the power of the sword in certain matters, circumscribed by the Ten Commandments. I think I know what is meant: though God has given authority to government, at times it is tyrannical, especially when it takes the innocent lives of its citizens, but the table does not say that.

And especially to the point, for anyone to think that we can obey our way into blessing means that by our moral works we can make the Triune God obligated to us, that we will earn God's favor by our own effort, that the Gospel of Jesus Christ, the crucified and resurrected Son of God, is irrelevant, that all we need is a generic "god" and a few generic moral "principles" to make things right. A human works salvation is Mormonism, but it is not the Gospel. This is a denial of the Triune God, a denial of His Ten Commandments that say that we are hopeless sinners, a denial that the only solution is through Jesus of Nazareth, by His death on the cross for our sins, and by His bodily resurrection, a denial that we receive His salvation, which means His forgiveness of sins, as a free gift as we repent.

But let us get back to our culture. Because all morality is personal, moral change only comes by *confrontation*. We must be willing to be vulnerable, to stand against those who hate God, to do so with love and compassion, giving the Gospel the whole time. We who know God through Christ have a debt to pay, and it is to share the Lord Jesus with those who hate Him, just as we also hated Him at one time.

Make no mistake, conservative politics of the kind mentioned above with "values" and "principles" will only invoke the wrath of God just like those who are making a frontal assault against the King of kings with abortion and sexual sins. The irony is that those who think they are doing the will of God by pursing morality without the Triune God and without His Ten Commandments are also at war with Him. But they think they have the moral high ground. This is Pharisaical self-deception.

I. Hypocritical "Christians"

Glenn Beck is part of the problem. He is always rightly denouncing the liberation theology of the left, which is a "gospel" of political salvation, especially prominent among African Americans, but he is offering a liberation theology of the right, which is also a political salvation. What is so sad is that many evangelicals are following him, which tells me they just want a political revival, to get things back to "normal" so they enjoy their peace, their quiet, and their toys. Beck speaks very highly of the tea party movement, but many of those are not pro-life, not pro-family but pro-gay, and what they want is fiscal responsibility, which means money, not Him. The Triune God is going to cram toys down our throats. Even Beck recently said that gays who practiced their "morals" in private would not bother him, but that contributes to our national character, our national immorality before God.

Even Christians are given to self-righteousness. The power of sin to self-deceive never ceases to amaze me (even in my own life, as much as I know it). If you ask a Christian why he is not attending worship, he will give some excuse like "I'm a good Christian because I go to church at Christmas and Easter." (We call them "Christers.") They will then think that God is pleased with this, stating that God knows their circumstances. But how do they know what the Triune God thinks? They make it up as they go, thereby creating a god after their own image, who just happens to excuse their disobedience. What God really thinks is that we are "not [to] forsake the assembling of ourselves together"

(Hebrews 10:25), and that must be done each Lord's Day (1 Corinthians 16:2). Again, here is what God says:

> There is a way that seems right to a man, but its end is the way of death (Proverbs 14:12).

Moreover, from a survey taken in March 2009, those who claim no religion in the USA are now 15 percent, up from 14 percent in 2001 and from 8 percent in 1990. This is because *there is a famine in the land*:

> [11] "Behold, the days are coming," says the Lord GOD, "That I will send a famine on the land, not a famine of bread, nor a thirst for water, but of hearing the words of the LORD. [12] They shall wander from sea to sea, and from north to east; they shall run to and fro, seeking the word of the LORD, but shall not find it (Amos 8:11-12).

We have fallen so far from the Triune God that I fear it may be too late, but only He knows. One thing is sure, our covenant God can be our covenant enemy when we have compromised our relationship to Him with so much unrighteousness, and He will fight against us. Isaiah said of the people of God in his day:

> But they rebelled and grieved His Holy Spirit; so [God] turned Himself against them as an enemy, *and* He fought against them (Isaiah 63:10).

We are at a point where we must do as King Jehoshaphat did when he was faced with enemies that he could not overcome. He went to the temple to pray and to confess the sins of the people, and he concluded:

> O our God, will You not judge [our enemies]? For we have no power against this great multitude that is coming against us; nor do we know what to do, but our eyes are upon You (2 Chronicles 20:12).

The problem is not God's power, for He could turn the hearts of the ungodly in our culture in a week, but here is the problem:

> But your iniquities have separated you from your God; and your sins have hidden *His* face from you, so that He will not hear (Isaiah 59:2).

Once again I give the solution that we began this book with, and the Lord God is speaking:

> 13 "When I shut up heaven and there is no rain, or command the locusts to devour the land, or send pestilence among My people, 14 if My people who are called by My name will humble themselves, and pray and seek My face, and turn from their wicked ways, **then** I will hear from heaven, and will forgive their sin and heal their land" (2 Chronicles 7:13-14).

Though this promise was made to Israel many centuries ago, God does not change. If Christians ("My people") would humble themselves in the confession of their sins; trust in the Messiah, Jesus Christ; and seek the Lord by loving His commandments, *then* He would forgive our sins, defeat our enemies by converting them to Christ, and restore our land to its greatness. Anything short of this will only continue to increase the judgment.

We must fall on our faces, confess our sins against this loving but just God, and trust in the Lord Jesus Christ and His death and resurrection. Anything short of this, personally, in our churches, and nationally, will only lead to more judgment.

II. Cultural Saturation with Sin

Indeed, our culture has almost completely abandoned the Triune God. Is God just waiting for our sins to completely saturate our land and then final judgment will come? I don't know, but He has done so with other nations:

> The iniquity of the Amorites is not yet complete (Genesis 15:16).

> And in the latter time of their kingdom, when the transgressors have reached their fullness, a king shall arise, having fierce features, who understands sinister schemes (Daniel 8:23).

> 31 [Jesus:] "Therefore you are witnesses against yourselves that you are sons of those who murdered the prophets. 32 Fill up, then, the measure of your fathers' *guilt.* 33 Serpents, brood of vipers! How can you escape the condemnation of hell? 34 There-

fore, indeed, I send you prophets, wise men, and scribes: *some* of them you will kill and crucify, and *some* of them you will scourge in your synagogues and persecute from city to city, [35] that on you may come all the righteous blood shed on the earth, from the blood of righteous Abel to the blood of Zechariah, son of Berechiah, whom you murdered between the temple and the altar" (Matthew 23:31-35).

[14] For you, brethren, became imitators of the churches of God which are in Judea in Christ Jesus. For you also suffered the same things from your own countrymen, just as they *did* from the Judeans, [15] who killed both the Lord Jesus and their own prophets, and have persecuted us; and they do not please God and are contrary to all men, [16] forbidding us to speak to the Gentiles that they may be saved, so as always <u>to fill up</u> <u>*the measure of*</u> <u>their sins</u>; but wrath has come upon them to the uttermost (1 Thessalonians 2:14-16).

We see the same fullness of wickedness in God's instructions to Israel to take the Promised Land. God said the reason He was giving the Israelites the land is that those in it had so given themselves over to wickedness that only judgment was left for them:

[24] Do not defile yourselves with any of these things; for by all these the nations are defiled, which I am casting out before you. [25] For the land is defiled; therefore I visit the punishment of its iniquity upon it, and the land vomits out its inhabitants (Leviticus 18:24-25).

[22] You shall therefore keep all My statutes and all My judgments, and perform them, that the land where I am bringing you to dwell may not vomit you out. [23] And you shall not walk in the statutes of the nation which I am casting out before you; for they commit all these things, and therefore I abhor them (Leviticus 20:22-23).

III. Liberal Arrogance

One definition of a liberal (regardless what side of the aisle) is one who hates the Triune God, His Commandments, and His people. What God loves they hate; what God hates they love. Liberals seek to please people and thus make war with God, while Christians seek to please the Triune God and thus incur the anger of non-Christians. They cannot hurt Him so they want to hurt Christians. Thus *the persecution of Christians has already begun* in the United Kingdom and in the USA. Young Christians are hammered in the university classrooms by professors who think it their duty to relieve high school graduates of their faith, while the liberals present their own irrational faith. This persecution may degenerate to all out murder of Christians, with the government's approval, of course. Unless things are turned around, there will be the "final solution" for Christians.

It has been reported in the national news in England that Christians are being pursued for hate speech when they presented the gospel.[2] (**You must listen to footnote 2 on the internet** if it is still there!) One man was suspended from his job when he refused to attend homosexual sensitivity training presented by a lesbian. The government is considering legislation to force affirmative action regarding gays to force employers to hire them.

Remember the timely film put out by Ben Stein, *Expelled: No Intelligence Allowed*, where he documented the extreme bias against Christians or any theists who would dare challenge the first commandment of the God-haters, "Thou shalt worship evolution as the creator." Make no mistake that this is the first commandment for many in our culture, especially the so-called intellectuals, but who cannot stand up to the challenge to prove their faith that chaos produced order. Christian professors are not being hired, and those that are accidently hired are being fired. So much for tolerance.

Moreover, a bill that would allow the state legislature in Connecticut to reconfigure the governing structure of the Catholic Church has

---

[2] http://downloads.cbn.com/cbnnewsplayer/cbnplayer.swf?aid=9425. **You must listen to this!**

been pulled, *for now*. This attitude by those who hate the Triune God indicates their true posture that the government god is over the Jesus God.

(Consider all the legislation to redefine marriage. See Chapter 13: What Is Marriage?)

For a very informed article on what is facing us, please send an email to service@footstoolpublications.com, and ask for the Focus on the Family Action article. I encourage all Christians to check with their web sites often for what is going on:

- http://www.citizenlink.org/focusaction/
- http://www.focusonthefamily.com/

From the persecution of Christians mentioned above, we see that all worship is exclusive; God-haters don't want anyone worshipping any other god than the politically correct god created by them. They are *extremely* intolerant. Consider (April 2009) the Miss USA pageant where one of the contestants was subjected to a question from a hostile liberal judge about gay "marriages." First, that was a "religious" question and should not have been asked, according to the rules of the pageant. Second, when she said such unions were ok, but that she preferred a traditional marriage, later the judge screamed obscenities on his video blog, which was later played on Fox News, saying that the reason she placed second was because she was a "stupid bi. . ." It would seem clear that he voted against her on religious grounds: she did not sign off on his immoral confession of faith. This manifested hatred will only increase as those who oppose God's Ten Commandments become increasingly more vocal. She was a graceful Christian, both during and after the contest, but he was vehemently hostile. We see which one had grace and tolerance.

IV. Statism

After rehearsing the hundreds of millions murdered by atheist regimes in the 20th century (Hitler, USSR, Bolsheviks, Chinese Communists, Khmer Rouge, Fidel Castro, Cambodia, Vietnam, Laos, North Korea, and many others), the former atheist Peter Hitchens insightfully states:

The delusion of revolutionary progress, and the ruthlessness it justifies, survives any amount of experience. This suggests that terror and slaughter are inherent in utopian materialist revolutionary movements. There will be another of these episodes along soon.[3]

But Atheists cannot bear to look their faith's faults full in the face. They cannot even admit that their dogmatic insistence that there is no God is in fact a faith, though they cannot possibly know if they are right. And so the escape clauses come think and fast. If atheism in practice appears at any point to have had bad consequences, that is because it took on the character of religion. So this murder, that massacre, that purge just do not count. If religious people do good things with good consequences, that is because they are really atheists without knowing it.

We are told by my brother [Christopher Hitchens] that Joseph Stalin's Soviet Union was in fact a religious state. In the mouth of any other person, serving a cause other than the comfortable West's rejection of self-restraint and divine law, such thin, self-serving stuff would produce scorn and mockery from the anti-religion advocates. . . . To say that Stalin used many of the outward forms of religion is perfectly reasonable and true. But to claim that the outward forms are more important than the inward character is plainly false. It is precisely the inward character — submission to an earthly authority instead of an eternal authority — that makes all the difference.[4]

This lack of integrity or complete self-deception of the New Atheists to their own assumptions is why I cannot take the New Atheists seriously. With all their name calling and arrogance, they and their books are very subjective.

Atheist regimes, who are materialists, make human idols of the elite, and believe in the ultimate goodness of themselves while rejecting

---

[3] Headed for the West and especially in the USA, I'm afraid.

[4] Peter Hitchens, brother to atheist Christopher Hitchens, *The Rage Against God: How Atheism Led Me to Faith* (Grand Rapids: Zondervan, 2010), pp. 154-155.

such of their opposition, which is what we see in the New Atheists. If others disagree with them, it is because they are defective, either genetically or in their reason. Either way, purging is the solution. Tyrants cannot tolerate rival authority with a rival moral law code. "Atheism is a license for ruthlessness, and it appeals to the ruthless."[5] In the USA, we could have government by emergency with some president taking over, suspending the Constitution on the alleged basis of some impending disaster, such as economic, military, or whatever they may dream up.[6]

If the twentieth century teaches us anything, it is that atheistic countries first verbally attack their opposition, religion, especially Christianity with Christ as Lord, before they engage in open persecution and murder. Elitists do not want the competition. If we Christians are called to suffer for Christ's sake, we must do so with patience toward God and love for those made in His image. But let us take courage. Though the USSR severely persecuted the church, Stalin is gone, and the churches are back. Leningrad is once again St. Petersburg. Because of the resurrection of Christ, we always win in the end — always.

V. What Must Christians Do?

Regarding whether to fight or not, we have no choice. The spiritual war is all around us. Consider the insightful words of Patrick Henry on the eve of the Declaration of Independence whether they should fight the British, whether there would be war:

> "It is vain, sir, to extenuate the matter. Gentlemen may cry peace, peace, but there is no peace. *The war is actually begun.* The next gale that sweeps from the north will bring to our ears the clash of resounding arms. Our brethren are already in the field. Why stand we here idle? What is it that gentlemen wish? What would they have? Is life so dear, or peace so sweet, as to be purchased at the price of chains and slavery? Forbid it, Almighty

---

[5] Hitchens, *Rage*, p. 160.
[6] See the insightful book by Gary North, *Government by Emergency* (Ft. Worth, TX: American Bureau of Economic Research, 1983).

God! I know not what course others may take, but as for me,
give me liberty or give me death!" [emphasis added]

The spiritual war is all around us. We are already in it. We will either be a casualty or a warrior; there are no other choices.

But we're collapsing under the weight of our own sins, like a rotten superstructure. We'll compromise almost anything for the sake of personal peace and prosperity. "Lord, just let my children grow up first." But those who put anything before the Lord are part of the problem. We must train our children to be righteous in believing the Gospel and to be faithful covenant seed, serpent slayers for Jesus (Romans 16:20). Remember that Daniel was only a teen when he was taken captive to Babylon, and he stood strong his whole life.

Moreover, we need good theology, the creeds, not hype, not positive confession, not entertainment on Sundays. Don't expect most popular ministers to take a stand; they have too much to lose in their mega-churches, mega-buildings, mega-ministries, and mega-bucks, though there have been exceptions, such as D. James Kennedy (who is now at home with the Lord). Christ has already won, has been enthroned on high, and Christ is the majority. All He needs is one person of faith, or for a few Christians to wake up, and fight the war that is all around us. It will cost us.

At this juncture in our battles with Satan in the USA, all Christians who adhere to the Nicene Creed must band together, which means Roman Catholic, Eastern Orthodox, and Protestant. We must put aside our internal differences for now, oppose the Goliaths that challenge us in our beloved nation, or we won't have *any* Christian freedoms. We'll be hauled off to the Gulag under the guise of some euphemism like "Fairness to Pagans."

But the persecution that is now here and increasing has its silver lining—it will (hopefully) cause the true Christians to wake up. The Church will be purified. We will march again, and it is the Church, not individuals or single families, that will storm the gates of hell with the Gospel and win (Matthew 16:18). Our weapons are not physical, not guns and knives, but they are spiritual:

> [3] For though we walk in the flesh, we do not war according to the flesh. [4] For the weapons of our warfare are not carnal but mighty in God for pulling down strongholds, [5] casting down arguments and every high thing that exalts itself against the knowledge of God, bringing every thought into captivity to the obedience of Christ, [6] and being ready to punish all disobedience when your obedience is fulfilled (2 Corinthians 10:3-6).

Yet these weapons are more powerful than physical weapons. The Triune God will punish "all disobedience" when the Church is obedient to Him, trusting Him for the battle, proclaiming His word. From now on, it will cost us something to serve Christ in the USA. Because our Christian ancestors preached the Gospel so strongly for so long, we've had a free ride. The ride is over. Now comes the cost, and we must sacrifice ourselves and all we have. We must pledge "our lives, our fortunes, our sacred honor" to Christ and to one another, being willing to die for the One who died for us. Even death cannot stop us, for our Lord has made it our friend, not our enemy. Sin is the enemy. Satan is the enemy. Those who hate us are Christ's enemies.

But *we Christians must repent*, which means we must do more than condemn others for their sins; anyone can do that. We must condemn ourselves for our apathy in sacrificing our children on pagan altars in public schools, for not loving those made in God's image as God loves them, for in loving His image, we love Him. We must demonstrate this love with such ministries as helping street people. If nothing else, we can get involved with the Salvation Army to help. Moreover, we must have more ministries to help those girls who have had an abortion or are considering one, to have more pro-life clinics. We must not condemn but love them for Christ's sake, to share His love with them. We must begin more ministries to those who engage in various sexual sins, such as recovery clinics for those who are hooked with porn on the internet, for prostitutes, for those in same sex unions, for those who have AIDS, and so on. It is time for us to get dirty, not only by confession of our own sins by admitting them, but also to demonstrate our repentance by getting involved to help deliver others from their sins as we seek to serve them with the love of Christ. We must love people more than our pastimes and more than our toys. If we don't stop being hypocrites, God will continue to increase the cultural pressure on us until we repent. Truly we deserve what is coming on us.

Finally, we Christians must stop compromising the Gospel for the sake of personal peace. We must not be like Esau who sold his birthright (Hebrews 12:16) for a few temporal morsels of bread and toys to play with while eternity roars down on us like a tyrannosaurus rex. The wrath of the Lamb only waits so long. But while the day of grace is still here, let us repent of all our sins against God's holy commandments, and let us go forth under the banner of the cross. The victory is His—and ours!

VI. What Must Non-Christians Do?

You must first realize that you have broken God's law. Until you admit that, there is nothing to do but meet Christ at the Last Day judgment, and it will not bode well. You must not engage in self-justification but in self-condemnation. But anyone who admits his sins, confesses them to God, while also trusting in the death and resurrection of Christ, will be acquitted. Moreover, you must be baptized into a church where God is honored, and seek to serve Him there.

Charles Colson, who was convicted at Watergate, was converted to Christ while in prison. Moreover, my homosexual friend "Steve" related to me how he knew there was a sovereign God when he came to Christ, for his desire for men was taken away. He was as surprised as anyone. And www.ExodusInternational.org works with gays who want out by leading them to know Christ. Since we are made in His image, though marred with sin, He knows how to change us, to make us new and whole, but we must be willing to confess that we need help. God loves us as we are, but He loves us too much to leave us as we are. He will not affirm us in our sins, but He will affirm us if we are willing to part with them. We cannot have the holy God and our unholy sins; we must choose which master we shall serve—Him or our sins (Matthew 6:24).

Remember, God will do with us what we do with His Son, Jesus Christ. If we throw Him away, God will throw us away. If we embrace

386 Not Ten Suggestions

Him as our Lord and Savior, God the Father will embrace us as His children. The choice is ours, but also His.

VII. Hope Beyond Measure!

As you little boy grows up and your inevitably take him to a funeral, what will you tell him? Will you tell him the only thing an atheist can say? "There is no hope. We live, die, and that is the end. You'll never see your dad again. Keep a stiff upper lip, life stinks."

For the Christian, life is wonderful. Even our sufferings have meaning because the sufferings of Christ had meaning, and we are identified with Him. He was raised from the dead, and His sufferings for our sins are applied to us. There is not one thing in the Christian's life that does not have meaning, even the worst suffering—death. Our Lord sanctifies our sufferings to us to make us better people, and then when we die, we reap the benefits of those sufferings, not as merits but as rewards. I can truly stand at a coffin with my loved one lying there (and indeed have!), and not be afraid, praise the Lord for His resurrection, and look forward to our reunion! Indeed, I have preached the funerals of close loved ones, knowing that we have the victory! There is no greater joy than living with hope that kills the grave! Here is the way the Apostle Paul put it:

> For to me, to live is Christ, and to die is gain (Philippians 1:21).

> We are confident, yes, well pleased rather to be absent from the body and to be present with the Lord (2 Corinthians 5:8).

> [16] Therefore we do not lose heart. Even though our <u>outward</u> man is perishing, yet the <u>inward</u> man is being renewed day by day. [17] For our light affliction, which is but for a moment, is working for us a far more exceeding and eternal weight of glory, [18] while we do not look at the things which are seen, but at the things which are not seen. <u>For the things which are seen are temporary, but the things which are not seen are eternal</u> (2 Corinthians 4:16-18).

> **AMEN** to the glory of the Triune God!

Appendix 1: Worship of Images and Prayers to Saints

Harold Browne was an Anglican theologian who wrote an exposition of the 39 Articles. He wrote over 100 years ago on the use of images in worship:

> In short, if the Roman Church had never approached nearer to idolatry than the Jews when they worshipped in the courts of the temple, within which were symbolical figures of oxen and cherubim, than the high priest, when once a year he approached the very ark of the covenant and sprinkled the blood before the mercy-seat, or than the people in the wilderness, when they looked upon the brazen serpent and recovered, there would have been no controversy and no councils on the subject of image-worship. But when we know, that the common people are taught to bow down before statues and pictures of our blessed Savior, of His Virgin Mother, and of His saints and angels; though we are told that they make prayers, not to the images, but to those of which they are images, yet we ask, wherein does such worship differ from idolatry? No heathen people believed the image to be their God. They prayed not to the image, but to the god whom the image was meant to represent. Nay! the golden calves of Jeroboam were doubtless meant merely as symbols of the power of Jehovah; and the people, in bowing down before them, thought they worshipped the gods "which brought them up out of the land of Egypt" (1 Kings xii. 28). But it is the very essence of idolatry, not to worship God in spirit and in truth, but to worship Him through the medium of an image or representation. It is against this that the second commandment is

directed: "Thou shalt not make to thyself any graven image, nor the likeness of anything that is in heaven or earth, or under the earth—Thou shalt not bow down to it, nor worship it." And it is not uncharitable to assert, that the ignorant people in ignorant ages have as much worshipped the figure of the Virgin and the image of our Lord upon the cross, as ever ignorant heathens worshipped the statues of Baal or Jupiter, or as the Israelites worshipped the golden calf in the wilderness. It must even be added, painful as it is to dwell on such a subject, that divines of eminence in the Church of Rome have taught unchecked, that to the very images of Christ was due the same supreme worship which is due to Christ Himself—even that *latria*, with which none but the Holy Trinity and the Incarnate Word must be approached. Bellarmine himself, who takes a middle course, states the above as one out of three current opinions in the Church, and as held by Thomas Aquinas, Caietan, Bonaventura, and many others of high name; and though he himself considers the worship of *latria* only improperly and *per accidens* due to an image, yet he says that "*the images of Christ and the saints are to be venerated, not only by accident or improperly, but also by themselves properly, so that themselves terminate the veneration, as in themselves considered, and not only as they take the place of their Exemplar.*" If this be not to break one, and that not the least of God's commandments, and to teach then so, it must indeed be hard to know how God's commandments can be broken, and how kept. Even enlightened heathenism seldom went so far as to believe the worship to be due *properly* to the idol itself, and not merely to its original and prototype.[1]

We agree with Browne in the abuses, yet symbols are allowed. (See Appendix 3: Bowing and Worshipping, and see the chapter on the Second Commandment.) Some say they *pray to* saints, which assumes their omniscience to hear multiple millions of prayers, their omnipotence to

---

[1] Harold Browne, *Exposition of the Thirty-Nine Articles of Religion*, CD version from www.foostoolpublications.com , p. 663.

answer the prayers, and their omnipresence to be with people all over the world at the same time.

Others say that they only *ask* Mary or Peter to pray *for* them, not pray *to* them, but there is not a single example of this anywhere in Holy Scripture, much less commanded, and 2 Timothy 3:16-17 states that Holy Scripture is all we need for belief, life, and godliness.

Browne states:

> It is desirable to observe the distinctions which Romanist divines make between the worship due to God, and that paid to the Blessed Virgin and the saints. They lay it down, that there are three kinds of worship or adoration: first, *latria*, which belongs only to God; Secondly, that honor and respect shown to good men; thirdly, an intermediate worship, called by them *dulia*, which belongs to glorified saints in general, and *hyperdulia*, which belongs to the human nature of Christ, and to the Blessed Virgin.[2]

This is not the place to go into this topic in detail, but it is enough to say that we do not give any kind of worship to creatures. We may honor martyrs in the sense of thanking God for their lives, and wanting to live like they did, which is precisely what we see done in Hebrews 11 with the martyrs of the Old Testament. What the Reformation has advocated is only one kind of worship and that is to God alone. We may honor godly people and reverence the cross in the sense of what it stands for, but there is no worship here, and honor to martyrs and reverence to the cross was the virtual universal practice of the early church, while worship of any kind was strongly condemned.

Moreover, we are forbidden to have contact with the dead (1 Samuel 28:7ff) or with those who have contact with the dead (Deuteronomy 18:10-11). This would eliminate prayers to saints.

> [19] And when they say to you, "Inquire of the mediums and the necromancers who chirp and mutter," should not a people inquire of their God? Should they inquire of the dead on behalf of the living? [20] To the law and to the testimony! If

---

[2] Browne, *Exposition of the Thirty-Nine Articles*, p. 650.

they will not speak according to this word, it is because they
have no light in them (Isaiah 8:19-20, ESV).

We are to seek God through His written word, not through the dead!

The doctrine of the Communion of the Saints only appeared in the
fifth century in the creeds and was absent from the Eastern versions at
that time. It does not teach that we can pray to the dead or have some
kind of personal communion with them in the sense of praying to
them. The Communion of the Saints is communion with the same God,
by the Holy Spirit, in Christ, whether on earth or in heaven, but not
talking to one another beyond the grave.

Moreover, the expression in Hebrews 12:1 that "we are surrounded by so great a cloud of witnesses" says absolutely nothing
about praying to them or asking them to pray for us. The Greek word
for "witnesses" is the same word used for "martyr" and in light of the
previous chapter (chapter 11), where many Old Testament martyrs
were just mentioned, the idea most likely is this: "we are surrounded
by so great a cloud of *martyrs.*" We are surrounded by them, not in the
sense that we talk to them or they to us, but in the sense that we profit
from their recorded witness in the Scriptures as just given in the previous chapter.

Then comes the theological problem why prayers to Christ who is
the only mediator (1 Timothy 2:5), God and man in one Person, the
Creator of all, are not sufficient so that one must have mere creatures
mediate for us to add to Christ's mediation for our salvation. What
sense does it make to add the finite prayers of Mary and the saints to
the infinite prayers of Christ for us as the mediator? Of course, as humans we do pray for one another on earth, but we do not plead our
blood or our so-called merits for one another, and we do not go to God
through any mediator but Christ, as the Bible explicitly says:

There is one God and <u>one Mediator</u> between God and men,
the Man Christ Jesus (1 Timothy 2:5).

When I was in electrical engineering at a private Roman Catholic
engineering college after high school, there was a notice on the bulletin
board about praying for the speedy release from purgatory of a professor who had been killed in a plane crash. The notice said something

about having the merits of the spiritual treasury of the church stored from the saints applied to him. As I turned away, I saw my calculus professor and asked: "Brother Jerome, what does it mean to add finite to infinite?" He said, "It means nothing. One does not get larger than infinite." To which I responded, "What sense can it make to add the finite merits of the saints to the infinite merit of Christ? Why can't professor (don't recall his name) go to heaven immediately based on Christ's merits?" He was stunned.

Appendix 2: The Incarnation

But God demonstrates His own love toward us, in that while we were still sinners, Christ died for us (Romans 5:8)

© Dec 2001

The Rev. Dr. Curtis I. Crenshaw[1]

The mystery of the incarnation is something that we shall never fathom. We can behold it, worship the Son, revel in His grace, wonder with awe at His love, but never exhaust its mystery.

At the time that the Father appointed,[2] the Son of the living God was joined with humanity, conceived in the Virgin's womb by the Holy Spirit. The Second Person of the Holy Trinity had *added* to His undiminished divine Person a perfect human nature, taken from Mary. His humanity came from Mary, as the Last Adam had to be in the lineage of the first Adam, of the fallen human race, not a new race created outside of the existing one. As redeemer He had to be one with us, yet outside us without sin. He took from her what was human as mankind was originally created, but not as fallen. He was fully human, having a real body and a rational soul. He got hungry, needed to sleep, had human emotions of joy and anger, but He never sinned. *He was fully human as if not God.*

The woman Eve was taken from the *side of Adam* and given to him as his bride. The woman led the man into sin. Now the Last Adam is taken from the woman to deal with sin, and on the cross His side is pierced so that His bride can come from Him!

He was also *fully God as if not human.* He was the second Person of the Trinity, God of God, light of light, very God of very God, the same

---

[1] This may be copied and handed out to small groups if and only if no changes are made, and it is not published for profit. Dr. Crenshaw may be reached at Service@footstoolpublications.com.

[2] Galatians 4:4

in essence as the Father in every way, existing from all eternity. When the Virgin conceived by the Holy Spirit, humanity was joined to His deity, not that His deity came into existence. Indeed, He was unchangeable[3] so that His deity did not change one iota at the holy conception. He *added* to His divine person perfect humanity, but nothing whatsoever was subtracted.[4] If He had ceased in any way to be God, there would have been no Trinity and no God, for God is Father, Son, and Holy Spirit. Giving up His deity would be incarnation by deicide. Or if Christ had ceased to be fully God, there would have been two "gods" left, the Father and the Spirit, which would mean the death of God. *A savior who is not fully God is a bridge broken at the far end, and a savior who is not fully man is a bridge broken at the near end. He would not reach fully either to God or man.*

Here we are confronted with one of the greatest mysteries of God's holy and infallible Bible. The infinite One adds a finite nature without in any way lessening the infinite. As Mary carried the babe in her womb, sustaining His life, He was giving her life as He upheld all things by the word of His power.[5] As she held Him in her arms after His birth, He was holding her and the whole universe in His "arms." She had originated, so to speak, His humanity. He had created all things whatsoever, making Himself the *originator* of creation.[6] He was not only the Word who spoke all things into existence, but He was the *sustainer* of what He had called into being from nothing. He was not only the originator and sustainer but also the *goal* of creation, the reason it was created, the end toward which all creation is moving, the one to be glorified.[7] Thus He is the origin, sustainer, and goal of creation as all moves to glorify Him.

The mystery of *the union of God and man* can only be understood by what has been revealed. We know that it was necessary for Him to be both God and man. He had to be a man to redeem man from his sin

---

[3] Hebrews 13:8

[4] The modern day heresy of kenosis states that Christ's incarnation was by *subtraction*, that He gave up something of either His deity or the use of His deity.

[5] Hebrews 1:3

[6] John 1:3; Colossians 1:16

[7] Colossians 1:16-17

and death, to be identified with the human race that lost relationship with God. As God He could not die, but as man He could. He had to be God to satisfy infinite holiness, to take an infinite penalty, an infinite curse. What He did in His atonement was absolutely dependent on who He was, the two aspects being inseparable. Adam sinned and died. Jesus must be one with the seed of Adam so that He could die.[8] Adam owed God perfect obedience. Jesus obeyed God perfectly for us.[9] Adam came under the penalty of sin, which was divine judgment. Jesus took our punishment.[10] We read:

> Inasmuch then as the children have partaken of flesh and blood, He Himself likewise shared in the same, that through death He might destroy him who had the power of death, that is, the devil, and release those who through fear of death were all their lifetime subject to bondage. For indeed He does not give aid to angels, but He does give aid to the seed of Abraham. Therefore, in all things He had to be made like His brethren, that He might be a merciful and faithful High Priest in things pertaining to God, to make propitiation for the sins of the people.[11]

He had to be *one Person* so that what one nature did would be united with the other nature in the one Person, thus joining the work of both natures. If He had only been a man indwelt by God, He would have been a great prophet, but not the One who could redeem; just one of the prophets of old. Under this circumstance, when He died, we would be left with a dead man and a distant God.[12] But as God-man in one person, when He shed His blood, it was the blood of God: "to shepherd the Church of God which He purchased with His own blood."[13]

------

[8] Hebrews 2:9

[9] Hebrews 2:10 (The grammar indicates that Jesus was bringing many sons to glory by His being made perfect.)

[10] Isaiah 53:5; Romans 3: 25; Galatians 3:13

[11] Hebrews 2:14-17

[12] From my student, Mark Bleakley.

[13] Acts 20:28

396 Not Ten Suggestions

If Christ were two persons, how could he shed His blood as man and offer infinite atonement as God and do both as one offering? It would be two offerings as two persons. He had to be one Person so that what one nature did would be united with the other nature in the one Person, thus joining the work of both natures.

If He had been two persons, we would not have a union of man and God doing a single work, but two persons doing a dual work. There would have been a human sacrifice to a God who could not accept such. Such a *moral* cooperation of a divine and human will would not give infinite value to the human or a human aspect to the divine. *There would be moral cooperation between two persons, but not an essential union of God and man.* God would still not be revealed personally but through a human only. But with a union of essence, a personal union[14] of man and God, what either nature did was attributed to the one Person. If He had been two persons, the natures could not have joined in one act but as two acts. But He was the God-man, not God and man; thus the two natures joined in Him as one work.

If the *natures had been mixed* in some way, He would have been less than God or more than man. If he had been less than God, He could not have offered sufficient atonement to the infinite God. If He had been more than man, He could not have represented us, not being "made like His brethren." He would have been a hybrid, but not the God-man who lived and died for us, being totally acceptable to God as His peer, and representing us as our peer, joined in one Person and working as one.

Yet if the two natures had not been joined in essence, a metaphysical union, what He did in one nature would not have affected what He did in the other nature. He would have acted as a human and then as God but neither act would have been united with the other as the one act of the God-man. We would have had the acts of man and the acts of God in separation, not in union in one Person. As it was, His atoning work brought man and God together in *Himself.*

Though the natures were joined in the Son, they were *not mixed together but distinct.* There was a Creator/creature distinction in Christ

---

[14] "Hypostatic" is the word theologians use.

Himself.[15] Consider the contrasts we have in this God-man of the two natures and one person with natures united but not merged:

> He was God yet man.
>
> He was infinite yet finite.
>
> He was a babe who needed nurturing yet God who upheld all things by His sovereign word.
>
> He had a human will that struggled with His mission in the garden yet a divine will that was unchangeable, impeccable, and absolutely determinative of all things. His human will was always obedient to His divine will.
>
> He had a human consciousness and a divine consciousness yet only a divine *self*-consciousness and divine *self*-awareness, the I AM, the One who forgave sins.[16]
>
> He had a human mind yet a divine mind. He could be known by humans face to face yet He and the Father knew one another uniquely, infinitely, and exhaustively: "No one knows the Son except the Father. Nor does anyone know the Father except the Son, and the one to whom the Son wills to reveal Him."[17] He could say humanly He did not know the time of His Second Coming,[18] but divinely He knew all things.[19] He read the hearts of men as easily as one reads a book.[20]
>
> As God He upholds all things; even His humanity is upheld by His own deity. His humanity is indwelt by His deity, by the Holy Spirit given to Him without measure.[21]

---

[15] Most of the Christological heresies of the ancient church were attempts to compromise the Creator/creature distinction in Christ.

[16] Matthew 9:1ff. There were not two self-consciousnesses in the Lord, for then He would have been two persons. Some struggle with how the one Person could both know and not know the time of His Second Coming, but the Church's teaching of two consciousnesses seems to answer this. In His human conscious, He did not know; in His divine consciousness, He did know.

[17] Matthew 11:27

[18] Mark 13:32

[19] Matthew 11:27; John 21:17

[20] Matthew 9:4

[21] John 3:34

As man He was limited to one place at a time yet as God He filled heaven and earth.[22]

As man He was limited in His abilities to perform works of feat yet as God He was (is) the Lord God omnipotent, raising the dead, stilling storms, upholding all things, the beginning and the end.

In these contrasts, it is not that a single nature was both infinite and finite, for that would be a contradiction, but that the single Person of the Son can be considered from either the human nature or the divine nature, each being distinct from the other.

As God-man He had (has) absolute authority in heaven and on earth. When Satan came to tempt Him as the Last Adam,[23] he instantly obeyed the Lord when He commanded him to leave Him. Even the wind obeyed, and demons immediately came out of the ones He commanded them to exit. The healings He performed were instantaneous and perfect, a wonder to behold, as He recreated human tissue. With one spoken word, or sometimes just the thought, He performed miracles in His own name, not the name of another.

The incarnation is love beyond measure. God became humble, as it were, submitting Himself to the now rebellious creation that He had originally made holy.[24] One's humility is measured by the degree of his exaltation. It would not mean much for a common laborer to help an old lady across the street, but if the president of the USA did, it would mean more. How much more is it for the infinite God to assume humanity and submit to those who hated Him! The judgment that God required, He now came to take. The holiness that we lacked, He wove by His perfect obedience to His own holy law and commandments. The curse and punishment due us, He joyfully assumed in our place on the

---

[22] John 1:48-50; 3:13 (This last text is supported throughout the manuscript history even though most modern versions leave out the words "even the Son of man who is in heaven.")

[23] Matthew 4:1ff. This is the only other time Satan appeared personally to tempt someone. In other words, he appeared twice in Scripture to tempt humans personally: the first Adam and the Last Adam. We are not suggesting that he had nothing to do with other temptations, but that Scripture only records two personal appearances to tempt.

[24] Philippians 2:8

cross: "Who for the joy that was set before Him endured the cross, despising the shame, and has sat down at the right hand of the throne of God."[25] Love manifested itself with infinite condescending. This was not a love in words only but primarily of doing.

Furthermore, *this love was particular*. It is easy to say: "I just love everyone." When we love everyone, there is no accountability for loving any one person. But take an oath to love one other person no matter what, such as in our wedding vows, to flesh out love for this other human for better or worse, giving up selfish orientation, to focus on the person's needs—that is another matter! But that is precisely what the Lord of Glory did for His people. The Father gave Him a bride,[26] whom He cherished to the point of death, even death on a cross.[27] There was nothing He would not do for His bride, even submitting to vile men, dying, and raising Himself from the dead.[28] He ascended to His home to prepare a place for His bride.[29]

In heaven we shall behold our loved ones who have known and served the King of glory. They will be beautiful and be whole, bodies restored,[30] no more suffering, sadness, or pain. We shall be "together with *them*," and "thus *we* shall *always* be with the Lord."[31] What joy we shall have as we are reunited with loved ones we have not seen for many years, especially knowing that no power can ever separate us again! A child lost in youth is beautiful. A godly grandmother who taught you the Bible at her feet greets you. A father who was faithful in bringing you up in the discipline and instruction of the Lord embraces you. A mother who prayed for you for years rejoices. A husband who was faithful to love his wife as Christ loved the Church is reunited with the one he cared for on earth.[32] Once in heaven, we can project ourselves a million millennia into the future, and at that projected time we will have been to-

---

[25] Hebrews 12:2

[26] John 17:6; Ephesians 5:22ff

[27] Philippians 2:8

[28] John 10:18

[29] John 14:2

[30] Paul indicates that we shall have some form of body in heaven (2 Cor. 5:1-8), but at the resurrection we shall have glorified bodies like the Lord's (Phil. 3:21).

[31] 1 Thessalonians 4:17

[32] Ephesians 5:22ff. But there will not be marriage in heaven (Matt. 22:30).

400 Not Ten Suggestions

gether only a finite period of time, with an infinite period still to come!
The finite past will always be but a dot; the infinite future a line that
reaches to the horizon.[33]

As much as we shall rejoice over being made whole and reunited
with loved ones, whom we shall easily recognize,[34] there is one exception to being whole in heaven: the hands, feet, and side of the Lord.[35]
Fixing our attention on Him, we worship the nail prints in His hands
and feet and the spear hole in His side. He has changed the crown of
thorns for a diadem, and His robe is whiter than snow for His purity.
All else fades as we behold the Lamb on His throne. Like a tidal wave,
we will be overwhelmed with such grace as we bask in His presence.
As never ending waves break on a shore, we shall forever have one
wave of grace only to be followed by another. We shall be filled with
praise, singing the song of the Lamb:

> And they sang a new song, saying: "You are worthy to
> take the scroll,
>
> And to open its seals;
>
> For You were slain,
>
> And have redeemed us to God by Your blood out of
> every tribe and tongue and people and nation,
>
> And have made us kings and priests to our God;
>
> And we shall reign on the earth."[36]

All anxieties will immediately evaporate in the security of His loving presence. Only what was done for the Son of God will carry over
from the past;[37] all else will be burned away.[38]

Then comes the Last Day judgment.[39] We shall approach the
throne of the Almighty Lamb, whose omniscient gaze will penetrate

---

[33] The same could be said of hell.
[34] 1 Thessalonians 4:17 ("with them")
[35] John 20:25-28
[36] Revelation 5:9-10
[37] Revelation 14:13
[38] 1 Corinthians 3:12-15; 2 Corinthians 5:20
[39] 2 Corinthians 5:10

our hearts, as "all things are naked and open to the eyes of Him to whom we must give account."[40] As we acknowledge one sin after another, we seem to hear the sound of a hammer against wood. We look up to behold every sin we committed nailed to the cross.[41] *Then we are openly acknowledged and acquitted* as children of the Lamb before God the Father, the holy angels, and all creation. Satan is forever banished to hell along with his angels and his seed who preferred him to Christ.[42]

But heaven is not automatic nor for everyone. Only the God-man is worthy of our faith. He *alone* has accomplished our salvation, not the saints or ourselves. We cannot offer anything that will satisfy God and make ourselves acceptable to Him. Jesus has already done so. It would be the highest possible insult and sin to think that we do not need this Jesus, that we can earn our way to heaven, that what He has done is a good start but that we must complete what He left out.[43] In this case, Jesus would be necessary, but not sufficient, and His death on the cross considered a failure. We are not the God-man and cannot accomplish the salvation of anyone. He alone must be the object of our faith, not Him *and* us. If we think we can attain heaven by our own efforts, it would be faith in ourselves.

Having said that, there is one thing that we contribute to our salvation, without which we cannot be saved, and it is a human work—*our sins*! If we come to the Father by faith alone in Jesus alone, confessing our sins to Him, falling completely on His mercy, He will accept us. For then we understand that only He could accomplish what we cannot do. He came to call sinners, not those who think they are acceptable as they are.[44]

In the person of the Son, we have a **substantial** *union of Creator and creature*, a union of Spirit and creation, or of the spiritual and the physical, as it were. Our salvation was accomplished by both aspects. Likewise, we look to the visible, "physical" Church to accept us into His body, to be baptized ("physical") and to be in spiritual union with Him.

---

[40] Hebrews 4:13
[41] Colossians 2:14
[42] Genesis 3:15; Matthew 25:46; 1 John 3:10
[43] Romans 4:1-8
[44] Matthew 9:13; Luke 18:9-14

We must not think that we can have one without the other. To think that we can have His spiritual salvation without the physical, visible Church[45] would be to have a docetic Christ, one who was God but only appeared to be human. It would also be spurning His authority in His Church, thinking we can make ourselves His bride our way. On the other hand, to think that we are necessarily saved because we are in the visible Church would be to have a human Christ who was not God. Just as the two aspects of human (or "physical") and divine (or "spiritual") were united in Him, so we have a united salvation, in union with Him by being in His Church by baptism. The Church leads us to worship God, who is spirit, using physical means, the sacraments. In the Church, the two aspects come together: physical and spiritual, just as they do in Christ: God and man in one person. Salvation is only for those who confess their sins to the Lamb, confessing faith in Him alone, submitting to Him in His Church by being baptized into His body, and persevering in His grace to the end. On the one hand, it is a free gift. On the other hand, the free gift comes in the context of His visible Church.

Let us worship the King who alone is our righteousness. **Amen**.

---

[45] A true Church is one that preaches the biblical gospel and administers the sacraments of baptism and Holy Communion according to God's Word.

Appendix 3: Bowing and Worshipping

(Technical chapter)

What does the Hebrew verb for "bowing/worship" mean? The root of the verb is somewhat debated, but generally it is recognized not as *shahâ* (שׁחה) as BDB and K&B (959) have it listed, but as *havâ* (חוה). But the usage is the important matter. It is used 170 times in the Old Testament, and almost always translated by *proskuneō* (προσκυνέω) in the Septuagint (hereafter LXX, the Greek translation of the Old Testament completed about A.D. 200), meaning variously according to context: bow, prostrate oneself, worship.[1] The action performed may be before humans as respect or before YHWH in prayer or worship. "Strictly speaking, therefore, the verb merely designates a gesture as part of a more inclusive action; but it comes to refer also to the inward attitude thus expressed."[2] Another authority is similar: "The verb always refers to an action/attitude directed toward a human or divine figure who is recognized . . . as being in a position of honor or authority. Depending on the figure and the situation, it may be a gesture or greeting, respect, submission, or worship."[3] Let us see if these preliminary definitions can be validated from biblical usage.

The Hebrew verb is used in two primary ways: (1) in secular greetings of *respect* (Gen. 18:2; 19:1; 23:7; 24:26; 33:3, 6ff; Ex. 4:31; 11:8; 18:7 Ruth 2:10 [Ruth to Boaz], 1 Sam. 20:41 [David to Jonathan]; 28:14 [Saul to Samuel], etc.) and in (2) cultic acts of *worship* of YHWH. It is often used with *bo'*, come, (בוא), *zabhach*, sacrifice, (זבח), or *'abhadh*, serve,

---

[1] TDOT, 4:249ff.
[2] Ibid.
[3] *New International Dictionary of Old Testament Theology and Exegesis*, 2:43.

(עבד). "Especially in the Psalms or other texts related to the [ritual], the verb can not only stand for 'pray,' but can also be rendered 'carry out a cultic action (before YHWH).'"[4] (See Psalm. 5:8(7); 95:6; 99:5, 9; 132:7; 138:2; Neh. 8:6; 9:3; 1 Chron. 29:20; 2 Chron. 7:3; 20:18; 29:28-30, etc.)

In Ez. 46 during the offering of sacrifice the prince shall stand by the gate and bow in worship at its threshold (v. 2), while the people (v. 3) assist in this act of obeisance (see. v. 9).

Deut. 26:10 (see 1 Sam. 1:3, 19, 28) requires that the Israelite who offers firstfruits shall bow in worship "before YHWH your God."

In 2 Kings 5:17ff, Naaman asked if it were permissible to bow to the false god Rimmon in Rimmon's temple when so required by his (Naaman's) master. Elisha gave him permission, for one can bow and not mean it: "Yet in this thing may the LORD pardon your servant: when my master goes into the temple of Rimmon *to worship* there, and he leans on my hand, and *I bow down* in the temple of Rimmon—when *I bow down* in the temple of Rimmon, may the LORD please pardon your servant in this thing" (2 Kings 5:18). Here the NKJV variously translates the same word *worship* (once) and *bow down* (twice), capturing the sense of the original. Naaman was only bowing, but his master was worshipping. This demonstrates that sometimes the word can mean to mechanically bow without the attendant idea of worship.

Moreover, it is instructive how often "bow/worship" *havâ* (חוה) and "serve" *ʿābad* (עבד) go together, as here in Exodus 20. "Serve" occurs before "bow/worship" in Deut. 8:19; 11:16; 17:3; 29:25 (26), Joshua 23:7, 16; Judges 2:19; 1 Kings 9:6, 9; 2 Kings 21:21; Jer. 8:2; 13:10; 16:11; 25:6; 2 Chron. 7:19, 22. "Bow/worship" occurs before "serve" in Deut. 4:19; 5:9: 30:17; Ex. 20:5; 23:24; 2 Kings 17:35; 21:3; 2 Chron. 7:22; 33:3; Jer. 22:9.[5] Thus we conclude that the verb *havâ* (חוה), especially as used in worship, does not simply mean bow but usually *carries the additional idea of serving* the object of "bowing/worship."

Exodus 32:8 (see especially Psalm. 106:19) instructs us that worshipping the molded calf was wrong. This was more than just bowing and more than respect; it was worship, as is seen by the explanation in

[4]TDOT, 4:252.
[5]Ibid., 4:254.

the verse itself: "This is your god, O Israel, that brought you out of the land of Egypt."

In the LXX, Ex. 20:5 is translated: ου προσκυνησεις αυτοις, ου δε μη λατρευσεις αυτοις ["You shall not *worship* them and neither shall you *serve* them"). We see here a distinction between the two words for "worship," which distinction the early fathers maintained. The first word *proskunêseis* (προσκυνησεις) can mean, like the Hebrew it usually translates *havâ* (חוה), polite bowing or worshipping. Obviously here it means worship. The second word *latreuseis* (λατρευσεις) only means to serve God in the sense of cultic or ritual worship. Thus the LXX translators were saying that we should not worship idols and should not serve them in a cultic sense. But nothing is forbidden in bowing to a symbol in worship.

In the New Testament, *proskuneō* (προσκυνεω) is almost always used of worshipping God only,[6] though in the LXX such was not the case. The Seventh Ecumenical Council at Nicea (787) distinguished between the two words, allowing *proskuneō* (προσκυνεω) of icons, but reserving *latreia* (λατρεια) of God only.[7]

Sometimes the Hebrew verb *havâ* (חוה) can be used of both YHWH and the king at the same time: "Then David said to all the assembly, 'Now bless the LORD your God.' So all the assembly blessed the LORD God of their fathers, and *bowed their heads* and <u>prostrated themselves</u> before the LORD *and the king*" (1 Chron. 29:20). It would seem obvious from the analogy of Scripture that they worshipped God but bowed before both, which is precisely what we do in worship; namely, we bow in the presence of a symbol (the cross), but we worship God only. Here the king was the symbol of God's authority and presence, and so they bowed to both but worshipped only the Lord.

The Hebrew word for bow *qadad* (קדד) is not the same as the word for worship *havâ* (חוה). *Qadad* means "I bow down," and according to TWOT

---

[6]As a quick look at a concordance will reveal. See also TDNT, 6:764.

[7]TDNT, 6:765; also *The Nicene and Post-Nicene Fathers*, "The Seven Ecumenical Councils," vol. 14, p. 526.

The root refers to the bowing of one's head accompanying and emphasizing obeisance. Hence, it has a very restricted use, unlike its Akkadian cognate *qadādu*. It is to be distinguished from all other words for "bow" by this restricted use. Our root occurs fifteen times (perhaps sixteen; cf. *qādar*). This root is used to emphasize devotion and thus occurs at especially crucial times. When Joseph's brothers return to Egypt with Benjamin, their obeisance is notably and understandably pronounced (Gen 43:28). Similarly, when Saul sees the vision of Samuel he is especially respectful (1 Sam 28:14). The deepest awe and reverence typifies one's attitude toward God at crucial times, for example, when Eliezer's prayer is miraculously answered (Gen 24:26), and when the people celebrated at Hezekiah's consecration of the temple (2 Chr 29:30). Israel reacted in this way when they saw Aaron's signs (Exo 4:31) validating the announcement that God had sent Moses to deliver them from Egypt, and when the Passover was initiated (Exo 12:27). God's giving the law a second time in spite of Moses' anger (sin) in the face of Israel's idolatry elicited this deep reaction from Moses. Each recorded dedication of the temple was met with this deepest worship (1 Chr 29:20; 2 Chr 29:30; Neh 8:6). [8]

Notice these occurrences of *qadad* (to bow, in italics below) used with the Hebrew *havâ* (to worship, underlined below). Besides 1 Chron. 29:20 given above:

> Then the man *bowed down his head* and <u>worshiped</u> the LORD (Gen. 24:26).

> And *I bowed my head* and <u>worshiped</u> the LORD, and blessed the LORD God of my master Abraham, who had led me in the way of truth to take the daughter of my master's brother for his son (Gen. 24:48).

> And they [Joseph's brothers] answered, "Your servant our father is in good health; he is still alive." And *they bowed their heads down* and <u>prostrated themselves</u> (Gen. 43:28).

---

[8] TWOT on *qadad*.

So the people believed; and when they heard that the LORD had visited the children of Israel and that He had looked on their affliction, then *they bowed their heads* and <u>worshiped</u> (Ex. 4:31).

It is the Passover sacrifice of the LORD, who passed over the houses of the children of Israel in Egypt when He struck the Egyptians and delivered our households. So the *people bowed their heads* and <u>worshiped</u> (Ex. 12:27).

So Moses made haste and *bowed his head* toward the earth, and <u>worshipped</u> (Ex. 34:8).

Then the LORD opened Balaam's eyes, and he saw the Angel of the LORD standing in the way with His drawn sword in His hand; and *he bowed his head* and <u>fell flat</u> on his face (Num. 22:31).

David also arose afterward, went out of the cave, and called out to Saul, saying, "My lord the king!" And when Saul looked behind him, David *stooped* with his face to the earth, and <u>bowed down</u> (1 Sam. 24:8 (Heb = v. 9)).

And Saul perceived that it was Samuel, and he *stooped with his face* to the ground and <u>bowed down</u> (1 Sam. 28:14).

And Bathsheba *bowed* and <u>did homage</u> to the king. Then the king said, "What is your wish?" (1 Kings 1:16; v. 31 is the same).

And Jehoshaphat *bowed his head* with his face to the ground, and all Judah and the inhabitants of Jerusalem bowed [this verb means fell] before the LORD, <u>worshiping</u> the LORD (2 Chron. 20:18).

Moreover King Hezekiah and the leaders commanded the Levites to sing praise to the LORD with the words of David and of Asaph the seer. So they sang praises with gladness, and *they bowed their heads* and <u>worshipped</u> (2 Chron. 29:30).

And Ezra blessed the LORD, the great God. Then all the people answered, "Amen, Amen!" while lifting up their hands. And *they bowed their heads* and <u>worshiped</u> the LORD with their faces to the ground (Neh. 8:6).

We should conclude: (1) "bowing" often goes with worship. (2) The Hebrew word for worship does not necessarily include bowing, for if it did we would not need the added word *bow*. (3) Sometimes the people bowed in the presence of symbols to worship the Lord. Therefore, when the Second Commandment says not to "bow down" or "serve" (our two words) carved images/idols, we notice that "bow down" means "worship," which is supported by the verb "serve." From the above verses quoted throughout the Old Testament, we see that we are not to worship or become devoted to the creation, but only to the Creator, but also we see that we can mechanically bow, which does not involve worship.

We see that Scripture itself calls for a distinction between respecting a king and worshipping Yahweh, even though the same word can be used for both. It would seem difficult to improve on the answer of an early bishop to the Jews about alleged idolatry among Christians:

> The bishop Leontius of Neapolis in Cyprus, who at the close of the sixth century wrote an apology for Christianity against the Jews, and in it noticed the charge of idolatry, asserts that the law of Moses is directed not unconditionally against the use of religious images, but only against the idolatrous worship of them; since the tabernacle and the temple themselves contained cherubim and other figures. . . . [9]

So what does the verb *havâ* mean here in Exodus 20:5? Keil and Delitzsch note:

> It is not only evident from the context that the allusion is not to the making of images generally, but to the construction of figures of God as objects of religious reverence or worship, but this is expressly stated in v. 5; so that even *Calvin* observes, that "there is no necessity to refute what some have foolishly imagined, that sculpture and painting of every kind are condemned here."

---

[9] *The Nicene and Post-Nicene Fathers*, "The Seven Ecumenical Councils," vol. 14, p. 568.

K & D go on to translate v. 5: "Thou shalt not <u>pray</u> to them and serve them," stating that the verb *havâ* (חוה) "signifies bending before God in prayer, and invoking His name" and ʿābaḏ (עבד) "worship by means of sacrifice and religious ceremonies."[10]

In light of the tabernacle, temple, and other passages mentioned above, we conclude that what is forbidden here is not using symbols, nor even bowing in their presence, but terminating one's worship on them.

One excellent example of this distinction is the bronze serpent. Moses had obeyed God's instruction to put a serpent on a bronze pole so that if the people looked to it they would be healed from the snake bites they were being judged with (Num. 21:8-9). This symbolized God's mercy, and those who did not look to it in faith were not healed! It was a required symbol. It was not good enough just to think about it. But when the serpent on the pole became an object of worship rather than a symbol, it was rightly destroyed by Hezekiah (2 Kings 18:1-4).

Jesus said that the serpent on the pole was a type of His death (John 3:14-15) and that everyone who looked to Him on the cross would be saved! We may use it in worship, and like the serpent look at it in the worship service, even reverence it, as long as it is a symbol, but no one is allowed to worship it. We are not required to bow to the cross in worship, but one is required to approach God by means of the original cross of Christ and by no other way. Thus there is nothing wrong with having a physical cross, with honoring it as the visible expression of what Jesus has done for us on a real cross 2,000 years ago. If we can have the mental image of it, we can legitimately have the physical expression of it. But as soon as one worships the cross or gives magical power to it, he has crossed the line.

As Paul states, we are not allowed to worship and serve the creature rather than the Creator (Rom. 1:25). Israel was not allowed to worship idols (Lev. 26:1) nor to make carved images for private worship (Deut. 27:15). **AMEN.**

---

[10]Keil and Delitzsch, (AP&A), 1:465. This set is numbered differently from most sets of K&D.

Annotated Bibliography

(This is an incomplete list of a few books that would be helpful for further reading. You may find these works at Amazon.com, Abebooks.com, or Christianbooks.com. Also, look for my blog (http://curtiscrenshaw.wordpress.com/) to find my longer comments on these books from time to time. I'm just now building out my blog so it may not be very far along when you see it.)

Atheism

David Berlinski, *The Devil's Delusion* (2009), is a take off on Dawkins's book, *The God Delusion*. Berlinski describes himself as a secular Jew, who is also a mathematician who has written books on math, and holds the Ph.D. from Princeton University. This book is soft cover and about 220 pages. It is absolutely hilarious to read as he ties up the materialist atheists in knots, accusing them of holding to creation by evolution and believing that science is inerrant. He demonstrates many times that modern atheists hold their views because of circular reasoning, metaphysical assumptions, and often just bad science. He displays vast learning in many fields.

Richard Dawkins, a leader in the New Atheist movement, wrote *The God Delusion*, and Christian scholar Alister McGrath, with a Ph.D. in molecular biophysics and another in historical theology, formerly an atheist, wrote an excellent and very readable work in response to Dawkins, *The Dawkins Delusion: Atheist Fundamentalism and the Denial of the Divine*. McGrath's work is much smaller because, as McGrath says, there is very little of substance to respond to. If Dawkins could sustain a rational argument, he would not need to resort to name calling and constant outburst of emotion. These New Atheists are like the Pharisees of Jesus' day: when He uncovered their assumptions, as Christians are doing today, especially in the intelligent design movement, they could not answer Him so they crucified Him.

Antony Flew, *There Is a God.* This book is soft cover and only about 220 pages of text. It is written by one who was for 50 years the foremost scholar for atheism in the world. He was a British philosopher who died about a month ago (April 2010) at age 87, and was noted for the many books he wrote on the philosophy of religion, promoting atheism. Much to the chagrin of his fellow atheists, in 2004 he changed his mind, and then wrote this book in 2007. All the work done by theistic scientists in intelligent design convinced him there was a super-intelligence who created the universe. This is the very readable, non-technical story of the reasons for his change. Flew became open to the Christian faith, and even had Christian scholar N. T. Wright add an appendix on the evidence for the bodily resurrection of Christ, which he said was "very powerful"! Whether he became a Christian will only be revealed at the Last Day, but this is a *very* encouraging read. He takes atheists like Dawkins (*The God Delusion*) to task, and the atheistic world is in a tizzy about this book!

Sam Harris, also considered a leader in the very militant and mean spirited New Atheism, wrote *Letter to a Christian Nation* (2006). Like Dawkins above, he is unwilling (or unable) to analyze his own assumptions and thus resorts to name calling, rage, and implied persecution of Christians. It is one of the most militant and arrogant books I've ever read with incredible ignorance of the Bible, though he thinks he really knows it. It is a quick, easy read of just over 100 pages. He refers to Christians as ignorant, dangerous, and just plain stupid. Who can take something like this serious? Of course, he considers himself brilliant, magnanimous, and educated. The logical conclusion to this book and to Dawkins's book above is the persecution of Christians. One gets the impression that he wants to see us all dead.

Peter Hitchens, a journalist, is the brother of the infamous Christopher Hitchens, who in turn is also a leader in the New Atheism, having written the popular *God Is Not Great* book. Like his brother, Peter was also an avowed atheist for many years, but he has now written a book titled: *The Rage Against God: How Atheism Led Me to Faith.* It is just over 200 pages, easy reading, and recommended. The book tells Peter's life story in atheism, and how he came to faith in the resurrection of the Christ. Peter also writes in an irenic spirit, unlike his brother, and many times he addresses his infidel brother with gentle challenges. Peter also demonstrates the rage that the new atheism has against Christians and Christianity. Particularly interesting are the three chapters where he deals with the three things often brought up by atheists. (1) Atheists claim that most wars are caused by religion, but Peter Hitchens shows that other factors dominate. Moreover, Peter shows how many millions atheistic governments have murdered in the last 100 years. (2) Atheists think they can have morality without the Triune God, but Hitchens demonstrates otherwise. (3) When atheists are confronted with the horrors of atheistic governments and all their murders, they claim such governments were not really atheistic but religious in disguise! (Sam Harris does this in his book mentioned above.) Take a look at this one!

Alister McGrath, Ph.D. wrote another work that is also very readable and recommended: *The Twilight of Atheism: The Rise and Fall of Disbelief in the Modern World*. This work traces the rise of intellectual atheism and its demise. I hope he's right.

Ravi Zacharias, Ph.D., *The End of Reason*, is a short work by a very fine Christian apologist; easy reading. Highly recommended.

Ethics

Robert H. Bork, *Slouching Towards Gomorrah: Modern Liberalism and American Decline*. Bork should have been on the Supreme Court, but the liberals hated him so much that they lied, connived, and did whatever it took to keep him off. This is a very insightful look at evil forces in our culture by one who was reared with the Presbyterian Shorter Catechism and became Roman Catholic in later life. He documents that two evils dominate the American culture: radical egalitarianism and radical individualism, accompanied by envy. Highly recommended.

Craig A. Boyd, *A Shared Morality: A Narrative Defense of Natural Law Ethics*. This is a very heavy philosophical work from St. Augustine to today, and it nuances every conceivable aspect of a theoretical ethic. Definitely not for the faint of heart. Its strength to me was the survey of so many modern views, but its weakness is how little it is based on Scripture. Boyd tries to build an ethic on who man is rather than who God is.

James Dobson, *Marriage Under Fire*, 2004, a short but powerful analysis of the implications of the gay attack on Christian marriage.

Dinesh D'Souza, Ph.D., *What's So Great About Christianity?* This a great evaluation of why we are where we are, especially intellectually. Generally easy reading and much good material.

John M. Frame, *The Doctrine of the Christian Life*. This is over 1,000 pages, and generally easy to understand. Frame covers the basic approaches to ethics for the first 400 pages, and then spends 450 pages on the Ten Commandments, with several fine concluding chapters of great interest to Christians, such as Christ and Culture. There are numerous appendices. Highly recommended.

Robert A. J. Gagnon, *The Bible and Homosexual Practice*, published 2001, over 500 pages. This is without a doubt the best book on the subject. Gagnon is a very competent scholar, and he delves into Greek from Plato to Philo and Josephus. He also researches what the Jews believed, not only in the Old Testament but also between the Old and New Testaments. He quotes dozens of sources demonstrating that "natural use" and "against nature" in Romans 1:26 were set phrases that referred to heterosexual and homosexual respectively. There is nothing left to be said once he is done. The one draw back to the book for most people is that if you don't like hundreds of quotes from scholarly literature and cannot handle serious Greek grammar, you will benefit little from this otherwise excellent work.

David Hazony, *The Ten Commandments: How Our Most Ancient Moral Text Can Renew Modern Life*, 2010. Hazony is an orthodox Jew, and though there are some keen insights here and there, for the most part he promotes pelagianism, salvation by our own efforts, completely misses the Messiah in the Old Testament, relies heavily on Jewish tradition and on the wisdom of the rabbis, and in general is not very helpful for Christians.

A very interesting book on original sin that surveys various persons and cultures is Alan Jacobs, *Original Sin* (New York, NJ: Harper Collins, 2008). This is not just a pragmatic approach, but he delves into various secular and Christian theories, along with great insight into how cultures stand or fall with their view of original sin. Highly recommended; Jacobs is evangelical.

Erwin W. Lutzer, *The Truth about Same-Sex Marriage*, 2004. This was written by a Christian pastor, extremely easy to read, but very powerful in many of its assessments of homosexuality, homosexuals, and the sometimes lack of compassion by Christians regarding these people. Everyone needs to read this one. He offers a way for us to minister to these people with compassion, love, and concern.

Patrick D. Miller, Ph. D., *The Ten Commandments*, was published in 2009. Dr. Miller taught Old Testament at Princeton Theological Seminary. These days one wants to ask if anything good can come out of Princeton, and Miller demonstrates that the answer is Yes. This is 500 pages of very scholarly but usually readable material that is full of exegetical insights, and still remains conservative. If he dealt with abortion or homosexuality, I did not see it. I can't image how one could write 500 pages on the Ten Commandments and not address the worst ongoing killings of our society and the worst ongoing sexual sins.

Mark F. Rooker, Ph.D., *The Ten Commandments: Ethics for the Twenty-First Century*, published 2010. Rooker is professor of Old Testament and Hebrew at Southeastern Baptist Theological Seminary. The book is very readable, follows the same format each chapter (Introduction, Old Testament, New Testament, and some other insights, Conclusion), very conservative man who believes the Bible to be God's word, but has some technicality from Hebrew throughout. His quotes from others, especially the early fathers, is very helpful. What is astonishing is that he does not mention abortion or homosexuality. Mildly dispensational. 240 pages

Education

Christian scholar Samuel Blumenfeld wrote the excellent work *Is Public Education Necessary?*,[1] and in it he traces the origin of public education back to New England liberals who wanted to evangelize the nation for

---

[1] This is one of the most incredible books I've ever read, and the historical research is superb. Get this book! Try www.abebooks.com.

liberalism (beginning in the early 1800s and gaining force the rest of the century).

Curtis Crenshaw, the author of this book, has a series of booklets to introduce you to this area: *Keeping Covenant and Educating Our Children*, *Keeping Covenant and Disciplining Our Children*, and *Keeping Covenant and Catechizing Our Children*. These may be ordered by asking for these by title in an email to service@footstoolpublications. You will be contacted.

Then there is William Kilpatrick's *Why Johnny Can't Tell Right from Wrong*, in which he shows that public education leaders are training teachers to say repeatedly to their students that they are the only judges of right and wrong for themselves. He points out that classes on values clarification teach students that moral compromise is legitimate in certain cases, and then desensitizing sex classes teach students how to engage in "safe" sex. Girls practice putting condoms on cucumbers.

R. J. Rushdoony, *Intellectual Schizophrenia: Culture, Crisis, and Education*, 1961. Outstanding analysis of why we need to be consistent in educating our children, not sending them off to public schools and then to church where they hear opposite things.

Evolution

Michael Behe, Ph.D., *Darwin's Black Box*, presents the idea that there is irreducible complexity to living organisms, which means many functioning "parts" had to be in place simultaneously for an organism to live. This stung his fellow scientists for at least two reasons: he is a professor of Biochemistry so writing from within the guild hurt, and it is impossible to refute his evidence. Now that we know more about the body and its chemistry, Darwin is defeated. Very technical in places on chemistry, but most people can get a lot from it. Behe is a conservative Roman Catholic. Recommended.

William A. Dembski (Ph. D. in philosophy and Ph.D. in mathematics from University of Chicago) edited *Darwin's Nemesis*. Each chapter is authored by a different and highly credentialed scientist in honor of Philip E. Johnson (see below), including a couple of writers who disagree with him. Authors are mostly favorable to intelligent design, and speak of how Dr. Johnson encouraged them to come out of the closet and be heard as scientists who believe. Highly recommended.

Thomas B. Fowler and Daniel Kuebler, *The Evolution Controversy*. This is very informative in presenting major positions, such as a history of Darwinism, Neo-Darwinism, Creationist School, Intelligent Design School, and Meta-Darwinism School. Good survey with many quotes from original sources.

Normal Geisler, Ph.D. and Frank Turek, Ph.D., *I Don't Have Enough Faith to be an Atheist*. If you need to give a book to someone who is skeptical, this is a good place to begin. They cover the gamut from the problem of origins to the problem of evil to who is Jesus and is the resurrection of Christ believable. Recommended if you need a faith lift or know someone else who does. A weakness is not challenging the pretended autonomy of human reasoning.

Stephen Hawking, Ph.D., *A Brief History of Time*, Ph.D. Hawking is not a Christian, and this little book is fascinating to read. Difficult and technical in places, but worth the effort.

Cornelius G. Hunter, *Science's Blind Spot: The Unseen Religion of Scientific Naturalism*. Good analysis of the assumptions of evolutionists.

In 1991 a man highly trained in logic and analysis of logical fallacies wrote a seminal work evaluating the arguments of evolutionists. It was explosive, as seen by the myriads of vitriolic responses to it. **Philip E. Johnson, Ph.D.**, *Darwin on Trial*, spawned the intelligent design movement with his challenges to the many fallacious arguments for evolution. **If you read only one book in this bibliography, make this it!**

Dr. Johnson wrote a sequel, Philip E. Johnson, Ph.D., *Reason in the Balance: The Case Against Naturalism in Science, Law, and Education*. Another very critical analysis of the pseudo-scientific character of much of what passes for science, education, and how atheists function by an anti-intellectual faith.

Geoffrey Simmons, M.D., *What Darwin Didn't Know*. This could be used in a high school anatomy class, for this medical doctor analyzes all the major functions of the body, showing how they work and how they all needed to be in place at once for the body to live. Outstanding read! Recommended.

Geoffrey Simmons, M.D., *Billions of Missing Links*. Demonstrates the impossibility of bridging the millions of missing links. Very readable and good for teens. Recommended.

Lee Strobel was a former atheist who has written a series of books that are good to give to skeptics or to those who need a faith lift. *The Case for a Creator* is very good indeed, and Strobel interviews former skeptics, all of whom are highly credentialed. Easy reading and highly recommended.

Jonathan Wells, Ph.D., Th.D., *Icons of Evolution: Science or Myth?* Dr. Wells began as a convinced evolutionist, having a Ph.D. in biology from the University of California, Berkeley. In this book he demolishes some of the common arguments for evolution. Very readable and highly recommended.

Historical Evaluations

Alexis de Tocqueville, *Democracy in America*, written in 1835 and 1840, two volumes. This is a fascinating study of the early history of our country by a French man who had incredible insights into our culture of the time.

C. Gregg Singer, Ph.D., *A Theological Interpretation of American History, Revised Edition*. I knew Dr. Singer as a friend, and he was one of the most underrated scholars in the USA. He was a tremendous Christian and historian, as well as a biblical scholar. This is one of the best books I've ever read on the rise and decline of the USA. By all means, get this one! He went home to be with Christ about 15 years ago.

I strongly urge the reader to obtain Richard Weikart, *From Darwin to Hitler: Evolutionary Ethics, Eugenics, and Racism in Germany*. It is extremely well researched, and recommended by a Who's Who of scholars. Footnotes abound, and one can find it on Amazon.com. The title says it all.

Law and Society

Robert H. Bork, *The Tempting of America: The Political Seduction of the Law*. This is another brilliant work by Judge Bork, and a timely analysis of why the original intent of the Constitution is the only perspective we should take, why our society is moving away from that original intent, and the moral implications of moving away from our historical roots.

Philosophy

Thomas Cathcart and Daniel Klein, *Plato and a Platypus Walk into a Bar* . . . This is a humorous and easy to understand introduction to philosophy. Short read.

William Lane Craig and Walter Sinnott-Armstrong, *God? A Debate between a Christian and an Atheist*. Craig is the Christian with two earned doctorates, one on Cosmology, the theory of origins. I would like to say this is an easy read, and though in places it is, one has to concentrate hard to keep up with the arguments pro and con. One weakness is that Craig does not challenge the origin of reason or origin of logic and allows Sinnott-Armstrong to pretend the autonomy of human thought.

Alistair Kee, *Nietzsche Against the Crucified*. This is an analysis of the philosophy of Nietzsche by a non-Christian. Very insightful and helpful into Nietzsche's thought.

Friedrich Nietzsche, *Joyful Wisdom*. Difficult reading at times, and convoluted, but if one wants to read him first hand, this is one of his more popular works.

Problem of Evil

Tammy Bruce, *The Death of Right and Wrong* (New York: Three Rivers Press, 2003). Ms. Bruce denies that she is a Christian, and she is pro-choice and a feminist. She was once heavily involved in the National Organized for Women and in leftist causes. Thus her insight from an insider's view is not only revealing, but her sense of right and wrong is usually on target, testifying to the remnant of the image of God within her. Sadly, though, she has no solution to the evils that plague our society, for that lies only in Christ. Only He can change people's hearts to want to practice the commandments of God, which change is a product of the Gospel, trusting in the substitutionary death of Christ for our sins and in His bodily resurrection. Ms. Bruce speaks of the "core values" of Christianity as ethics, which is typical of those who do not want a supernatural God. The theological core is hidden from her. The moral ethics of Christianity is secondary to Christ Himself. She does not see that her approval of murdering babies and her lesbianism are violations of God's law, and that she needs to be delivered from these by trusting in Christ. My heart goes out to her.

Alvin Plantinga, *God, Freedom, and Evil*. This is not for the faint of heart, as Plantinga is heavy on formal logic, but it is a Christian approach.

N. T. Wright, *Evil and the Justice of God*. This is not a heavy weight book, and he does not tell us why God allowed evil. Yet it is a good summary of the biblical teaching on evil with the solution in the cross of Christ.